AA CAR CARE

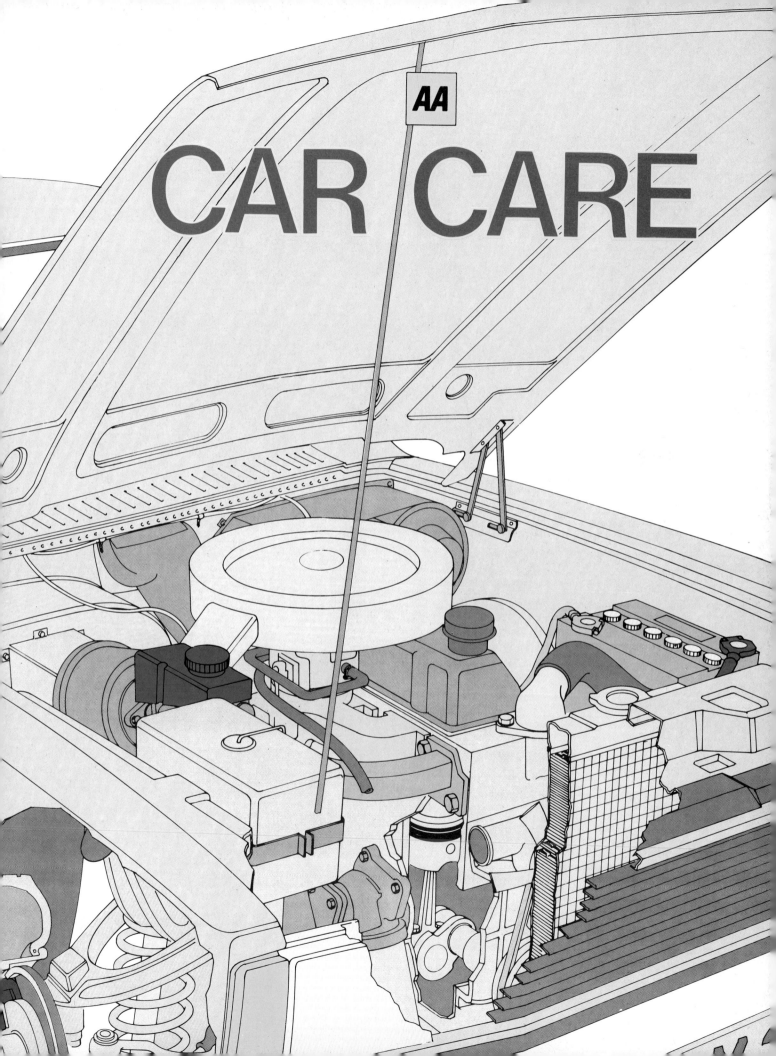

CAR CARE

Produced by the Publications Division of the Automobile Association

Technical Advisers: Les Sims/Manager, AA Technical Services
Charles Surridge/Head of AA Mechanical and Electrical Research
Editors: Roland Weisz   Chris Webb
Barry Francis/technical
Mark Fensome/assistant   Neil Davis/index
Art Editors: Michael Preedy MSIAD   Michael Clack
Paul McNeil/designer
David Harris/illustrator   Michael Wilkins/photographer
Phototypeset, printed and bound by Purnell & Sons Ltd
of Paulton, Bristol BS18 5LQ

Published by The Automobile Association, Fanum House,
Basingstoke, Hampshire, RG21 2EA

The AA is grateful to the following for their help and advice,
and in many cases, for supplying material and illustrations for this book.

AC Delco Ltd, Armstrong Patents Co Ltd, Austin-Morris, Robert Bosch Ltd,
BP Oil Ltd, Britax-Excelsior Ltd, British Insurance Association, Burmah-Castrol Co,
Champion Spark Plug Co Ltd, Citroen Cars Ltd, Datsun UK Ltd,
Alexander Duckham & Co Ltd, Dunlop Tyre Group, Esquire Kleindienst & Co Ltd,
Ferodo Ltd, Fiat Motor Co (UK) Ltd, Firestone Tyre & Rubber Co (Great Britain) Ltd,
Ford Motor Company Ltd, General Motors Ltd, GKN Group,
Goodyear Tyre & Rubber Co (Great Britain) Ltd, Gray-Campling Ltd,
Holset Engineering Ltd, Honda (UK) Ltd, Intec Ltd, Jaguar Rover Triumph Ltd,
Kenlowe Accessories & Co Ltd, Lloyds Industries Ltd, Loctite (UK) Ltd,
Lucas Electrical Parts & Service, Lucas Girling Parts and Service, Lumenition Ltd,
Mobil Oil Co Ltd, 'Practical Motorist', Pressed Steel Fisher, Renault Ltd,
Smiths Industries Ltd, SU-Butec Sales & Marketing Centre, Trico-Folberth Ltd,
Triplex Safety Glass Co Ltd, Vauxhall Motors Ltd, Volkswagen (GB) Ltd,
Volvo Concessionaires, Watford Motor Accessories, Wilmot Breedon Ltd,
WWWebber Ltd, Zenith Carburettor Co Ltd, Ziebart (GB) Ltd

ISBN 0 86145 0221

AA
CAR CARE

HOW THIS BOOK WILL HELP YOU

This book explains in simple language how a car works and how to put it right when something goes wrong. The book covers not only the theory of motor car engineering, but also gives practical step-by-step advice on the easiest way to tackle common repair jobs, most with only a basic set of tools. There are 100 projects, and although some of them require a degree of technical skill, they are well within the capabilities of most car owners who want to carry out their own servicing.

The book is divided into four main sections:

1 Under the Bonnet:
the engine and all the support systems needed for it to function properly.

2 Electrical Systems:
the numerous uses of the energy supplied by the battery and generator.

3 On the Road:
the parts that affect the handling and braking of the car.

4 Outside and In:
methods of keeping the body and furnishings in top condition.

There is also a section on diagnosing the cause of trouble in an emergency.

Each section is divided, under clearly identifiable headings, into chapters explaining the working of the systems, followed by a series of practical projects. The accompanying photographs are numbered to correspond with the steps in the text. In some cases, where alternative procedures apply, the step numbers are shown with a star.

At the start of every project, an assessment is given of the time the job will take to complete, the tools needed for the job and the materials required. In addition, every project is given a rating, expressed in

spanners ✧✧ to indicate how easy it is to do the work. (These spanners are in no way related to the spanner symbols used by the AA in appointing garages). ✧ indicates a straightforward job, suitable for the inexperienced; ✧✧ a job requiring some knowledge of car mechanics; ✧✧✧ a more complex job requiring a comprehensive set of tools and the skills to use them properly.

The figures quoted for the times taken to do the projects are only approximate, and do not take into account unexpected snags which may arise, or any procedure which is made complicated because of the type of car under repair, or its condition.

This book is not intended as a professional workshop manual. The projects have been picked because they represent a typical cross-section of the repairs and adjustments that most cars need from time to time.

Although most component types are covered, some components are bound to be different from those illustrated. In those cases it may be advisable to consult the car maker's workshop manual—many of these are available on loan from public libraries, or can be bought from the manufacturer.

Measurements throughout are quoted in inches and, where appropriate, the metric equivalent is also given.

On pages 8 and 9 there is a list of tools that are sufficient to deal with most projects and that can easily be acquired for a modest outlay.

The most important tool for the DIY man, however, is not on the list. It is here—ready to be used: **Car Care**. Its pages will open up the secrets to car maintenance and make your motoring more reliable—and safer, too.

CONTENTS

See overleaf for full list of Projects

CONTENTS: 100 PROJECTS

⚒
for the inexperienced

⚒⚒
for those with some knowledge of car mechanics

⚒⚒⚒
for those with a comprehensive set of tools and the skills to use them properly

The tool kit

You cannot tackle car care without a good set of tools. Your kit need not be as comprehensive as a professional mechanic's, but it pays to buy individual items of the best quality that you can afford. Cheap tools or equipment that are not designed to do the job you are tackling, can cause injury to yourself and damage to the car. Before collecting a set of tools check with the car's handbook, a workshop manual or, if necessary, with the main agent to find whether the type that you will require is AF (across flats) or metric.

Generally, up to the mid-70s, British cars used AF sizes. After that date British manufacturers joined European and Japanese makers in using mainly metric nuts and bolts. There are some cars that require both types of spanner.

Spanners

Although open-ended spanners are still commonly used for nuts and bolts, a more positive hold is obtained by using ring or socket spanners. In either case, a sensible range is $\frac{5}{16}$in-$\frac{7}{8}$in AF (or 8mm-19mm metric). Ring spanners are also sold as a combination set with a ring at one end and an open-ended jaw at the other. Whichever sets you buy, always have some duplicate sizes to hold a bolt while turning a nut (an adjustable spanner is useful here, too).

Sockets are very versatile and can be bought in sets with useful extras like extension bars (to reach deep into recesses), ratchet handles and plug sockets. The most suitable type for general maintenance and repair are those connecting to $\frac{1}{2}$in drive handles.

Never be tempted to use an extension to the handle of a spanner not designed for this purpose. A light tap can be used to start a nut turning (see Stubborn Brutes, pages 10 and 11), but never bludgeon a spanner continuously.

Screwdrivers

A selection of cross-point and straight-blade screwdrivers of various sizes is essential to deal with the variety of screw sizes on every car. Keep screwdriver blades in good condition by using them only on screws, not as convenient scrapers and levers. Do not throw away old screwdrivers though; they can be used for these purposes.

Pliers

Standard engineers' pliers will cope with most gripping and holding jobs on a car, but there are special types of pliers designed for specific jobs. Keen DIY mechanics will find long-nosed pliers useful for fiddly electrical work, and bigger jobs will be better managed with the wide-jawed, adjustable, multi-grip type. Another very useful pliers-like tool is a self-grip wrench.

Allen keys

A few cars have Allen bolts on engine and transmission components. These have hexagonal sockets in their heads, and are undone and tightened with Allen keys, which are available in AF and metric sets. For some larger Allen bolts there are $\frac{1}{2}$in drive adapters to provide extra torque.

Spark-plug spanner

Plugs are best removed with a special socket spanner. This has a rubber insert to prevent damage to the fragile insulating porcelain, and a short handle to guard against over-tightening.

Feeler gauge
and spark-plug gap tool

A set of feeler gauges for valve gear, spark plug and contact-breaker points adjustment can be bought cheaply at most accessory shops. A more sophisticated set of feelers for setting the spark-plug gap includes a small tool for bending the side electrode, and often a file for cleaning.

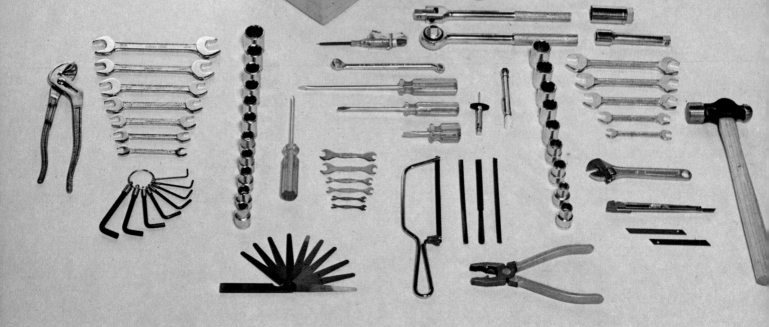

Electric test lamp

A small test lamp for 12-volt car systems is invaluable for diagnosing electrical faults and when fitting accessories. Ready-made ones consist of a 12-volt test bulb inside a probe handle, and a wire with a crocodile clip. To use it, connect the crocodile clip to clean body metal and touch the probe on the electrical terminal that you want to test. If the bulb lights, the terminal is live.

Cutting, filing and scraping

A number of do-it-yourself jobs – fitting a radio, for instance – involve making a hole in the body metal. A two-speed power drill with a chuck capacity up to $\frac{1}{2}$in (12.5mm) is ideal for this. Use high-speed bits in the drill, starting with one of about $\frac{1}{8}$in (3mm) diameter, and enlarging the hole with larger bits. If the hole needs to be bigger than $\frac{1}{2}$in diameter, it is best to enlarge it with a round (rat-tail) file.

For rust repairs, tin-snips are used to cut away corroded metal, and a flat file and a rasp speed up the rough shaping of filler (used for body repairs). Other cutting tools that should be included are a hacksaw (the Junior type is often most useful) and a handyman knife. For removing flaky paint, dirt and rust from underbody components, a wire brush is needed.

To light up obscure corners under the car an inspection lamp is required. If you are using a mains type, the bulb should be enclosed in a protective cage to prevent accidental breakage. Alternatively, use a 12-volt lamp which clips to the car battery – this can also be used in roadside emergencies.

A few cars have grease nipples on the suspension and steering joints. For these, buy a lever-operated grease gun.

All cars have hinges and locks that need oiling at service intervals – a lever-type oil can is best for these.

Hammers, often misused but nevertheless essential for some work, come in a confusing variety, but a $\frac{3}{4}$lb ball-pein engineering hammer, or one that has interchangeable heads for various types of work, is most useful.

After work, clean all spanners – petrol or paraffin will wash off grease, underbody sealant and grime – and lightly oil non-stainless tools, except files, to prevent them from going rusty.

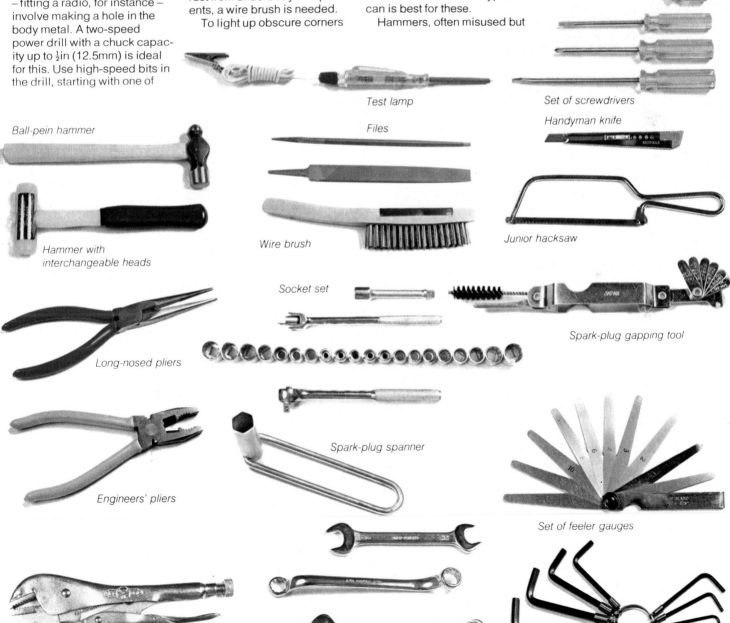

Test lamp

Set of screwdrivers

Handyman knife

Ball-pein hammer

Files

Hammer with interchangeable heads

Wire brush

Junior hacksaw

Long-nosed pliers

Socket set

Spark-plug gapping tool

Engineers' pliers

Spark-plug spanner

Set of feeler gauges

Self-grip wrench

Open-ended and ring spanners

Set of Allen keys

Stubborn brutes

On every car there are always odd-shaped or odd-sized adjusters or plugs, corroded bolts, seized joints and steadfast rivets to deal with in the course of car-care work. Removing these stubborn brutes can take as long as the job itself unless you use a few simple tricks or some of the special tools designed to take on the rough work.

Brake adjusters and drain plugs

On many cars the means of brake adjustment is a small splined or square-headed screw in a less than easily accessible position. Inexpensive spanners, specially designed to reach the adjusters and cope with the unusual shape of the head, are available at car accessory shops.

Drain plugs in radiators, sumps and the transmission system vary enormously. A universal tool to deal with all drain plugs with internal square drives can be bought.

Rusted bolts

When rust attacks bolt threads, the corroded material expands and locks the threads in place. Penetrating oils and fluids liberally applied to rusted nuts and bolts will help to free them. The fluid should be left to soak in for a few hours. At this stage do not exert too much force on a bolt—there are a few more tricks if fluids do not work.

Heating the seized bolt is the next possibility, but be careful. Clean off any inflammable sealant around the bolt, and never apply heat near the fuel tank, carburettor or fuel lines. Do not play a flame near the flexible brake pipes either. Heat the bolt, using a butane gas blowlamp with a fine-flame attachment. For maximum effect, try the spanner on it while it is hot. Smart taps on the spanner with a hammer may make it possible to gain the first break in the corrosion lock.

If these mild measures do not work, there are two further possibilities. When the area to which the bolt is fixed is solid, a sharp cold chisel and a hammer can be used to shear off the bolt head or split the nut.

Do not use this method if you are dealing with a bolt tapped into a casting or with a nut screwed on to a stud unless it is absolutely necessary.

A nut on a bolt or stud is much better tackled with a nut-splitter. This is a device available from tool-hire shops. It consists of a collar into which a blade is tightened, using a fine-thread bolt. It splits the nut, leaving the bolt or stud thread undamaged.

If you are left with a section of snapped-off bolt rusted into a casting, leave it to soak in penetrating oil for as long as possible. Mark the centre of the bolt with a centre punch and hammer and, with a drill half

Fine blowlamp flame may free seized nuts

Cold chisel, held at about 30°, will chop the head off a rusted bolt

Nut-splitter can be hired to crack open the nut, leaving the bolt undamaged

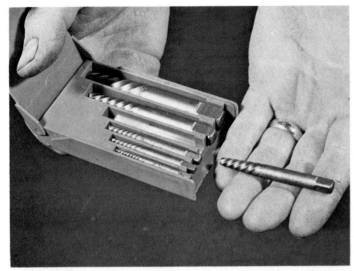

Stud extractor is a tapered, reverse-thread bolt

the diameter of the bolt, drill as accurately as possible down the centre of the seized part. You can then use a stud extractor (sometimes called an 'easy-out') which is a tapered reverse-thread bolt. Screw it into the new hole and turn it with a spanner. As it begins to bite, it will probably extract the old stud or bolt. Be careful, however, because a broken extractor is often impossible to remove. Failing this, get the broken section drilled out by a garage. The hole may require rethreading for a larger bolt.

Screws and rivets
Seized screws lend themselves to treatment by many of the same methods as bolts. Soaking in penetrating oil is very often a lot more successful with screws because the parts that they secure are more lightly held, and the oil can actually get to work quicker. When using the screwdriver, a couple of smart taps on the handle will sometimes help to free the screw, or you can turn it in the tightening (clockwise) direction before backing it off. If the screw slot becomes burred it may be possible to cut it deeper with a hacksaw.

An impact driver is a special tool to deal with stubborn screws. Usually supplied with interchangeable blades to suit different screws, the impact driver is designed to impart a turning motion to the screw when it is hit with a hammer.

Rivets are best drilled out, but they can be tackled, like rusted screws, with a cold chisel and a hammer.

Taper joints
On many cars, parts of the steering and suspension mechanisms are joined by taper joints, a conical section tightened into a tapered cup. It is necessary first to undo the securing nut and then separate the two interlocked parts. A simple but effective method is to strike each side of the joint with two very heavy hammers simultaneously. This is called impact hammering. If you can get a helper to exert some downward pressure on one of the joint components at the same time, so much the better. If this method fails, there are special joint-splitting tools on the market for the DIY man.

The simplest, and cheapest, are joint-splitting wedges. These are mating wedges cut out at the centre so that they can be placed on each side of the joint. As they slide together, the wedging effect increases until the joint parts.

Other joint-splitters are clamped round the joint so that a threaded bolt can be tightened on to the inner component to force it out of the tapered cup. Ball joints on steering mechanisms can be split apart by using similar screw-down removers.

Impact screwdriver

Seized rivets can be drilled out carefully

Clamp holds the joint and forces out the taper-shaft

TAKING CARE
Car cleaning

A neglected film of dirt on car bodywork eventually discolours the paint. It also holds moisture which can set up corrosion in crevices and at body joints.

To keep paintwork in good condition, it should be cleaned once a week. It is important to use plenty of water as the dirt film contains tiny particles of grit which will scratch the surface if they are removed with a dry cloth. Always clean the car away from direct sunlight and when the bonnet top is cool. Hot surfaces cause smearing.

The equipment needed is simple: a plastic bucket, two large sponges, a soft-bristled brush, a garden hose and a chamois leather.

First close all the car windows and doors, and soak the body with plenty of cold water from a hose or by pouring several buckets of water over it. Then fill the bucket with tepid water and add a car shampoo (washing-up liquid gets off dirt, but it leaves smears).

Load the sponge with plenty of water and wash the bodywork. Start at the roof, then move to the bonnet, the boot lid or tailgate, followed by the sides, the front, and the rear. Do not clean the windscreen with a shampoo containing a wax as this will cause the wipers to smear.

Use a soft brush dipped in car shampoo to clean dirt from between the grille crevices and the wheel rims. Stubborn marks on the wheels can often be removed with a stiff brush dipped in paraffin before cleaning the wheels with shampoo. If its paint is badly chipped, a wheel can be repainted with an aerosol spray (see Project 90).

After cleaning, rinse the paintwork with clean water, preferably using a soft-bristled brush attached to a garden hose. In winter, direct a powerful jet from the hose under the wheel arches and the underside of the car to flush away road salt and mud.

Empty the bucket and refill it with clean water. Load the second sponge with clean water, lift the wipers, and wash the windscreen, using plenty of water to float off the dirt. Gently

sponge clean the edges of the wiper-blade rubbers. If the rear window has a wiper, wash this and its wiper in the same way.

Dip the chamois leather into clean water, wring it out and use it to remove water droplets from the glass and then the bodywork.

Once the paint is clean, any small blemishes will show up. Tar spots can be removed with a proprietary cleaner or with white spirit. Small areas of chipped paint should be retouched with brush-on touch-up paint (see Project 87). Minor rust spots must be treated with a rust remover and repainted before they grow any larger.

Brightwork
Chrome should be cleaned with car shampoo and rinsed off with clean water, but if it has surface marks, a chrome cleaner, which contains a mild abrasive, can be used to remove them. Wax polish the chrome afterwards to give

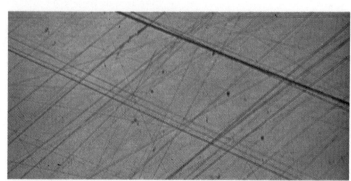
Careless washing can leave scars on paintwork

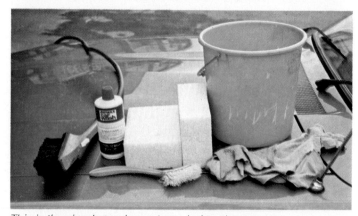
This is the simple equipment needed to clean a car

Use car shampoo to lather bodywork

Remove stubborn grime on wheels with a stiff brush

Wash off soap with hose brush

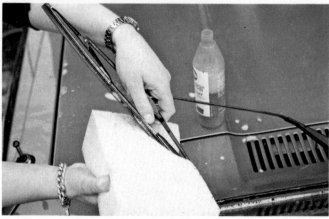
Gently sponge the edges of the wiper blades

Dry the surface with a good chamois leather

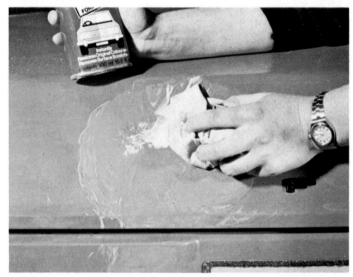

Use haze-remover to restore shine to paintwork

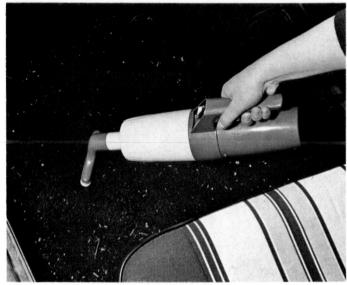

Vacuum the interior with a nozzle-headed cleaner

an extra protective gloss.

From time to time, clean the inside of the bumpers and apply a coat of the tacky sort of rust preventive sold in aerosols. This will discourage rust from forming.

Anodised aluminium brightwork should be cleaned with a sponge and shampoo, then rinsed with clean water. Aluminium trim that has tarnished can be brightened up with an alloy cleaner.

Removing ingrained dirt

If a car is parked in the open for most of its life, dirt in the atmosphere gradually discolours the paint and eventually the gloss dulls. Weekly cleaning will retard the process, but will not eliminate it altogether.

Dull paint can be restored to its original shine and colour by using a haze remover or mild cutting compound. These fluids contain very fine abrasive particles, and when applied with a soft cloth they remove a very thin layer of paint, uncovering fresh colour underneath and restoring the gloss.

When using a cutting compound, take care not to rub too hard, especially on external corners and edges. Paint on these areas is likely to be thin and it is easy accidentally to rub through to the primer coat. Treat a small area of the body at a time, about 18in square, applying the compound with only moderate pressure, and polishing it off with a dry cloth before moving on to the next area.

Cleaning the interior

Empty the ashtrays and remove unwanted material from the glove box, door pockets and oddments trays. Take out any rubber floor mats and shake them clean, then use a nozzle-type vacuum cleaner (the portable type is convenient) or a small dustpan and stiff brush to remove grit and dirt from the carpets and from cloth-covered seats. Stains on cloth-covered seats may respond to a proprietary cleaner, although old, ingrained stains can be difficult to remove. Sometimes a carpet shampoo, lightly

applied, will lift out a stubborn stain. If it does not, the seat cover may have to be removed (see Project 96) and soaked in a biological detergent to remove the marks.

Leather seats are best wiped with a damp cloth. If they are dirty they can be sponged with tepid soapy water, worked up into thick suds. Wipe off with a damp cloth, and rub dry.

PVC trim panels, seats and interior paintwork can be freshened up with a damp cloth. Do not use a lot of water on side trim panels, as the backing board will warp if it gets wet. Remove dust from the facia and steering column with a damp cloth, then add a shine with polish.

Fabric headlinings are best cleaned with a portable vacuum cleaner or a soft-bristled brush. Clean vinyl headlinings with a damp cloth.

If PVC upholstery and trim or a vinyl roof lining are really grimy, there are several proprietary emulsifying cleaners which can be used to good effect. These are available in either foam or liquid form. Apply the cleaner, if necessary working it into the surface with a sponge or brush. Wait a few minutes for it to eat into the dirt, then wipe the trim clean with a damp cloth. Do not use a detergent or any cleaner containing bleach, as this may damage the upholstery.

Clean the inside of the windscreen and rear window with a cloth dipped in a 50/50 mixture of water and methylated spirit. On heated rear windows, take care that you do not accidentally catch and break one of the elements. Finger marks can be removed from side windows by using a proprietary window cleaner.

Do not forget to clean the inside of the boot or luggage compartment. Remove the carpet or floor covering and vacuum clean it, after having shaken out the dust. Sweep out any dirt from under the carpet.

Finally, ensure that the toolkit, jack and wheelbrace are complete and properly stowed, and that the spare tyre is serviceable and correctly inflated.

Safety under the car

Do-it-yourself car maintenance and repairs sooner or later involve climbing underneath the vehicle. Since the average family car weighs a ton, it is essential that it is supported securely so that there is no chance of the car slipping and causing a serious accident.

Never get under a car supported only by a jack—even a new one can collapse. The car should be held up by axle stands or drive-up ramps standing on a firm, level surface, with the wheels that are on the ground securely chocked to prevent them rolling.

Do not use house bricks to support the car, they can crumble without warning.

Jacking
Most cars are supplied with a side-lift or scissor jack that raises the car when a screw thread is turned. The side-lift jack has a long pin which engages with a socket on the car, usually under the side. If the socket is near a door, the jack will probably prevent the door from being opened once it is in position. If you need to open the door, do so before jacking up.

The scissor jack is extended by turning a horizontal screw. It has a rectangular, self-supporting base and a head which engages with a jacking recess in the suspension or bodywork. See the car handbook for the location of these recesses.

If you want to support certain parts of the car, such as the engine or gearbox, while the wheels remain on the ground, or on drive-up ramps, you will need a free-standing jack which has a vertical lift and a reasonably large base.

To prevent damage to the underside of the car, place a piece of hard wood on the jack head before lifting. To locate the jack firmly, the head can sometimes be raised by hand on its screw adjustment up to the timber at the jacking area before the operating lever or T-handle has to be used.

When buying a bottle jack, make sure that it will fit under the lowest part of the car when it is fully retracted.

Small trolley jacks suitable for home use are sold by accessory shops. They can be used, where there is a convenient jacking point, to raise one end of the vehicle in a single lift.

The lifting action of the trolley jack must move either the car or the jack in respect to the ground. If neither moves, the jack will slip off the car's lifting point, causing damage.

Sometimes the car cannot be lifted high enough for an axle stand to be fitted, except with a trolley jack. Extra height can be gained if the base of the jack is rested on a piece of stout timber, but ensure that such an arrangement is stable.

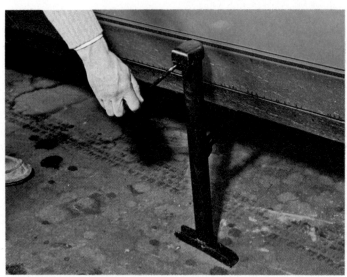
Side-lift jack: *Its lifting pin engages with a socket*

Scissor jack: *Height is adjusted by turning a horizontal screw*

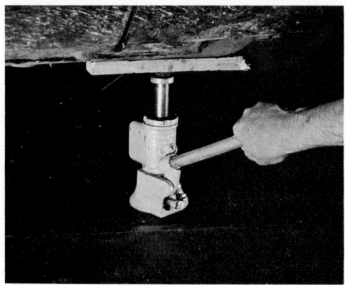
Bottle jack: *It must clear the lowest part of the car*

Trolley jack: *It raises the car in a single lift*

Strong points

The strongest areas on today's one-piece car bodies are the jacking points, the mountings for the suspension, and the rear axle casing. These are the only points that should support the car when jack or axle stands are used.

The pictures show jacks and stands in use at some of the most convenient strong points.

Axle stands

Axle stands are steel tripods, adjustable for height. Two can be used to support one end of the car, or four if the whole vehicle has to be lifted off the ground.

Use axle stands only at the strong points under the car. If they are not used, considerable damage can be done. When fitting a stand, jack up the car and insert the stand carefully, making sure that your body is at no time under the car.

Once the stand is in position, lower the jack slowly. When the weight of the car is on the stand, its three legs should be firmly on the ground. If they are not, raise the car again and re-position the stand.

Drive-up ramps

These are used for raising the front or rear of the car. Place the ramps centrally against the front or rear wheels, making sure that the front wheels are straight. Drive slowly and carefully up them until the wheels are firmly on the flat top. Apply the handbrake and chock the wheels remaining on the ground.

Sometimes ramps skid away from the car when the tyres touch them. When this happens, loop a short length of old carpet round the bottom rung of each ramp, with the ends of the carpet towards the wheel. This will prevent the ramps from moving away when the tyres meet the slope.

If the ramp has a solid slope, wrap the carpet sideways over and under the slope; this should help to stop it from sliding away.

Ramps, of course, cannot be used when working on the suspension system or wheels.

Wheel chocks

These prevent the wheels on the ground from rolling when the opposite end of the car is being raised. Some car makers include triangular chocks in the toolkit.

Your local timber yard can make four chocks very quickly from a thick piece of timber. A 45° chamfer is cut along one edge with a circular saw and the timber is then cut into 6in (152mm) lengths. Use one chock in front, and another one behind each grounded wheel, with the chamfer pushed up firmly against the tyre.

When positioning axle stands, take care not to place your body under the car

Drive slowly up the ramps until the wheels are on the flat top

Loop a short length of carpet around the bottom rung to prevent the ramps from skidding

Weekly checks

Service plan

Every car should be given a series of simple checks once a week. They take very little time and involve the use of virtually no tools.

Engine oil level

The engine has a dipstick to indicate the level of oil in the sump. With the engine switched off, check the level after the car has been standing for a few minutes on a level surface. Withdraw the dipstick and wipe the end with a clean cloth. Insert it fully into the engine and withdraw it again. Note the oil level.

Most dipsticks have maximum and minimum marks, and the oil should not be allowed to fall below the minimum marking. If the level is near the minimum, add oil. Allow it to run down into the sump, checking the level from time to time with the dipstick and adding oil until the level reaches the maximum mark. Do not overfill.

Checking oil level on dipstick

Coolant level

When the engine is cold, check the level of the coolant against the recommended level on the side of the radiator expansion bottle, or, if the radiator has a filler cap, take it off and check the water inside. It should be about ¾in below the bottom of the filler neck. Add water if necessary to top up the level. In winter, top up with an anti-freeze mixture (see Project 8) to maintain frost protection in the cooling system.

Checking coolant level

Battery electrolyte level

Use only distilled water to bring the battery electrolyte level to just above the plate separators. If the battery needs topping up every week, have it checked by an auto-electrician (see Project 31).

Screenwasher reservoir

In winter, add specially formulated screenwasher anti-freeze to the water. Do not use coolant anti-freeze as this can cause streaking on the screen and may damage the paintwork.

Lighting

Side and rear lights and headlights can be checked by switching them on and walking round the car. Brake lights, however, will work only when the brake pedal is depressed, and often only when the ignition is switched on. Have a helper operate the pedal while you watch from behind the car.

If a brake light has failed, remove the light lens and change the bulb. The lens is usually held in place by external screws, but if in doubt, check the method of removal in the car handbook. A combined stop and rear light bulb has offset fixing pins. Note the position of the pins on the old bulb as you take it out and insert the new bulb in the same position.

Removing rear light lens

Fitting new rear light bulb

Brake fluid level

Fluid in the master cylinder reservoir should be between marked levels. Use only fresh fluid for topping it up.

Clutch fluid level

If the car has a hydraulic clutch top up the reservoir if necessary, using the same fluid as the car maker recommends for the brakes. If the clutch repeatedly needs topping up, have the hydraulic system examined by a garage.

Tyre pressures and tread depth

Check tyre pressures when the tyres are cold (see Project 67) and if necessary inflate them with a tyre pump to the manufacturer's recommended pressure. If a tyre loses more than 4lb/sq in (0.28kg/sq cm) of pressure each week, have a tyre specialist check the tyre to find out why.

Topping up clutch fluid

Servicing the car at home

The average car needs servicing about once every 5,000 or 6,000 miles. With a comprehensive tool kit a major service can be carried out at home. If you have not done this sort of work before, allow a full day for it.

The projects throughout this book detail the service jobs that most cars require. Use the guide on the next page to locate them. A guide to the particular service operations that your car needs will be given in the handbook.

At higher mileage intervals, cars need more complicated service operations. For instance, most car makers recommend changing all the brake fluid after 18 months. Jobs of this nature are not detailed here and should be left to a garage.

Before you start servicing your car you will need certain information, including the recommended spark plug gaps, contact-breaker points gap, the ignition timing and valve clearances. These details should be given in the handbook, or, failing that, they can be obtained from the local dealer.

Most of the service operations in the guide are in addition to the weekly checks. Where possible the jobs have been listed in the order in which they should be tackled. This may not be convenient in all cases. For instance, where the valve clearances have to be checked with the engine cold, the car should, ideally, be left overnight before these checks are made. Remember, too, that before draining the oil, the engine must be warmed up.

All manufacturers issue to their dealers regular service bulletins, some of which are safety conscious. Without this information no one, no matter how competent, can be sure that his car is safe. It is strongly recommended that a car should be checked by a franchised dealer at least once a year.

Inspecting the underside

The underside should be inspected during servicing for damage and oil leaks. Support the vehicle securely on axle-stands or, one end at a time, on drive-up ramps before getting underneath. Remember to chock the wheels.

The main areas to check are:

Brakes

Clean dirt from all hydraulic metal pipes with a soft wire brush and check for fluid seepage and corrosion. A thin covering of surface rust that is removed by wire brushing is not dangerous, but if the pipe surface is pitted, have a new pipe fitted by a specialist. If there is any trace of leakage, let a brake specialist check the hydraulic system.

Brake hoses must be renewed if there is the slightest sign of surface damage. Bend them sharply near the ends and look for cracks on the surface. Also check for any rubbing marks which suggest that the hose has been fouling the suspension.

Cleaning brake pipe with a wire brush

Assessing the condition of a brake hose

Oil leaks

Traces of oil on the underside of the engine and transmission are not unusual and can be ignored, but a substantial leak that leaves a pool of oil on the ground after the car is parked must be investigated.

Clean the oil from the area of the leak using paraffin and a paint brush, and dry it with a clean cloth. Run the engine or drive the car to identify the source of the leak. Leaks from the valve cover gasket are easy to cure (see Project 23), but other leaks may be more complicated to put right. These are best left to a garage.

Exhaust system

Pull the system downwards to make sure that the mountings and rubber hangers are sound. Run the engine at tick-over speed, and listen for blowing exhaust gas, usually heard as a 'chuffing' noise, which will pinpoint a leak. Any holes in the system can be temporarily patched (see Project 100), but have the system repaired by an exhaust specialist as soon as possible.

Grease nipples

Some cars have grease nipples on the suspension joints. To lubricate each joint, attach a grease gun to the nipple and operate the lever to pump grease in until lubricant can be seen seeping from the joint.

If grease is unwilling to enter the joint, unscrew the nipple

Checking exhaust hangers

and clean any hardened grease from the inside with a piece of stout wire. Try the nipple on the grease gun and when grease can be passed through it, refit it and try lubricating the joint again. If grease still refuses to enter, have the joint overhauled by a garage.

ROUTINE SERVICING GUIDE

CHECK LIST	Project no
1 Check engine valve clearances	12-15
2 Change engine oil, change filter	19-22
3 Check under-bonnet fluid levels	see opposite page
4 Check fanbelt tension	1
5 Clean carburettor air filter	25
6 Service carburettor	26
7 Check spark plugs	53
8 Service distributor and check contact-breaker points gap	54 and 57
9 Check condition of HT cables	58
10 Check ignition timing	59
11 Clean crankcase ventilating system	24
12 Check clutch cable adjustment	76
13 Check disc brake pads for wear	73-73A
14 Adjust drum brakes	74
15 Check handbrake adjustment	75
16 Check brake pipes for leaks/corrosion	See this page for Inspecting the underside
17 Check the underside for oil leaks	
18 Check exhaust system	
19 Lubricate grease nipples	
20 Check gearbox and rear axle oil level	80
21 Check steering joints for wear	71
22 Check dampers for leaks	69-70
23 Check wiper blades rubbers for wear	81
24 Check operation of windscreen washers	82

Greasing a Mini rear suspension arm

Steering-box mountings

The bolts fixing the steering unit are normally locked by tab washers. During inspection, try to move the bolt head with an open-ended spanner. There should be no trace of movement. If there is, unlock the washer and fully tighten the fixing with a ring spanner.

Tightening steering rack mounting bolt

Under the bonnet

Cooling system

The internal combustion engine is not very efficient. Of the energy that is released by burning a mixture of petrol and air in the cylinders, less than a quarter goes to work pushing down the pistons and turning the crankshaft. The remainder is converted into heat.

About half this heat goes down the exhaust pipe. The remainder builds up in and around the cylinder block, and if it was not dissipated, the engine would eventually reach a temperature where moving parts would expand and seize up, or aluminium-based components such as pistons would begin to melt.

All internal combustion engines therefore have a cooling system. In its simplest form it may be no more than fins which increase the surface area round the cylinders and dissipate more heat. Most motorcycle engines are cooled by air passing through their cooling fins as the machine moves along the road.

However, relying on road draught does not suit all engines, and a hard-working, air-cooled agricultural engine will usually have a fan to force air through the cooling fins so that it does not have to rely on forward motion for its air-flow.

A car engine needs to operate within fairly accurate temperature limits, and a cooling system, where the cylinders and combustion chambers are surrounded by a jacket containing water, offers an easy way of doing this job efficiently.

From the jacket, water passes to a radiator which is usually placed in the airstream caused by the forward motion of the car. Air-flow through the radiator, especially when the car is standing still, is assisted by a fan.

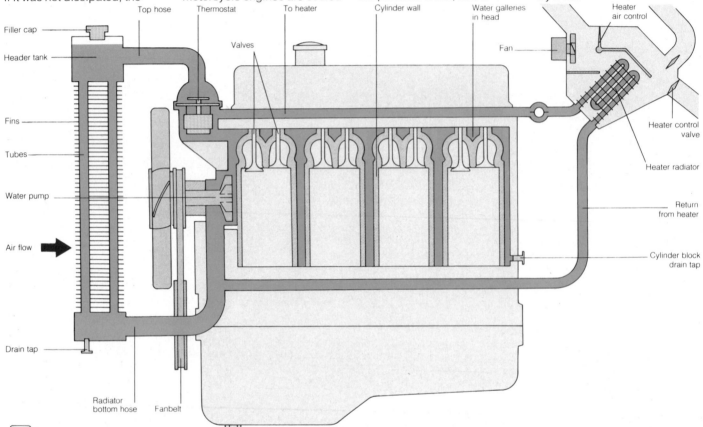

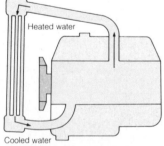

Originally cars relied on the thermo-siphon principle to circulate water between the jacket and the radiator. Hot water naturally rises, and if a tall radiator was used, water heated in the jacket passed of its own accord up the top hose to the top of the radiator, then gradually sank down the radiator as the air-flow cooled it. It eventually re-entered the water jacket through the bottom hose from the radiator.

Thermo-siphon systems are not very quick-acting, and are too inefficient for today's high-output engines. Current practice is to use a water pump to circulate coolant from the engine through the radiator. Besides giving a greater rate of cooling, the pump allows smaller radiators to be used.

On its own, the pumped system would prevent the engine from overheating and destroying itself, but might over-cool the engine. Better economy, performance and driveability are obtained if the coolant temperature can be maintained at a few degrees below boiling point.

One of the risks when operating with the coolant near its boiling point is that it will literally boil over if the engine gets a fraction too hot. To give a greater safety margin, the system is pressurised by a spring-loaded cap. Increasing the pressure raises the boiling-point—for every 1lb/sq in (0.07kg/sq cm) increase in pressure the boiling point rises about 1.7°C. A car with a 14lb/sq in (0.98kg/sq cm) pressure cap should not boil its coolant until it reached 124°C.

To help warm up the engine quickly, a temperature-sensitive valve—the thermostat—is placed next to the water pump, usually where the top hose meets the cylinder head. When the engine is cold, the thermostat blocks off the top hose and no water can pass to the radiator. Instead, the water pump circulates the coolant through a by-pass circuit around the water jacket. As the water temperature in the engine jacket increases, the thermostat opens and allows water to pass to the radiator.

How the thermostat works

On old cars with low-pressure cooling systems the bellows-type thermostat, which had a flexible metal casing that looked like a miniature concertina, was used. The bellows were filled with a low boiling-point fluid which vaporised or boiled at the appropriate temperature, stretching the bellows and opening the valve.

Wax-filled thermostats are used on most current cars because they are not as sensitive to the pressure inside the system as a bellows type.

The heart of this thermostat is a small, sealed capsule of wax. In the centre of the capsule is a rubber compartment enclosing a pin attached to a bridge

across the top. As the appropriate temperature is reached, the wax melts and expands, forcing the pin away from the capsule. Because the pin is fixed to the bridge piece it cannot move upwards, so the capsule, attached to the valve, moves down, allowing water to flow into the radiator.

The wax thermostat needs a heavy coil spring to return it to the closed position when the wax cools and contracts, and here lies its only disadvantage. If the wax leaks, the spring will shut the valve, isolating the radiator and allowing the engine to overheat. The bellows unit, on the other hand, will fail in the open position if it develops a leak.

What is in a fanbelt?

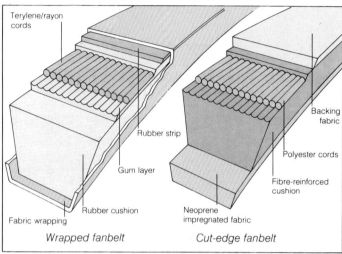

Wrapped fanbelt *Cut-edge fanbelt*

At peak engine speeds, a fanbelt that is turning a water pump, alternator and cooling fan may be transmitting as much as 6 brake horsepower—as much power as can be obtained from a good 70cc motorcycle. The fanbelt must be tough, yet flexible enough not to jump off the small pulley fitted to the average alternator; it must not stretch and it should run silently.

Wrapped belts have terylene or rayon cords inside which resist stretching. The V-section

which drives the pulleys is of synthetic rubber and the complete belt is wrapped with fabric to minimise abrasion.

Cut-edge belts do not have any outer wrapping, and this allows a few extra anti-stretch cords to be fitted in. The cords are made from polyester and the plastic V-section contains several plies of strengthening fabric which are abrasion-resistant.

Cut-edge belts are said to have a longer life than an equivalent wrapped belt.

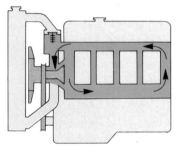

Thermostat shut: Water is trapped in the engine jacket

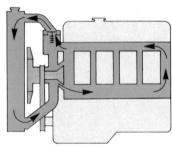

Thermostat open: Hot water is allowed to flow to the radiator

Pressure cap

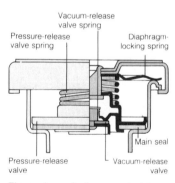

The main seal allows coolant to boil at a higher temperature than normal. Release valve prevents hoses collapsing when system cools

This has two valves. The pressure valve is the large spring-loaded one with a sealing ring that sits on a ledge in the radiator filler neck or the neck of the expansion tank.

Inside the ring is a smaller valve which is spring-loaded in the opposite direction—it is pulled by spring pressure

towards the top of the cap. Its purpose is to allow air to enter the cooling system when the water cools and contracts. Without it, the hoses and radiator would be sucked inwards as the engine cooled.

Because the pressure cap allows the coolant to boil at a higher temperature than normal, an apparently dormant cooling system may well burst into sudden activity and boil over vigorously if the cap is removed when the engine is fully warmed up.

It is advisable, therefore, not to take off the cap while the engine is hot. Even if the engine has been allowed 15-20 minutes to cool, always wear a heavy glove or use several layers of old cloth to protect the hand that releases the cap. The radiator cap has a 'safety' position. Undoing it a quarter of a turn will exhaust any steam through the overflow pipe. Wait until all the steam has escaped before releasing the cap fully.

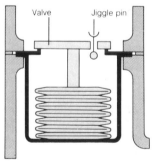

Bellows thermostat shut: Cold water in the engine contracts the bellows, closing the valve

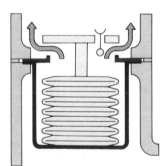

Bellows thermostat open: Hot water expands the bellows and water flows to the radiator

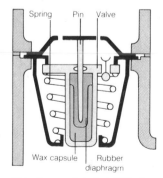

Wax thermostat shut: With the engine cold, a heavy coil spring closes the valve

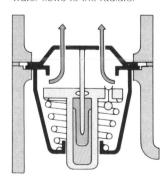

Wax thermostat open: When hot, the wax expands, and in trying to expel the pin it opens the valve

Cooling system

The radiator and cooling fan

The radiator contains a large number of thin-walled tubes carrying hot water from the engine, surrounded by a larger number of cooling fins. Air-flow through the fins draws heat from the pipes and cools the water inside.

The water tubes may run from top to bottom, but on more modern cross-flow designs the tubes run from side to side. Radiators with a pressure cap are provided with a small overflow pipe to allow any excess water to escape as it expands —often to an overflow reservoir (see illustration below).

A cooling fan is provided to pass air through the radiator, especially when the car is stationary or crawling in a low gear. Because the fan absorbs a good deal of power at higher engine speeds—often when it is not needed—many small cars are now fitted with thermostatically-switched electric cooling fans. These operate only when the engine temperature has reached a pre-determined level, and cut out once the temperature is lowered satisfactorily.

The amount of power lost in driving a fan can be reduced by providing a degree of 'slip' at the hub. Fans with a viscous drive use a silicone fluid coupling at the hub, which binds the fan and its drive together at low engine speeds, but as engine speed rises and the air drag on the fan blades builds up, the fluid allows the fan to slip.

Another system uses a magnetic clutch .The magnet is switched on electrically and couples the fan to the engine when triggered by a thermo-static switch linked to the cooling system.

A development is expected to be a self-contained fan that uses wax to lock on to its driving hub when it is needed. When the air passing through the radiator and flowing over the fan reaches a pre-determined temperature, wax inside the fan hub will expand and operate a clutch, bringing the fan into service. When the radiator has cooled, the wax inside will contract, disengaging the clutch. The fan will then free-wheel.

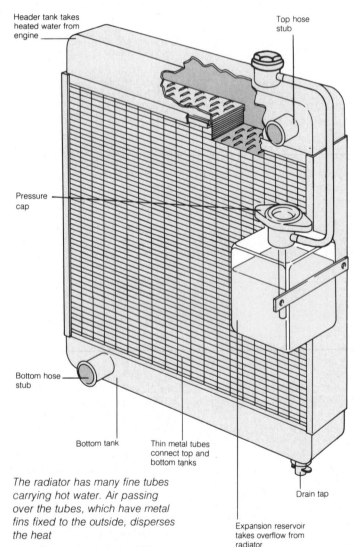

The radiator has many fine tubes carrying hot water. Air passing over the tubes, which have metal fins fixed to the outside, disperses the heat

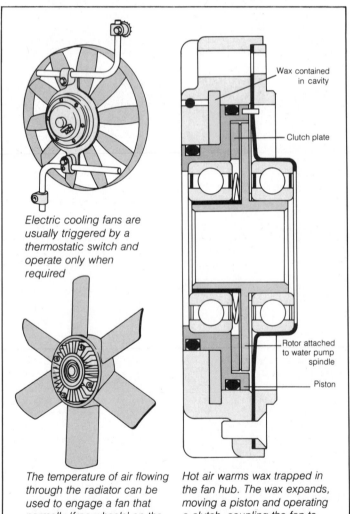

Electric cooling fans are usually triggered by a thermostatic switch and operate only when required

The temperature of air flowing through the radiator can be used to engage a fan that normally 'free-wheels' on the water pump spindle

Hot air warms wax trapped in the fan hub. The wax expands, moving a piston and operating a clutch, coupling the fan to the drive

Semi-sealed systems

All cooling systems have to allow for the expansion and contraction of the water as it heats and cools. Some manufacturers provide a small additional reservoir near the radiator which eliminates the need for regular topping up and thus prevents dilution of the anti-freeze. On these systems, the radiator may not have a filler cap at all, or it will have an air-tight cap or plug and the pressure cap will be on the reservoir.

With the engine cold, the coolant level should be at the manufacturer's mark, where one is provided; otherwise the reservoir should be about one-third full. As the system warms up, the surplus water caused by expansion travels down an overflow pipe into the reservoir. When the system cools, the partial vacuum created draws water into the radiator again.

Anti-freeze

Even though a car is kept in a heated garage in winter, its cooling system may freeze up when the car is used. The first sign of a frozen engine will be the squeal made by the fanbelt trying to turn the frozen water pump.

If the car is driven straight from its heated garage when the air temperature is below freezing point, the thermostat will stay shut and the water in the radiator will not circulate. In a short time, soft, mushy ice will form in the radiator tubes, and they will become blocked.

Once this happens, even though the thermostat opens, no additional radiator cooling is available and the engine overheats. This is the reason why so many cars without anti-freeze are seen boiling on a freezing morning.

A good quality anti-freeze will prevent the cooling system from freezing. The higher the concentration of anti-freeze, the greater the protection. In Britain a 33% anti-freeze/water mixture gives adequate protection. In addition it contains inhibitors which discourage rusting or corrosion, particularly of aluminium components, and so gives benefits all year round. Over a period (some anti-freezes have a claimed life of 2 or 3 years), the inhibitors lose their effect, and after the recommended lifetime the cooling system should be drained and the anti-freeze renewed. Remember that topping up with water alone will weaken the anti-freeze mixture.

Air-cooling

Multi-cylinder air-cooled engines buried under a bonnet or boot must have some form of fan cooling and ducting in order to cool all cylinders evenly. The cylinders and heads are heavily finned, and each fin is tapered because heat always flows to the thinnest part of a mass of material. The hotter areas, near the exhaust ports on the cylinder heads, will have bigger fins than elsewhere.

The fan-blown air will be ducted by a metal cowling so that it stays close to the finned areas; usually air-flow will be regulated by a thermo-statically-controlled flap-valve. During warm-up, the flap will be closed to restrict the movement of air and permit the engine to reach its operating

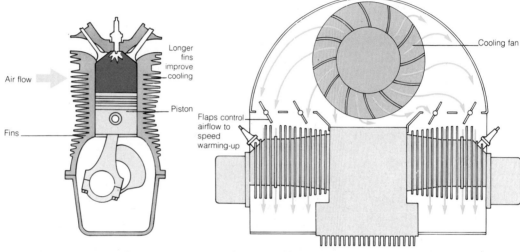

Air-cooled engines have fins to increase the surface area of hot sections and dissipate the heat. On cars these engines have a fan to blow air over the fins whenever they are running

temperature quickly. Once the air is fully warm, the flap will open and promote more air-flow through the cooling fins.

On engines where a fanbelt drives the fan, it is important that the belt is renewed at the first sign of wear. Always carry a spare belt.

The heater—something for nothing

It is only sensible that some of the engine's dissipated heat should be used to heat the car's occupants. On a water-cooled engine, the heater consists of a miniature radiator which is plumbed into the cooling system and has its own air supply.

The most primitive heater is the recirculatory type. This has the radiator mounted inside the car. A small electric fan blows air from the car interior through the radiator to heat it. The fresh-air heater works on the same principle, but, as the name suggests, the air is drawn from outside—usually from an intake just ahead of the windscreen, clear of exhaust fumes—and passed through the radiator. Most fresh-air systems rely on the car's motion to force air through the radiator. A booster fan is provided to increase the air-flow for demisting.

Temperature control methods vary. Most fresh-air systems use a flap-valve to regulate the flow of air, and have a remotely-controlled water valve to adjust the flow of hot water through the heater radiator. These methods give a slow response to temperature adjustments.

A faster heater response can be obtained by keeping the heater radiator hot all the time and arranging flap valves to direct air flow through or round it—or to mix the two. Most manufacturers today use this air-blending system of heater control.

Air-cooled engines do not give up their excess heat so easily. The most usual method of interior heating is to pass the exhaust down-pipe through a large canister which acts as a heat-gatherer. Air is diverted from the engine cooling fan and blown through this heat-exchanger into the car interior. These heaters are not as easily controlled as a water-heated system.

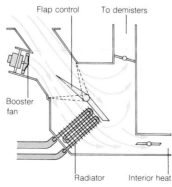

Recirculatory heater

Air-blending heater

A recirculatory heater (left) takes in air from inside the car, and fan-blows it through a small radiator connected to the engine cooling system. Flap valves are used to direct the flow of warm air

In the air-blending fresh air heater, the flap ahead of the radiator can be adjusted to divert air through it or past it – or a mixture of both. This allows instant alterations to be made to the temperature of the air entering the interior

Cooling system projects

Most car makers rely on the fanbelt to cool the engine. Although it may not drive a radiator cooling fan, on most water-cooled engines it drives the water pump; on air-cooled engines it often drives the fan that blows air through the cooling fins. In either instance if the belt breaks the engine overheats.

Fanbelts stretch a little in service and should be checked for damage and correct tension at each service interval. Proper tensioning is important—an over-tight belt will put too much strain on the bearings of the water pump and generator, while a loose belt will slip and in time the battery will go flat because the generator is not turning fast enough. Methods

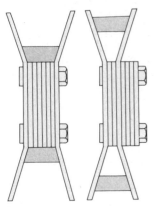

The split pulley method of belt tensioning. Removing shims from between the pulley halves makes the belt run wider and increases the tension.

of tensioning a slack fanbelt vary: on most engines the generator is moved away from the cylinder block to take up any slack. On a few cars, however, the generator is fixed and on these a split pulley is used to adjust belt tension. Removing spacers from the centre of the pulley makes the belt run nearer the edge and increases the tension. If the belt cannot be tensioned fully, it has stretched and must be renewed.

When fitting a new belt, slacken off all the tensioning adjustment and fit it on the pulleys by hand, taking care not to twist the belt. Once it is fitted to all pulleys, tension it as shown.

Project 1: Checking fanbelt tension

Step 1. First twist the belt and look for cracks or cuts on the vee-section that touches the pulleys. If it is damaged, fit a new belt.
2. If the belt is sound, see the car handbook for the correct method of checking the ten- sion. If one is not mentioned press the belt firmly mid-way between the two most widely spaced pulleys; there should be about ½in (12mm) deflection in the belt.
***2.** If your car has an unortho- dox fanbelt arrangement, as on the Peugeot 104, you must check the maker's recom- mended tensioning system. Tension is correct when there is approximately ⅝in to ¾in (15mm-20mm) between the belts when they are squeezed together firmly.

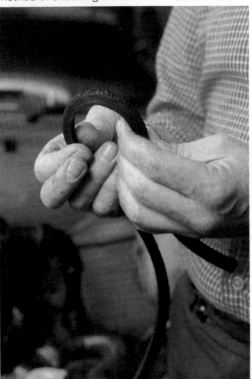

Step 1.

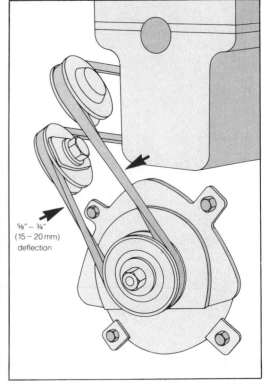

⅝" – ¾" (15 – 20 mm) deflection

*Step *2.*

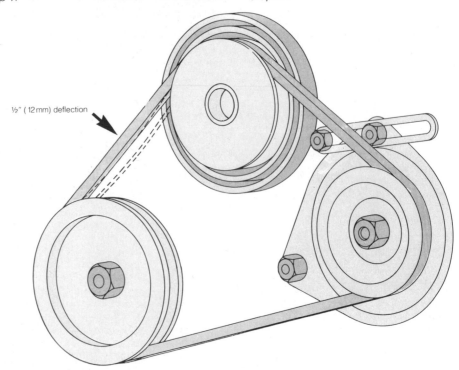

½" (12mm) deflection

Step 2.

Project 2: Adjusting fanbelt tension

Grading: 🔧
Time: Hinging generator
10min–15min
Split pulley 15min–25min
Tools: Spanners (some-times an Allen key) to fit
generator or pulley nuts
Materials: Wooden lever to
tension generator against
belt

Step 1. Where the generator tensions the belt, use two spanners to loosen the hinge fixings, and slacken off the clamping bolt.
2. Swing the generator away from the engine to tension the belt. Use a wooden lever (a hammer handle will do) between the generator and engine block to get the right tension.
3. While the belt is held under tension, tighten the clamp bolt. Re-check the tension and if it is correct re-tighten the hinge fixings.
*1. On cars with split pulley adjustment, undo the nuts holding the pulley together and take off the outer half.
*2. Remove one packing piece from the centre and refit the outer half, with the displaced packing piece on the outside; re-tighten the nuts, taking care not to trap the fanbelt near the hub.
*3. With the pulley assembled, rotate the engine one revolution before checking the tension.

Step 2.

Step * 1.

Step * 3.

Project 3: Fitting a new fanbelt

Grading: 🔧
Time: Hinging generator
15min–20min
Split pulley 20min–30min
Tools: As for Project 2

Step 1. Loosen all adjustments, remove the old belt, and fit the new one over the pulleys by hand. It sometimes helps to loop the belt over the crankshaft and generator pulleys first, and to rotate the water pump pulley to 'wind on' the belt in the same way as one fits a bicycle chain. Do not use a screwdriver or sharp implement to lever on a tight belt. If it will not fit by hand, the belt is the wrong size, or all the adjustments have not been fully slackened off.
*1. Some cars, like early BL Minis, have a close-fitting shroud round the cooling fan. On these a small cut-out provides just enough space to thread the belt over the fan, one blade at a time.
2. With split pulley adjustment, first fit the belt with all the spacers between the pulley halves, then if necessary subtract spacers until the correct tension on the belt has been obtained.
3. All new belts stretch a little when first used and the tension should be re-checked after 100 miles, or sooner if stated in the handbook.

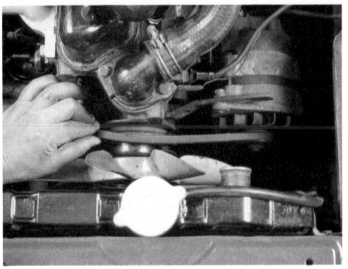

Step 1.

Cooling system projects

It is advisable to check the water-cooling system at least twice a year or every 6,000 miles, removing any dead insects or dirt blocking the air flow through the radiator fins and inspecting hoses for cracks, kinks or perishing—all signal weakness.

Most anti-freeze solutions are good for two years' use, but before winter starts, the strength of the anti-freeze should be checked—a garage can do this by measuring its specific gravity with a special hydrometer—and fresh anti-freeze added if necessary. When the time comes to change the anti-freeze any deposits in the cooling system should be flushed out after draining.

Project 4: Draining the cooling system

Grading: 🔧
Time: Approx 15min
Tools: Screwdriver; spanner if hoses need removal; spanner to fit drain plugs
Materials: Washing-up bowl; cloth

Step 1. Place the heater control to 'hot', or fully open the cylinder head water valve to prevent air locks. If the anti-freeze is to be re-used, an old bowl will catch the coolant.
2. Remove the radiator cap or plug slowly, using a large pad of folded cloth to protect your hands if the system is hot. Undo any air bleed valves (but do not remove them).
3. Open the radiator drain plug or tap, if fitted, and the plug or tap on the cylinder block—the handbook will show its location. If there is no radiator plug or drain tap, disconnect the bottom hose to let the water out.

4. If water trickles slowly from a tap or plug, it is probably blocked by sediment which can be dislodged by prodding with a piece of wire.

Step 3.

Project 5: Flushing and cleaning the cooling system

Grading: 🔧🔧
Time: Approx 1hr
Tools: Spanner; pliers; screwdriver to fit hose clips; spanners to fit thermostat housing fixings
Materials: Thermostat gasket; new hose clips; brush; garden hose-pipe

Step 1. Look through the radiator filler hole. If the tubes are covered with scale deposits, use a proprietary cleaning compound to loosen them, following the maker's instructions.
2. Flush the radiator by hosing water at mains pressure through the filler hole. If the flow through the bottom hose stub is restricted, it will be necessary to back-flush the radiator. Push a garden hose into the bottom radiator stub (wrap it in rag to prevent leakage). Turn on the tap and run it until the water runs out of the filler hole. In some cases it may be necessary to remove the radiator, turn it upside down and again back-flush it by hosing water in through the bottom hose stub. If this does not improve the flow of water and the engine persistently overheats, consult a radiator specialist—he may be able to de-scale it using a powerful alkaline solution.
3. Clean the outside of the

Step 4.

Step 5.

Step 6.

radiator with plenty of water and a soft-bristled brush to remove any debris blocking the air flow.
4. To flush the heater, disconnect the two heater hoses at the engine. One will be clipped to the cylinder head or inlet manifold, and the other will be attached near the water pump. With the heater control on 'hot', or the cylinder head water valve open, fit the mains hose to the heater hose disconnected from the pump. (When

you turn on the water there should be an unrestricted flow from the other heater hose.) Continue flushing until clear water emerges.
5. The thermostat must come out in order to flush the cylinder block. On most cars it is located under a housing at the cylinder head end of the top hose. Unbolt the housing, remove it, and scrape away the gasket round the edge of the thermostat. The thermostat should now lift out. It may, how-

ever, be corroded firmly in place. If so, scraping debris from the edge of the thermostat, using a small screwdriver, will allow it to be lifted.
6. Disconnect the bottom radiator hose at the water pump end. Insert the mains hose in the thermostat hole and turn on the water. There should be an unrestricted flow from the bottom hose stub. Flush until clear water emerges. Reassemble by reversing the sequence.

Cooling system projects

Project 6: Checking the thermostat

Grading: 🔧🔧
Time: Approx 30min
Tools: Long-nosed pliers
Materials: Thermostat gasket; saucepan

Step 1. Remove the thermostat (see Project 5). Hold the flange with pliers and submerge it in a pan of boiling water. The valve should open within approximately 30 seconds. When fully open the thermostat valve will be about ¼in from its seating.

2. To refit, scrape clean the seating on the cylinder head. Some thermostats are marked with the word 'radiator' or 'rad' on the flange. This marking goes nearest to the radiator.

3. Fit a new gasket after the thermostat, smear with high-melting-point grease, replace the cover and tighten the fixings evenly.

Step 2.

Step 3.

Project 7: Changing a hose

Grading: 🔧
Time: Approx 30min
Tools: Box-spanner, pliers, screwdriver to fit hose clips
Materials: New hose; hose clips; washing-up liquid; knife; emery cloth

Step.1. Drain the cooling system (see Project 4) and loosen the clips at each end of the hose.

Depending on the make of car the clips may be of sprung-wire, of the split-pin variety, or the worm-drive type. They are loosened in different ways.

2. Sprung-wire clips loosen their grip when the ends are carefully squeezed together with pliers. To loosen a split-pin clip, use a small screwdriver in the pin eye·as a tommy bar to unwind it. Screwed-wire clips and worm-drive clips can often be loosened with a screwdriver, but some makers use a hexagon-headed screw—usually 7mm—and a small box-spanner or socket is best for these. It is sometimes difficult to re-fit sprung-wire clips and split-pin clips once they are loosened, and they are best replaced by new worm-drive clips.

3. Pull the hose off the stub. A twisting action will usually free it. If it is tight, cut it off—this is better than putting a lot of force on a radiator-hose stub and running the risk of cracking the joint.

4. Use emery cloth to clean dirt or deposits from the hose stub, lightly smear the inside of the hose ends with washing-up liquid, thread on the hose clips and push the hose firmly on the stubs.

5. Position the hose so that it follows its natural curve and is not twisted, then tighten the clips firmly.

Spring wire

Worm drive

Screwed wire

Split pin

Hose clips

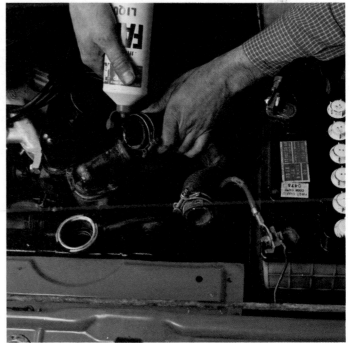

Step 4.

Cooling system projects

Project 8: Refilling/adding anti-freeze

Grading: 🔧 🔧🔧
Time: 20min-1hr
Tools: Hose clamps (on cars with bleed valves); watering-can
Materials: Anti-freeze

Water alone should not be used for filling a cooling system as it causes corrosion. A proprietary anti-freeze mix will not only prevent the coolant freezing, but contains additives that discourage corrosion and the build-up of scale deposits.

Step 1. Check that all drain points are closed and that the hose clips are properly tightened. Set the heater control to 'hot' or ensure that the heater water valve is open.

2. Dilute the anti-freeze with tap water or, better, clean rainwater in a watering-can, according to the protection required—see the manufacturer's instructions.

3. If there is an expansion reservoir, fill this one-third full, or to the level marked on the side. Where the cooling system has bleed valves, they should be fully opened.

4. On cars without bleed valves, pour the anti-freeze through the filler hole, pouring slowly to avoid air locks. When the coolant level reaches the filler neck, leave the cap off, and run the engine at a fast idle speed. As the water pump circulates the coolant, air locks will be released at the filler hole. After about five minutes, stop the engine, top up the coolant, and refit the filler cap. Run it again until normal temperature is reached and check for leaks.

*4. On cars with bleed valves it may be necessary to clamp the circuits incorporating the valves, using a hose clip, in order to force out pockets of air from the heater and inlet manifold.

*5. The method Renault recommends for its 5 and 12 models is fairly typical. When the water reaches the top of the radiator filler neck, the return hose from the heater and the hose from the inlet manifold are clamped near the water pump. Renault makes special clamps for this purpose, but Girling brake-hose clamps or two self-grip wrenches, applied with care, will do. Pack small pieces of hardboard under the jaws to prevent them cutting the hoses.

*6. With the bleed screws open, run the engine at a fast idle speed. The level in the radiator will drop. Keep filling it until water flows from a bleed valve continuously without a trace of air. Close each bleed valve when this happens.

Remove the clamps, top up the radiator, run the engine to normal temperature and check for leaks.

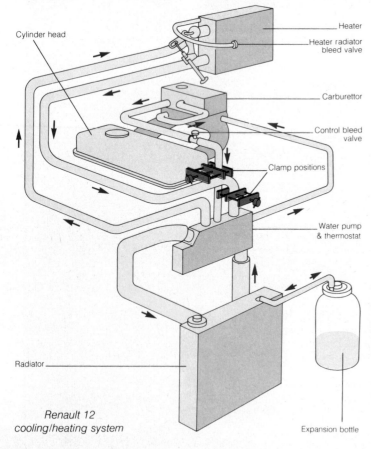
Step 2.

Step 3.

Step 4.

Step *5.

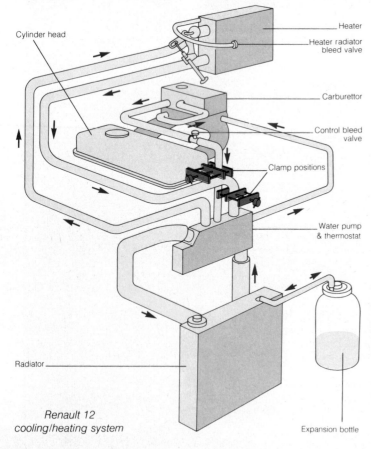
*Renault 12
cooling/heating system*

Cylinder head

Heater

Heater radiator bleed valve

Carburettor

Control bleed valve

Clamp positions

Water pump & thermostat

Radiator

Expansion bottle

Project 9: Checking a radiator pressure cap

Grading: 🔧
Time: 5min
Tools: Small screwdriver

A leaking radiator cap, or one with a weak pressure spring, will prevent pressurisation of the cooling system, allowing the coolant to boil at a lower temperature than it should. When this happens, coolant overflows and the engine is likely to overheat. There are two seals in the radiator cap which can be checked visually.

Step 1. Remove the cap from the radiator and inspect the pressure seal. If it has a damaged surface or has stretched so that it overlaps its seating, fit a new cap.

2. Gently lift the vacuum seal in the centre of the pressure seal and make the same checks on the sealing washer.

3. Caps are usually stamped with their spring pressure on the top. This should agree with the maker's recommendation (a dealer will know). If you suspect that the pressure spring is weak, a garage can check it.

Step 1.

Step 2.

Project 10: Replacing a water pump

Grading: 🔧🔧
Time: Approx 1hr 20min
Tools: Spanner; pliers; screwdriver for hose clips; spanner for radiator fixings, fan bolts and generator mountings; wrench; socket for pump fixings
Materials: Water pump; gasket; sealing compound; mallet; scraper; by-pass hose, if necessary

Step 3.

Step 4.

Step 2.

Step 5.

Step 6.

Although a defective water pump will leak coolant, this is not always obvious because it is dispersed around the engine bay by the drive pulley or fan.

If there is a persistent water loss, but checks on hoses show no apparent leaks, it is possible that the seal on the pump spindle is damaged and is allowing water to leak through the pump bearings. As a rough guide to pump condition, loosen the fanbelt (see 'Looking After the Fanbelt') and try to rock the pump spindle by moving the pulley up and down. If there is more than a fraction of free play, the pump is probably leaking. Leaking pumps sometimes make a squeaking sound, but a squeaking pump is not necessarily leaking—carry out the spindle test before deciding to renew it.
Step 1. Drain the coolant (see Project 4) and remove the top and bottom radiator hoses at the pump.
2. Slacken the generator mounting bolts and remove the drive belt. Where the pump has the radiator cooling fan attached, undo the fan-blade attachment bolts from the pump pulley and remove the fan. If there is insufficient clearance to remove the fan blades, undo the radiator cowl, or if necessary, remove the radiator.
3. Using a suitable socket extension bar and wrench, undo the attachment bolts or nuts round the outer edge of the pump. If the pump is linked to the cylinder head by a small-bore by-pass hose, remove this. Draw the pump from the engine, if necessary lightly tapping it sideways with a mallet to jar it free.
4. Scrape any dirt and the remains of the old gasket from the front of the engine. Fit a new gasket to the new pump, holding it in place with non-setting sealant. Smear sealing compound on the gasket seating on the engine. If the pump has a by-pass hose fit a new one, with new clips, first attaching it loosely to the pump stub.
5. Offer up the pump to the engine, if necessary fitting the by-pass hose on the cylinder head stub—thread the hose clip on the hose first.
6. Tighten the securing bolts or nuts evenly round the edge of the pump.

If appropriate, tighten the by-pass hose clips, then refit the radiator hoses, fan and radiator, re-tension the fanbelt and top up with coolant.

Project 11: Checking an air-cooled engine system

Grading: 🔧
Time: Varies with the amount of work
Tools: Spanners, screwdriver to fit air hose clips; spanners to fit drive belt adjuster; oil can

A fault in an air-cooled system is not as easy to trace as on a water-cooled layout because the engine is surrounded by ducting.

It is advisable that the following areas be checked every 6,000 miles.
Step 1. If the fan is belt-driven, check the belt for cracking or fraying and renew it at the first sign of such deterioration. (See Project 3).
2. Ensure that the air intake at the fan housing is clear of obstructions. A mis-shapen air hose may have collapsed internally—if you are suspicious, unclip it and check inside.
3. Support the car on ramps and check underneath for any looseness of fixings holding the ducting, or any damage to the ducting.
4. Lubricate and check the action of any flap valve linkages.

Producing the power

Internal combustion

Most cars are powered by a piston engine that burns a mixture of petrol and air. The mixture is burned in a combustion chamber within a cylinder above a piston.

When it burns, the mixture expands rapidly and the pressure that this exerts on the top of the piston forces it down the cylinder.

The underside of the piston is connected by a rod (the connecting rod) to a cranked shaft (crankshaft) and this arrangement allows the downward path of the piston to be transformed into rotary movement of the shaft. From the crankshaft the power is transmitted to the wheels that drive the car through the clutch (or torque convertor), gearbox and final drive.

Inlet and exhaust valves at the top of the cylinder control the entry of the petrol/air mixture and the exit of burned gases into the exhaust system. The valves are operated by eccentric lobes on a camshaft, driven from the crankshaft.

The mixture is ignited in the combustion chamber by a spark plug. The high-voltage, or high-tension current necessary to produce a spark is generated within a separate ignition system and usually fed to each cylinder as required by a distributor, normally driven by the camshaft.

To start the engine it must be rotated. This is done electrically by a starter motor which rotates the crankshaft, usually by engaging a small pinion (or gear wheel) with the gear teeth round the outer edge of a flywheel, bolted to the end of the crankshaft. Besides providing a means of starting the engine, the flywheel smooths out the power pulses from the pistons and allows the crankshaft to turn relatively smoothly.

Once the starter is rotating the crankshaft, the up and down movement of the pistons sucks mixture into the cylinders, and when the ignition is switched on, combustion begins and the engine starts.

In addition, the internal combustion engine will have a water- or air-cooling system, and its own lubrication system.

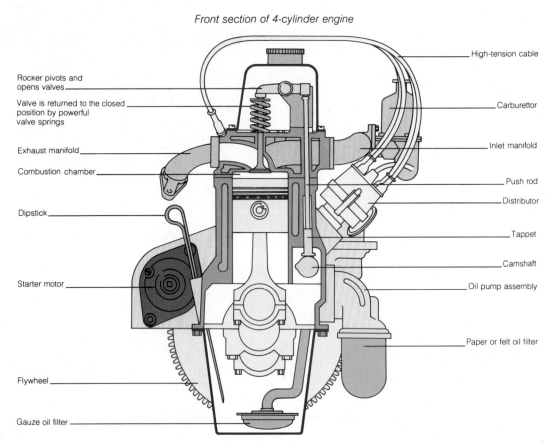

Front section of 4-cylinder engine

Rocker pivots and opens valves

Valve is returned to the closed position by powerful valve springs

Exhaust manifold

Combustion chamber

Dipstick

Starter motor

Flywheel

Gauze oil filter

High-tension cable

Carburettor

Inlet manifold

Push rod

Distributor

Tappet

Camshaft

Oil pump assembly

Paper or felt oil filter

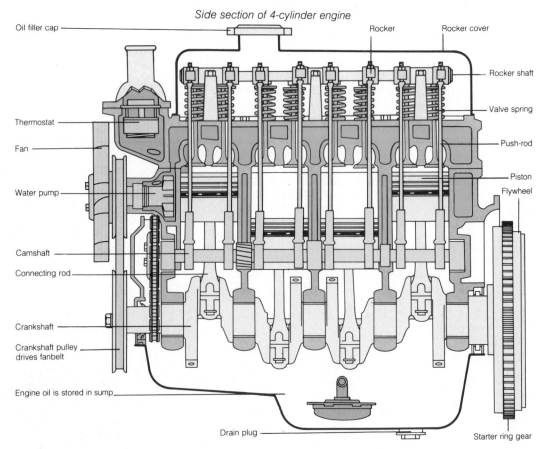

Side section of 4-cylinder engine

Oil filler cap

Thermostat

Fan

Water pump

Camshaft

Connecting rod

Crankshaft

Crankshaft pulley drives fanbelt

Engine oil is stored in sump

Drain plug

Rocker

Rocker cover

Rocker shaft

Valve spring

Push-rod

Piston

Flywheel

Starter ring gear

From the outside

The components that transmit the power—the pistons, connecting rods and crankshaft—are hidden inside the cylinder block, and the outside of the block and cylinder head carries a number of vital ancillary components.

These include the inlet and exhaust manifolds, which carry fuel and air to the cylinders and pipe exhaust gas out, carburettor, distributor, starter motor, generator and usually the petrol pump. The positions of these components vary a little depending on the layout of the engine. The drawing shows where they are located on four-cylinder engines found on the majority of small cars.

Some of the outside components are hard to find. The carburettor is usually beneath a big air filter, and the exhaust manifold may be half buried in a heat box that directs warm air to the carburettor.

In addition, there will be a number of small diameter hoses. Besides taking water to and from the interior heater, hoses often feed water from the cylinder block to a jacket round the inlet manifold, where warmth helps to vaporise the mixture. They also pipe crankcase fumes to the inlet manifold.

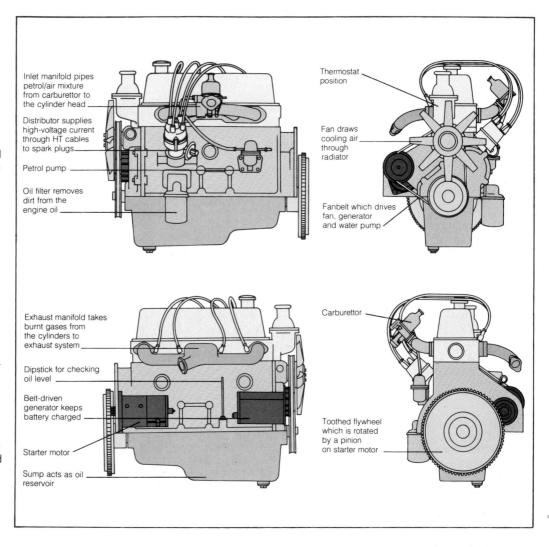

Inlet manifold pipes petrol/air mixture from carburettor to the cylinder head

Distributor supplies high-voltage current through HT cables to spark plugs

Petrol pump

Oil filter removes dirt from the engine oil

Thermostat position

Fan draws cooling air through radiator

Fanbelt which drives fan, generator and water pump

Exhaust manifold takes burnt gases from the cylinders to exhaust system

Dipstick for checking oil level

Belt-driven generator keeps battery charged

Starter motor

Sump acts as oil reservoir

Carburettor

Toothed flywheel which is rotated by a pinion on starter motor

The heavy metal

Because substantial temperatures and forces are generated within an internal combustion engine, the components in direct contact with these loads must be extremely rigid and very strong to withstand the demands made upon them.

There are three major assemblies:

The cylinder head contains the combustion chambers, the valves—there are usually two to each cylinder—the springs that close the valves and the valve gear that opens them and the inlet and exhaust ports.

The cylinder block contains the cylinders and houses the crankshaft, pistons and connecting rods.

It may also carry the camshaft, but on some engines this is mounted above the cylinder head, and where this is done,

the engine is known as an overhead camshaft (OHC) engine.

In water-cooled engines, both the cylinder block and cylinder head contain passages through which cooling water circulates.

The crankshaft assembly includes the pistons, connecting rods and the crankshaft. The shaft is carried in main bearings mounted between the cylinders at the bottom of the cylinder block.

At one end of the crankshaft is the flywheel.

At the base of the engine a pressed steel or cast aluminium sump provides a reservoir for lubricating oil. At the top, a cover keeps in the oil that lubricates the valve gear and, on modern engines, provides a seal against atmospheric air.

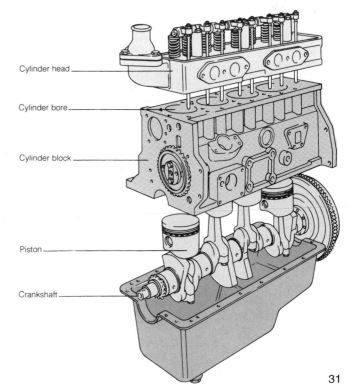

Cylinder head

Cylinder bore

Cylinder block

Piston

Crankshaft

Producing the power

Basic principles: the four-stroke cycle

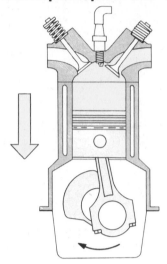
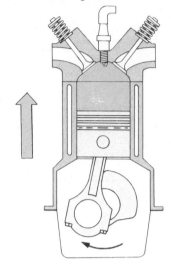
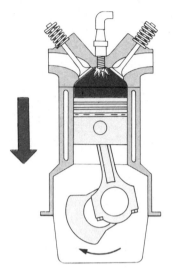
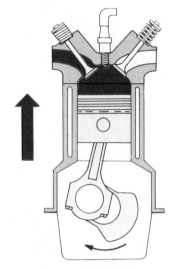

1 Induction   *2 Compression*   *3 Power*   *4 Exhaust*

The internal combustion engine in most cars works on the four-stroke principle. This means that to produce one pulse of power the piston must travel up and down the cylinder four times.

Each stroke of the piston performs a separate function in the cycle as follows:

Induction stroke Begins the process. The inlet valve is open and rotation of the crankshaft is moving the piston down the cylinder, sucking in a mixture of fuel and air which travels from the carburettor, along the inlet manifold and past the open valve.

Compression stroke Both valves are shut and the rotating crankshaft now raises the piston, compressing the mixture above it into the combustion area.

Power stroke Both valves remain shut, and a spark jumping across the electrodes of the spark plug has set the mixture alight. It burns rapidly, expanding very quickly just as the piston begins its downward movement. The energy released rams the piston to the bottom of the cylinder, driving round the crankshaft half a turn.

Exhaust stroke Spent gases from the power stroke leave the combustion chamber through the open exhaust valve, helped out by the pressure created by the rising piston.

When the piston reaches the top of the cylinder at the end of this stroke, the exhaust valve will close, the inlet valve will open and the cycle begin again with another induction stroke.

During the four strokes, the crankshaft rotates twice, but since the valves only need to operate once during each cycle, the camshaft that opens them is driven at half crankshaft speed and rotates only once every four strokes.

Compression ratio

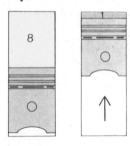

The engine compression ratio

The power that an internal combustion engine develops depends on how much energy can be released above the piston at each power stroke. This in turn depends on the quantity of fuel/air mixture in the cylinder and the efficiency with which it is compressed.

The amount that the mixture is squeezed up is referred to as the compression ratio. This is the difference between the volume of the mixture in the cylinder when the piston is at the bottom of its stroke, and the volume when the piston is at its highest position. If the upward movement of the piston reduces the mixture to one-eighth its original volume, the compression ratio is 8:1.

In theory the more the mixture is compressed, the more energy it releases when it burns. In practice, however, very high compression ratios result in knocking or pinking in which some of the mixture furthest away from the spark plug explodes or detonates causing uneven burning, overheating and loss of power. For maximum efficiency, burning of the mixture should occur rapidly but smoothly.

Valve overlap

So far we have assumed that the incoming mixture rushes past the inlet valve as soon as it opens. In practice, the mixture is slow to accelerate, and in order to fill the cylinder as completely as possible, the inlet valve is opened a little early, when the piston is near the end of the exhaust stroke, and while the exhaust valve is still open. This is called valve overlap.

It might seem that opening the inlet valve early would offer an alternative exit for the exhaust gas, but provided the amount of overlap is carefully chosen, the opposite happens and the last wisps of exhaust leaving the cylinder help drag the fresh mixture in past the inlet valve.

Once it is moving, the inlet mixture does not stop automatically when the piston reaches the bottom of the cylinder, and if the closing of the inlet valve is delayed, the cylinder fills more completely, even though by now the piston has started to rise on the compression stroke.

In practice, in order to make the most of the momentum of fresh mixture and exhaust gas flowing in and out of the cylinder, the exhaust valve opens before the piston reaches the bottom of the cylinder and closes after it has reached the top. Similarly, the inlet valve opens before the piston reaches the top of the cylinder and closes after the piston reaches the bottom.

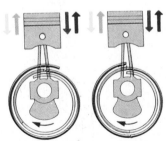

Theoretical valve timing (right) with no valve overlap. In practice, (left) inlet and exhaust valves are open together as the coloured lines show

'Gas flow'

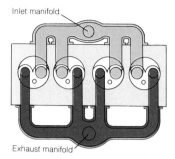

Crossflow cylinder head

Crossflow engines have the inlet manifold on one side of the cylinder head and the exhaust system on the opposite side, so that during the four-stroke cycle, the inlet charge and exhaust gas flow across the combustion chamber—an arrangement that gives efficient cylinder filling during the period of valve overlap.

Engines with the inlet and exhaust manifolds on the same side of the cylinder head have a reverse flow arrangment. This is a little less efficient during the valve overlap period, but means that the heat from the exhaust can be easily and cheaply used to warm the inlet manifold and so improve vaporisation of the mixture inside. On a crossflow engine it is necessary to pipe water from the cooling system to heat the inlet manifold.

Smoothing out vibration

On a four-cylinder engine, if the firing order were 1,2,3,4, the crankshaft and the engine mountings would be subject to considerable stress and vibration. The stress is minimised if the firing impulses are spread more evenly along the crankshaft, and the firing order of four-cylinder units is either 1,3,4,2 or 1,2,4,3.

In addition to distributing the load as evenly as possible the engine designer adds webs to the crankshaft in order to counterbalance the mass of each piston and connecting rod assembly—this helps the engine to produce a smooth power output. Engines are fitted to rubber mountings which reduce the amount of vibration passed on to the car body.

Pistons and connecting rods

The driving force that transmits the expansion of the burning fuel/air into half a turn of the crankshaft is the piston. Since at maximum engine speed it may be sliding up and down the cylinder at 100 times a second, it must be light, yet strong enough to take the shock-loads of combustion and of sudden and frequent reversals of direction.

In most cars the pistons are made of aluminium alloy, and have a number of hardened steel piston rings sitting in grooves round the upper portion of the piston. The rings fill the small gap between the piston and the cylinder bore. Usually two of them are compression rings and seal the gap, while lower down an oil control ring scrapes excess oil from the cylinder walls and prevents it from being burned in the combustion chamber.

The piston's up and down movement is converted to the circular motion of the crankshaft by a forged steel connecting rod that pivots on a gudgeon pin (sometimes called a wrist pin) where it connects to the underside of the piston, and is bolted at its bottom end to the orbiting crankpin of the crankshaft.

The end of the connecting rod that embraces the gudgeon pin is called the small end, and the bottom end, which is larger, and is normally split so that it

can be bolted round the crank-pin, is the big end.

On most cars the big end encloses a two-piece plain bearing, a shell bearing, which has a soft metal surface in contact with the crankpin. It is this soft, relatively cheap bearing material, and not the finely ground crankpin, that is the first to fail if the lubrication system breaks down.

A few car engines, developed from motorcycle units, have ball- or roller-type big end bearings, which cannot be split. As a consequence, these engines have multi-piece crankshafts which must be separated and re-assembled, using a powerful hydraulic press, when a connecting rod or bearings have to be changed.

Cast iron rings fitted in grooves near the top of the piston prevent combustion gases leaking past. The lower ring is slotted to remove oil from the cylinder wall.

The piston is attached to the connecting rod by the gudgeon pin which floats in the little-end bearing.

Crankshaft and bearings

Most crankshafts are forged or cast in one piece. They have two sets of bearing surfaces—journals and crankpins—which are very accurately ground. The journals are spaced along the shaft and rotate in main bearings fixed to the bottom of the cylinder block. Crankpins revolve inside the connecting rod big-ends. The crankshaft is either hollow or drilled, allowing lubricating oil under pressure to flow from the journals to the crankpins.

Lubricating oil for the main and big-end bearings passes through holes drilled in the crankshaft

Producing the power

Valves

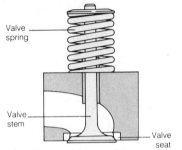

Valve spring

Valve stem

Valve seat

Most four-stroke engines use two poppet valves to allow the mixture into the cylinder and let the exhaust out.

As they are in direct contact with the combustion process, both valves are made from heat-resistant material.

Of the two, the inlet valve, which is cooled by the inrush of petrol/air mixture on each induction stroke, runs cooler. The exhaust valve, which in normal use runs at a red-hot 800°C, is usually made of a higher-temperature alloy steel than the inlet, and transfers much of its heat to the cylinder head when it is closed.

Both valves are shut by a powerful spring, usually in the form of a coil round the outside of the valve stem. The bottom of the spring rests on the cylinder head casting and the top presses against a retainer fitted to the end of the valve stem. Some valves have two coil springs, fitted one inside the other, to shut them.

A valve is opened simply by being pushed down against spring pressure, and there are several methods of doing this.

Valve adjustment

Metal expands when it is heated, and to make sure the valves are able to shut fully when the engine is hot, a small amount of play or clearance is allowed for in the valve gear.

The clearance reduces as the engine gets hot, but should never disappear altogether. On pushrod and rocker layouts where the camshaft is a long way from the valve, a larger clearance is needed than on a direct-acting overhead camshaft system. The valve clearance is measured when the valve is fully shut by checking the slack in the operating linkage with a feeler gauge. The manufacturer will specify

Valve-operating systems

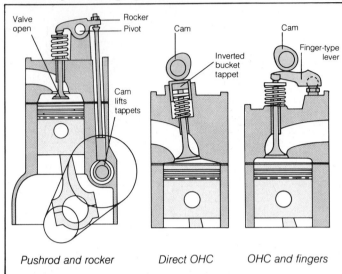

Valve open — Rocker — Pivot

Cam lifts tappets

Cam

Inverted bucket tappet

Cam

Finger-type lever

Pushrod and rocker   *Direct OHC*   *OHC and fingers*

Pushrod and rocker. The camshaft is mounted in the cylinder block and is chain- or belt-driven from the front of the crankshaft. A hardened steel block rests on each cam and as the camshaft rotates the tappet lifts each time the lobe of the cam travels underneath it.

From the tappet block, the lifting motion is transmitted along a pushrod to a rocker pivoting above the valve. As the pushrod lifts one side of the rocker, the other side presses down the valve and opens it. Once the cam lobe has passed underneath the tappet, the spring shuts the valve and the rocker, pushrod and tappet return to the at-rest position.

The main disadvantages of pushrod and rocker systems are noisy operation at high

whether the clearance should be checked with the engine hot or cold. It is important that the recommended clearances and checking system are used, since incorrect adjustment can cause valve damage and lead to an expensive overhaul.

A few engines have hydraulic tappets which have two parts, one sliding within the other. Oil under pressure expands these tappets and takes up the clearances when the engine is running. On these engines, no valve adjustment is needed.

The way valve clearances are adjusted to take up wear depends on the design of the

speeds and wear of the large number of moving parts. Putting the camshaft directly above the valves reduces the number of parts and gives quieter operation.

Overhead camshaft. A direct-acting overhead camshaft works more or less directly on the end of the valve stem, eliminating a pushrod and rocker. A tappet mounted upside-down, called an inverted bucket-tappet sits in a guide over the valve stem and spring.

An alternative arrangement is to use levers (fingers) or rockers bearing on the camshaft to operate the valves. Some high-performance engines use two camshafts, one to operate the inlet valves and one the exhaust valves.

valve gear. Most pushrod and rocker systems use an adjusting screw, usually with a lock-nut, at the pushrod end of the rocker. Turning the screw anti-clockwise increases the valve clearance, turning the screw clockwise reduces it. Alternatively, the rockers may pivot on a ball mounting on the underside of a lock-nut. Turning the lock-nut adjusts the clearance.

Because of the fewer moving parts, direct-acting overhead camshaft systems need less adjustment. In fact on some engines the only way in which adjustment can be made is by dismantling the camshaft and

Driving the camshaft

Until the development of the internally-toothed rubber belt, most overhead camshafts were chain-driven. Because of the length of chain involved, a tensioner was needed to prevent whipping. The tensioner was in the form of either a synthetic rubber pad, spring-loaded or hydraulically pressed against the side of the chain, or a spring blade or rubber-faced steel strip bearing on one side of the chain.

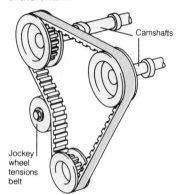

Camshafts

Jockey wheel tensions belt

Belt-driven overhead camshaft

A toothed-belt camshaft drive is quieter than a chain and, since it needs no lubrication, it can be mounted externally. The oil-resistant rubber is moulded on to non-stretch cords and on the inside has a series of square-section teeth that accurately match cut-outs in the crankshaft and camshaft pulley wheels. The belt is usually tensioned by a jockey wheel which bears on its smooth side.

tappets and altering the thickness of small packing shims between the bucket tappet and valve stem.

Some manufacturers avoid dismantling the camshaft by making a recess in the upper face of the bucket tappet and fitting a thick shim or 'biscuit' into it. To change these, a special tool is used to lever down the tappet, but it is not necessary to remove the camshaft.

Another method is to provide an adjusting screw inside the tappet. The screw, which bears on the end of the valve stem, is turned by inserting an Allen key through a small hole in the side or end of the tappet.

Combustion chamber

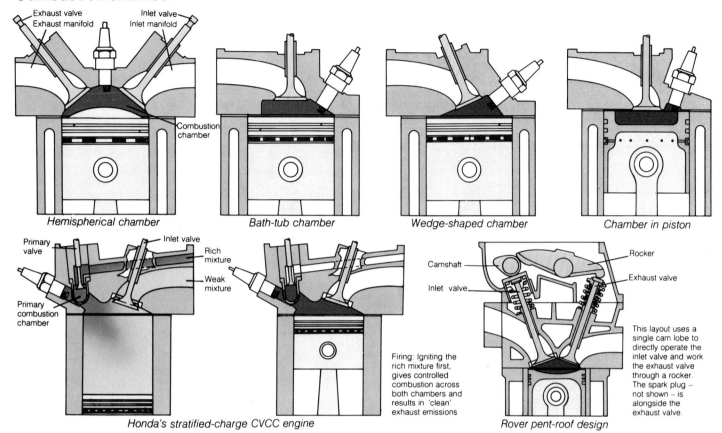

Hemispherical chamber

Bath-tub chamber

Wedge-shaped chamber

Chamber in piston

Honda's stratified-charge CVCC engine

Firing: Igniting the rich mixture first, gives controlled combustion across both chambers and results in 'clean' exhaust emissions

Rover pent-roof design

This layout uses a single cam lobe to directly operate the inlet valve and work the exhaust valve through a rocker. The spark plug – not shown – is alongside the exhaust valve.

The shape of the combustion chamber in which the fuel/air mixture is burned, has a considerable effect on the power output. Ideally the chamber should be compact, so that the minimum of heat is lost to the cooling system, and shaped in such a way that the mixture burns evenly, producing a progressive increase in pressure.

The dome-like, hemispherical combustion chamber, with the valves inclined at 90° to each other and a centre spark plug, has long been recognised as the most effective design.

The layout leaves room for a large, free-flowing inlet tract from which the mixture swirls easily into the space above the piston. The exhaust valve is opposite the inlet in a cross-flow layout. This gives the most efficient filling and emptying of the cylinder, while the angling of the valves permits large valve sizes to be used which admit a larger volume of mixture.

The generous power output from a hemispherical combus-tion chamber means that it is often used in high-performance engines. Its drawback is that valves inclined at 90° need two overhead camshafts—or one overhead camshaft and a complex linkage—to operate them. The expense of this sort of valve gear makes it uneconomical to produce for cheaper cars.

Placing the valves more upright and turning the hemispherical chamber into a shallow pent-roof shape reduces the efficiency a little, but allows the use of simpler valve gear, and a single overhead camshaft and rockers.

The designers of mass-produced cars try to get the advantages of a hemispherical chamber more cheaply and usually opt for one of these alternatives:

Bowl in piston. The cylinder head is flat or nearly flat and the combustion chamber forms in the top of the piston. When used on an over-square engine (where the diameter of the piston is greater than its stroke) large valves can be fitted.

At the top of the stroke, the rim of the piston very nearly touches the cylinder head, providing a degree of 'squish', a squeezing action that forces mixture at the edge of the cylinder towards the centre. This assists burning and helps to compensate for the offset position of the spark plug.

Bathtub combustion chamber. This is formed in the cylinder head and has two vertical valves and a side-mounted spark plug. Mixture in the 'squish' area between the piston and the flat face of the head provides some turbulence within the mixture, which helps it burn smoothly. Some bathtub chambers have a shaped projection between the valves, giving the chamber a heart-shaped plan view. This swirls the incoming mixture, helping to atomise it further.

Wedge shape. Both valves are inclined at the same angle in the sloping roof, allowing a slightly smoother inlet tract compared with the vertical-valve bathtub shape. The 'squish' action is the same as in a bathtub chamber.

Future trends. If a weaker mixture (less fuel to air) can be burned in the combustion chamber, this reduces the amount of noxious fumes emitted from the exhaust. Normally a weak mixture causes overheating, knocking or pinking and can be difficult to ignite.

Engine designers are solving these problems by using more sophisticated combustion chambers. In Japan, where exhaust emission regulations are more stringent than in Europe, Honda uses a two-stage combustion chamber which is fed with mixture in two strengths. A rich mixture is introduced to a small primary chamber round the spark plug, while a separate stream of weak mixture is fed to the main chamber below it. When the plug fires, the rich mixture ignites, and the burning spreads smoothly to the weak mixture in the other chamber.

Honda says this CVCC (Compound Vortex Controlled Combustion) unit easily meets emission regulations without the need to use a complicated exhaust system to filter the exhaust further.

Producing the power

Multi-cylinder engines

A single-cylinder four-stroke piston engine spends three-quarters of its running time exhausting burned gas, drawing in fresh mixture and compressing it.

On only one of the four strokes—the power stroke—is any energy produced, and this makes the output of a single-cylinder four-stroke engine very uneven.

This can be smoothed out if more cylinders, with their pistons driving a common crankshaft, are used. A twin-cylinder four-stroke, for instance, will produce one power stroke for each revolution of the crankshaft, instead of every other

revolution as on a single-cylinder engine.

If the engine has four cylinders it produces one power stroke for each half-turn of the crankshaft and at no time is the crankshaft 'free-wheeling' on one of the three passive strokes.

Even better results can be obtained using six cylinders, as the power strokes can be made to overlap, so that the crankshaft receives a fresh impulse before the previous power stroke has died away—on an in-line six-cylinder engine the crankshaft receives three power impulses each revolution.

In theory, the more cylinders you can use to drive the crankshaft, the smoother the power output, and 8- and 12-cylinder engines are used on some of the more expensive cars.

A large number of cylinders can pose practical problems. An engine with eight cylinders in a straight line for instance would have a very long crankshaft which would tend to twist and be more likely to break at higher engine speeds. The car would also need a long bonnet to enclose the engine.

So in the interests of crankshaft rigidity and compactness, 8- and 12-cylinder engines have their cylinders

arranged in a V, with two cylinder heads and a common crankshaft.

There are also V-6 and V-4 cylinder engines.

The other layout in popular use is where the cylinders are horizontally opposed in two flat banks, with the crankshaft between them. Its low build makes the 'flat' engine particularly suitable for rear installation. In 4- or 6-cylinder form, the flat engine has excellent mechanical balance as movement of a piston assembly in one direction is perfectly balanced by movement of similar components operating in the opposite direction.

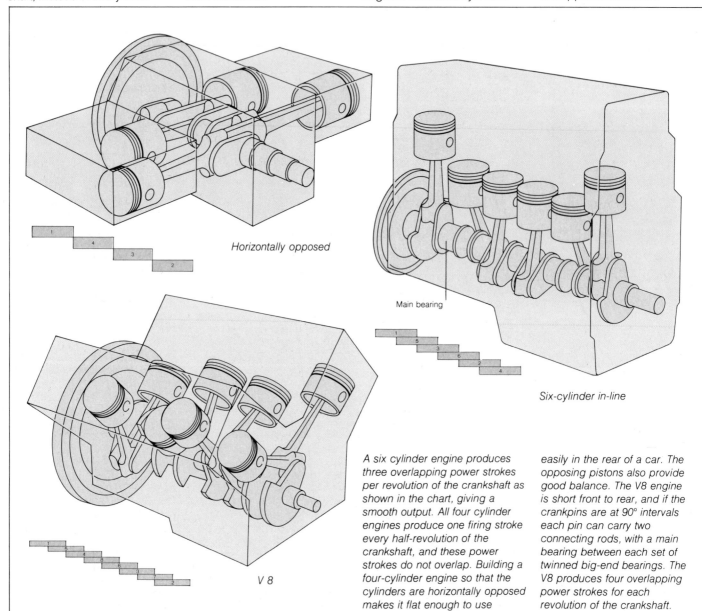

Horizontally opposed

Main bearing

Six-cylinder in-line

V 8

A six cylinder engine produces three overlapping power strokes per revolution of the crankshaft as shown in the chart, giving a smooth output. All four cylinder engines produce one firing stroke every half-revolution of the crankshaft, and these power strokes do not overlap. Building a four-cylinder engine so that the cylinders are horizontally opposed makes it flat enough to use

easily in the rear of a car. The opposing pistons also provide good balance. The V8 engine is short front to rear, and if the crankpins are at 90° intervals each pin can carry two connecting rods, with a main bearing between each set of twinned big-end bearings. The V8 produces four overlapping power strokes for each revolution of the crankshaft.

Producing the power

The diesel engine

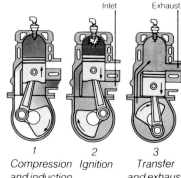

Inlet valve Exhaust valve

1 Induction *2 Compression* *Injection* *3 Power* *4 Exhaust*

Using similar mechanical components to a piston petrol engine, the diesel burns fuel oil. It has no spark plugs—instead the air is compressed in the cylinder until it heats up, and so ignites fuel that is injected into the combustion chamber.

This compression-ignition process works as follows:

Suction. Exhaust valve shut, inlet valve open. The descending piston draws in atmospheric air.

Compression. Both valves shut. The rising piston highly compresses the air (the compression ratio on a diesel engine may be around 22:1), substantially raising its temperature.

Injection/power. As the piston approaches the top of its stroke, fuel is injected into the combustion chamber, meets the hot air and ignites. Combustion forces the piston to the bottom of the cylinder, turning the crankshaft.

Exhaust. The exhaust valve opens, and the rising piston pushes out the burned gas.

The very high compression ratio of the diesel engine results in greater efficiency, and as a result, diesel engines use less fuel than a comparable petrol engine—particularly in traffic. The disadvantages of the diesel are higher initial cost, noisier operation, slower acceleration and a lower maximum speed. Despite the drawbacks—some of which are being eliminated by improved design—the diesel engine is being fitted to greater numbers of private cars because of its energy-saving potential.

The Wankel engine

When it was first produced in 1964 the Wankel rotary engine, with its turbine smoothness, light weight and very few moving parts, was expected to challenge seriously the supremacy of the piston engine. Since then, problems with internal sealing, a heavy thirst for fuel and difficulty in meeting exhaust pollution regulations have meant that it has become a rarity.

Inside, instead of pistons, it has a three-pointed rotor which makes tip contact continuously with the inside of a chamber which has the shape of a wide-waisted figure-of-eight. As the rotor orbits within the chamber, three working spaces between the rotor sides and the chamber expand and contract.

Two ports in the chamber admit the petrol/air mixture and let out the exhaust. A spark plug (sometimes two) fires the mixture. The engine has no valves, and relies on the movement of the rotor to provide a four-stroke sequence. On a

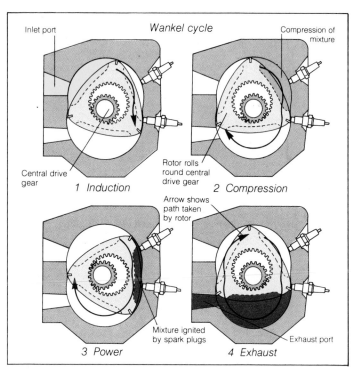

Wankel cycle

Inlet port

Compression of mixture

Central drive gear

Rotor rolls round central drive gear

1 Induction *2 Compression*

Arrow shows path taken by rotor

Mixture ignited by spark plugs

Exhaust port

3 Power *4 Exhaust*

single rotor engine there are three power strokes for each single rotation of the rotor—it is usual to link two or more rotors together. An output shaft geared to the centre of the rotor turns at three times rotor speed and takes the drive to the gearbox.

The two-stroke engine

1 Compression and induction *2 Ignition* *3 Transfer and exhaust*

Inlet Exhaust

Exhaust emission requirements have made the two-stroke piston engine obsolete in new cars, although a few older models use it.

Combustion occurs on each downward stroke of the piston. There are no valves; instead the descending piston uncovers ports which let out the exhaust gas and then replace it with a fresh charge of fuel/air mixture.

Most two-strokes use a small quantity of lubricating oil in the fuel, which produces a smoky exhaust. They are less efficient than a four-stroke engine.

Power and torque

The output of an engine is expressed in two ways. One measure is its maximum power output, expressed in bhp (brake horsepower) or kilowatts and is an indication of its rate of doing work. The figure will be quoted alongside the engine speed at which the power is delivered—for instance '60bhp at 5,500rpm'. The majority of modern engines are capable of 50bhp per 1000cc of engine capacity. Most cars are geared so that the engine develops maximum power at maximum road speed.

The other measure of engine output is torque, loosely defined as 'pulling power'. A car needs high torque from low engine speeds, helping to eliminate frequent gear changing. Torque is a measure of leverage, and is quoted in lb-ft (pounds-feet) or kg-m (kilogram-metres) at the engine speed at which maximum torque occurs, usually around half the speed at which maximum power is produced.

Producing the power projects

Checking and adjusting valve clearances

For maximum economy and performance it is important that the valve clearances are correct; most manufacturers recommend that they are checked at regular service intervals, usually every 5,000–6,000 miles. Some engines have hydraulic tappets which automatically provide the correct setting, and these do not need checking. Some engines need special tools to check the valve clearances, and in this instance valve checking and adjustment should be left to a garage.

Hot and cold adjustment

The car manufacturer will indicate in the handbook or workshop manual whether the valve clearances are to be checked and adjusted with the engine hot or cold. For practical purposes, a cold engine is one that has stood idle overnight, whereas a hot engine is one at normal operating temperature, which is achieved after driving at least four miles. On a few engines the manufacturer will recommend a specific engine temperature for checking and adjusting valve clearances. If this is the case the job is best left to professionals.

Making adjustments

The direct-acting overhead camshaft system is the easiest to check, but can be the hardest to adjust, because on some engines the camshaft must come out and the bucket tappets lifted so that adjusting shims can be fitted underneath —a major dismantling job. To keep servicing costs down, manufacturers of these engines may specify a minimum valve clearance. Provided the gap does not go below this figure, the engine will operate satisfactorily. On most other valve mechanisms, adjustment of the clearances is made by turning an adjusting screw or nut and is straightforward.

Inlet and exhaust clearances

Many engines have a different clearance figure quoted for inlet and exhaust valves. Since all valves look the same when viewed from the stem end, they can be distinguished by tracing the line of the two manifolds.

The inlet manifold branches will aim at the inlet valves, and the branches of the exhaust manifold will point towards the exhaust valves.

Turning the engine

Because each valve clearance must be checked with the valve in the *fully* closed position, it will be necessary to turn the engine to check them all. On in-line engines it is possible to 'pair' the valves and save a lot of engine turning. On four-cylinder in-line engines the 'rule of nine' is used. Number the valves from the generator end. Turn the engine until one valve is fully open. Subtract its number from nine, and the answer is the valve to check. For instance, when valve no.2 is fully open, 9−2=7, so valve no. 7 is the one to check. The same principle applies to six-cylinder in-line engines, using the 'rule of 13'. The crankshaft can be turned by using a spanner on the crankshaft pulley nut.

Using a feeler gauge

If the clearances are incorrect, on most engines it is only a matter of turning an adjusting screw to put each one right. The clearance is correct when a clean feeler will slide into the gap with only moderate end pressure. If the gauge is a loose fit the gap is too wide. If the blade buckles under pressure, it is too small.

Project 12: Shim-adjusted overhead camshaft

> **Grading:** 🔧
> **Time:** 45min–1hr
> **Tools:** Spanner and screwdriver to remove valve cover, and, if necessary, spanner to turn engine; feeler gauge

This arrangement is used on a number of cars including the Austin Maxi and Allegro 1500 and 1750 models, the Princess 2200 range and Hillman Imp engines. The 2000cc and 1700cc 'O' series overhead camshaft engines used since 1978 in the four-cylinder Princess and Marina 1700 models need special tools and equipment to hold the camshaft while clearances are checked, and these engines are best left to professionals.

Step 1. Refer to the handbook to see if the valve clearances are to be checked with the engine hot or cold.

2. Remove the camshaft cover.

On some engines this means disconnecting the high-tension cables at the spark plugs (mark them with sticky tape for correct reassembly). It may also involve disconnecting the fuel pipe at the carburettor (block the end with a pencil), and removing the air cleaner from the carburettor.

3. Turn the crankshaft until one cam lobe is pointing directly away from the tappet.

4. Check the manifolds to ascertain whether the valve is for inlet or exhaust, then use a feeler gauge—laminating two together if necessary—to check the clearance between the tappet and the heel of the cam lobe. Make a note of the valve (number them from the generator end of the engine), and make a note of the clearance.

5. Turn the engine until the next cam lobe is pointing directly away from the tappet and repeat Step 4. Continue this

Project 13: Pushrod and rocker

> **Grading:** 🔧🔧
> **Time:** 45min–1hr
> **Tools:** Spanners or screwdriver to remove rocker cover; feeler gauges; screwdriver or spanner to fit adjuster; spanner for locknut; if necessary, spanner to turn engine

The valve clearance is checked between the tip of the valve stem and the rocker pad, with the engine hot or cold as recommended, and with the valve fully closed.

As the camshaft is out of sight inside the block, you must calculate when the cam lobe is pointing directly away from the tappet and the tappet is resting on the cam heel.

This is done by turning the crankshaft until the valve to be adjusted is fully open, and then turning it again one complete revolution. This will rotate the camshaft half a turn, putting the tappet on the heel of the cam lobe. It helps to put a chalk mark on the crankshaft pulley to show when it has rotated one revolution.

Step 4.

procedure until all the valve clearances have been checked and noted.

6. Compare the clearances with the manufacturer's recommendation. On single-carburettor Maxi engines, for instance, the manufacturer states that no adjustment is necessary until the valve clearances are less than 0.012in (0.30mm).

7. If clearances do need adjusting, have the job done professionally.

Step 1. Identify the inlet and exhaust valves.

2. Turn the engine, using the rule of nine or thirteen, until the valve is fully closed.

3. Insert the appropriate feeler gauge into the gap. It should slide in under moderate pressure. If it is too loose or too tight, move to Step 4.

4. Where the rocker has an adjuster on one end, loosen the lock-nut, and turn the adjusting screw clockwise to reduce the clearance, or anti-clockwise to increase it. Some engines have purpose-made, stiff adjusting screws which do not have a lock-nut.

5. Some pushrod engines have the adjusting nut at the centre of the rocker, and the valve clearances are set with the engine at normal operating temperature and running. Do not use an ordinary feeler gauge for this—dealers sell long feeler strips for the purpose. Make sure that you have no loose clothing; it could be caught in the engine or fanbelt.

6. Run the engine at idling speed. Put a socket or box spanner on the adjusting nut. Insert the feeler blade between the moving rocker pad and valve stem. If the gap is too small, the feeler will be difficult to fit and the engine will run unevenly when it is in position. If the blade rattles, the gap is too wide.

7. Adjust the nut until the engine runs smoothly and any feeler blade rattle disappears. If you find this difficult, stop the engine and check the gap statically.

Step 4.

Step 6.

Project 14: Overhead camshaft and fingers

Grading: 🔧🔧
Time: 45min–1hr
Tools: Spanners/screwdriver to remove valve cover; feeler gauges; spanners to fit valve adjusting stud and lock-nut; if necessary, spanner to turn engine

On some engines a finger or follower is interposed between the valve and camshaft lobe.

On engines with this arrangement the clearance is checked between the heel of the cam and the finger.

Step 1. Identify the inlet and exhaust valves.

2. Check the gap using a feeler gauge.

3. If the clearance needs altering, loosen the lock-nut, and turn the stud anti-clockwise to close the gap, clockwise to enlarge it.

*Ford uses this camshaft and finger arrangement on its single overhead camshaft engines (see illustration right). With this type of engine you might find it difficult in some cases to turn a lock-nut near the carburettor. Garages use a special 'crowsfoot' spanner to get over this problem, but the lock-nut can be turned with an ordinary spanner if the carburettor is removed.

Step 2.

Step 3.

Producing the power projects

Project 15: Checking externally-adjusted OHC clearances

> **Grading:** 🔧🔧
> **Time:** 45min–1hr
> **Tools:** Spanner or screw-driver to remove valve cover, and, if necessary, spanner to turn engine; feeler gauges; Allen key

To overcome the problem of dismantling the camshaft and tappets to make valve adjust-ments (as on Jaguar and Hill-man Imp engines), some manufacturers—Fiat and Vaux-hall among them—provide an easier method of adjustment.

On Fiat OHC engines, the adjusting shims—called 'bis-cuits'—are recessed in the top face of the tappet. If a clear-ance is incorrect, a special tool is used to lever the tappet away from the camshaft, the old bis-cuit is removed and a new one of the correct thickness is inserted in its place.

On Vauxhall OHC engines, no shims or special tools are needed. This means that adjustment is a straightforward DIY job. The gap is altered by a small transverse Allen screw in the tappet, with a ramp on one side. The illustrations show how the gap is adjusted.
Step 1. Identify the inlet and exhaust valves.

2. Check the clearance on each one with the cam lobe pointing away from the tappet.
3. To alter the clearance, rotate the tappet until a niche appears. The access hole for the screw lies below the niche and aligns with a cut-out in the head casting.
4. Use a small Allen key to turn the screw one full turn at a time, anti-clockwise to increase the gap, or clockwise to decrease it. Each complete revolution of the screw alters the gap by 0.003in (0.08mm).
5. After adjustment, re-check the gap with a feeler gauge.

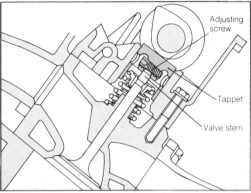
Step 1.

Adjusting screw
Tappet
Valve stem

Step 2.

Step 3.

Step 4.

Project 16: Renewing engine mountings

> **Grading:** 🔧🔧
> **Time:** 45min–1hr
> **Tools:** Pillar or trolley jack; spanners to fit mounting nuts or bolts; if required, screwdriver, pliers or span-ners to undo hose clips and remove radiator or fan fixings
> **Materials:** New engine mounting; timber for packing

The rubber mountings that help to prevent engine vibrations from being transmitted to the bodyshell can actually cause vibration if they are damaged or softened by leaking oil. The weakened rubber allows the engine to rock excessively, and the engine and transmis-sion judders when the clutch is engaged.

To change a mounting under the engine or gearbox, a pillar or trolley jack is used to take the weight while the old mount-ing is undone. The engine or gearbox is then lifted, the old mounting removed, and a new one inserted.
Step 1. Place a jack under the engine sump. Put a piece of timber at least 1in thick and measuring about 9in ×6in on top of the jack.
2. Raise the jack until it just takes the weight of the engine.

The timber will spread the load and prevent damage to the underside of the engine.
3. Remove the nuts or bolts securing the damaged mounting.
4. Slowly raise the engine, watching that the radiator hoses do not over-stretch, and that an engine-driven fan does not move dangerously near the radiator. If the hoses show signs of strain, drain the cool-ing system and remove them (see Project 7). Remove the radiator or fan if necessary.
5. Remove the mounting and insert the new one, putting on the mounting nuts or bolts finger-tight.
6. Lower the engine slowly. When the weight is on the mounting, fully tighten the fixings.

Step 2.

Step 3.

Producing the power projects

Project 17: Fitting new steady-bar rubber bushes

Grading: ✦
Time: 20min–30min
Tools: Spanners to fit fixing bolts
Materials: New rubber bushes; washing-up liquid

Worn steady-bar rubbers will allow an engine to rock excessively, causing clutch judder and putting an unnecessary strain on the exhaust system. The illustrations show how the job is done on a Mini.
Step 1. Remove the fixing bolt and loosen the cover bracket bolt on the cylinder head.
2. Swing the steady bar clear, and push the old rubbers from the eye.
3. Fit the new rubbers and sleeve by hand. If they are difficult to fit, coating them in washing-up liquid will help them into the eye.
4. Fit the centre sleeve, re-assemble the bracket and fixing bolt, and tighten both bolts.

Step 1.

Step 2.

Step 3.

Step 4.

Project 18: Changing an exhaust manifold gasket

Grading: ✦✦
Time: 30min–1hr 30min depending on the type of engine.
Tools: Spanner, socket and extension or box spanner to fit manifold nuts/bolts; if required, spanner to fit downpipe clamp bolts; old kitchen knife; where applicable, spanners/screwdriver to remove air cleaner and carburettor controls
Materials: New gasket; penetrating oil

If an exhaust manifold gasket leaks—usually because a nut or bolt has worked loose— exhaust fumes may drift into the car.

A leak makes a distinct chuffing sound and the hot, escaping gas can be felt with the palm of the hand. Renewing the gasket cures the trouble.

A few cars have a combined inlet and exhaust manifold. On these the carburettor air cleaner must be taken off, and it may be necessary to disconnect the throttle and choke controls at the carburettor if they are anchored to the manifold.
Step 1. If the manifold has never been removed, put penetrating oil on the fixing bolts or nuts and leave it overnight to work into the threads.
2. Remove the nuts or bolts securing the manifold, using a socket and extension or a box spanner, if necessary.
3. Move the manifold away from the cylinder head and extract the old gasket. On a few cars, the downpipe to the exhaust system will restrict movement of the manifold. On these, loosen the clamp between manifold and downpipe.
4. Scrape off all traces of old gasket material from the manifold and head faces.
5. Insert the new gasket, refit the manifold and do up all fixings finger-tight. Then tighten them firmly with a spanner or socket, working outwards from the centre.
6. If the downpipe joint has been loosened, re-tighten the fixings. Reconnect throttle and choke controls, and refit the air cleaner if it has been removed.

Step 2.

Step 4.

Step 5.

Lubrication

How the oil circulates

Under a microscope even the smoothest engine components have a surface that looks like a ploughed field. If these surfaces made rubbing contact without a film of oil between them, they would grind together, overheat and destroy themselves.

To prevent this happening, all engines have a built-in lubrication system that pumps, sprays or drips a constant supply of oil on all the moving metal components.

In addition to reducing friction, engine oil has the vital task of helping to cool components such as pistons and valves that are in direct contact with the blow-torch temperatures within the combustion chambers. It also helps to make a gas-tight seal between the piston rings and cylinders, and carries away harmful combustion waste products.

The path that the oil takes through the engine is shown in the illustration. From the sump, a reservoir under the crankcase, it is drawn through a wire strainer into the pump. Most pumps have an output of several gallons per minute and can produce pressures of more than 60psi (4.2kg sq.cm). A relief valve limits the pressure in the lubrication system, usually to between 40 and 60psi (2.8 and 4.2kg sq.cm).

From the pump, oil passes through a filter and into a main gallery drilled in the side of the crankcase. Drillings connect the gallery to the crankshaft main bearing housings and, once the engine is running, oil under pressure is forced between the rotating crankshaft journals and the bearings.

The crankshaft will be hollow or drilled so that the oil supply to the main bearings is also linked to the big-end bearings at the bases of the connecting rods. In this way all crankshaft bearings are pressure-fed.

The connecting rods take the oil a little further. The rod may be drilled near its base so that a jet of oil sprays the cylinder walls and the underside of the piston as the crankshaft rotates.

Alternatively the connecting rod may be drilled along its length so that pressurised oil from the big-end bearing is taken direct to the gudgeon pin to lubricate it. The surplus then spills out to cool the underside of the piston and cylinder.

The camshaft operates at half engine speed, but it needs effective lubrication because of the high rubbing loads on the cams. It is usual to pressure-feed the camshaft bearings, and to splash or spray oil on the cam lobes.

A push-rod engine with its camshaft mounted low in the crankcase, has oil piped to the hollow rocker shaft, from where it lubricates the rocker bearings and push-rod ends. The surplus then drips down the push-rod openings and coats the camshaft lobes on its way back to the sump.

On engines with an overhead camshaft, two systems are in popular use. In the simplest system the rotating camshaft lobes dip into a trough of oil.

An alternative is to spray the cam lobes with oil. This is usually done by a perforated oil pipe alongside the camshaft. Small holes drilled in the side of the pipe aim a jet of oil on to each rotating lobe. The surplus splashes over the valve assembly before dripping back to the sump.

On cars where an internal chain drives the camshaft, a small tapping from the main gallery sprays oil on the chain links as they move past.

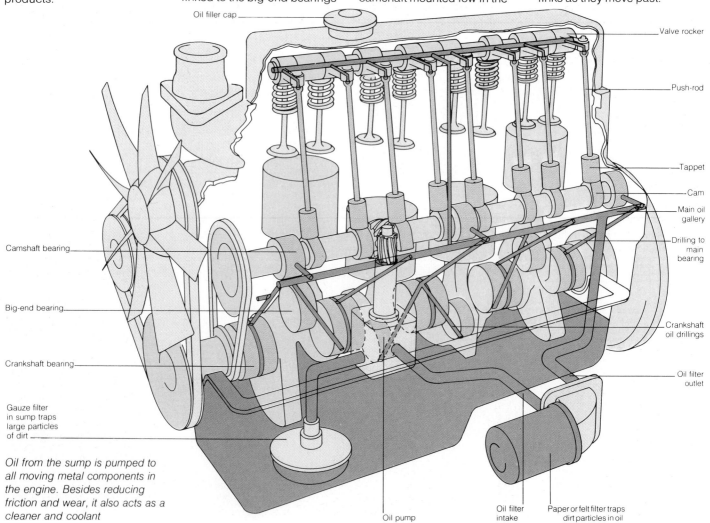

Oil filler cap — Valve rocker — Push-rod — Tappet — Cam — Main oil gallery — Drilling to main bearing — Crankshaft oil drillings — Oil filter outlet — Camshaft bearing — Big-end bearing — Crankshaft bearing — Gauze filter in sump traps large particles of dirt — Oil pump — Oil filter intake — Paper or felt filter traps dirt particles in oil

Oil from the sump is pumped to all moving metal components in the engine. Besides reducing friction and wear, it also acts as a cleaner and coolant

Oil pump

In its simplest form an oil pump consists of two gear wheels meshed together in a tight space so that oil cannot escape past the sides. One wheel is driven by the engine and, as the gears rotate in opposite directions, the dwell or recess between each tooth in each wheel traps a small quantity of oil from an inlet port. The trapped oil is carried round by each wheel towards an outlet port on the opposite side of the casing, where it is forced out by the meshing teeth.

The principle of squeezing oil from an ever-decreasing space is used in the rotor-type pump. Here an inner and outer rotor are mounted on different axes in the same cylinder.

The inner rotor, which commonly has four lobes, is driven by the engine. It meshes with an outer rotor which has five lobes. As they rotate, the spaces between them vary in size. The intake port is placed at a point where the space between the rotor lobes is increasing, drawing oil in. It is then carried round the pump, and as rotation continues, the space between the lobes gets smaller, compressing the oil which is then ejected through the outlet port.

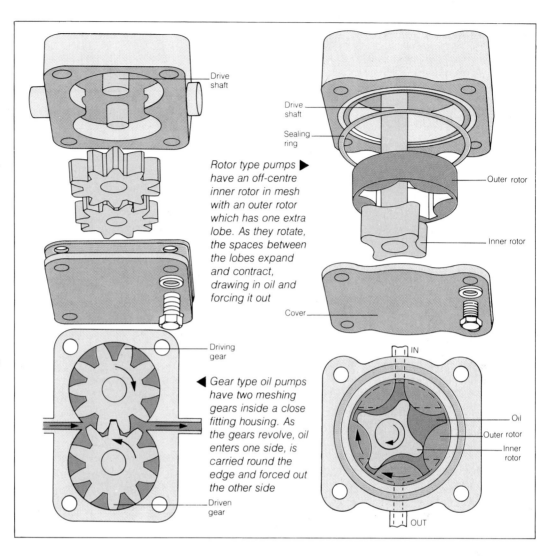

Rotor type pumps ▶ *have an off-centre inner rotor in mesh with an outer rotor which has one extra lobe. As they rotate, the spaces between the lobes expand and contract, drawing in oil and forcing it out*

◀ *Gear type oil pumps have two meshing gears inside a close fitting housing. As the gears revolve, oil enters one side, is carried round the edge and forced out the other side*

How the crankshaft floats in oil

To enable a shaft to rotate easily, every bearing has a small clearance—a crankshaft bearing 2 inches (50.8mm) in diameter, for instance, would have a clearance of 0.003in (0.076mm).

When the engine is at rest the heavy crankshaft sits in the bottom of its bearings, leaving most of the clearance at the top. Once the engine is started, for the first few seconds, a thin film of residual oil prevents metal-to-metal contact until oil under pressure arrives from the pump.

Once the bearing is full of oil, the rotating shaft drags oil molecules round with it. As they approach the narrowest clearance near the bottom of the bearing, they pile up and form a wedge which forces the

shaft and bearing apart.

The action of the oil wedge —shown in exaggerated form in the illustrations—means that the crankshaft literally floats in oil once the engine is running. In theory, this floating action means that the crankshaft bearings should never wear out, but they do. How does this happen?

One reason, for example, is a low oil level in the sump. When a car with a sump only partly full of oil is cornered, the oil moves away from the pump pick-up and for a few seconds, air instead of oil is pumped to the bearings.

If this happens often enough, the metal-to-metal contact increases the bearing clearance and eventually most of the oil spills out of the side of

the bearing instead of forming the oil wedge that supports the crankshaft. Once this stage is reached the engine makes a rumbling or deep knocking sound on acceleration as the

bearing surfaces hammer together, and it is usually necessary to regrind the crankshaft journals and fit new undersized bearings to get things back to normal.

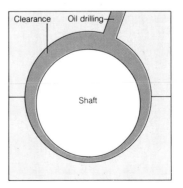

A stationary crankshaft journal rests on a thin oil film in the bottom of the shell bearing

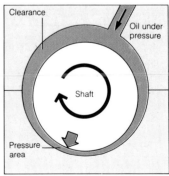

Once rotating, the shaft drags oil into the pressure area which lifts the shaft off the bearing

Lubrication

Oil filters

Even new engines sometimes contain small particles of metal left over from the manufacturing process, or grains of sand which have not been removed from the crankcase after casting. Old engines continually deposit in the sump tiny fragments of metal worn from highly-loaded components such as the piston rings. To prevent any of these lodging in close-fitting bearings or blocking oil drillings, engine oil is filtered.

The simplest filter is a wire mesh strainer that prevents solids from entering the oil pump—most engines have one of these.

In addition, many engines have an extra filter that traps very fine particles. The most common type has a pleated paper or felt element, and pumping oil through it removes all but microscopic solids from the lubricant.

Another way of separating particles is to pump the oil into a fast-revolving cylinder. Centrifugal force then throws the particles to the outer edge while uncontaminated oil passes through the centre.

Most engines use a full-flow system to filter all the oil after it leaves the pump. The most popular method is to pump the oil into a bowl or canister containing a cylindrical filter. From the inner walls of the bowl, oil flows through the filter and out from the centre to the main gallery.

Full-flow filtration works well provided the filter is renewed at regular service intervals. If it is left in service too long it may become blocked. When this happens, to prevent oil starvation, the build-up of pressure of oil inside the filter forces open a spring-loaded relief valve in the housing and the oil by-passes the filter. The valve prevents immediate engine failure, but the engine will be lubricated with unfiltered oil until the filter is renewed.

Rarer now is a by-pass filtration system in which only a proportion of the oil pump output goes through a filter. The remainder is fed directly to the oil gallery.

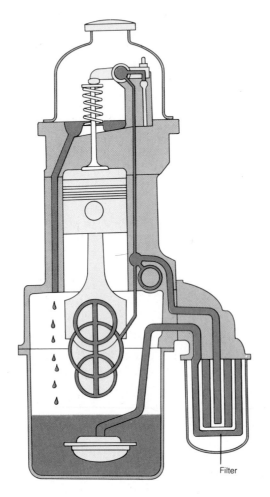

Full flow filtration: The oil pump passes all its output through the filter on its way to the engine

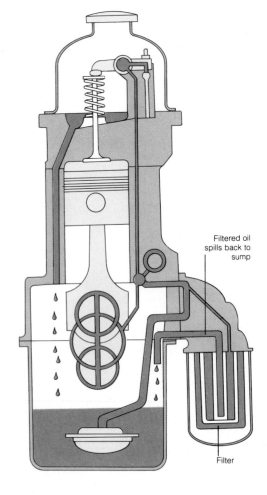

Filtered oil spills back to sump

By-pass filtration: The filter is fed only a small quantity of oil from the pump. The remainder by-passes the filter

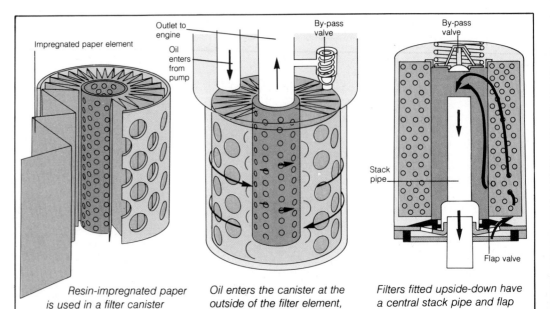

Impregnated paper element

Outlet to engine

Oil enters from pump

By-pass valve

By-pass valve

Stack pipe

Flap valve

Resin-impregnated paper is used in a filter canister to trap dirt. The canister must be changed periodically

Oil enters the canister at the outside of the filter element, passes through the filter and leaves from a central outlet

Filters fitted upside-down have a central stack pipe and flap valve to prevent oil draining when the engine is stationary

Oil seals and gaskets

Oil has a habit of creeping through small openings into areas where it is not wanted and, to contain it, the engine has a number of oil seals and gaskets.

A gasket is simply a piece of soft, oil-resistant material that is sandwiched between metal joints to prevent oil seeping out. The gasket may be made of cork, a composition material, or, in some instances, may be a silicone-based compound that is squeezed from a tube.

Virtually all engines have a cork or composition gasket between the valve cover and the cylinder head. If oil leaks from this joint, it is possible that the gasket has been damaged during fitting, or is not properly located. Many engine oil leaks from the valve cover are caused by the fixing screws or bolts being over-tightened, distorting the cover by bending it into the soft gasket material. Straightening the valve cover and fitting a new gasket will make it oil-tight.

Where metal surfaces have to make close contact and yet provide an oil seal, some car manufacturers specify a thin layer of mastic sealant on the mating surfaces. During tightening, any excess sealant is squeezed out, leaving a very thin film behind to discourage oil seepage. Oil

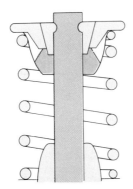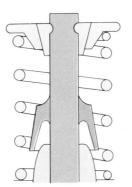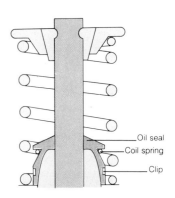

Oil seals on the sliding valve stems prevent excess oil from being drawn into the combustion chambers. With increasingly stringent exhaust emission regulations, the efficient lip-type seal, which is clipped to the top of the valve guide, is now widely used

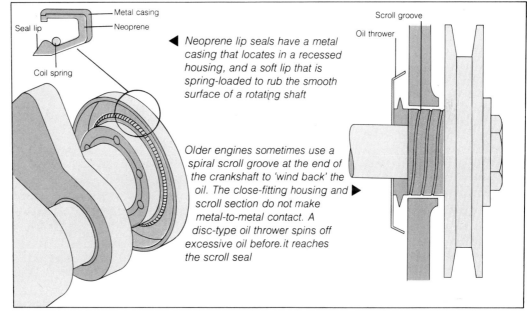

◄ *Neoprene lip seals have a metal casing that locates in a recessed housing, and a soft lip that is spring-loaded to rub the smooth surface of a rotating shaft*

Older engines sometimes use a spiral scroll groove at the end of the crankshaft to 'wind back' the oil. The close-fitting housing and ► scroll section do not make metal-to-metal contact. A disc-type oil thrower spins off excessive oil before it reaches the scroll seal

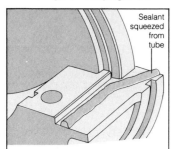

In some areas, sealant squeezed from a tube provides an oil-tight film between close fitting components, such as this bearing cap

seals are necessary where oil must be prevented from entering or leaving a moving component.

The stems of valves at their upper end work in an atmosphere where oil is being continually dripped or squirted on to the camshaft or rockers that operate the valves. It is important that excess oil cannot dribble down the valve stems into the combustion chambers because burning it will dramatically increase oil consumption.

To prevent this happening valve stems have oil seals. Depending on the engine, the seal may be in the form of a tight-fitting O-ring, an inverted mushroom shape threaded on the stem, or a spring-loaded seal clipped to the top of the valve guide and spring-loaded to hold its sealing lip against the sliding valve stem.

All perform the same function—they deflect, or wipe, most of the oil from the valve stem to prevent it being burned in the combustion chamber. A small film of oil does get through, and this lubricates the valve guides.

Where a rotating shaft pro-trudes from the engine, an oil seal is used to prevent oil from being thrown out. It is particularly important that oil does not reach the clutch linings and cause clutch slip, so the rear of the crankshaft passes through some form of oil seal, where it emerges from the crankcase behind the flywheel.

Engines with road draught crankcase ventilation systems quite often use a scroll (see page 47).

This is a spiral groove machined on the crankshaft surface that works in a close-fitting housing and 'winds' the oil back into the engine as the shaft rotates. Frequently, a disc fitted to the crankshaft, on the engine side of the scroll, is used as an oil thrower, to spin off excessive amounts of oil and prevent it reaching the scroll. With the

increasingly widespread use of closed circuit crankcase breathing systems, which can cause a small build-up of pressure in the crankcase (see page 47), neoprene lip seals are more usually fitted to seal both ends of the crankshaft. The lip seal is moulded into a metal casing that is pressed into a register. At the rear of the crankcase, a recess is provided for the seal, and the soft lip around its inner circumference rubs against a machined face on the shaft. The lip faces towards the oil, and a circular coil spring around the lip acts like a rubber band and presses it against the rotating shaft.

Lip seals rely on making contact with a perfectly smooth moving surface in order to provide an oil-tight seal—any damage to the rotating shaft surface will cause an oil leak.

Lubrication

Oil viscosity

Straight lubricating oil becomes thick and stodgy at low temperatures, but gets very much thinner when it is hot. The thickness, or 'body' of an oil, is called its viscosity and is expressed as a number prefixed by the letters SAE which stand for the Society of Automotive Engineers, the American organisation that devised viscosity standards.

Since oil viscosity alters according to the temperature, two standards are popularly used, one indicating viscosity at engine working temperature and the other when the oil is cold.

The working viscosity is calculated with the oil at 99°C (210°F), and the grade of oil is written SAE 20, 30, 40 or 50. The higher the number, the thicker the oil.

Oil with a very good high-temperature viscosity works well in warm climates, but when the air temperature drops below freezing it thickens and puts so much drag on the moving parts that the starter has difficulty in turning the engine.

For improved cold-starting an oil with a good low temperature viscosity is needed. These winter-grade oils have their viscosity checked at – 18°C (0°F), and their grade is written with a W suffix, SAE 5W, 10W and 20W, to indicate this.

The snag with these very thin oils is that once the engine has started and reached operating temperature, they become so

thin that they sometimes allow metal-to-metal contact.

The breakthrough came when technologists developed multigrade oils that gave the best of both worlds. An SAE 20W/50 oil, for instance, has the cold-weather fluidity of a 20W winter grade oil, and the 'body' of a straight SAE 50 at 99°C (210°F). Although it appears from the figures that the oil actually gets thicker as it

heats up, this is not so: a multigrade just becomes thinner more slowly than a monograde oil.

The need to conserve energy has led to the development of low-viscosity oils. Although these are multigrades, they are made deliberately thin so they cause the minimum drag on moving parts. On an engine in good condition, controlled tests show that using an SAE

10W/30 low-viscosity oil results in a 5% to 7% improvement in fuel consumption.

On a worn engine, the economy is not as good. Worn piston rings and bores result in oil getting past and burning in the combustion chamber. The increased oil consumption will more than offset any fuel savings. An engine in this condition is better off with SAE 20W/50 multigrade oil.

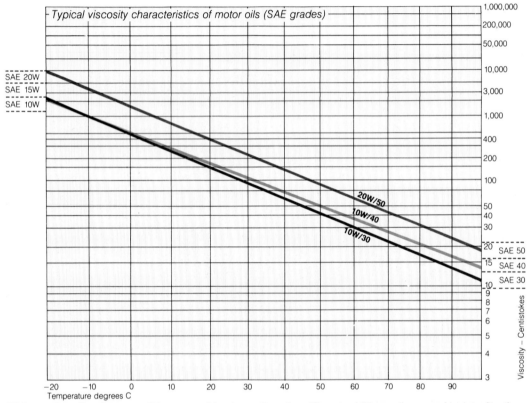

Oil loses viscosity – becomes thinner – as it heats up. By using different additives, oil companies can alter the behaviour of oil blends so they are as thin as possible to make the engine easy to rotate when cold, and retain sufficient "body" to provide effective lubrication when hot. The chart shows how the viscosity of three popular grades of oil alters as they warm up. Centistokes are units of viscosity which indicate the rate of flow of a fluid.

Additives

The inside of an engine is an extremely hostile environment for the lubricating oil. It has to cope with extremes of temperature, acids corrosion and dirt, so additives are used to ensure that it can withstand them.

The first problem, immediately after the engine starts up, is cold corrosion. Each gallon of petrol used gives off its own volume of water as it burns. In a cold engine some of this dribbles from the exhaust pipe, but the rest remains in the combustion

area, combining with other products to form a weak acid that tends to eat into the cylinder walls. A good engine oil contains alkaline inhibitors to neutralise the acid, although the wear cannot be eliminated entirely. Cold corrosion can be reduced by driving the car, putting load on the engine, to warm it up as quickly as possible after a cold start.

Combustion gases leaking past the pistons deposit soot in the oil. Left alone this would form a sludge that would block oilways. Top quality oils

contain dispersants that 'wrap up' tiny particles of soot and hold them in suspension. This is why engine oil looks dirty only a short time after it has been changed.

High temperature dispersants discourage a hard lacquer from forming near the top of the pistons and sticking the piston rings; anti-oxidants prevent air in the crankcase from combining chemically with the oil and making it thicker, while multigrade oils contain a viscosity improver which provides them with

the appropriate amount of 'body' at high operating temperatures.

Engines that are run for short distances and rarely warm up fully, often build up deposits on cool areas such as the inside of the valve cover. Aptly named 'mayonnaise', these deposits are caused by oil dispersants 'wrapping up' condensed water droplets. Apart from some localised rusting, the deposits do no harm. They can be cleaned off very easily with a rag soaked in paraffin when the valve adjustment is checked.

Controlling crankcase fumes

On each compression and firing stroke, some combustion gases inevitably escape past the pistons into the crankcase. This is known as piston blow-by. The fumes consist mostly of unburned fuel (hydrocarbons). As an engine wears, piston blow-by increases.

Because unburned hydrocarbons form an explosive mixture, dilute the sump oil and form sludge, car makers ventilate the crankcase to let them out. Until emission control regulations took effect, the 'road draught' system was used, in which forward motion of the car created a vacuum at the outer end of a ventilation tube from the crankcase. Fresh air was drawn in—usually through the oil filler—to replace the vented crankcase fumes.

Unfortunately 'road draught' ventilation was ineffective below 25mph and oil contamination was high in engines used mostly in town traffic.

Positive crankcase ventilation was introduced to control emissions (unburned hydrocarbons are poisonous) and provide ventilation regardless of road speed. A positive system uses the vacuum in the inlet manifold to suck fumes from the crankcase and pass them to the combustion chamber where they are burned.

The system contains a positive crankcase valve (PCV) that acts as a fire precaution and adjusts the flow of fumes taken in by the engine. If a back-fire occurs in the manifold, the back-flow pushes the valve down, blocking the route to the crankcase. When manifold vacuum is high, at idling speed or small throttle openings, the valve lifts against spring pressure, reducing the flow of fumes and air to the manifold. This prevents an over-weak mixture from stalling the engine.

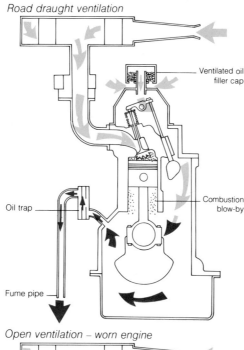
Road draught ventilation
Ventilated oil filler cap
Oil trap
Combustion blow-by
Fume pipe

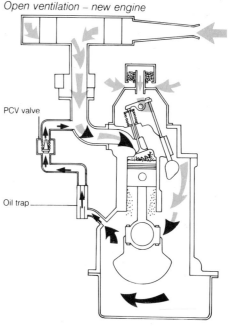
Open ventilation – new engine
PCV valve
Oil trap

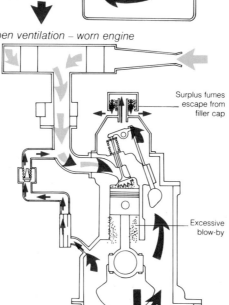
Open ventilation – worn engine
Surplus fumes escape from filler cap
Excessive blow-by

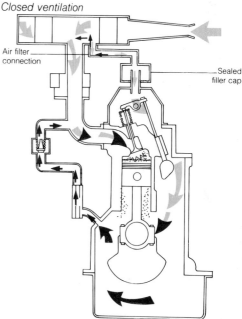
Closed ventilation
Air filter connection
Sealed filler cap

The road draught system pipes crankcase fumes directly into the air stream under the car. Later engines use an open ventilation system, drawing in fresh air through a vented oil filler cap and exhausting crankcase fumes into the inlet manifold through a positive crankcase ventilation (PCV) valve. When the engine became worn, under load, the inlet manifold could not cope with all the fumes and the surplus escaped to the atmosphere through the filler cap vent. A closed ventilation system avoids this. The filler cap is sealed and air enters the engine from the carburettor air cleaner – the same air cleaner connection draws off any surplus fumes under load and feeds them into the carburettor barrel

Open ventilation

This works by taking in fresh air through a ventilated oil filler cap and feeding crankcase fumes into the engine air-intake system.

On new engines it works well, but worn engines can overload the system by producing more piston blow-by at full throttle than the inlet manifold vacuum can cope with. If this occurs, surplus fumes escape to the atmosphere through the filler cap.

Closed ventilation

Fresh air is taken from inside the carburettor air cleaner body to a sealed oil filler cap or direct to a sealed valve cover. If the crankcase of a worn engine cannot be cleared by inlet vacuum, the surplus fumes are vented into the air cleaner where they enter the carburettor and eventually are conveyed to the combustion chambers. Carburettor settings are arranged to allow for this extra air.

Lubrication projects

Changing the engine oil and filter

Most car makers recommend that engine oil is changed and the oil filter renewed at 5,000-6,000-mile intervals, or every six months. The figures for your car can be checked in the handbook.

Oil is drained after removing a plug at the base of the sump. Before beginning, look underneath at the drain plug—if it has a hexagonal or square recess or a squared end, a special tool may be needed to loosen it.

Oil flows more readily when hot and is best drained after the engine has been warmed up. The sump is designed to drain when the car is on level ground.

If necessary, raising one side of the car a few inches with the jack will provide enough room to reach underneath and loosen the plug, but do not get under the car unless the vehicle is properly supported. Lower the jack once the plug is loose.

Use a shallow container to catch the oil. If the sump holds more than five litres (check in the handbook) an old washing-up bowl will do. Better is an empty 5-litre oil tin laid on its side with a large square hole cut in the upper side. The tin-plate is thin enough to cut with an old pair of stout scissors, but be sure to turn over the edges of the metal with pliers —this prevents cut fingers when the tin is moved. Purpose-made plastic drain cans are also available.

It is illegal to pour old engine oil down the drain; it should be poured into a container (the filler neck on the cut-out oil tin helps here) and taken to the nearest local authority rubbish area. A discarded filter can be wrapped in a plastic bag and put in the dustbin.

Current practice is to fit a one-piece 'throw-away' cartridge-type filter which screws directly on to the crankcase or on to a filter housing.

Earlier engines use bowl-type filters which must be dismantled to remove the filter element inside, cleaned, and a new element inserted.

Not all engines have external filters. Volkswagen air-cooled engines have an internal strainer (see Project 19), while as well as an external filter, some engines also have a centrifugal filter, which is usually incorporated in the crankshaft pulley. These are generally serviced only at long intervals—around 24,000 miles.

Project 19: Changing the oil

> **Grading:** 🔧
> **Time:** 10min-20min
> **Tools:** Drain-plug spanner or key; container to catch waste oil
> **Materials:** Engine oil

Step 1. Warm up the engine by driving the car for about a mile.
2. Remove the oil filler cap from the top of the engine to allow the oil to drain more quickly.
3. Loosen the drain plug about half a turn.
4. Put the container in position and unscrew the plug by hand —be careful not to drop it in the container.
5. If the plug is magnetic, wipe off the metal particles that have collected on it with a clean cloth.
6. Once the oil has drained, wipe clean the drain plug hole, and refit the plug securely.
***7.** On air-cooled Volkswagen engines, the drain plug plate should be removed and the wire gauze oil strainer underneath cleaned in petrol and dried. Refit the plate using a new gasket, and replace the drain plug.
8. On engines with an external filter, fit a new one. See next project.
9. Add a little less oil than is necessary to fill the sump. The capacity and grade of oil required will be given in the handbook. On some cars the oil must be poured slowly to avoid overflowing.
10. Take out the dipstick and wipe the end. After allowing the oil a few minutes to reach the sump, check the level. Add oil to the correct level.

Project 20: Changing a cartridge filter

> **Grading:** 🔧
> **Time:** 5min-15min
> **Tools:** Strap wrench; container to catch waste oil
> **Materials:** New filter

Step 1. Although they are fitted hand-tight, most cartridge canisters require a strap wrench to loosen them. If you do not have a wrench, one can be made from a piece of strap wrapped around a socket set extension bar and used to turn the canister. Use a drip tray to catch spilled oil.
***1.** On some cars the canister is fitted inverted, and loosening it will spill oil all over the engine. Very little can be done to prevent this, except by removing it quickly and turning it open end upwards. The spilled oil can be prevented from soiling the floor with a drip tray.
2. Remove the canister.
3. Wipe the sealing face on the block with a clean cloth.
4. If necessary, fit the new rubber sealing ring to the flange on the inner end of the new cartridge (on most the ring is fixed in place). Lubricate the ring with a smear of engine oil.
5. Screw the filter into position by hand until the ring makes firm contact. Refill the engine with oil, start up (the oil-pressure warning light will stay on a little longer than usual as the filter fills up) and check at the filter for leaks.

Step 1.

Step 4.

Step 9.

Step 4.

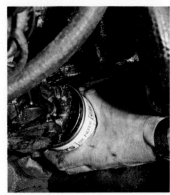

Step 5.

Project 21: Cleaning a bowl-type filter

Grading: 🔧
Time: 15min-20min
Tools: Spanner to fit securing bolt; skewer or other pointed instrument; mirror; waste-oil container
Materials: New filter element

Step 1. Place a drip tray under the filter, and undo the securing bolt. This will be at the base of the bowl, or on top of the filter housing.
2. Remove the bowl and tip the contents into a suitable container. Note the arrangement of any springs and washers around the centre bolt.
3. There will be a sealing ring in a groove in the filter housing. Use a skewer or some other pointed instrument to spear it and ease it out.
4. Clean dirt from the groove with a corner of cloth and insert the new rubber ring supplied with the filter element. Take care not to twist the ring—if necessary using a mirror to check it.
5. After washing the filter bowl in paraffin to remove any sludge, insert the new element.
6. Position the bowl against the sealing ring and hold it firmly in place while the fixing bolt is hand-tightened. Finally tighten the bolt with a spanner.
7. With the engine sump filled with oil, check for leaks at the filter while the engine is running. Leaks are usually caused by a loose fixing bolt, or an improperly seated or twisted sealing ring.

Step 1.

Step 2.

Step 3.

Step 5.

Project 22: Cleaning a centrifugal filter

Grading: 🔧
Time: 30min-40min
Tools: Spanner to fit fixing bolts; brush and touch-up paint; scraper, cleaning brush
Materials: New gasket or sealing ring

These operate by throwing any deposits in the oil to the outside as they rotate. To clean them, they are separated and the deposits are scraped out. After washing in paraffin, the two halves are reassembled.

Some centrifugal filters carry ignition timing marks; these should be marked with a dab of paint so that they can be refitted in exactly the same position in relation to the engine-driven half, otherwise the ignition timing settings will be lost.

Step 1. Place a drip tray under the filter unit.
2. Mark the cover for reassembly in the same position. Loosen the bolts.
3. Remove the bolts and cover. Clean the interior with a brush and paraffin. Reassemble.

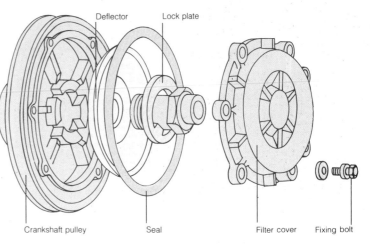

Deflector   Lock plate

Crankshaft pulley   Seal   Filter cover   Fixing bolt

Lubrication projects

Project 23: Renewing a leaking gasket

Grading: 🔧
Time: 20min–40min
Tools: Spanners to fit valve cover fixings; scraper; light hammer; mirror; block of hardwood, if necessary
Materials: Gasket; silicone sealant

Gaskets are often used between metal surfaces to make an oil-tight joint. If the gasket is displaced or damaged, or the metal surfaces are distorted, oil will leak.

The gaskets most likely to leak are those that are frequently disturbed, such as the one under the valve cover which has its oil-tight seal broken each time the valve settings are checked. Ideally a new gasket should be fitted each time the cover is taken off.

The most complex gasket in the engine is between the cylinder head and block. The cylinder head gasket has the difficult job of sealing off combustion gases, water in the cooling system and high-pressure lubricating oil. If it leaks, the cylinder head must come off—a complicated job that is best left to a garage. The pictures show how to renew a valve cover gasket.

Step 1. If necessary, move away the air cleaner, spark plug cables and any hoses overhanging the valve cover.
2. Undo the fixings and lift off the cover.
3. Peel off the gaskets.

Cork gaskets may be positioned by the shaping of the cover flange, or extensions on the gasket may engage with cut-outs in the flange, or the gasket may be struck with jointing compound.
4. Clean all traces of old gasket from the flange and the mating surfaces.
5. Many oil leaks are caused by over-tightening the fixing bolts or screws and distorting the cover. Resting the bent flange on a hardwood block and gently tapping it with a light hammer will straighten out the distortions.
6. Slight imperfections can be sealed using a silicone sealant on the surface before fitting the new gasket.
7. If a cork gasket is distorted soak it in warm water to regain its shape.
8. With the gasket attached, place the valve cover carefully in position on the cylinder head. Use a mirror to check hidden areas, in case the gasket has slipped out of position.
9. Refit the cover screws or bolts with any sealing washers. If damaged washers are fitted, oil will seep out. Using new washers, tighten the bolts sufficiently to just compress the gasket. Refit any components that you have removed, start the engine and check all round the gasket for leaks. Small leaks can be cured by parting the joint and applying silicone sealant.

Step 2.

Step 3.

Step 6.

Step 9.

Project 24: Cleaning the crankcase ventilating system

Grading: 🔧🔧
Time: Approx ½hr
Tools: Screwdriver to fit hose clips; old paint brush; stiff wire
Materials: Paraffin; clean cloth

To discourage oil from being thrown into the combustion chambers and to prevent any chance of fire, modern crankcase ventilation systems incorporate an oil separator and a valve, or a flame trap.

In time, these restrictors can become clogged with deposits carried by the oily fumes, and if they are not unblocked, the resulting pressure build-up causes oil leaks.

Most car makers recommend cleaning the breather assembly at 10,000-12,000-mile intervals. As most cars now have a closed or semi-closed breathing system which includes a spring-loaded ventilation valve, these types are dealt with here.

Step 1. Remove the oil filler cap. If it has ventilation holes and contains a gauze filter, rinse it in paraffin and shake off the surplus before refitting it.
2. On caps without ventilation holes, check that the rubber sealing ring is sound and able to make an airtight joint. If the ring is damaged, fit a new cap.
3. Locate the ventilation valve —on most cars it is at one end of the ventilation hose joining the crankcase to the inlet manifold or carburettor air cleaner.
4. Remove the valve assembly and clean it with an old paintbrush dipped in paraffin. Test its action by gently pressing the valve into the housing; it should move easily and freely against slight spring pressure. If it has a sticky action that cannot be improved by cleaning, fit a new valve. This may not be necessary as some valves can be dismantled after removing a circlip at the end (see diagram).
5. Disc-shaped valves, mounted on the inlet manifold, must also be dismantled for cleaning. These valves have a spring-loaded diaphragm inside, and a top cover held by a spring clip. Move the clip aside, remove the cover and lift out the diaphragm and spring underneath. Clean all parts and reassemble in reverse order.
6. Undo the hoses and check them for blockages.

To clean a sludged-up hose, make a 'pull-through' by hooking the end of a length of stiff wire round a small piece of cloth. Thread the wire through the hose and use it to draw through the cloth.
Renew any damaged hoses.
7. On reassembly, make sure that all hoses fit firmly and make an airtight joint. Air leaks cause erratic engine idling.

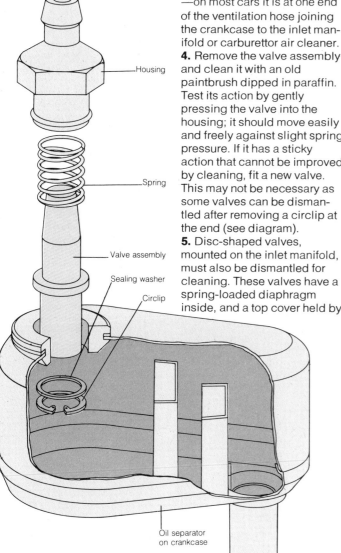

Housing

Spring

Valve assembly

Sealing washer

Circlip

Oil separator on crankcase

Step 1.

Step 3.

Step 4.

Step 6.

Fuel system

In order to convert petrol from the liquid that pours from the pump in a filling station to a vapour that can be burned in the engine, it passes through a number of stages in a fuel and induction system.

In older cars the petrol tank was mounted high up in the engine bay so that fuel could be gravity-fed to the engine. Because of the fire risk, fuel tanks in modern cars are remote from the engine.

To show the petrol level in the tank, there is a float which rides on the fuel and is connected by a long hinge to a variable electrical resistance. As the float rises and falls, a contact moves across the resistance and the varying current is taken to a gauge on the dashboard which indicates the fuel level. The gauge is usually electrically damped, so that it does not fluctuate rapidly as the fuel surges inside the tank.

A pump, driven by the engine, or electrically oper-ated, feeds petrol from the tank to the carburettor, a device that accurately mixes the fuel with air.

On some engines fuel is accurately metered and injected directly into the ingoing airstream by a fuel injection system which takes the place of the carburettor.

An engine running at speed consumes great quantities of air, and it is important that this contains no solid or dust particles that will cause wear or damage inside the engine. To prevent this the air intake is protected by a filter. It may be an 'oil bath' type where air passes over oil before being drawn through a fine wire mesh; a metal mesh filter, where an oil-wetted gauze collects any solid particles, or a 'paper element' type with a replaceable pleated paper cartridge.

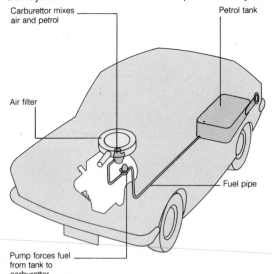

Carburettor mixes air and petrol

Air filter

Petrol tank

Fuel pipe

Pump forces fuel from tank to carburettor

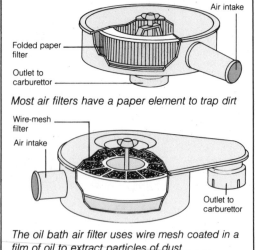

Folded paper filter

Outlet to carburettor

Air intake

Most air filters have a paper element to trap dirt

Wire-mesh filter

Air intake

Outlet to carburettor

The oil bath air filter uses wire mesh coated in a film of oil to extract particles of dust

The simple carburettor

The carburettor and air filter are usually mounted on an inlet manifold, a branching pipe feeding the fuel-and-air mixture from the carburettor to the inlet ports of the cylinder.

All air drawn into the engine on the induction strokes passes through the main bore of the carburettor, known as the carburettor barrel. At one point, the diameter of the barrel is reduced by means of a waisted restriction called a venturi.

When it meets this restriction, the air flow speeds up and a slight vacuum is created.

Fuel pumped from the tank enters the carburettor and fills a reservoir known as the float chamber. As the fuel level rises, a float in the chamber lifts until it closes off a valve which controls fuel entry. As fuel is used, the float falls, allowing the chamber to be replenished. In this way, whenever the engine is run-ning, the amount of fuel in the float chamber remains approximately the same.

If the float chamber is connected by a small drilling to the narrowest part of the venturi, and the fuel level in the chamber is put slightly below the fuel outlet into the venturi, the engine will suck petrol into the air stream while it is running.

This 'venturi effect' is the operating principle of all con-ventional carburettors used on modern engines.

Fuel entering the air stream as a liquid is broken down into tiny droplets by the turbulent air flow in the barrel and is vaporised by the heat present in the manifold and cylinder head.

The speed of the engine is regulated by the amount of fuel-and-air mixture drawn in, and is controlled by a pivoted disc, known as a throttle valve, mounted on a spindle passing through the lower part of the carburettor barrel.

When the throttle is moved to a vertical position, parallel with the sides of the barrel, it provides practically no restriction and the engine runs up to full speed. If the spindle is turned slowly to close the flap, mixture flow is increasingly obstructed. By altering the position of the throttle, the engine can be held at any required speed.

So far, basic principles have been explained, but even with a speed throttle, the carburettor so far described is too crude to be used on a modern car engine, and needs some extra refinements.

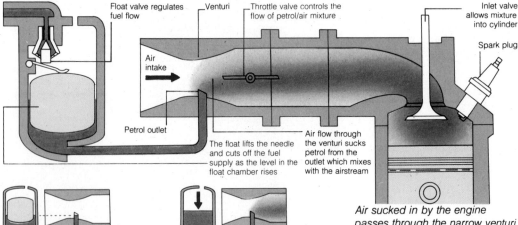

Float valve regulates fuel flow

Venturi

Throttle valve controls the flow of petrol/air mixture

Inlet valve allows mixture into cylinder

Spark plug

Air intake

Petrol outlet

The float lifts the needle and cuts off the fuel supply as the level in the float chamber rises

Air flow through the venturi sucks petrol from the outlet which mixes with the airstream

The float chamber maintains fuel at the correct level in the venturi

Atmospheric pressure forces fuel into the venturi

Air sucked in by the engine passes through the narrow venturi which creates a partial vacuum and draws in petrol. A throttle valve controls the flow of petrol/air

Fuel system

Fuel/air mixture

Fuel and air will only ignite and burn efficiently if they are mixed together in the correct proportions, but the precise ratio depends on a number of outside factors. Under steady load conditions, a mixture ratio of about fifteen parts air to one part petrol by weight—known as the chemically correct ratio—ensures burning of the fuel. For cold starting, however, engines need a mixture with a greater proportion of petrol—a rich mixture—sometimes as rich as one part air to one part petrol by weight. For maximum economy, a smaller proportion of fuel, or a weaker mixture, of around 16:1 air/fuel is needed. During hard acceleration a richer mixture of around 12:1 must be supplied.

With the simple carburettor described above, it is possible, in theory, to alter the bore of the petrol outlet into the airstream, eventually arriving by trial and error at the ideal mixture strength. Calibrating the carburettor in this way, however, would give the correct mixture at only one particular engine speed, since the delivery of fuel at the venturi does not automatically keep in step with the flow of air through it when the throttle is opened and closed.

If we opened the throttle and doubled the engine speed, for instance, the air flow could double but the increased vacuum would draw a greater proportion of fuel from the outlet, making the mixture too rich. Conversely, halving the engine speed would reduce the fuel flow by more than half and the mixture strength would be too weak.

Over-rich and over-weak mixtures must be avoided. When the mixture is too rich, the oxygen in the air is used up before all the fuel is burned, and some unburned fuel is thrown out of the cylinder on the exhaust stroke. If the mixture is too weak, all the fuel is used while there is still oxygen available.

Both conditions reduce engine output and efficiency. The mixture is correct when all fuel and oxygen are burned completely during combustion.

Constant fuel/air ratio

All carburettors are designed to provide a correct mixture strength regardless of engine speed, the most commonly used device being the emulsion tube. Here, fuel from the float chamber passes through a main jet, which limits the rate of flow, and then into a vertical well, with an outlet in the upper part opening into the venturi. In the top of this well is another jet which allows air to enter and flow down a thin 'emulsion' tube, which mixes air with the petrol and is mounted in the centre of the well. It contains cross-drillings at different heights which allow the fuel and air to mix.

Fuel is drawn from the outlet, causing the level in the well to fall below that of the float chamber. When this happens, air is drawn in through the top jet, mixing with the fuel and diluting the output.

As speed rises further, the level continues to fall, uncovering more of the air holes in the central tube, thus weakening the mixture. The jet sizes and the layout of the central tube are chosen so that the mixture ratio will be correct and constant.

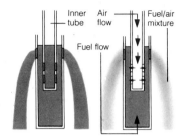

Petrol flows into an emulsion tube before it is discharged into the carburettor barrel. As the engine speeds up, air is drawn through the air correction jet into the cross-drilled inner tube and mixes with the petrol, weakening the mixture

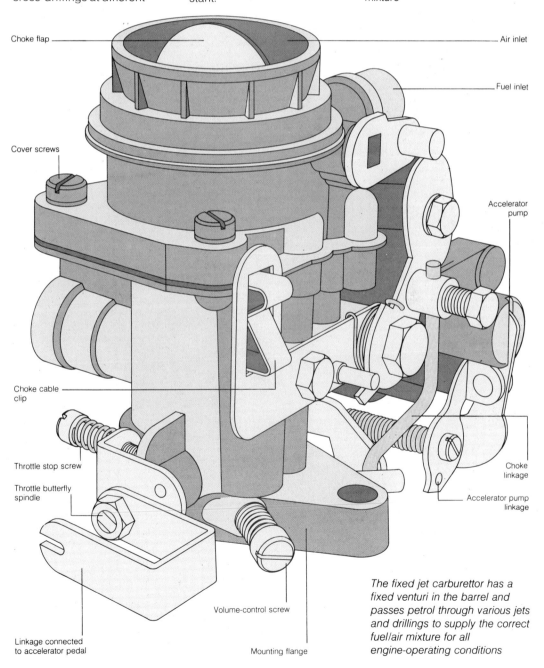

The fixed jet carburettor has a fixed venturi in the barrel and passes petrol through various jets and drillings to supply the correct fuel/air mixture for all engine-operating conditions

Fuel system

Slow-running system

At very low engine speeds there is insufficient vacuum to draw any fuel from the venturi outlet, but there is a high vacuum on the engine side of the throttle valve because the engine is trying to draw in air.

This high vacuum is used to suck a mixture of fuel and air through a separate idling circuit which has its outlet on the engine side of the throttle valve. In this way the engine keeps running when the throttle is closed.

The flow from the idling circuit outlet is adjusted by a tapered screw to obtain the smoothest idling speed. The presence of an air entry point in the circuit prevents it siphoning petrol when the engine has stopped.

There may be other small progression drillings adjacent to the throttle valve. These bridge the gap between the slow-running circuit and main outlet by supplying fuel which mixes with the first rush of air past the valve as it opens.

Because the idling circuit needs a high vacuum to operate it, once the throttle has opened past the progression drillings, it automatically stops working.

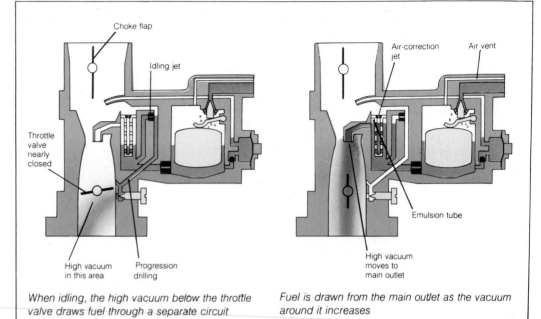

When idling, the high vacuum below the throttle valve draws fuel through a separate circuit

Fuel is drawn from the main outlet as the vacuum around it increases

Cold starting

To provide the very rich mixture for cold starting, a choke flap is used to block the entry of air into the barrel. When the engine is cranked over, it creates a high vacuum below the flap, drawing a rich mixture from the outlets.

As soon as the engine fires, the flap must be partially opened. Most manually-operated choke flaps are spring-loaded into the shut position and automatically open a little when the engine starts. As the engine warms up, the choke should be gradually disengaged by the driver.

Cold engines will not idle at normal speed, so a mechanism is provided to open the throttle valve slightly and give a fast idle when the choke is in use.

Automatic chokes usually have a metallic coil attached to the choke flap spindle. When the engine is cold the spring contracts, holding the flap fully shut. When the engine starts, heat from the exhaust, cooling system, or an electrical element, is directed at the spring. The heat expands it, causing it to unwind and gradually open the flap. It will also have a linkage to provide a fast idling speed when the choke is in use.

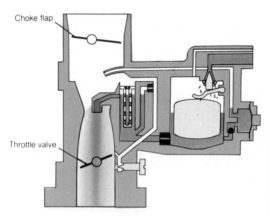

A flap is used to partially block the barrel for cold starts. It increases vacuum around the fuel outlet and draws more fuel to provide a rich mixture

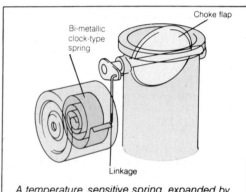

A temperature sensitive spring, expanded by the warming-up of the exhaust or cooling system, is used to operate the choke flap on an automatic choke

Accelerator pumps

The accelerator pump provides an additional supply of fuel which prevents the engine from temporarily cutting out or losing power when the throttle is suddenly opened for acceleration.

A piston or diaphragm, acting on a well filled with fuel, is connected to the throttle linkage, and sprays a jet of neat fuel into the carburettor barrel when the throttle is opened.

The injected fuel mixes with the 'gulp' of incoming air and provides a smooth increase in power by eliminating any fuel lag.

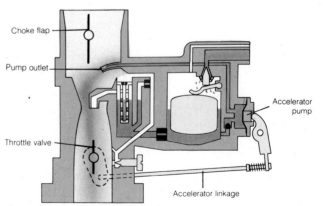

The accelerator pump squirts an enrichening shot of fuel down the barrel to provide a quick response when the throttle is opened quickly

'Economy' circuits

A cruising engine can accept a weaker mixture than an engine running under heavy load. To exploit this 'economy' devices are used. A common layout is a spring-loaded diaphragm which obstructs a channel leading to the main jet circuit. The space above the diaphragm is connected by a drilling to the carburettor barrel below the throttle. When the engine is cruising, the increased vacuum below the throttle lifts the diaphragm against spring pressure, unblocking the channel and bleeding extra air into the main jet circuit to weaken the mixture. If the throttle is opened for additional power, the vacuum below the throttle falls, the diaphragm again blocks the channel, and the main jet supplies a richer mixture.

An alternative is to use the diaphragm to open and close an additional fuel supply running to the main outlet. The principle is similar, the diaphragm being operated by manifold vacuum, but the supply is obstructed on cruising, and extra fuel is allowed to flow to enrich the mixture on wide throttle openings.

Variable-choke carburettors

Fixed choke carburettors require many different jets and circuits in order to maintain a fuel supply that is in step with the constantly changing vacuum in the venturi. Variable choke carburettors avoid this by altering the size of the venturi according to the air flow. This results in a constant vacuum in the venturi and it is only necessary to have one fuel jet, the size of which is varied to provide the correct mixture for all operating conditions.

Variable choke carburettors are usually of a horizontal design. They have a conventional float chamber, but the single outlet from this leads to a jet mounted in the lower part of the carburettor barrel, in the centre of a raised section which partially obstructs the airway.

The upper part of the carburettor has an enclosed housing or suction chamber containing a two-diameter piston, or air valve. In its lowest position, when the engine is stationary, the narrow base of the piston rests on the raised section in the carburettor barrel, while in the highest position, it unblocks the carburettor barrel completely, allowing unobstructed airflow. The piston is hollow, and small drillings in its base on the engine side permit air to enter and leave the suction chamber above its larger upper diameter.

When the engine is started, the obstruction of the piston creates a vacuum in the engine side of the carburettor barrel. The holes in the piston transmit this vacuum to the suction chamber above the larger diameter of the piston, which causes the piston to rise. The amount of piston lift depends on airflow, and the vacuum acting on the jet remains constant.

To vary the amount of fuel flowing into the carburettor barrel, there is a tapered needle, attached to the base of the piston, and moving vertically in a petrol jet. At low engine speeds, when the piston practically blocks the carburettor barrel, only a small quantity of fuel emerges to mix with the proportionally small airflow. As engine speed increases, however, and the piston rises, the obstruction in the jet becomes progressively less and more fuel flows out to mix with the extra air.

The taper of the needle is designed so that the ideal mixture can be supplied at all speeds. This type of carburettor does not need a separate idling circuit, but provision for cold starting is provided by a linkage which lowers the jet from the needle, thus giving a rich mixture.

As with a fixed choke carburettor, the variable choke design needs enrichment for acceleration and this is provided by a hydraulic damper which resists sudden upward movement of the piston when the throttle is opened. This brief delay allows extra vacuum to act on the jet and draw out a richer mixture.

There are two basic types of variable choke carburettor in common use. The main difference between them is in the way in which an air seal is provided around the piston rim.

One has a piston which is a very close fit within the suction chamber, whereas the other uses a flexible diaphragm clamped around the piston top and the rim of the suction chamber.

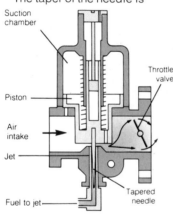

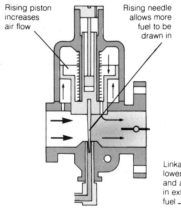

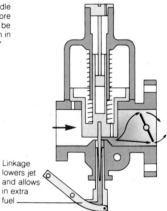

Throttle shut: Lack of vacuum in the barrel allows the piston to fall, restricting mixture flow

Throttle open: Engine vacuum lifts the piston, providing an increased flow of fuel and air

Cold starting: Operating the choke lowers the jet, allowing more fuel to be drawn into the barrel

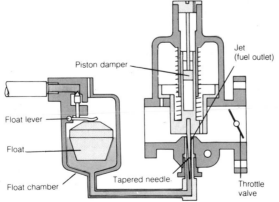

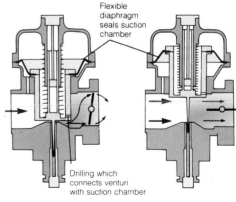

As with the fixed-jet carburettor, the float chamber supplies petrol at the correct level to the outlet. The piston controls the air flow and a tapered needle meters the flow of fuel

The Zenith Stromberg carburettor also has a tapered needle to meter fuel flow, but uses a diaphragm instead of a piston to raise or lower the air valve that adjusts the flow of air

Fuel system

Compound and twin-choke carburettors

Modern engines are required both to operate at motorway speeds and to perform satisfactorily in heavy traffic.

On some engines it is difficult to provide a carburettor which is large enough to supply sufficient air for high-speed running, yet small enough to maintain the operation of the main circuit correctly at low speed. For this reason, compound carburettors, which have two or more barrels side by side, have been developed. These are of the fixed choke type and, in effect, are two carburettors in one.

At lower speeds, opening the throttle works only one barrel, the second barrel remaining closed. The venturi action within the first barrel provides sufficient vacuum to operate the main circuit efficiently. At higher speeds, where the small diameter of the first barrel would limit engine power, a vacuum-operated device automatically opens the second barrel.

Alternatively there is a mechanical linkage which operates the second barrel when the first is open more than a certain amount. These are known as 'progressive twin-choke carburettors'.

True 'twin-choke' or twin-barrel carburettors have two throttles that open simultaneously. They are commonly used on 'V' engines, where each barrel supplies one bank of cylinders.

Multiple carburettors

An engine may have two or more separate carburettors, each serving one or more of the cylinders. This arrangement normally produces slightly more power than a single installation, because it gives better distribution of the fuel/air mixture.

With a single carburettor, the fuel/air mixture leaving the carburettor is usually drawn through a multi-branch inlet manifold to each cylinder in turn, resulting in the mixture continually having to change direction and negotiate sharp corners.

In some cases the cylinders may not all receive the same amount of mixture, so that the carburettor has to be set wastefully rich to feed the weakest cylinder properly.

With multiple carburettors less complex manifolds are used, and, where each cylinder has its own carburettor barrel, or one barrel feeds two or three cylinders, the problems of unequal supply and awkward manifold shapes are avoided.

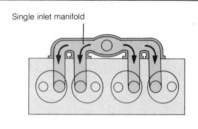

Single inlet manifold

On single carburettor engines, a multi-branched manifold takes the mixture to each cylinder. This arrangement inevitably has a number of sharp bends

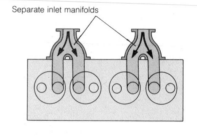

Separate inlet manifolds

On a multiple carburettor layout, simpler manifolds allow a smoother flow of mixture which is distributed more evenly to the cylinders, increasing engine efficiency

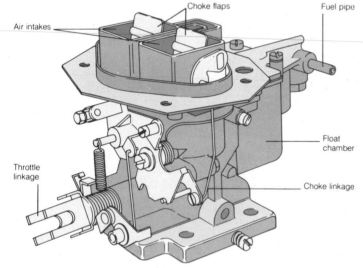

Air intakes — Choke flaps — Fuel pipe

Float chamber

Throttle linkage

Choke linkage

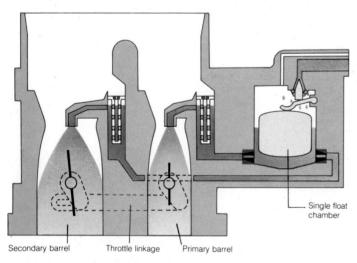

Secondary barrel — Throttle linkage — Primary barrel

Single float chamber

A compound twin-choke carburettor offers big-carburettor performance with small-carburettor economy. The throttle valves are linked so that the secondary throttle opens only when full power is required

Emission control

The internal combustion engine pollutes the atmosphere. The chief pollutants are unburnt or partially burnt fuel (hydrocarbons), oxides of nitrogen (NOX) that are formed at very high temperatures in the combustion chamber, and carbon monoxide (CO) which is present in the exhaust.

A major contributor to pollution is imperfect carburation, and since the early 1970s carburettors have been redesigned or modified to produce a more accurately metered fuel/air mixture. Compared with earlier models, these 'emission'-type carburettors produce a weaker fuel/air mixture—particularly at idling speeds—to ensure complete combustion of the fuel. A weak mixture tends to give an uneven or 'lumpy' tick-over and, to avoid this, engines designed to produce a less harmful exhaust are usually set with a faster idling speed than 'non-emission' engines.

To discourage private owners from making carburettor adjustments that would upset the in-built settings, external adjusters that control mixture strength and engine idling speed are concealed or capped to prevent tampering on carburettors made after 1972. Currently, no penalty exists for altering the controls on a 'tamper-proofed' carburettor, but it has been suggested that a check of the idle mixture ratio should become part of the annual MoT test for cars that are three years old or more. If this happens, it is probable that cars found to have harmfully pollutant exhausts will need to have their carburettors reset by authorised agencies.

Poppet 'by-pass' valves

Pollution is also high when an engine is decelerating on a closed throttle. With the throttle shut, any fuel clinging to the manifold walls as a liquid will suddenly be sucked into the cylinders. For a moment this makes the mixture far too rich, then, when this fuel has been used, the mixture becomes too weak. Each extreme gives a sharp increase in the pollutants in the exhaust gas.

A simple cure for this is to place a spring-loaded poppet valve in the throttle plate. Under all other conditions but deceleration, the poppet valve remains shut; during deceleration, the particularly high vacuum in the inlet manifold opens the poppet valve, allowing a moderate amount of mixture to enter. This avoids the sudden burst of liquid fuel being drawn into the cylinders, and enables the engine to continue to fire cleanly.

A similar result is achieved by a 'by-pass' valve. A channel is built into the carburettor which runs from the atmosphere side of the throttle plate to the engine side. Flow through the channel is obstructed by a diaphragm-operated valve connected to the inlet manifold. At very high vacuum levels, the diaphragm unseats the valve, allowing a certain proportion of mixture to flow down the channel into the manifold. Once again, the rich 'snap' followed by excessive weakness is avoided.

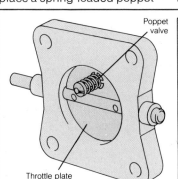
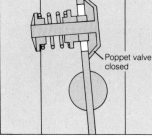
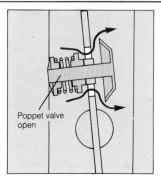

High vacuum in the inlet manifold can produce toxic exhaust fumes. On some carburettors a spring-loaded poppet valve on the throttle lifts off its seat when the throttle is closed, relieving the vacuum

Temperature compensation

Like most liquids, petrol flows more easily when hot. Therefore in hot weather or in slow-moving traffic, when under-bonnet temperatures are high, fuel flow from the carburettor increases, producing a rich mixture.

Emission carburettors employ various adaptations to prevent this. On the constant-vacuum SU HIF carburettor, the main jet is carried at the end of a bi-metallic strip. This strip bends as the temperature rises and is so arranged that, as the temperature increases, the strip pushes the jet upwards, positioning it at a wider part of the metering needle and weakening the mixture. Alternatively, the base of the main jet may incorporate a wax capsule which expands when heated with a similar result.

Zenith CD and some fixed-choke carburettors use a bi-metallic blade attached to a conical valve. As the blade heats up and bends, the valve is drawn outwards, opening a channel which allows extra air to enter the carburettor barrel, slightly weakening the mixture. All emission control devices are non-adjustable and operate automatically.

Some recent carburettors make use of the fact that a turbulent flow of fuel is not affected by variations in temperature. By adding a small quantity of air to the fuel before it leaves the jet, the flow becomes turbulent and needs no temperature compensation.

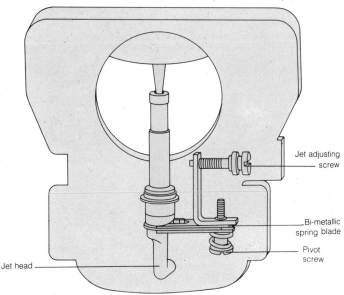

As it gets hot, fuel flows more easily. To prevent over-richness, the SU HIF carburettor uses a bi-metallic spring in the fuel that bends upwards as the temperature rises, raising the jet to maintain the correct mixture

Thermostatic air-intake valves

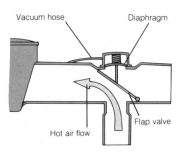

Thermostatic air intakes pick up exhaust-heated air when the engine is cold

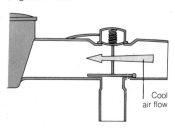

Once the engine is hot, a flap is moved to admit cool air. This system improves fuel economy

To help warm up the engine as soon as possible and reduce the need for choke, many cars now have a dual air intake to the air cleaner, one taking cool air from the front of the engine bay and one taking hot air ducted from the exhaust area.

On starting from cold a valve at the joint of the two intakes blanks off the cold air pipe and allows the carburettor to take only hot air from the exhaust ducting. The warm air helps vaporise the fuel and enables the choke to be dispensed with more rapidly. When the engine is warmed up, the valve, which may be wax-operated or worked by a temperature-sensitive bi-metallic blade, switches to the cold intake. Cold air occupies less space than hot air, and the cold intake charge fills the cylinders more efficiently, enabling the engine to develop more power.

Engines without automatic air intake control usually have a 'summer' and 'winter' manual setting for the air cleaner pick-up pipe. The 'winter' setting, which picks up warm air from near the exhaust manifold, should be selected during the colder months.

Fuel system

Fuel pumps

Because the carburettor is usually higher than the fuel tank, a pump is used to push the fuel under fairly low pressure to the carburettor float chamber.

There are two types of pump, a mechanical one which is driven by the engine camshaft, and an electric one, often fitted close to the tank.

Mechanical pump

A mechanical pump consists mainly of a chamber divided by a diaphragm. The top portion, which holds petrol, contains a filter and sediment bowl and has two spring-loaded valves to control the flow of fuel. Underneath, a diaphragm has a central rod connected to an operating link and rocker arm which is operated by a lobe on the camshaft. A coil spring loads the diaphragm upwards and regulates the pressure of the pump output.

When the engine is running, the diaphragm is alternately pulled down by the link and pushed up by the spring. On the downstroke, fuel enters the upper chamber through the one-way inlet valve, and on the upstroke, leaves through the outlet valve. When the float chamber is full and its needle valve is closed, the spring-loaded diaphragm pressurises the fuel in the line and remains at its lowest position. A one-way pivot on the link allows the rocker to continue operating without forcing up the diaphragm.

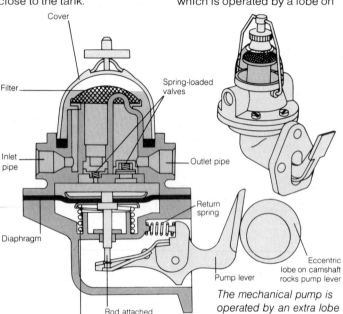

Cover

Filter

Inlet pipe

Diaphragm

Spring-loaded valves

Outlet pipe

Return spring

Eccentric lobe on camshaft rocks pump lever

Pump lever

Rod attached to pump lever

Spring

The mechanical pump is operated by an extra lobe on the camshaft

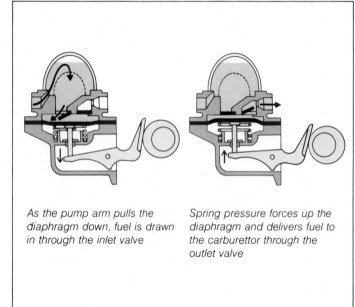

As the pump arm pulls the diaphragm down, fuel is drawn in through the inlet valve

Spring pressure forces up the diaphragm and delivers fuel to the carburettor through the outlet valve

Electric pump

An electric pump uses a spring-loaded diaphragm and valve arrangement similar to that used on the mechanical pump, but the diaphragm is moved against spring pressure by a solenoid, an electro-magnetic switch.

Switching on the ignition energises the solenoid which pulls the diaphragm against spring pressure, drawing petrol from the tank. At the end of its travel, a rod connected to the centre of the diaphragm opens two electrical contacts, de-energising the solenoid. The spring pushes the diaphragm in the opposite direction, pumping petrol to the carburettor.

At the end of the spring-loaded stroke, the electrical contacts are closed by the diaphragm rod and the process restarts. When the float chamber is full, fuel pressure holds the contacts open.

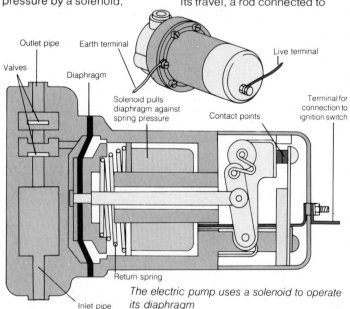

Outlet pipe

Valves

Diaphragm

Earth terminal

Live terminal

Solenoid pulls diaphragm against spring pressure

Contact points

Terminal for connection to ignition switch

Return spring

Inlet pipe

The electric pump uses a solenoid to operate its diaphragm

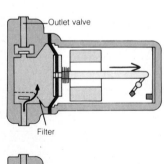

Outlet valve

Filter

Switching on the ignition energises the solenoid, pulling the diaphragm against spring pressure and drawing in fuel. Diaphragm movement eventually opens the electrical points

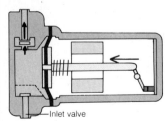

Inlet valve

Once the electrical points have opened, a coil spring returns the diaphragm, pumping fuel through the outlet valve. At the end of the pumping stroke, the points close, re-starting the cycle

Fuel injection

In theory fuel injection provides ideal combustion by spraying the required quantity of fuel directly into the inlet manifold or inlet port so that it is in exactly the correct proportion to the air flow.

Most fuel injection systems employ electronic triggering which, though complex and relatively expensive, has superseded the less reliable mechanical type of injection.

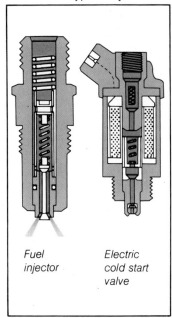

Fuel injector   *Electric cold start valve*

Mechanical fuel injection

A typical system uses a high-pressure pump to deliver fuel at 100psi to a fuel distributor mounted on the engine and driven at half engine speed. The distributor is sensitive to throttle position and inlet man-ifold vacuum, and delivers appropriate quantities of fuel to each of the injectors in turn.

The injector nozzles are held closed by spring-loaded valves until fuel pressure forces them open, when a metered, highly-atomised spray of petrol is delivered to the back of the inlet valve. A facia-control is used to adjust the fuel distributor to deliver a rich mixture to a separate valve for cold starts.

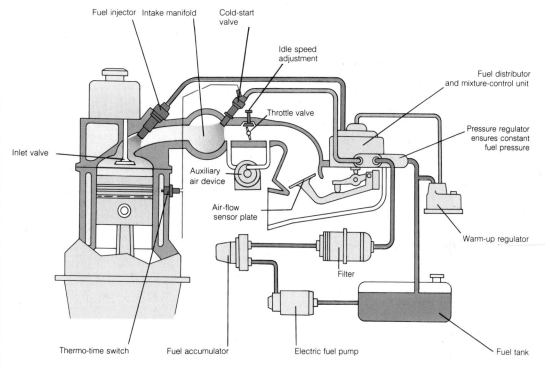

Mechanical fuel injection systems are triggered by the throttle, engine speed and manifold vacuum. Efficiency drops as engine wears

Electronic fuel injection

The injection of fuel in these systems is governed by a complex electronic control unit, or computer. The Bosch system illustrated has an electrically driven pump that draws more fuel than is needed from the tank. A pressure regulator limits pressure in the fuel lines to 25-30psi (1.75-2.10kg sq.cm) and returns the surplus to the tank, reducing the chances of a vapour lock.

Each injector is spring-loaded in the closed position and opened by a solenoid. The amount of fuel sprayed into the intake port depends on how long the solenoid holds the injector nozzle open. Solenoid duration is signalled by the computer which is linked to a number of sensing devices. The computer determines injector duration after sensing manifold vacuum, air and water temperatures, rate of acceleration and throttle position.

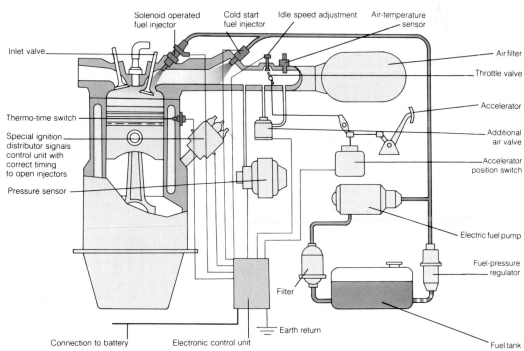

Electronic fuel injection relies on a computer to meter the fuel supply

Fuel system projects

Project 25: Servicing the air filter

Grading: 🔧
Time: 5min-15min
Tools: Spanner or screwdriver to fit air cleaner lid fixings
Materials: New air filter at service intervals

Most cars now use a folded paper element inside the carburettor air cleaner to filter the air and prevent dust from being drawn into the engine. Manufacturers usually recommend that the element is checked every 5,000-6,000 miles and changed every 12,000-18,000 miles.

A few cars have a wire mesh filter or an oil-bath air cleaner. These need cleaning and replenishing with oil at service intervals.

Step 1. A paper element will be sealed inside the carburettor air cleaner. Depending on its type, it will be necessary to remove bolts, screws or undo clips to remove the air cleaner lid.

2. Lift out the element. If it has been in use for less than 12,000 miles, surface dirt can be removed by tapping it lightly against a garage wall.
3. If the element is coated with oil, renew it, but also check where the oil is coming from —probably the crankcase breather system needs cleaning (see Project 24).
4. Wipe any dirt from the inside of the air cleaner before fitting a new element. Refit the air cleaner lid.
* To service a wire mesh air filter, dismantle the air cleaner, extract the mesh; wash the mesh in petrol to remove dirt, then dip it in engine oil and allow it to drain for 30 minutes before refitting it.
** An oil-bath air cleaner must be removed from the carburettor. Remove the lid and pour away the old oil. Clean it with a paint brush soaked in petrol, dry the inside, and refit it to the carburettor. Refill with oil to the level marked inside, before replacing the lid.

Step 1.

Project 26: Servicing the carburettor

Grading: 🔧🔧
Time: 1hr-2hr, depending on carburettor
Tools: Oil can; spanners or screwdrivers for removing air cleaner and carburettor top, carburettor plugs and jets; if necessary, tyre pump
Materials: Sketch pad and pencil; tissue or lint-free cloth; jam jar

Many carburettors fitted to cars made after 1976 cannot have their mixture settings altered without special tools because they do not have conventional adjusting screws. However, even these emission-type carburettors need occasional maintenance. The maintenance procedure differs, depending on whether the carburettor is of the fixed-choke type or a variable-choke unit.

Variable-choke carburettor
Step 1. Using an oil can, lubricate the throttle and choke controls at the carburettor with engine oil; check that the choke mechanism returns to the 'off' position when the knob is pushed in.
2. Unscrew and lift the damper cap to check the oil level.
3. If necessary add engine oil to within $\frac{1}{2}$in of the top.
* Some dampers are restrained in the piston guide rod by a clip, which is dislodged if the damper assembly is pulled right out. While this should be avoided when topping up, the retaining clip can be refitted by removing the air cleaner and lifting the carburettor piston fully with the fingers. This puts the guide rod end level with the top of the suction chamber and the clip can then be refitted. If it is not seated properly, heavy fuel consumption can result.

Step 1.

Step 3.

*Step ***

Fixed-choke carburettor
This type of carburettor has a number of small jets that are likely to become blocked if sediment builds up in the float chamber. The chamber should be cleaned at major service intervals.

Step 1. Remove the air cleaner.

2. Undo the screws securing the top of the carburettor. Before lifting it off, make a sketch of any external linkages so that they can be reassembled in the same position.

3. Disconnect the fuel pipe and remove the top. Take care not to knock or bend the float if it is pivoted on the upper section, otherwise the fuel level will be upset.

4. Some fixed-choke carburettors have a drain plug in the float chamber to let out accumulated petrol. Undo the plug and catch the petrol in a jam-jar. Clean any sediment from the bottom of the chamber using clean tissue or a lint-free cloth.

5. The main jet is submerged in the float chamber. Unscrew it and check that it is unblocked by holding it up to the light. Blocked jets can be cleared by blowing through them with a tyre pump.

Alternatively a brush bristle can be used to probe out any stubborn dirt. Never use wire to clean a jet. Refit the main jet.

6. On a carburettor with an idling jet, remove the jet and check that it is clear.

7. Check the action of the float valve by gently holding it shut and sucking the end of the fuel pipe. If the tongue is placed over the end of the pipe, it should hold its vacuum for 20 seconds if the valve is in good order. If it leaks, unscrew the old valve and fit a replacement.

8. Refit the upper section of the carburettor, if necessary reconnecting the external linkage. Check manual choke systems by operating the choke knob at the facia. When the knob is fully out the choke flap should blank off the choke tube. Push the knob fully towards the facia. This will enable the choke flap to return smoothly to the vertical position.

Step 2.

Step 3.

Step 4.

Step 5.

Project 27: Checking an automatic choke

Grading: 🔧
Time: 5min-15min
Tools: Spanner or screwdriver to remove air cleaner lid

Step 1. With the engine cold, remove the air cleaner lid. The choke flap (there are two flaps on a twin-choke carburettor) should completely block the carburettor barrel(s).

2. Refit the air cleaner, start the car and drive it for at least four miles until the engine is at normal operating temperature.

3. Remove the air cleaner lid with the engine hot. The choke flap(s) should be in the vertical position. If the automatic choke does not operate correctly, get a garage to check it.

Step 1.

Fuel system projects

Project 28: Cleaning a mechanical fuel pump

> **Grading:** ✔
> **Time:** 15min-25min
> **Tools:** Spanners and screw-drivers to remove cover
> **Materials:** Cloth; clean paint brush

Mechanical pumps contain a filter to prevent grit being passed to the carburettor. The filter should be cleaned at major service intervals—every 10,000 or 12,000 miles.

Step 1. Disconnect the battery.
2. Place a piece of cloth under the pump to catch spilt petrol.
3. On pumps with a glass bowl, slacken the screw at the top of the wire retainer, swing the retainer to one side and lift off the bowl.
4. On later pumps a metal cover is used. Remove the centre screw and lift off the cover.
5. Lift off the wire mesh filter and wash it in petrol.

6. Dip a clean paint brush in petrol and remove any dirt from the sediment chamber, then wipe clean.
7. Refit the filter and glass bowl or cover. Make sure that the sealing ring is in good condition.
8. Tighten the bowl or cover screw just sufficiently to compress the sealing ring and form a petrol-tight seal. Reconnect the battery, run the engine and check for leaks.

Project 29: Renewing a mechanical fuel pump

> **Grading:** ✔✔
> **Time:** 30min-45min
> **Tools:** Spanner or screw-driver to disconnect battery and undo fuel pump fixings
> **Materials:** New pump; pump gaskets; one sharpened pencil; scraper

Step 1. Disconnect the battery.
2. Remove the fuel pipes at the pump.
  Plug the end of the inlet pipe with a pointed pencil to prevent fuel leaks.
3. Undo the nuts or bolts holding the pump to the engine.
4. Withdraw the pump.
  If the pump is operated by a short push-rod, pull out the rod.
5. Clean the remains of any gasket from the pump mounting area with a scraper. If there is a spacer between the pump and engine, take care not to damage the spacer surface when removing old gasket material, otherwise oil leaks may occur.
6. Fit new gaskets on both sides of the spacer and offer up the new pump, taking care that the operating lever fits over the camshaft.
7. Fit the fixing nuts or bolts, screwing them in finger-tight. While the pump is still loose, push it towards the block. If it is fitted correctly, the spring inside will press the pump away from the block. Provided this happens, tighten the fixings. If there is no spring resistance, the pump lever has been pushed underneath the camshaft and will not operate. Remove the pump and try again.
8. Where the pump is operated by a push-rod, fit the rod and then fit the pump using new gaskets. There is no need to carry out Step 7 (above) on this sort of pump.
9. Remove the pencil from the fuel pipe and refit the unions to the pump, taking care not to cross-thread them.
10. Reconnect the battery, run the engine and check for leaks at the pipes.

Step 3.

Step 5.

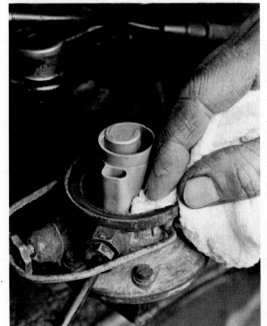

Step 6.

Step 8.

Fuel system projects

Project 30: Renewing an electric fuel pump

Grading: 🔧🔧
Time: 30min-1 hr, depending on the location of the pump
Tools: For under-car pumps, ramps or jack and axle stands to raise the car; spanners and screwdrivers to disconnect battery; pump wiring, fuel pipes and bracket
Materials: New electric pump or reconditioned unit; two sharpened pencils for blocking fuel pipes

Depending on the car, an electrical fuel pump will be mounted under the floor at the rear, inside the boot or under the bonnet.

As different types of pump are used, depending on their location, it is important to quote the make and model of car, and engine and chassis numbers when ordering a replacement.

Step 1. Disconnect the battery.
2. Depending on the location of the pump, either raise and support the rear end of the car, lift the bonnet or remove a trim panel in the boot to gain access to it.
3. Release the pump fixing clamp and lift the pump clear. If a plastic pipe is attached to the end cover, detach it.
4. Disconnect the live cable and remove the earth wire from the pump body.
5. Undo the fuel pipe clips and disconnect the pipe which comes from the tank. Block the end quickly with a pencil-point to prevent fuel leakage. Remove and block the other pipe with a pencil.
6. Fit the new pump to the clamp, ensuring that it is at the correct attitude (the body may be marked 'top').
7. Reconnect the live feed and earth wire; correctly fit the fuel pipes (one pipe stub on the pump will be marked 'inlet'), and, if necessary, reconnect the breather pipe to the end cover.

Reconnect the battery and switch on the ignition to test the pump—it will click for several seconds as it fills with petrol. Lower the rear end of the car, if necessary.

Step 2.

Step 3.

Step 4.

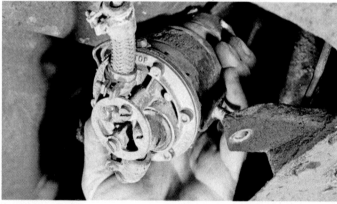

Step 3.

Step 4.

Electrical systems

ELECTRICAL SYSTEMS

Battery and charging

Every car is fitted with a battery. It is charged while the engine is running and provides the vehicle's electrical needs while the engine is stopped. It also produces the very high current demanded by the starter motor to re-start the engine. This means that the battery must be capable of being charged and discharged a great number of times without loss of performance, and be able to provide a lot of electrical energy (as much as that used by a three-bar electric fire) for the few seconds that the starter motor is in use. The failure of the battery to turn the starter motor is usually the first indication of a fault.

A battery consists of a number of separate 2-volt cells. The cells are joined so that their individual voltages are added together—a 6-volt battery has three cells and a 12-volt battery, six. Each cell has a voltage potential of only 2 volts, whether it is as small as a torch battery or as big as a one-gallon container—the size of each cell determines only how long it can provide a given amount of current.

A cell consists of a number of lead plates which are alternately connected to its positive and negative terminals. They are insulated from each other by synthetic separators and immersed in a solution of sulphuric acid diluted with distilled or de-ionised (chemically-filtered) water known as electrolyte. The number of lead plates in each cell varies, but the total is always an odd number because each cell starts and finishes with a negative plate. This is because the positive plates work harder and are usually sandwiched between negative plates in order to realise their full potential. In most car batteries the cells contain seven, nine or eleven plates—the more plates there are, the greater the capacity of the battery.

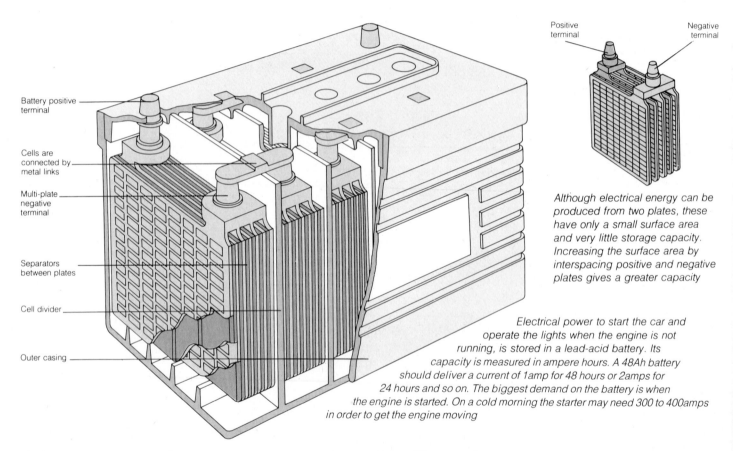

Battery positive terminal

Cells are connected by metal links

Multi-plate negative terminal

Separators between plates

Cell divider

Outer casing

Positive terminal

Negative terminal

Although electrical energy can be produced from two plates, these have only a small surface area and very little storage capacity. Increasing the surface area by interspacing positive and negative plates gives a greater capacity

Electrical power to start the car and operate the lights when the engine is not running, is stored in a lead-acid battery. Its capacity is measured in ampere hours. A 48Ah battery should deliver a current of 1amp for 48 hours or 2amps for 24 hours and so on. The biggest demand on the battery is when the engine is started. On a cold morning the starter may need 300 to 400amps in order to get the engine moving

How the battery works

The negative plates are made from spongy lead material and the positive plates from lead dioxide. When an external circuit is connected to the battery, the acid in the electrolyte enters the plates, gradually turning them to lead sulphate, and this chemical action generates electricity. The battery can continue to discharge until all the plates have been converted to lead sulphate, at which time the battery is said to be 'flat'.

If, instead of taking electrical power from the battery, the battery is connected to a charger, or charging system, and current is passed through it at a voltage slightly in excess of its normal output, the chemical process is reversed. The acid leaves the plates, making the electrolyte stronger, and the plates gradually revert to their original composition of lead dioxide and spongy lead. This process is known as recharging and can be continued until no further chemical change in the plates occurs.

Specific gravity

The amount of acid in the electrolyte is directly proportional to the state of charge of the battery. This can be measured if a sample of electrolyte is, in effect, weighed and its specific gravity (SG) is determined. This is done with an instrument called a hydrometer which compares the weight (density) of a sample of electrolyte with an equal volume of water.

The hydrometer consists of a glass tube with a rubber bulb at one end and a thin rubber tube at the other. Inside the glass tube there is a float which is calibrated from 1.100 to 1.300. When the rubber tube of the hydrometer is inserted into a battery cell below the surface of the electrolyte, a sample can be taken by pressing and releasing the rubber bulb. The float sinks in the sample, and the specific gravity can be read from the point where the float breaks the surface of the electrolyte. Do not use a hydrometer within an hour of topping up, because it will show a false reading.

Temperature

The battery is a chemical device, and does not, in fact, store electricity. Instead, it stores chemicals capable of producing electricity, and so it is affected by temperature. All chemical changes are assisted by an increase in temperature and retarded by a temperature reduction—this is why a freezer keeps food fresh for long periods of time. The ability of a fully charged, serviceable battery to give the high current required by the starter motor is reduced by approximately 40% at freezing point (0°C) (32°F) and by as much as 60% at −18°C (0°F) when compared with its performance on a summer day at 27°C (81°F). Also, cold weather makes engines harder to turn, calling for more battery current. This is why a battery which has performed without problems for a year or two usually starts to give trouble during the winter months.

Capacity

The number and size of the lead plates in each cell determine the capacity of a battery. In practical terms, capacity indicates the battery's ability to provide current. For instance, a battery with a high capacity will still provide starter current if the side lights have been left on all night, while a low-capacity battery would be 'flat' – ie have no current left

The capacity of a battery can be difficult to judge, but physical size is usually a good indication. Stamped or printed on most batteries will be figures—33 or 38 for instance —indicating its capacity. Sometimes the figures are followed by the letters Ah (ampere-hours)—the unit of measurement of capacity.

The manufacturer determines the ampere-hour capacity of a type of battery by testing samples. If it is capable of providing 3.5amps for 10 hours before becoming discharged, it is rated as 35Ah (3.5amps × 10 hours), and in the battery specification it will have its capacity shown as 35Ah at the 10-hour rate.

Because battery capacity is affected by the rate at which it is discharged, the same battery will be capable of providing 2amps for 20 hours and so its capacity could also be quoted as (2amps × 20 hours) or 40Ah at the 20-hour rate.

Therefore, when making comparisons, it is important to find out at which hour rate the Ah capacity figure was determined.

In practice the capacity will reduce as a battery grows older and loses some of the active material from its plates. Provided the battery fitted to a vehicle is replaced with one of the same capacity, no problem should be experienced.

Battery life

The life of most batteries is two to three years, but this depends to a large extent on their operating environment, including temperature, vibration, charging system performance, and on how well they are maintained.

When a battery is discharged, the plates in its cells are changed to lead sulphate. Unless it is recharged without delay the lead sulphate will become hard and leave parts of the plates beyond recovery, reducing the battery's capacity.

If the battery is left 'flat' for a day or two, crystals start to form. These expand and force active materials from the plates into and through the separators, causing internal short circuits. Once a cell has been damaged in this way, no amount of recharging will bring it to life—it is useless and cannot be repaired.

Older batteries which have areas of non-reversible lead sulphate on their plates can be damaged by indiscriminate fast or boost charging. The plates get hot and lumps of lead sulphate fall off them, taking areas of useful material with them. This not only reduces the battery capacity, but the material which has fallen off can jam into the separators and cause short-circuits between the plates.

The water used for topping up is also important. If it contains impurities such as lime or chlorine, the plates will be damaged or become coated. Coated plates prevent the electrolyte from making contact with the active material. Distilled or de-ionised water is cheap and should always be used for topping up. Rain water or melted ice from the freezer compartment of a refrigerator are not suitable as both are likely to be contaminated.

If a battery is thought to be faulty it can be tested by an auto-electrician, but first make sure that it is fully charged because a 'flat' battery will always appear to be faulty. A battery is fully charged when, while it is on charge, three hourly checks with a hydrometer show no change in the specific gravity of the electrolyte in any of its cells.

Never add anything other than distilled or de-ionised water to the battery. Acid will be lost only by the spillage of electrolyte—often the result of over-filling. Acid replacement must be left to a specialist.

The charging system

All vehicles have a charging system which provides for their electrical needs, such as ignition, lights, heater and electrical accessories, while the engine is running, as well as charging the battery. It consists of a generator, driven by a belt, and an automatic control system. Cars made in the last five or six years are fitted with a type of generator known as an alternator; older cars and some commercial vehicles have a different type, known as a dynamo.

In both the alternator and the dynamo, electricity is generated in the same way as it is at a power station. Either, coils of wire are moved near a stationary magnet (dynamo), or the magnet is moved near coils of wire (alternator). In each case the moving lines of magnetic force generate electricity in the coils of wire. The amount of electricity generated depends on the speed at which the coils and magnet move relative to each other, how close they are to each other, the strength of the magnetic field and the number of turns of wire in each coil.

As the speed of a car engine changes continually, but the electrical requirements for such items as headlights or a heated rear window are constant, a method of controlling the generator output is necessary. This is achieved by an automatic control system which alters the strength of the magnetic field.

An alternator can produce a higher output for longer periods of time than a dynamo. This is because the generating windings in an alternator are stationary and are not restricted in size, nor are they as difficult to cool as those of a dynamo, which rotate in its armature.

In practice, both the alternator and the dynamo start to produce a useful current output at armature speeds in excess of 1,500rpm. However, the maximum speed of a dynamo armature is limited to about 6,000rpm. This is because of the effects of centrifugal force on its complicated windings, and also because at high speed, constant brush contact with the commutator is difficult to achieve. The armature, or rotor, in an alternator is not as complicated and can be turned at least three times as fast as a dynamo. This means that the drive-belt pulley fitted to a dynamo has to be quite large to prevent the armature turning too quickly, and the engine must be turning quite fast for it to produce a useful current. The alternator is fitted with a much smaller pulley and can produce a useful current at engine tick-over speeds.

Battery and charging

Dynamo

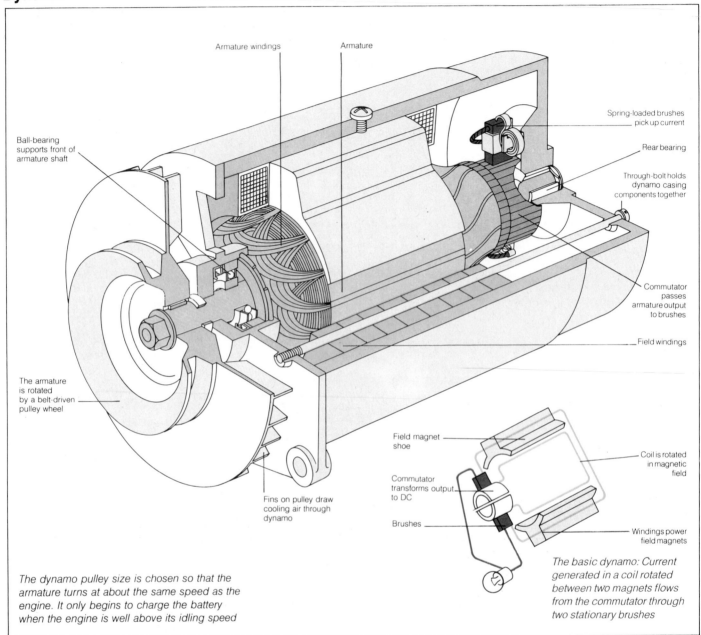

Armature windings

Armature

Ball-bearing supports front of armature shaft

Spring-loaded brushes pick up current

Rear bearing

Through-bolt holds dynamo casing components together

Commutator passes armature output to brushes

Field windings

The armature is rotated by a belt-driven pulley wheel

Fins on pulley draw cooling air through dynamo

Field magnet shoe

Coil is rotated in magnetic field

Commutator transforms output to DC

Brushes

Windings power field magnets

The dynamo pulley size is chosen so that the armature turns at about the same speed as the engine. It only begins to charge the battery when the engine is well above its idling speed

The basic dynamo: Current generated in a coil rotated between two magnets flows from the commutator through two stationary brushes

The dynamo has its rotating armature mounted between two stationary coils of wire, known as the field windings, wound on soft iron shoes. When current is passed through the field windings the shoes become the poles of a magnet, with its lines of force passing between them through the armature. Each armature winding terminates at a copper strip which is part of the commutator. Each coil is joined to the next, producing, in effect, one very large coil which has a connection to a copper strip on the commutator every few turns. As the armature rotates, electricity is generated in these windings, most of it in the windings directly adjacent to the two magnetic shoes. Each winding becomes negative as it passes one shoe and then positive as it passes the other. By having a graphite brush rubbing against the commutator in line with each shoe, current can be taken from the armature. In this way one brush is always negative and the other positive, so the output is direct current, suitable for charging the battery and operating the car's electrical equipment.

Control box

Left to itself, a dynamo would produce too high an output voltage, resulting in damaged light bulbs and other components. To correct its tendency to overproduce, a control box is used.

The control box contains a regulator which limits the output voltage. It also has a 'cut-out' which connects the dynamo to the battery when its output is sufficiently high, and disconnects it when the engine is stopped, so preventing the battery from discharging through the dynamo.

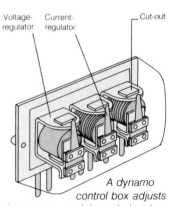

Voltage-regulator

Current-regulator

Cut-out

A dynamo control box adjusts dynamo output. It is sealed at the factory and should only be adjusted by an auto-electrician

How the regulator works

Some of the dynamo output passes through a set of contacts in the regulator to the field windings, increasing the magnetic field and the dynamo output. The output current also passes through the voltage regulator winding, and when this output reaches a pre-set value, the magnetic field it produces is sufficiently strong to pull open the regulator points against spring pressure. This begins a chain reaction, and once the contacts separate, the magnetic field in the dynamo reduces and so its output falls. This means that the magnetic field produced by the regulator winding is also reduced and when it drops to a certain value, the spring-loaded regulator points close again, increasing the output. This cycle of operation occurs hundreds of times a minute, and controls the output voltage of the dynamo irrespective of the speed of the engine.

The 'cut-out'

Output current is also passed through the cut-out winding which has a pair of contacts normally spring-loaded in the 'open' position. When the dynamo output exceeds that of the battery, the magnetic field produced by this winding closes the cut-out points and the dynamo starts to charge the battery and provide current for the electrical system. When the engine is switched off and the dynamo stops generating, the magnetic field produced by the cut-out winding reduces, allowing the cut-out points to open, automatically disconnecting the battery.

Most control boxes also have a third relay which controls the output current. This relay is connected in series with the voltage regulator and operates in the same way to prevent excessive current from being produced, which would damage the generator.

Although control boxes have provision for adjustment, they cannot be adjusted correctly without expensive instruments and detailed manufacturer's data. Work of this kind should be entrusted to an auto-electrician.

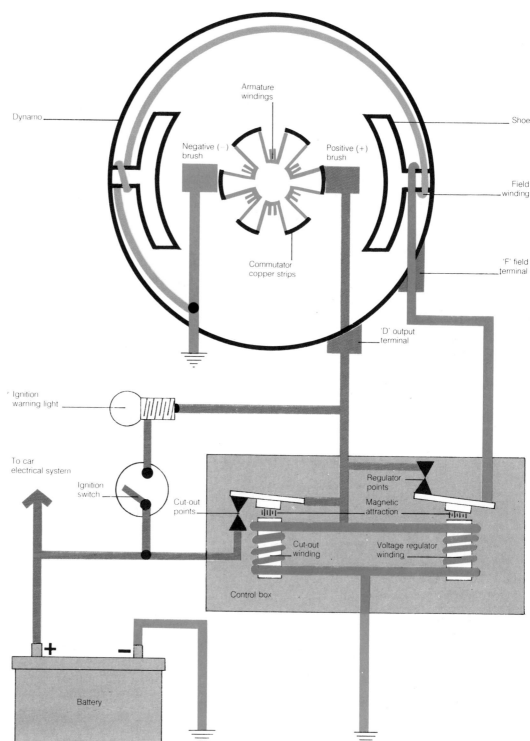

To prevent the dynamo from overloading itself, its output is adjusted by a control box which limits the voltage output by controlling the strength of the magnetic field in the dynamo field windings.
Current from the output terminal is fed to the control box which contains two relays. When dynamo output exceeds battery voltage, a proportion of it flowing through the cut-out winding generates a magnetic field strong enough to close the cut-out points and feed the bulk of the output to the car's electrical system. Also, as the voltage increases, a proportion of it flowing through the regulator winding generates sufficient magnetism to open the regulator points. This shuts off power to the field windings and the magnetic field within the dynamo diminishes, reducing the output. The lower output reduces the magnetism of the regulator winding, allowing the points to close and the process to begin again. The regulator points open and close several hundred times a minute

Battery and charging

The alternator

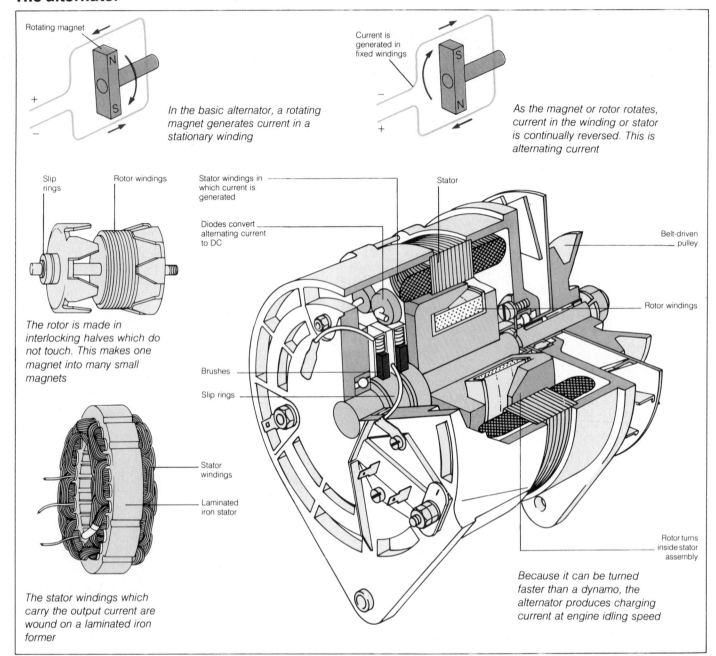

In the basic alternator, a rotating magnet generates current in a stationary winding

Rotating magnet

Current is generated in fixed windings

As the magnet or rotor rotates, current in the winding or stator is continually reversed. This is alternating current

Slip rings

Rotor windings

Stator windings in which current is generated

Stator

Diodes convert alternating current to DC

Belt-driven pulley

Rotor windings

The rotor is made in interlocking halves which do not touch. This makes one magnet into many small magnets

Brushes

Slip rings

Stator windings

Laminated iron stator

The stator windings which carry the output current are wound on a laminated iron former

Rotor turns inside stator assembly

Because it can be turned faster than a dynamo, the alternator produces charging current at engine idling speed

The alternator generates current in the same way as the dynamo. The field winding, however, is incorporated in the armature (called the rotor), and current is generated in stationary windings mounted around the outside cover, and called the stator. Current is fed to the rotor winding through two stationary graphite brushes, which make contact with two smooth slip-rings formed on one end of the rotor. Each end of the rotor is formed into fingers which mesh together but do not touch. When current is passed through the rotor windings, one end of the rotor and its fingers become the north pole of a magnet, and the other end and its fingers, the south pole. As the rotor turns, each stator winding is subject to a change in the magnetic field as each finger moves past it. The succession of magnetic north and south poles passing the stator winding generates alternately positive and negative current in the stator.

As the stator windings in which current is generated are stationary, the alternator cannot use a commutator and brushes to sort out the polarity. The positive and negative output from each stator winding —there are normally three of them—is alternating current, which varies according to the speed of the rotor. Because a number of components, such as a radio, will be damaged if they are fed with alternating current, and also because alternating current cannot be used to charge the battery, the polarity must be rectified to produce direct current. Rectification is achieved by using small electrical 'one-way valves' known as diodes. These will allow only positive current to pass through them in one direction and negative current in the other.

By connecting a number of diodes into a circuit known as a rectifying 'bridge', the alternating current can be rearranged so that positive current is fed to the battery positive terminal and negative current to its negative terminal, changing the alternator output into direct current. Most car alternators have nine diodes in a rectifier pack, as shown in the wiring diagram of the alternator.

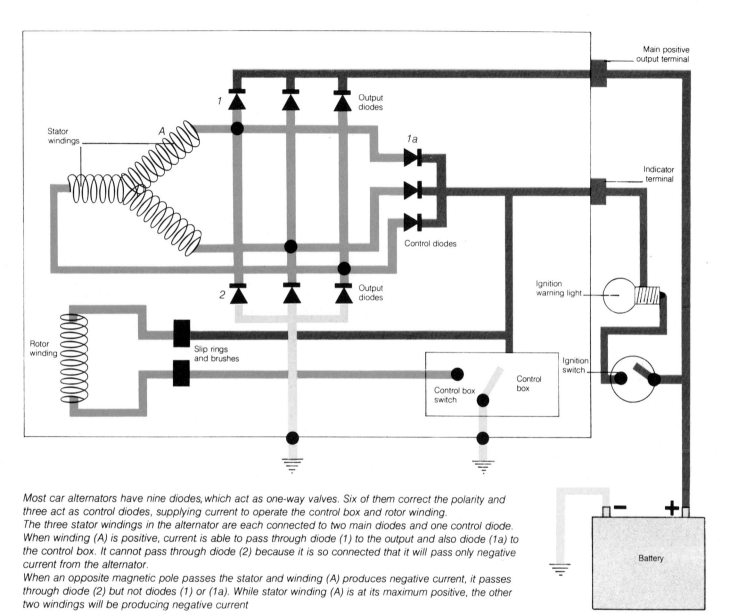

Most car alternators have nine diodes, which act as one-way valves. Six of them correct the polarity and three act as control diodes, supplying current to operate the control box and rotor winding.
The three stator windings in the alternator are each connected to two main diodes and one control diode. When winding (A) is positive, current is able to pass through diode (1) to the output and also diode (1a) to the control box. It cannot pass through diode (2) because it is so connected that it will pass only negative current from the alternator.
When an opposite magnetic pole passes the stator and winding (A) produces negative current, it passes through diode (2) but not diodes (1) or (1a). While stator winding (A) is at its maximum positive, the other two windings will be producing negative current

Alternator control box

This is usually fitted inside the body of the alternator. It works in the same way as a dynamo regulator to limit output voltage, but often, instead of having contact points, it uses a transistor as a solid-state switch. It receives current from the control diodes which also supply the rotor winding, and are at the same voltage as the output terminal.

When the output voltage rises above a pre-set limit, the transistor switch operates and disconnects the rotor windings. The rotor magnetic field reduces, and so does the output, and this causes the transistor to switch the rotor winding on again, and the output rises. This cycle of operation occurs many hundreds of times a second to

control the alternator output within fine limits.

It can be seen from the alternator control diagram that while the six main diodes allow current from the stator windings to reach the battery positive and negative terminals, they will not allow the battery current to pass in the opposite direction through them into the stator windings. For this reason

no cut-out is required.

Diodes have little electrical resistance, and if the battery or 'jump start' leads are wrongly connected, the diodes will conduct an excessive current and there will be a short circuit which will cause them to 'blow' like a fuse. This will mean an expensive repair or a replacement alternator.

Warning light

In most cars there is a charge warning light, often known as the ignition warning light. This is a bulb connected between the ignition switch and the generator. In the wiring diagram it can be seen that if the

engine is stopped and the ignition is switched on, current from the battery passes through the bulb to earth in the generator. This causes the bulb to light because one side of it is connected to earth and

the other to a 12-volt supply. When the engine is started the bulb goes out. This is because it now has 12 volts from the battery on one side of it and 12 volts from the generator on the other, so nothing passes

through it. At engine idling speed it may glow very dimly, indicating that some current is passing from the battery through the bulb because the generator output is not as high as that of the battery.

Battery and charging projects

Project 31: Looking after the battery

Grading: 🔧
Time: Varies, depending on the state of the battery
Tools: Spanner and screwdriver to fit terminal fixings; wire brush; hydrometer
Materials: Topping-up fluid; petroleum jelly; household ammonia or baking soda; cloth; paint

Step 1.

Step 2.

Step 3.

Step 4.

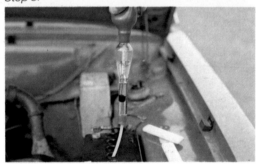
Step 5.

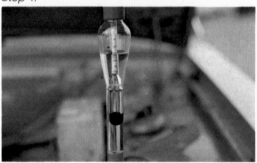
Step 6.

Over a period, a lead-acid battery loses distilled water from its electrolyte. If this is not replenished, the level eventually drops below the top of the plates, reducing efficiency.

The electrolyte is topped up using distilled or de-ionised water, sold by garages and accessory shops as topping-up fluid. Tap water, which may contain mineral traces, should not be used.

The correct level for the electrolyte is marked on the translucent case of modern batteries. On batteries with a black case, the electrolyte should just cover the splash shield over the top of the plates, or the separators between the plates.

If the battery terminals or the metal parts securing the battery are covered in acid corrosion, this must be neutralised before it eats into the metal. Undo the battery connections and take the battery out of the vehicle and wash corroded parts of the battery holder in household ammonia, or baking soda, and hot water. When the acid is neutralised, give the exposed metal a coat of paint. Battery terminals should be cleaned to bare metal with a wire brush.

As a battery discharges, the electrolyte solution becomes weaker. The state of charge of the battery can be found by testing the specific gravity of the electrolyte with a hydrometer. When the electrolyte temperature in the battery is 60°F (15°C), a discharged battery gives a reading of 1.110 to 1.130, a reading of 1.230 to 1.250 indicates the battery is 70 per cent charged, and a fully charged battery gives a reading of 1.270 to 1.290.

However, many hydrometers will have only coloured bands

on the float, representing the different charge states. Where figures are given, the decimal point may not be shown.

For really accurate readings, a battery specialist uses a temperature compensation scale, as shown here, to allow for the electrolyte temperature of the battery, if it is above or below 60°F.
Step 1. Once a week, remove the battery caps or vent cover and check the level of the electrolyte. If it is below the minimum mark, or the splash shield or separators between the plates are uncovered, top it up with distilled water. Do not overfill it, otherwise acid may leak out of the vent holes while the battery is being charged, causing corrosion. After topping up, dry the battery with a clean cloth.
2. Corroded battery connections make poor contact, and

reduce electrical output. Remove the terminals for cleaning. If they are tight, do not use force; instead, wrap a rag soaked in hot water around the terminals. This will expand them and ease their removal.
3. Clean the battery posts and terminals to bright metal with a wire brush, making sure that you keep the dust out of your eyes. Apply petroleum jelly to the mating surfaces.
4. Reconnect the terminals and smear the outside with petroleum jelly to discourage further corrosion.
5. The state of charge can be tested with a hydrometer. Insert the dip tube into the electrolyte, then squeeze and release the bulb to draw a sample of electrolyte into the tube.
6. Note the reading on the calibrated float riding on the surface of the sample.
* Hydrometer readings should

be taken only after the battery has been charged or used on the car for 30 minutes. If the readings fluctuate by more than 0.040, the cells may be faulty. Have an auto-electrician check the battery.

Centigrade			Fahrenheit
+0.021	45	110	+0.020
		100	+0.016
+0.014	35	90	+0.012
+0.007	25	80	+0.008
		70	+0.004
0.000	15	60	0.000
		50	−0.004
−0.007	5	40	−0.008
	0	30	−0.012
−0.014	−5	20	−0.016

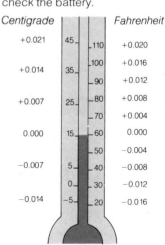
Electrolyte temperature compensation scale

Battery and charging projects

Project 32: Using a battery charger

Grading: 🔧
Time: 5min
Tools: Battery charger

In winter, when cold weather makes the battery less efficient, a car used on many short stop-start journeys will consume a great deal of battery power each time the starter is operated, but the car may not travel far enough for the generator to put back the lost energy.

Under these conditions, a mains-operated battery charger that puts a 'trickle' of current into the battery while the car is garaged overnight, will do the same job as a generator.

As most home chargers have a low output, it is not necessary to remove the battery filler caps or vent cover. Modern batteries must never have the vents removed during charging as the electrolyte will overflow. Inflammable hydrogen gas is given off through the vent holes during charging, so battery charging should be carried out only in a well-ventilated area, and anything likely to cause a spark should be at least six feet away from the battery.

Here, the battery has been removed from a car, but battery charging can, if required, be carried out with the battery connected up and in position on the car.

Step 1. Check the electrolyte level and top it up if necessary. Replace the filler plugs or vent cover.

2. Connect the charger clips to the battery terminals. The positive clip (+), usually joined to a red cable, goes to the battery positive (+) terminal. The negative (−) clip, generally joined to a black cable, is clamped on the negative battery terminal.

3. Plug in the charger to the mains and switch it on. It should indicate the rate of charge on a dial, or illuminate a working lamp. Most chargers make a humming sound. If the charger does not work, switch it off and check its fuse. If this has blown, check that the connections on the battery are correct. Accidentally touching them together when the charger is working will blow the fuse.

4. When charging is complete, switch off the charger at the mains.

5. After the mains supply has been switched off, disconnect the clips from the battery. A 'live' charger should never be disconnected at the battery, as a spark at the terminal may cause the hydrogen gas to explode.

Step 2.

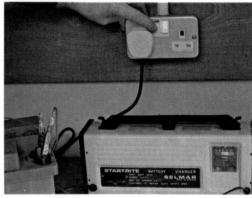

Step 3.

Dynamo maintenance

If the ignition warning light stays on during normal driving, either the fanbelt is broken or needs adjustment (see Projects 1, 2 and 3) or the dynamo needs attention. The dynamo brushes, commutator and armature can be examined after removing the unit from the engine and dismantling it.

The dynamo depends for maximum output on firm contact between two spring-loaded carbon brushes and its commutator. When new, brushes are about ¾in (19mm) long, but over a period the rotating commutator wears them down. When they have been reduced to about ⅜in (9.5mm) long, they should be renewed.

An armature which has lost solder is almost certainly burned out—have an auto-electrician check it. Although armatures can be renewed, it is often quicker and cheaper to fit a reconditioned dynamo bought on a service exchange basis.

Most dynamos are held together by two long through-bolts.

Project 33: Removing and dismantling the dynamo

Grading: 🔧🔧
Time: 30min-45min
Tools: Spanners to fit dynamo fixing nuts and bolts; large screwdriver; if necessary, medium vice

Step 1. Loosen the clamping bolts on the engine and swing the dynamo body towards the cylinder block. Disconnect the fanbelt.

2. Disconnect the two cables from the end of the dynamo.
3. Take out the fixing bolts and clamp bolt and take the dynamo to a work-bench.
4. Unscrew the two through-bolts. If they are very tight, up-end the dynamo and grip the sides of each bolt-head in a vice, and twist the dynamo to loosen them. Remove the bolts.
5. The main dynamo components—the commutator end bracket, casing and armature with the pulley bracket attached—can now be pulled apart. Reassembly is a reversal of the above procedure. Note that the end brackets each have a small protrusion at the edge that engages with a notch at the end of the casing to provide correct alignment. The cables cannot be refitted wrongly as the terminals are of different sizes.

Step 3.

Step 5.

Battery and charging projects

Project 34: Fitting new brushes

Grading: 🔧🔧
Time: 10min, once dynamo is dismantled (see previous Project).
Tools: Screwdriver to fit terminal screws; fine file
Materials: New brushes; fine glasspaper; cloth

Step 1. Both carbon brushes are fitted in oblong holders on the inside of the commutator end bracket. Remove each terminal screw holding the brush wire, swing each spring clear of the holder and take out the brushes.

2. Use a small piece of cloth moistened in petrol to clean inside each holder. Remove traces of petrol with a dry cloth.

3. Fit each new brush into its holder with its wire screwed tightly to the end bracket. The brush should slide in the holder without sticking. If it does stick, remove any high-spots from the carbon with a fine file. Fit the wires to the terminals.

4. The ends of the brushes should be concave to match the commutator. If they are not, wrap some fine glasspaper round the commutator, abrasive side outwards. With the brushes in their holders, fit the end bracket up to the commutator and twist it back and forth to shape the ends of the brushes.

5. Check and clean the commutator (see Project 35).

6. Pull each spring away from the holder and lift each brush until it no longer protrudes from the bottom. Prop it in place by resting the spring against the side of the brush.

7. Refit the end bracket and reassemble the dynamo. Use a small screwdriver through the ventilation holes in the end bracket to lift each spring and reposition it so that it rests on the end of the brush.

Step 1.

Step 3.

Step 6.

Step 7.

Project 35: Checking and cleaning the commutator

Grading: 🔧
Time: Approx 20min
Tools: Calipers
Materials: Fine glasspaper; old hacksaw blade

The commutator that the brushes bear on can be examined after removing the dynamo casing from around the armature. It is not necessary to disconnect the armature bracket at the pulley end.

Step 1. If the commutator is mis-shapen it will cause excessive brush wear and will reduce dynamo output. Check its diameter with calipers and check that the same gap fits all round the commutator. If it is badly worn, consult an auto-electrician. It may be necessary to obtain a service-exchange dynamo.

2. Provided the commutator is in good condition, use a strip of fine glasspaper (not emery cloth) to clean off surface dirt from the copper segments.

3. The gaps between the segments should be slightly undercut, using an old hacksaw or a sharp screwdriver blade.

Wipe off all filings and dirt with a clean dry cloth when you have finished.

Step 2.

Step 3.

Battery and charging projects

Project 36: Removing a dynamo pulley

Grading: ✦
Time: 10min-15min
Tools: Spanner to fit pulley nut; 1lb hammer; small-bladed screwdriver; if necessary, a medium vice; nylon or copper-faced hammer

Dynamo pulleys rarely break, but because most replacement dynamos are sold without one, it is usually necessary to transfer the old pulley to the new dynamo before it can be fitted to the engine.
Step 1. Loosen the pulley nut. Sometimes this is very tight. If so, do not hold the pulley in a vice—it will bend or break. Instead, dismantle the dynamo, pack the jaws of a vice with cloth and use it to gently hold the armature while the pulley nut is loosened.
2. Undo the nut until it is just above the end of the armature shaft. Then support the pulley and tap the nut gently with a hammer to drive out the armature.
3. If the new dynamo does not have a Woodruff key locking the pulley to the shaft, use a small screwdriver to prise the old one from its slot. Transfer the key to the new dynamo, tapping it into the slot with a nylon or copper-faced hammer. Fit the pulley, tightening the nut firmly.

Step 2.

Step 3.

Renewing alternator brushes

The alternator is more complicated than the dynamo, and if the ignition warning light refuses to go out and the fanbelt is operating correctly, its brushes may be worn out.

Replacing brushes is about the only alternator job that the DIY motorist should tackle.
Alternator brushes do not carry such heavy loads as those on a dynamo and are

smaller. Depending on type, they may be mounted in a holder fixed on the outside of the alternator rear body or under a plastic cover. Both types are illustrated here.

Project 37: Removing the alternator from the engine

Grading: ✦
Time: 15min-30min depending on alternator position
Tools: Spanners to fit alternator mounting nuts and bolts

Like the dynamo, the alternator should be removed from the car to fit new brushes.
Step 1. After disconnecting the battery, loosen the mountings, push the alternator towards the engine and disconnect the fanbelt.
2. Note the position of any

separate feed wires before disconnecting them from the rear of the alternator. Plug-and-socket cable connectors are usually made so that they can be fitted only one way round.
3. Remove the mounting bolts and take the alternator to the work-bench.

Step 2.

Step 3.

Project 38: Changing external brushes

Grading: ✦✦
Time: Approx 15min
Tools: Screwdriver to fit holder-fixing screws; spanner to fit terminal nuts; small-bladed screwdriver; long-nosed pliers
Materials: New brushes

Step 1. Undo the fixing screws and terminal nuts and withdraw the brush holder from the back of the alternator.
2. In the type shown, two external spade terminals must be

pushed inwards to release the old brushes. Depress the retaining tag on the terminal with a small screwdriver and push the terminal in the direction of the brush. Repeat the operation with the other terminal.
3. Thoroughly clean the holder, removing all the carbon dust. Press the spade terminal of the new brush assembly into the holder from the brush side. Pull the spade end into position from the other side using long-nosed pliers, until the tag

locks. Fit the other brush terminal in the same way.
4. Refit the holder to the alternator.

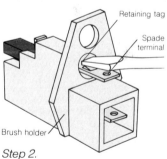
Step 2.

Project 39: Changing internal brushes

Grading: ✦✦
Time: 15min-20min
Tools: Socket to fit cover-fixing screws; screwdrivers to fit brush holder and brush tag-fixing screws
Materials: New brushes

Step 1. Use a socket or box spanner to remove the fixing screws. Lift off the rear cover.
2. Note the position of wires between the rectifier pack and brush holder. Remove the wires.
3. Undo the screws holding the

brush holder and remove it.
4. The brushes are fixed to metal terminal strips (as illustrated) at their outer ends. Take

out the screws holding these strips and pull out the brushes and springs. Fit replacement brushes and strips.

Step 1.

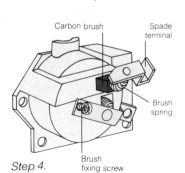
Step 4.

ELECTRICAL SYSTEMS

Wiring and electrical components

All the components in the car's electrical system are joined through their respective switches to the battery and generator. These supply the power that is converted by the components into light, heat and movement.

Each component must be connected to the power source by two conductors, one joined to the battery or generator positive terminal and the other to its negative terminal. This is because an electrical current will flow in a circuit only when a path for it exists from the power source, through the component and back to the power source again. For this reason, the action of turning on a switch is often referred to as 'completing a circuit', and turning it off as 'breaking the circuit'.

Nearly all cars have a steel bodyshell which is used as one of the two conductors and is known as the 'earth' connection. This reduces by half the amount of wire required and simplifies the electrical circuits.

Cars with glass-fibre bodies and special vehicles such as petrol tankers, where there is a fire risk, do not use the bodywork as a conductor, but have 'earth' return wires which should be occasionally checked for tightness.

How electricity flows

All substances and materials are made from atoms, each of which has a positively-charged nucleus and a number of negatively-charged particles called electrons which orbit around it in much the same way as the moon moves round the earth.

The number of electrons in an atom depends on the material of which it is part. Normally the negative charge of the electrons balances the positive charge of the nucleus. How-ever, if an atom loses an electron, it has a positive charge, and if it gains one it has a negative charge.

In a battery the positive plates have a great many atoms which have lost electrons to the negative plates by the chemical action of the battery. This results in a condition of imbalance. The imbalance creates a pressure (voltage) which is trying to return the excess electrons from the negative plate to the positive plate.

If an electrical circuit is connected to the battery and switched on, electrons from the atoms of the conducting wire are attracted into the battery positive plate, and at the same time electrons are pushed into the wire connected to the negative plate. The movement of electrons through the circuit can be likened to a long, thin tube filled with balls. If an extra ball is pushed in at one end, another ball will immediately fall out of the other end. Electrical current flowing in a circuit follows this principle—but at the speed of light.

Some substances, such as copper, have atoms from which electrons can be moved without too much difficulty. These are called conductors. Other substances, where the bond between the electrons and nucleus is very strong and from which electrons cannot be moved, are known as insulators.

Polarity

The polarity of a car indicates which terminal of the battery is connected to the bodywork and 'earthed'. Most cars have the negative terminal joined to the body and are termed 'negative earth' vehicles. It is important to know your car's electrical polarity, for if components such as radios, tape players and alternators, which are designed for negative earth cars, are fitted to a car with a positive earth system (where the battery positive terminal is connected to the body), they will be damaged. Heater or washer motors connected to cars of the wrong polarity may run backwards.

Electric cables

The cable used in a car is purpose-built with insulation that is unaffected by petrol, oil or high under-bonnet temperatures. Its copper conducting core is made up of a number of strands twisted together to make it flexible and to prevent it from breaking, even if it is repeatedly bent backwards and forwards.

Household wire should not be used in cars—it is not suitable.

Most of the wiring in a car is made into a 'loom', either by bundling the cables together and wrapping them with tape, fitting them into a plastic sleeve, or by laying them side by side and welding their insulation to a backing strip.

A cable's current-carrying capacity is determined by the number and thickness of the copper strands inside the insulation. A 17.5amp cable, for instance, has 28 strands of wire, each 0.30mm thick and is expressed as 28/0.30. The table identifies other wire capacities.

Because cable capacities are quoted in amps and the current consumption of an accessory is usually given in watts, the watts must be converted to amps by dividing them by the battery voltage. For example, on a 12-volt system, a 60-watt fog lamp would draw $60 \div 12 = 5$amps, and a cable of at least 5amps capacity must be used when connecting it.

Grade	Conductor Cross-Section	Maximum Continuous Current	
14/0.25	0.7 mm^2	6 amps	
14/0.30	1.0 mm^2	8.75 amps	*Cable grades are quoted as*
19/0.30	—	11.75 amps	*the number and thickness*
21/0.30	1.5 mm^2	12.75 amps	*of the copper conductor*
28/0.30	2.0 mm^2	17.5 amps	*strands inside. A 6 amp*
35/0.30	2.5 mm^2	21.75 amps	*14/0.25 cable has 14*
44/0.30	3.0 mm^2	27.5 amps	*strands, each 0.25 mm in*
65/0.30	4.5 mm^2	35 amps	*diameter*
97/0.30	7.0 mm^2	50 amps	

Colour-coding and wiring diagrams

Because car manufacturers bunch their cables together in a loom, different coloured insulation is used to identify individual wires. Unfortunately there is no international standard colour code for vehicle wiring, but most manufacturers use one principal colour for each electrical system, such as headlights, sidelights and ignition switch-controlled accessories. They then use different coloured stripes to identify sub-circuits in each system.

For instance, on a headlamp circuit using blue-coloured cables, blue cables with a red stripe (or tracer) may feed current to the dipped beams, while blue cables with a white stripe feed the main beams.

Although colour-coding helps identification, fault-finding requires some sort of map of the wiring system—a wiring diagram. Only a few car makers include such a diagram in the handbook, and it is usually necessary to obtain a workshop manual to study it in full.

At first sight a wiring diagram looks almost impossible to use, but if time is taken to identify the symbols, and a magnifying glass is used to identify circuits where the wires are close together or overlap, it can be a great help when fault-finding.

Wiring and electrical components

Amps, volts and resistance

The amp is a measurement of current flow. When one amp is passing through a circuit, 6,250,000,000,000,000,000 electrons are passing through any given point in the circuit every second. Voltage is the pressure which causes the electrons to leave their parent atoms and move. Voltage does not actually flow like current. The amount of electricity a component needs to operate it is quoted in watts (see Electric cables, page 76).

All conductors offer some resistance to the flow of electricity because they contain impure atoms which are non-conductors. These resist electron movement and therefore hinder the current flow. Resistors are deliberately made in this way by mixing conducting and partially-conducting materials.

Serious resistance to current flow also occurs when too much current is passed through too thin a conductor. The reason for this is apparent if electrons are likened to tennis balls. A hundred balls can be dropped through a six-foot diameter pipe all together with very little collision and time delay. If the same number of tennis balls were dropped through a pipe only one foot in diameter collisions would occur and hinder their progress.

The average family car has about 200 ft of electrical cable joining its electrical components. To identify individual circuits, all cables, except battery leads, earth straps and ignition HT cables, are colour-coded. The key to the code is with the car's wiring diagram given in the workshop manual, or sometimes in the handbook

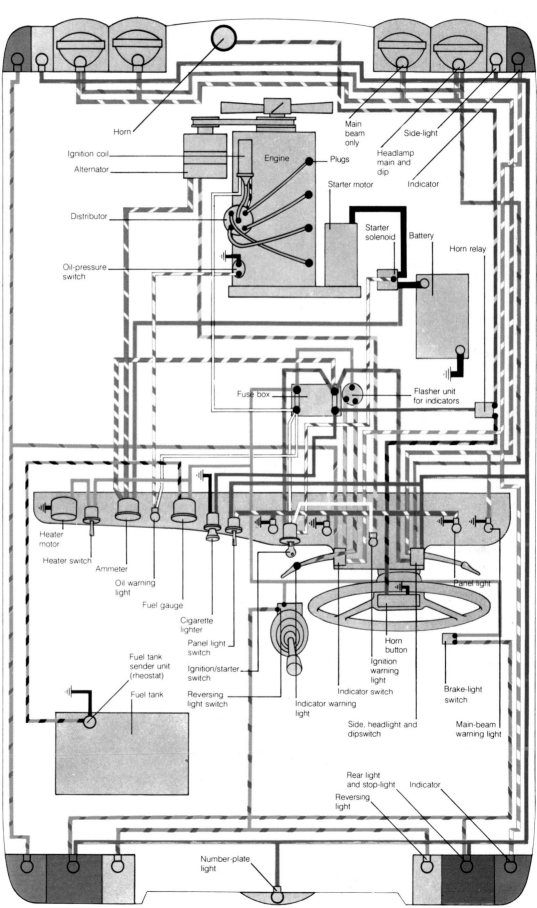

Horn

Ignition coil

Alternator

Engine

Plugs

Main beam only

Side-light

Headlamp main and dip

Starter motor

Indicator

Distributor

Oil-pressure switch

Starter solenoid

Battery

Horn relay

Fuse box

Flasher unit for indicators

Heater motor

Heater switch

Ammeter

Oil warning light

Fuel gauge

Cigarette lighter

Panel light switch

Fuel tank sender unit (rheostat)

Ignition/starter switch

Reversing light switch

Fuel tank

Indicator warning light

Horn button

Ignition warning light

Indicator switch

Side, headlight and dipswitch

Panel light

Brake-light switch

Main-beam warning light

Rear light and stop-light

Indicator

Reversing light

Number-plate light

Wiring and electrical components

Connectors

Most wiring is joined using sleeve or spade-type connectors. Sleeve connectors are frequently used where the main wiring loom joins shorter sections, such as where a separate loom feeds the headlamps or steering-column switches.

Spade connectors are used on most components, including the generator, control box and switches, and in most multiple plug-and-socket connections, where perhaps ten cables or more are linked together. The plastic connector housing these multiple units is usually made so that it cannot be assembled the wrong way round.

Spade and sleeve-type connectors are readily available for connecting accessories. Also popular is the 'splice' connector—a snap-together plastic connector intended for joining an extra wire into an existing cable. Contact is made by squeezing a metal blade with pliers. The blade cuts through the insulation and connects the conductors together.

Splice connectors should not be used where the wires are too thick to enter and should be avoided where a malfunction could be dangerous —causing the engine to cut out, or the headlamps to fail, for example.

Headlamps

The headlamp system provides two types of light beam: a main beam which throws the maximum amount of light well ahead of the car, and a dipped beam which is deflected downwards so that it will not dazzle oncoming drivers.

On cars with two headlamps, separate filaments in a single bulb provide the main and dipped beams. In a four-headlamp arrangement, two of the lamps —one on each side—emit only a main beam and are extinguished when the dipswitch is operated. Twin-filament bulbs on the other two lights then provide the dipped beams.

Light from the headlamp bulb is thrown forward by a reflector and passes through a number of prisms in the glass lens that shape it into a suitable beam.

Separate pre-focus bulbs are used in the majority of current headlamps. They have a locating flange which is shaped so that the bulb can be fitted in only one position, so putting the main beam filament at the focus point of the reflector. Depending upon the design of the bulb, the dipped beam filament may be shielded so that its light shines only on the upper part of the reflector, which reflects it downwards. Alternatively, the dip filament may be placed off-centre, which gives a similar result.

Standard headlamp bulbs have twin tungsten filaments, filled with inert gas. The disadvantage of this type of bulb is that if a filament becomes too hot, molecules of tungsten 'boil' off, slowly weakening it. In addition, the molecules build up on the inside of the glass, gradually blackening it and reducing the light output.

Quartz-halogen bulbs produce a higher light output than standard bulbs for the same given current. They, too, have tungsten filaments, but because they are surrounded by a halogen gas which 'bounces' the molecules back on to the filament, the filaments can run at a much higher temperature and produce more light. To withstand the extra heat, these bulbs have a quartz-glass envelope.

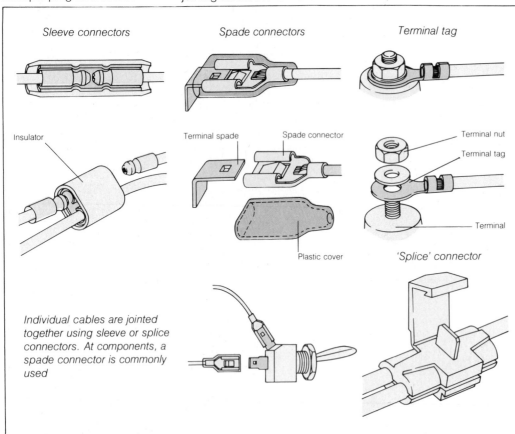

Sleeve connectors   *Spade connectors*   *Terminal tag*

Insulator

Terminal spade   Spade connector

Terminal nut
Terminal tag
Terminal

Plastic cover   *'Splice' connector*

Individual cables are jointed together using sleeve or splice connectors. At components, a spade connector is commonly used

Fuses

If a short-circuit occurs and the current rating of a fuse in the circuit is exceeded, it will 'blow'—melting its internal connecting wire. Current supply to the short-circuit will be cut because the circuit is broken. This prevents wires in the loom becoming red hot and catching fire.

The sort of fuse fitted to a car can take short periods of overload without failing. For instance, when lights are switched on, their cold filaments have very little resistance, so there is an initial current surge for the short time that it takes them to become hot.

Eventually these overloads can 'wear out' a fuse and it will fail. So, when a fuse fails for no obvious reason, it should be replaced with another of the same value. If the replacement blows immediately, or within a few weeks, a short-circuit or an overload may exist. This should be investigated and the fault rectified as soon as possible.

Fusible links

Although most electrical circuits are fused, it is possible that in an accident wires will be trapped by twisted metal. This can cause a short-circuit and result in a fire.

To prevent this, many manufacturers fit a fusible link. This is a high-value fuse connected into the main supply wire close to the battery, and is designed to fail if a massive short-circuit occurs. Some fusible links are easy to replace, but others have to be soldered in place with great care, because the heat of the soldering iron can damage them.

In theory, halogen bulbs should not wear out, but since tungsten molecules cannot be guaranteed to return to their original spot on the filament, failures do occur. All bulbs are likely to fail when they are hot, due to vibration.

The other sort of headlamp is a sealed-beam unit, in which the headlamp itself is, in effect, a large bulb with its reflector and front lens unit built in. Its major advantage is that reflector corrosion cannot occur, and because its filaments can be positioned very accurately a correct beam pattern is guaranteed. Because of the wide variety of headlamp shapes now in use, sealed-beam units are comparatively rare on new cars.

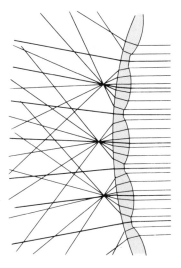

Prisms formed in the headlamp lens – here seen from above – shape the beam pattern

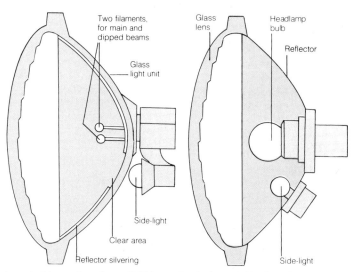

A sealed beam headlamp (left) is made of glass and is like a large bulb with a built-in reflector. Where a side-light bulb is fitted, it shines through a clear section in the silvered reflector. Bulb-type headlamps incorporating side-lights have two plug-in bulbs

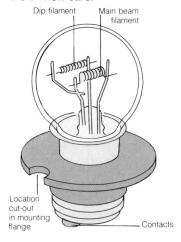

Pre-focus bulbs have a cut-out in their mounting flange so they will fit in only one position. This ensures the filaments are correctly placed in relation to the reflector

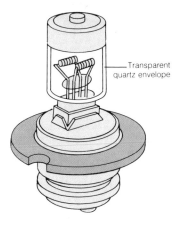

The smaller halogen bulb runs at a higher temperature and gives a brighter light than a normal tungsten filament bulb

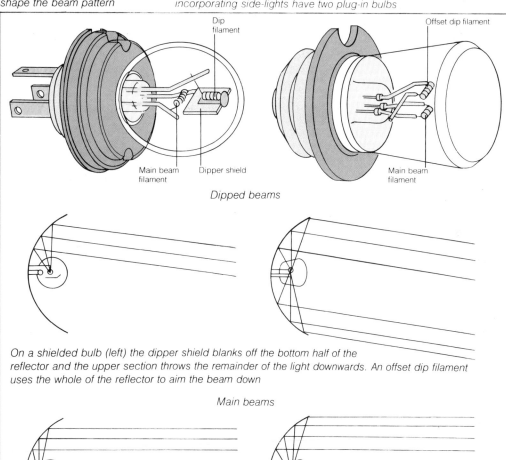

Dipped beams

On a shielded bulb (left) the dipper shield blanks off the bottom half of the reflector and the upper section throws the remainder of the light downwards. An offset dip filament uses the whole of the reflector to aim the beam down

Main beams

The bulb filament at the focus point of the reflector provides the main beam. Where the bulb has a dipper shield (left) the shield blankets part of the centre beam

Wiring and electrical components

Side and rear lights

In addition to headlamps, most cars are legally required to have front side lights, rear lights, stop lights, rear reflectors, flashing direction indicators and a light to illuminate the rear number plate. New cars must now be fitted with a high-intensity rear fog lamp. All lights should be in full working order.

Many cars incorporate 5-watt front side lights in the headlamp shells. Where the side light is separate, it is usually housed with a 21-watt flashing direction indicator bulb in a light unit. The side light is behind a diffusing white lens, and the indicator bulb is behind an amber lens.

At the rear, a typical lamp assembly will include a 21-watt direction indicator bulb behind an amber lens, a 21-watt reversing light bulb behind a diffused white lens, and probably a combined stop/rear lamp bulb with 5-watt (rear light) and 21-watt (stop-light) filaments. The red lenses will incorporate reflectors. New cars may also have a separate, high-intensity rear fog lamp, usually fitted with a 21-watt bulb behind a red lens.

On most cars the side, rear and number plate lights are controlled by a single switch that is wired independently of the ignition, so that the lights can be left on when the car is parked. This switch will also provide the supply to the instrument lighting, sometimes through a separate switch and with a dimmer control which allows the intensity of instrument lighting to be varied.

The headlamps have three switches—an on/off switch that is usually incorporated with the side lights switch, a dip/main-beam switch that diverts current to the main filaments or dip filaments as required, and a spring-loaded switch that by-passes all other lighting switches and operates the main beams for signalling. On many cars the headlamp flasher switch and dipswitch do not pass current to the headlamps themselves, but operate relays.

A relay is a rapid electro-magnetic switch. If fitted to a headlamp flasher circuit, it would be placed near the headlamps in the circuit between the battery and headlamp main-beam filaments.

Operating the headlamp flasher switch sends a small current to a coil in the relay. This current generates a magnetic field and causes a soft iron flap, mounted above the coil, to move and close two contacts.

These contacts feed the comparatively heavy current from the battery to the main-beam filaments.

Thanks to the relay, current travels to the main beams by the shortest route from the battery, thus reducing the amount of resistance. This gives brighter lights, and allows the use of smaller contacts on the interior flasher switch.

The stop-lights receive their current from a circuit that is live only when the ignition is switched on, and work only when the brake pedal is depressed. Pedal movement works a button-type switch or a hydraulic switch in a brake-pipe union.

Because there are usually two or more bulbs in each light unit and they share a common earth connection with the car body, it is possible for a bad connection between a twin-filament bulb and its holder, or the light unit and the car body, to produce some strange happenings.

A poor earth can cause the indicators to come on when the rear lights are switched on; alternatively, the side lights may come on when the brake pedal is pressed. What happens is that the lack of a nearby earth connection causes the current to seek out other routes to earth in order to complete the circuit.

Where these routes pass through a nearby light filament, the filament will glow dimly during the process. The problem can be cured by ensuring that all earth connections to the body are sound, and that all bulbs are clean and making a good connection with their holders.

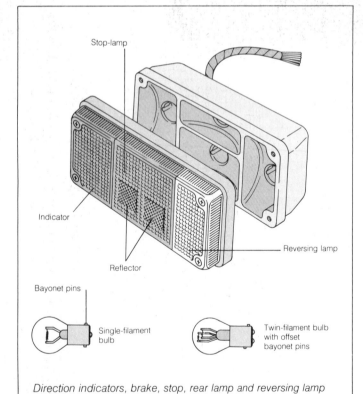

Direction indicators, brake, stop, rear lamp and reversing lamp bulbs are often incorporated in a single tail-lamp assembly.
Where a twin-filament combined stop/rear lamp is used, its offset bayonet pins prevent incorrect assembly

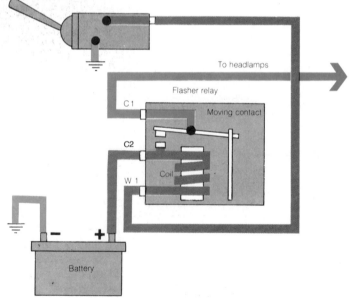

A relay is an electro-magnetic switch. This is the sort that may be used in a headlamp flasher circuit. When the flasher switch on the steering column is operated, battery current passes through the relay winding and completes its circuit to earth through the flasher switch. As current in the winding builds up, it generates a magnetic field that pulls the moving contact towards it and closes the points. A heavy current then flows from the battery, through the closed contacts to the headlamp main beams. Releasing the flasher switch collapses the magnetic field, the relay contacts separate and the headlamps go out. The relay action is virtually instantaneous

Wiring and electrical components

Inside a flasher unit

The most commonly used flasher unit is the two-terminal type, which has almost entirely replaced the older, cylindrical, three-terminal variety. Instead of the flasher bulbs being switched on and off by a set of contacts, pulled open and then allowed to close again by the expansion and contraction of a taut resistance wire, a 'clicker'-type mechanism is now employed.

The 'clicker' diaphragm is held bent by a piece of resistance metal strip stretched across it. At the centre of the strip there is a contact-breaker point which makes contact with one of the flasher unit terminals. When the indicators are operated, current passing through the contact-breaker points to the indicator bulbs heats the metal strip. This causes the strip to expand, allowing the diaphragm to straighten suddenly, thus opening the contact-breaker points. This switches off the flasher bulbs. Current ceases to flow through the metal strip, which cools and contracts, allowing the clicker diaphragm to bend back again, so closing the contacts and restarting the cycle. The Construction and Use Regulations require that the indicators flash between 60 and 120 times per minute.

If a trailer or caravan is towed, a heavy-duty flasher unit must be fitted, otherwise the flashing rate is unlikely to conform to the Construction and Use Regulations.

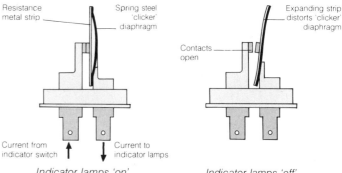

Modern flashing indicator switches use a 'clicker' spring-steel diaphragm and a metal resistance strip to interrupt the flow of current to the indicator lamps. With the switch 'off', the cool resistance metal contracts, bending the diaphragm and holding the contacts shut. Operating the switch sends current across the contacts and through the resistance metal to the lamps. The resistance metal heats, expands and the click-action of the diaphragm opens the contacts, extinguishing the indicator lamp. The resistance then cools, contracting and snapping the contacts shut, putting on the lamps and repeating the cycle

Instruments

The speedometer is the only instrument required by law. It is a mechanical device which is worked by a rotating cable driven by the gearbox. The speedometer needle is fixed to a metal drum which can rotate through about 270° and, while the vehicle is stationary, is held in the zero position by a hair spring. A magnet is turned inside the drum by the speedometer cable while the car is moving, and eddy currents set up by the magnet moving inside the drum produce attracting and repelling magnetic fields. These cause the drum and speedometer needle to turn against the pressure exerted by the hair spring. The amount of movement is determined by the speed of the magnet inside the drum, which, in turn, is determined by the speed of the car.

An additional instrument in the speedometer is the mileage indicator, called the odometer. This is operated by a gear, driven directly by the speedometer cable, and provides a lasting record of the distance the vehicle has travelled. Trip mileage recorders are also often incorporated.

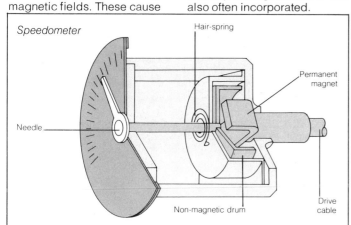

A flexible drive cable, usually connected to the gearbox, rotates a permanent magnet close to, but not touching, a metal drum, usually made of aluminium. Magnetic eddy-currents cause the drum to move against the pressure of a light spring in the same direction as the magnet. The faster the magnet rotates, the further the drum moves, moving a needle across a dial to indicate car speed

Fuel and temperature gauges

All cars are fitted with a fuel gauge and most have a temperature gauge. They are operated by, and display a reading which is proportional to, the current passing through them.

In the petrol tank there is a variable resistor which is operated by a float resting on the surface of the petrol, while in the engine cooling system there is a resistor which changes in value with temperature. These are known as sender units.

The higher the resistance of the fuel tank or cooling system sender unit, the less current will flow and so the lower the gauge will read. The gauges fitted in older cars work on a magnetic principle. The more current passing through a winding in the gauge, the stronger the magnetic field produced, and the further the needle moves across the scale. These instruments can be identified because they show instantly the amount of petrol in the tank and the temperature of the coolant, when the ignition is switched on. The more modern instruments, which take time to show a reading, contain a bi-metallic strip which bends as it is heated. Current is passed through a heater winding wound on the bi-metallic strip, which causes it to bend and operate a linkage to move the needle across the instrument face. The amount that it bends is dependent on the resistance of the sender unit.

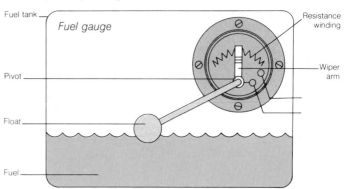

A float on the surface of the fuel is linked by an arm to a metal wiper that moves across a variable resistance. Alterations in fuel level make the float rise or fall, altering the resistance and adjusting the current fed to the fuel gauge, which indicates the fuel level

Wiring and electrical components

Voltage stabiliser

Because changes in generator output voltage would cause more or less current to pass through the heater windings and produce inaccurate readings, a voltage stabiliser unit is used. The stabiliser also contains a bi-metallic strip with a heater winding round it. Current passing through the heater winding from the ignition switch causes the strip to bend and open a pair of contacts, which provide current to the fuel and temperature gauges. This switches off the gauges, but because it takes their bi-metallic strips some time to lose the heat stored in them, the needles scarcely move.

Opening the contacts also switches off the current passing through the stabiliser's heater winding, so its own bi-metallic strip cools and the contact-breaker points close again, switching on the instruments. This cycle continues at a frequency dependent on the generator output voltage. The higher the voltage the longer the instruments are switched off each time. In practice, the instruments receive an average of about seven volts, and because of the action of the voltage stabiliser this does not vary much, even though the supply voltage may alter between 10 and 14 volts.

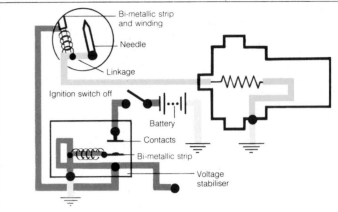

Current from a sensor – in this instance a temperature sensor, but it could be a fuel tank unit – sends regulated current to the gauge which passes through a winding round a bi-metallic strip

Wipers, heater, engine-cooling fan

Electric motors used to drive the wipers, heater and, when it is fitted, the engine cooling fan, are small but very powerful. In older cars these motors had field windings and worked the same way as the starter motor (page 110). More recent motors have permanent magnets instead of field windings. They also work on a similar principle to the starter motor but, because they have permanent magnets, their direction of rotation depends on how they are connected. If the armature of a permanent magnet motor is rotated, it then becomes a

generator. This means that by joining the input leads together, a permanent magnet motor can be made to stop quickly when, for instance, parking the wiper blades.

The electric engine-cooling fan is usually held in a bracket close to the radiator and replaces the engine-driven cooling fan. It is normally switched on and off automatically by a relay, controlled by a temperature sensor in the engine or radiator.

The heater motor—sometimes there are two—is designed to blow air into the

car and is normally controlled by a two- or three-position switch, which is used to connect the motor through resistors and so alter its speed.

The wiper motor is the most complex. It often has two speeds and needs a controlling mechanism which will allow it to continue to operate briefly, in order to park the wiper blades at the base of the windscreen, even after the motor is switched off. This is done by a switch, which is part of the wiper motor, and operates each time the blades are in the parked position.

Battery condition indicator

This is a device which indicates the voltage of the electrical system—typically 12 volts when the engine is stopped, and 13-14 volts with the engine running. It is similar to the fuel and temperature gauges, having a bi-metallic strip and a heater winding, but it is not used with a stabiliser. Its heater winding is supplied by the ignition switch, so that while the ignition is switched on, current at battery voltage passes through it.

Variations in battery voltage directly affect the current passing through the heater winding. This decides the amount that the bi-metallic strip bends, and so the instrument needle indicates the system voltage.

Tachometer

A tachometer, commonly referred to as a rev counter, indicates engine speed.

Some tachometers are driven by a rotating cable and work in the same way as the speedometer.

Modern electronic tachometers, however, are connected into the ignition system and, by producing a voltage pulse each time a spark occurs and averaging it against time, a current proportional to engine speed is produced. The tachometer displays a reading which is proportional to the current on a face marked in hundreds of engine revolutions per minute.

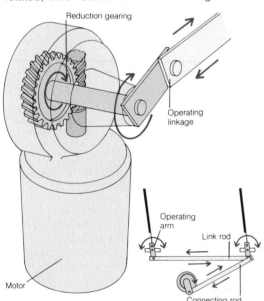

An electric motor drives the wipers, usually through a series of operating arms and connecting links which convert the rotary movement of the motor into the back-and-forth action of the wiper blades

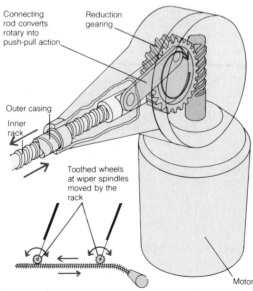

Some cars use a connecting-rod in a wiper motor gearbox to push-and-pull a flexible rack to-and-fro. The rack engages with toothed wheels at the base of the wiper arms which operate the blades

Wiring and electrical components

Horns

All cars are required to be fitted with an audible warning device, so that the driver can warn other road users of his approach.

Construction and Use Regulations require that the horn should make only a single tone.

The electric horn works in much the same way as a buz-

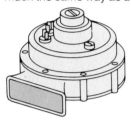

zer or a telephone bell. When the horn button is pressed, current passes through a set of contacts and a winding in the horn. The winding produces a magnetic field which attracts a metal armature attached to a taut metal diaphragm. As the armature moves towards the magnetic field, it stretches and bends the diaphragm until it

has moved far enough to push open the contacts. This switches off the magnetic field and the diaphragm pulls back the armature allowing the points to close again. This cycle of operation continues at a frequency dependent on the distance that the armature travels. The noise is produced by the diaphragm flexing back-

wards and forwards very rapidly.

A few cars use an air horn. This is normally driven by a high-pressure electric pump, which, when the horn control is pressed, provides air pressure to diaphragms fitted to one or more trumpets. Air horns produce a more strident sound than the conventional horn.

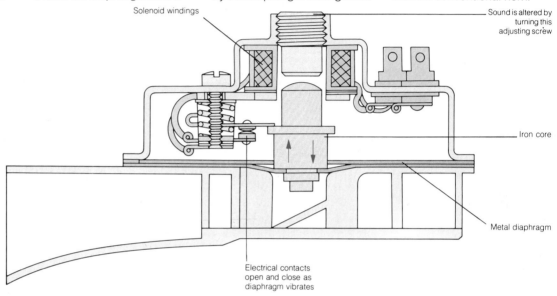

Solenoid windings

Sound is altered by turning this adjusting screw

Iron core

Metal diaphragm

Electrical contacts open and close as diaphragm vibrates

Electric horns produce their sound by vibrating a metal diaphragm very quickly. When the horn is operated, current passes through the contacts into windings which generate a magnetic field. An iron centre core attached to a diaphragm moves upwards, attracted by the magnet, and opens the points. As soon as this happens, the magnetic field collapses and the core drops, closing the contacts again. The cycle is repeated very rapidly

Wiring accessories

When adding an electrical accessory to a car, one problem which must be solved is where to connect it into the vehicle's electrical system.

The earth connection is usually simply achieved by using one of the bolts holding a component to the bodywork. But the supply is often more difficult.

First check the fitting instructions. They will indicate whether the accessory normally operates only when the ignition is on, or if it needs to be connected to a wire which can supply current at all times. You must also discover whether or not the circuit you connect to has a fuse, and whether this is an advantage or disadvantage.

For instance, an electronic ignition system should not be connected through a fuse because, if the fuse 'blows', the engine will stop without warn-

ing. This is potentially dangerous. It must also be connected to a circuit which is controlled by the ignition switch. On the other hand, a clock needs to be connected to a continuously live circuit, and it is a good idea for it to be fused.

Although wiring an accessory through an ignition-controlled circuit is a good way of preventing it from being left on by accident, accessories with a high current consumption, such as a rear window heater, or two powerful auxiliary lights, should not be connected to an ignition-controlled circuit unless a relay is used. This is because the ignition switch is not designed to supply high-current components, and will overheat or be damaged.

To decide where to make accessory connections, use the wiring diagram in your car handbook as follows:

Ignition switch-controlled connections

Check the colour of the wires from the ignition switch to the ignition coil and fuse box. Most cars have an ignition/steering lock, which has wires leaving it that are reasonably accessible. Unfused connections can be made to the identified wire.

Connections to a fused igni-

tion switch supply wire can usually be made at the fuse box or at the brake light switch; both are normally fairly accessible.

Again, the wire colouring should be checked on the diagram to determine which wire on this switch is 'live'.

Constant live connections

It is, of course, possible to make connections directly to the battery or starter solenoid, but if the connection should be made to a 'fused' supply, then, again, the wiring diagram is needed to trace the colour code of the most suitable wire or fuse to use. A component which is often fused (and to

which connections can usually be made) is the interior light supply wire, found entering one of the windscreen pillars.

It may be necessary to unwrap part of the loom's outer cover to find and identify the wire, because often the rear light cluster wires also pass over the top of the headlining.

Radio connection

It is important when connecting a radio set to follow carefully the instructions supplied. Normally the set is connected to an extra terminal on the ignition

switch which is provided for the purpose. Making connections to any other source of supply is likely to cause radio interference.

Wiring and electrical components

Project 40: Changing a sealed-beam headlamp

Grading: 🔧
Time: 10min-30min
Tools: Screwdriver

Sealed-beam headlamps do not have a separate bulb, or lens. If the lens becomes cracked or a filament burns out, the complete light unit must be renewed.
Step 1. Uncover the screws round the edge of the light unit by removing a circular trim or radiator grille. Trims have a fixing screw underneath, or are prised off. Some grilles are held by cross-head screws.
2. The all-glass, sealed-beam unit is trapped between a two-piece rim. Undo the screws round the outside to release it. Do not disturb the beam-setting screws (see Project 42).
3. Unplug the sealed-beam unit from the wiring connector. If a side light is incorporated, the bulb may be a press fit into a socket behind the reflector and can be pulled out.
4. Connect the new sealed-beam unit to the wiring plug and plug in the side light. Lugs moulded into the edge of the glass reflector engage with slots in the rearmost rim. With these located, refit the outer surround and its fixing screws.
5. Refit the grille or trim, and check the alignment of the new lamp (see Project 42).

Step 1.

Step 2.

Step 3.

Project 41: Changing a headlamp bulb

Grading: 🔧
Time: 5min-15min
Tools: Screwdriver

Many headlamps use separate twin-filament bulbs. These are fitted into the rear of a light which is made up of a reflector and lens. Tungsten bulbs, which have a glass 'envelope', tend to blacken with age and should be renewed as soon as this is apparent. Quartz-halogen bulbs do not blacken.

Light units that project into the under-bonnet area do not need to be taken out to change a bulb—the job can be done with the unit in position.
Step 1. If the light unit cannot be reached from behind, remove any trim, release the fixing screws and pull the unit forward. Note the position of any location lugs where the lamp fits into the aperture, so that it can be refitted correctly.
2. Unplug the wiring from the bulb.
3. Turn the fixing ring anti-clockwise and lift it from its seating. Then remove the bulb from the headlamp shell.
4. The fitting flange round the base of the bulb has projections which allow it to fit in only one position. Make sure that these align with mating notches in the lamp reflector, then fit the bulb.
5. If the bulb is of the quartz-halogen type, avoid touching the glass—oily traces from the skin will damage the quartz. If the glass is touched accidentally, wipe it clean with a cloth moistened in methylated spirit.
6. Reassemble in reverse order. Check the alignment of the new lamp (see Project 42).

Step 1.

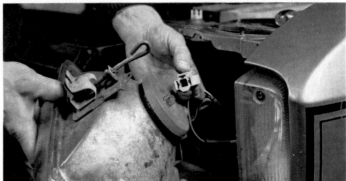
Step 2.

Step 3.

Step 4.

Wiring and electrical components

Project 42: Checking headlamp alignment

Grading: 🔧
Time: 15min-30min
Tools: Screwdriver, if necessary, to turn adjusting screws

When a new headlamp is fitted or an existing headlamp has been disturbed, its alignment should be checked. Ideally a garage beamsetter should be used when adjustments are made, but if the undisturbed lamp was correctly aligned, it is possible to use it as a guide to the correct alignment of the other lamp. The car should be laden as normally driven.

Step 1. Find a wall on a piece of level ground. Drive the car close up and square to the wall. Mark the wall with chalk at two points corresponding to the centre of each headlamp.

2. Reverse the car in a straight line for about 25ft. Draw two bold crosses on the wall, using the first chalk marks as their centres.

3. Switch on the headlamps.

On main beam, round sealed-beam units will produce two well-defined, bright areas. Their centres should be slightly below the horizontal line of the crosses, and be centred on the vertical lines.

4. If one of the lamps is off-target, as in the left beam in the picture, check that it is fitted correctly. If it is, turn the adjusting screws to aim it—the upper screw moves the beam up and down, the screw on the side moves it from side to side.

5. On some lamps the adjusters are mounted behind the light unit and are accessible from under the bonnet, but a cover may have to be removed. Refer to the car handbook if the adjusters are not obvious.

6. Continental beam patterns require adjusting on dipped beams, which have a chevron-shaped cut-off. When both lamps are out of alignment, as shown, adjust them as in Step 3, placing the centre of the cross slightly above the chevron.

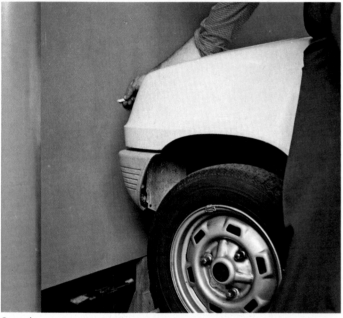

Step 1.

Step 2.

Step 4.

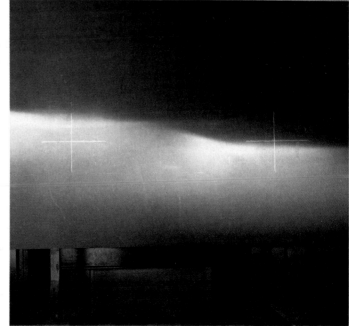

Step 6.

Wiring and electrical components

Project 43: Fitting rear fog-warning lamps

Grading: 🔧🔧🔧
Time: 1hr-2hr depending on the type of car
Tools: Drill, $\frac{1}{8}$in (3mm) and $\frac{5}{16}$in (8mm) bits; rat-tail file; spanner to fit lamp.fixings; screwdriver and spanner to disconnect battery; pliers; test lamp

Rear-mounted red fog-warning lamps usually have a 21-watt bulb which produces three times the light output of conventional rear lights, and makes the rear of the car more easily seen in fog.

These lamps must be fitted so that no part of them is closer than 4in (100mm) to a stop light lens. They must be used only in poor visibility, and should be wired so that they can be switched on only when the side lights are on. A 'tell-tale' warning light, to remind the driver that the lamps are in operation, must be fitted.

Step 1. Find suitable mounting points on the rear bumper or just above or below it.
2. If fitting the lamps to the bodywork, first check that there is room behind the panel for the lamp fixing, then drill a hole, as when fitting a radio aerial (see Project 47).
3. Fit the lamp, tightening it firmly to make a sound earth connection.
4. Disconnect the battery.
5. Inside the car, drill a hole, if necessary, in the facia. Loosely fit a switch which incorporates a warning light.
6. Remove the lighting switch (see Project 48).
7. Use the wiring diagram to identify the cable feeding the sidelights. If no diagram is available, make sure that the switch terminals are well clear of any body metal, reconnect the battery, and use a test lamp to check which wire becomes 'live' when the side lights are switched on (see pages 8 and 9). Disconnect the battery again.
8. Use a splice connector to join a cable to the side light feed wire, and connect the other end of the cable to one terminal on the rear fog-lamp switch.
9. From the other terminal of

Step 2.

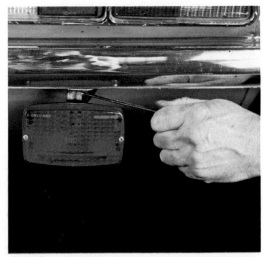

Step 3.

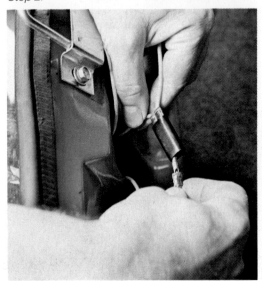

Step 12.

Step 14.

the rear fog-lamp switch, run a long cable under the carpets and into the boot of the car. Try to route this wire alongside the main wiring loom, which is usually found under the carpets close to the body sill. Fit the facia switch permanently.
10. Route the cable round the inside edge of the boot to the nearer fog lamp. Cut the cable so that it reaches the lamp without being either too tight or too slack.
11. Cut another piece of cable to link the lamps.
12. Bare the end of the switch cable and one end of the linking cable. Join the two wires with 'bullet' connectors.
13. Put an insulated connector on the other end of the linking cable and join it to the other lamp terminal—the diagram shows the wiring arrangement,

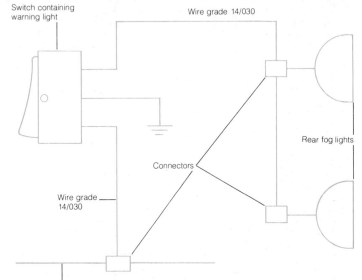

with recommended cable sizes.
14. Reconnect the battery, switch on the side lights and operate the facia switch. Check that both the fog lamps and the warning light work.

Wiring and electrical components

Project 44: Fitting front fog lamps

Grading: 🔧🔧
Time: 2hr
Tools: Centre punch; drill and bits for fitting lamps and relay; if necessary, round file; wire-connector crimping tool or pliers; wire-cutting and stripping tool; screwdriver for self-tapping screws; spanner for fog-lamp mounting nuts
Materials: Fog lamps, suitable relay and connectors; switch, self-tapping screws; grommets; grade 28/030 wire (from relay to fog lights and battery), 14/030 grade wire (to switch and side light circuit)

The Vehicle Lighting Regulations state that when fog lamps are fitted, they should be positioned so that their total light area is within 15¾in (400mm) of the outer edge of the car and that their centre is not more than 24in (609mm) above the road. They should be used only in fog or falling snow, when, provided two are fitted, they may be used instead of headlights. Their light can be yellow or white.

Where two fog lamps are to be fitted, a relay should be used to prevent the switch contacts from being damaged by arcing. This is because each lamp will have a bulb of at least 50 watts, which results in a total current consumption of 8amps when two lamps are fitted. The relay is operated by the panel switch and in turn feeds current directly from the battery to the fog lamps.

The relay must be of a type which is continuously rated, that is, designed to be left operating for long periods of time. Some relays are intermittently rated and are designed for use with headlight flashers and horns—this type will overheat and fail if used with fog lamps.

Most modern cars have blanked off holes in the facia into which switches for accessories can be fitted. These switches can be bought from any car accessory shop.
Step 1. Select a position on the front of the car to fit the fog lamps. Ideally they should be behind the front edge of the bumper so that they are given some protection.
2. Mark out and drill holes large enough to accept the fog-lamp mounting bolts. If necessary, also drill holes for the connecting wires and their grommets. It may be necessary to remove other light units to gain access to a box section, as shown in the picture.
3. Having fitted the lamps, mount the relay close to the battery, drilling the holes necessary for the self-tapping screws.
4. Connect the fog lamps to the relay, and the relay to the panel switch, as shown in the diagram. The fog lamp earth connections should be well made, and if a suitable panel switch is not available, an auxiliary panel and switch can be fitted on the lower edge of the facia. Make sure that all the wires passing through panels are protected by rubber grommets.
5. Make the final connection to the battery, incorporating a 15amp line fuse in the cable, and tidy up any loose wiring.

Step 2.

Step 3.

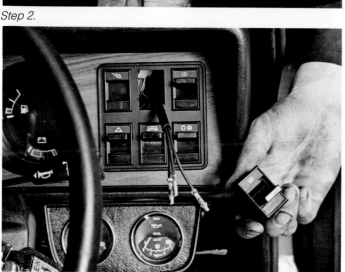

Step 4.

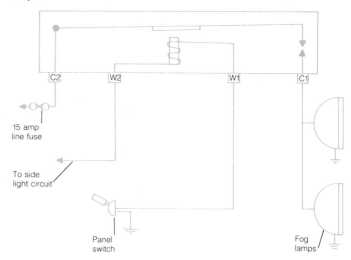

Wiring and electrical components

Project 45: Fitting a radio/tape player

Grading: 🔧🔧🔧
Time: 1hr-2hr
Tools: Screwdriver and spanner to disconnect battery; test lamp; pliers; screwdriver and spanner to fit receiver-mounting screws and nuts and suppressor mounting bolt
Materials: Radio or radio/tape player kit; one 1MFD suppressor

Most cars have a blanked off hole in the facia to accept a radio receiver. Fitting a radio or radio/tape player is easiest if you use one recommended by the car manufacturer, because it can be guaranteed to fit.

If you decide to use a non-standard receiver, it is worth-while measuring the hole and the space behind it to ensure that you buy a receiver that is not difficult to fit.

Many cars have a spare wire in the loom, situated behind the facia aperture, to power the radio. It can be identified from the wiring diagram or by using a test lamp (it should be live when the ignition is on). If no spare power supply is provided, the radio can be connected through an ignition-switch accessory circuit.

Step 1. Remove any trim panel covering the radio aperture. If it is not secured by nuts, prise it out with a screwdriver.

2. Disconnect the battery, identify the radio feed wire and connect it to the radio power lead. This will have a line-fuse holder which may be supplied with a spare end unit to hold the fuse in place and prevent it from being lost, or a short circuit occurring.

3. Check that when the radio is fitted, the supply and speaker wires cannot become trapped in the heater controls.

4. Remove the front panel from the set and fit the set in the aperture. Mark the positions of any metal mounting strips or supports.

5. Fit the mounting supports (see diagram), connect the power lead by reassembling the line fuse and its connector, plug in the aerial connection, and fit the receiver into position. Make sure that the casing makes a good earth contact with the metal supports.

6. Fit the front panel and control knobs.

7. Under the bonnet, loosen an ignition-coil mounting bolt, slip the mounting bracket of the suppressor under the bolt head and retighten the bolt to earth the suppressor. Join the suppressor cable to the coil's current supply lead from the ignition switch.

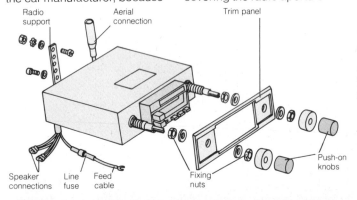

Radio support — Aerial connection — Trim panel — Push-on knobs — Speaker connections — Line fuse — Feed cable — Fixing nuts

Step 1.

Step 2.

Step 5.

Step 6.

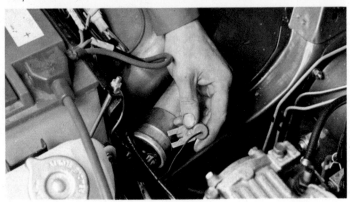

Step 7.

Project 46: Fitting speakers

Grading: ✗✗
Time: 1hr–1½hr
Tools: Screwdrivers to remove door furniture and trim; drill and bits; keyhole saw; screwdriver and spanner to fit mounting screws and nuts; pencils; if necessary, rat-tail file to enlarge cable holes in door
Materials: Speaker kit; adhesive tape

Stereo radios and tape players have two speakers, one for the left side and one for the right. Being identical, however, they become 'left' or 'right' only after they are wired up. Playing a test tape will confirm whether they are correctly connected. If they are not, their feed wires should be transposed.

Some speakers have been designed for fitting to the rear parcel shelf, although most car makers now leave room for a speaker on each side, behind a trim panel.

An electrical specialist or a dealer for your make of car can tell you the best position for the speakers.

Door-mounted speakers should have some waterproof protection at the back (do not use ordinary speakers) and need a plastic sleeve to protect the wires where they bridge the door-hinge gap.

Step 1. Remove the side or door panel (see Project 98) and check that there is room behind it for a speaker. Remember to allow for the position of the window glass and winder mechanism when the glass is wound down into the door. Roughly mark the speaker position on the back of the trim panel.

2. Use a speaker as a template to mark its size accurately on the back of the panel. Offer up the panel again into position and check that the speaker will not foul anything.

3. Make a hole within the marked outline the same size as the speaker cone. Drill a $\frac{5}{16}$in (8mm) hole first, then use a keyhole saw to cut out the big hole.

4. Drill the mounting holes and fit the speaker to the back of the panel and the grille to the front, using screws and nuts with shake-proof washers. If the panel fits to the body side, tape the wires behind it so that they emerge at an inconspicuous corner and can be led away under the outer edges of the carpet to the receiver. Tape the wires to the floor under the carpet to prevent them from fretting.

5. For door-mounted speakers, drill a hole in the door near the hinge and a corresponding hole an inch above or below it

in the door-post. Fit grommets to the holes, join them with a plastic sleeve, and pass the speaker wires through the sleeve. Drilling the holes out of line prevents the sleeve bending double and squashing when the door is closed. Remove the side trim panel ahead of the door and lead the wires through a body aperture to the receiver. Replace the trim.

6. Connect the ends of the wires to the appropriate terminals at the receiver.

7. If the speaker cables are too

long, coil the excess tidily under the facia, secure the centre with a rubber band, and tape the coils to the car body-work. Do not cut off the extra cable; it may be needed if the system is later transferred to another car.

8. Extend the aerial, reconnect the battery and switch on the radio. Tune to a distant station and adjust the radio-trimming screw (its position will be given in the radio instructions) until the best reception is obtained. The radio is now matched to the car aerial.

Step 2.

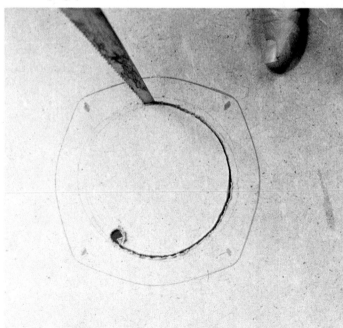

Step 3.

Step 4.

Wiring and electrical components

Project 47: Fitting a radio aerial

Grading: 🔧🔧
Time: 1hr-2hr
Tools: Drill; ⅜in (9.5mm) and ⁵⁄₁₆in (8mm) bits; rat-tail file; spanner to fit aerial nut
Materials: New aerial; old knife to use as scraper; masking tape

Most car radio aerial positions are a compromise. Ideally an aerial should be positioned as far away from the ignition system as possible to avoid electrical interference.

Many car makers solve the problem by providing a ready-drilled aerial position, often in the front wing. If in doubt, follow the recommendations of the car manufacturer.

On some cars—the Fiat 127 for instance—it is not possible to fit an aerial to the front wing, and the aerial must be fitted at the rear of the car. In this case, a good quality extension lead will also be required. The fitting of roof-mounted aerials, which involves disturbing the headlining, should be left to professionals.

Remember that when buying, the better the aerial, the better the reception.

Step 1. Check that there is sufficient space under the aerial-mounting position to accommodate the aerial tube.
2. Select a spot to make the fitting hole, and cover it with masking tape. This helps to prevent the drill from slipping and marking the paintwork.
3. Unscrew the aerial nut and use this as a rough guide to the size of hole required.
4. Drill a ⅛in (3mm) diameter pilot hole.
5. Enlarge the pilot hole to about ⁵⁄₁₆in (8mm) diameter.
6. The hole is further enlarged with a hole-cutting tool or a rat-tail file. Wrap masking tape round the tip of the file; this will help to prevent damage to the surrounding paintwork if it slips out of the hole.
7. File the hole evenly all round. Check the progress of the work frequently by trying to fit the aerial. The hole is the correct size when the aerial mounting is a snug fit.
8. On most aerials the components shown assembled on the aerial in the picture are mounted from under the wing. The metal earthing bracket has points on the corners that dig through the paint to make a good connection. If the underside of the wing is coated with sealant, scrape it away from the edges of the hole.
9. Assemble the plastic spacers so that the aerial can be angled backwards and slightly towards the centreline of the car. Hold the aerial tube from underneath, and tighten the fixing nut. Adjust the length of the lower stay, which is attached to the lower end of the aerial tube, and fix it to the inside of the wing with a self-tapping screw.
10. When an aerial is mounted in a front wing, drill a hole in the inner wing (see Steps 4-7), fit a rubber grommet, and thread the aerial lead into the under-bonnet area.
11. From under the bonnet,

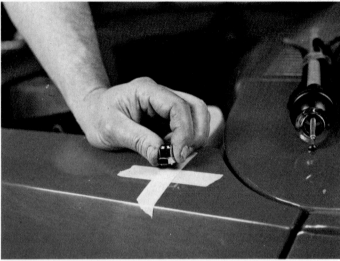
Step 3.

Step 4.

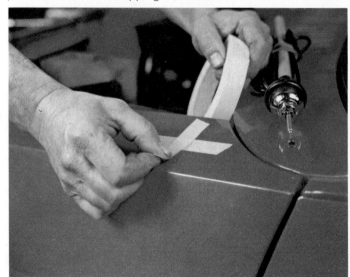
Step 2.

Step 5.

Wiring and electrical components

route the lead away from the wiring loom to the receiver position in the car. To reach the receiver, it may be necessary to drill another hole and fit a grommet.

Step 7.

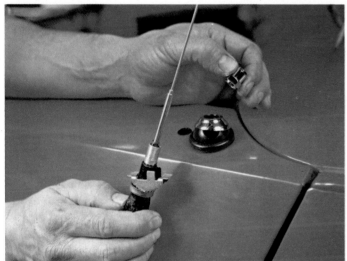

Step 8.

Step 9.

Project 48: Removing a switch

Grading: 🔧
Time: 5min-10min
Tools: Spanner or screwdriver to disconnect battery; spanner or long-nosed pliers to fit switch nut; stiff wire; screwdriver

It is not always obvious how a switch is fitted into the facia, although nowadays, in the interests of speedy production, most are simply a push-fit. Always disconnect the battery before removing a switch.

Step 1. Rocker switches are retained behind the facia panel by plastic or metal spring-clips. To remove the switch, reach behind the facia, squeeze the upper side clips between finger and thumb and push out the top of the switch. Repeat the operation with the lower clips. The switch should then come out. On some switches the clips are fitted top and bottom.

2. Tumbler switches, found on older cars, are fitted from behind the facia and are secured from the front by a nut screwed on to a threaded section. Loosen the nut and push the switch through the facia to release it.

If the nut cannot be turned with a spanner, use long-nosed pliers in the cut-outs to unscrew it.

3. Rotary switches are also fitted from behind but, before they will come out, the knob must be removed. It is usually held by a spring-loaded pin. Press this inwards with a piece of stiff wire and pull off the knob. The fixing nut can then be unscrewed.

4. Courtesy light switches, which operate an interior light, are usually a push fit into the door pillar. The switch body can be prised from the door with a screwdriver blade. A few are secured by an external screw. Undo this and pull out the switch.

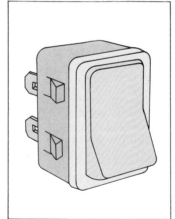

Step 1.

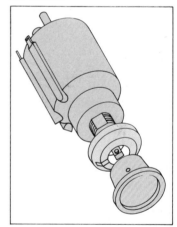

Step 3.

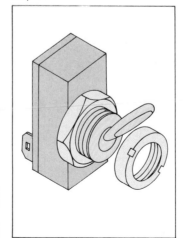

Step 2.

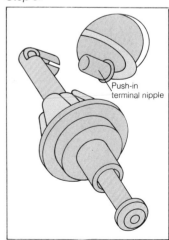

Push-in terminal nipple

Step 4.

Wiring and electrical components

Project 49: Adding a rear window wiper and washer

Grading: ⚡⚡⚡
Time: 3hr–4hr
Tools: Screwdrivers to fit pump-fixing screws and motor-terminal screws; drill and appropriate bits; rat-tail file; screwdriver or spanner to disconnect battery; pliers; test lamp; 3ft (1m) length of stiff wire
Materials: Rear wiper and washer kits; plastic insulating tape

Rear vision, particularly on hatchbacks and estate cars, is improved in the wet if a wiper is fitted to the back window to remove spray. A washer should also be fitted to remove dirt. Note that a front-mounted pump must be powerful enough to pressurise a long length of pipe, and that the pipe itself must be strong enough not to collapse.

The wiper and washer kits shown (pictures A and B) were fitted to a hatchback. The washer takes its water supply from the existing screenwash reservoir.

Step 1. If necessary, remove the interior trim panel from the tailgate (see Project 98).
2. Rear wiper kits are usually supplied with a template which shows exactly where to drill the motor spindle hole. Stick the template to the tailgate and drill a pilot hole where marked. Enlarge the hole to the indicated size with a larger drill and, if necessary, a rat-tail file. Remove the template.
3. Thread the motor shaft through the hole from the inside, fit the appropriate washers and seals on the outside, and tighten the external nut to fix it in position.
4. Disconnect the car battery.
5. If a washer and wiper are fitted at the same time it is best to use a two-position switch to operate them both—the first switch position turns on the wiper, the second, spring-return, position works the washer. Its power supply should be ignition-controlled. If no wiring diagram is available, temporarily reconnect the battery and use a test lamp to identify an ignition-controlled

supply—when it is connected to a suitable feed terminal, the lamp will light with the ignition switched on, but not when it is turned off. Disconnect the battery when you have identified a suitable supply wire.

A short cable is shown being used to make a suitable supply connection with another switch.
6. Connect two other cables —one for the wiper motor and one for the under-bonnet washer motor—to the remaining switch terminals. Fit the switch into the facia. Route the washer motor cable from the switch through the bulkhead into the engine bay.
7. Under the bonnet, fix the washer motor near the existing reservoir.
8. Drill a hole in the top of the reservoir, fit a grommet and insert a plastic pipe through it to the bottom of the reservoir.
9. Take the other end of the pipe and connect it to the motor inlet stub—arrows on the inlet and outlet stubs indicate the direction of water flow. Connect a long plastic pipe to the outlet stub and through the bulkhead into the car. Connect the pump wires. The switch wire goes in the positive motor terminal, the other terminal is connected to earth (one of the bracket-mounting screws) by a short black wire.
10. Inside the car, lift the carpets and route the wiper motor wire from the switch and the long plastic pipe together towards the rear of the car. If possible, follow the same route as the wiring loom. Tape them together and make sure that the pipe is not flattened or kinked.
11. Near the tailgate, the wire and pipe can be threaded up the rear pillar to the tailgate hinge. Drill a hole of the recommended size near the top of the pillar. Thread a stiff wire through the hole, hook it round the wire and pipe, and draw them through. Wrap plastic insulating tape round about 6in of exposed wire and pipe, then thread on a rubber grommet. Drill a hole the same size in the tailgate, fit another grommet on the wire and pipe and thread it on to the tailgate. Insert the grommets into both

holes and open the tailgate fully to check that the wire and pipe are not under strain.
12. Route the wire through the double skin of the tailgate to the motor, fit a connector and

join it to the live terminal. If the motor has an earth terminal, connect a cable between it and the tailgate shell—if necessary earthing it with a self-tapping screw.

A

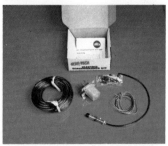
B

Step 2.

Step 3.

Step 5.

Step 6.

Step 7.

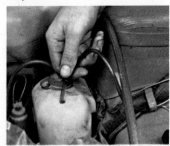
Step 8.

Step 9.

Step 11.

13. Drill a hole for the rear washer jet, fit the jet and from inside, join a short length of tube to it with a non-return valve at the end. The valve allows water to flow towards the jet, but will not let it return in the opposite direction. It can be tested by sucking on the end of the valve.

14. Draw the tube from the pump through the tailgate and connect it to the non-return valve.

15. Reconnect the battery.

16. Switch on the ignition, operate the wiper switch, stop the motor at the extreme of one arc and fit the wiper arm and blade.

Test the wiper and washer action, and re-adjust the arm and the aim of the jet as necessary.

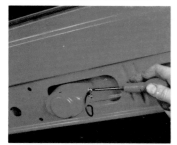
Step 12.

Step 13.

Step 14.

Step 16.

Project 50: Replacing a screenwash electric motor

Grading: 🔧
Time: 15min-1hr
Tools: Drill and bits to make mounting holes and hole in reservoir; screwdriver or spanner to disconnect battery; screwdriver to fit pump mounting screws; pliers
Materials: Replacement pump kit; woodscrew

If an electric screenwash motor breaks down, a replacement can be fitted from a ser-vice kit without the need to change any other components.

Step 1. If the washer motor does not work, first check the power supply with a test lamp and ensure that the earth con-nection is sound. If so, test the motor by disconnecting the outlet pipe, switching on the ignition, and asking a helper to operate the washers. If water spurts out, the pump is sound —check the jets and the rest of the pipework for blockages.

2. If the pump is faulty, a replacement can be fixed in its place. Disconnect the battery, and transfer the pipes and wires from the old pump to the new one.

*1. Many cars have a gravity-fed pump fitted at the base of the reservoir, as shown. If an exact replacement is not available, buy a pump service kit. Remove the outlet pipe from the old pump and block the stub with a tight-fitting woodscrew.

*2. Mount the new pump close to the reservoir.

*3. Disconnect the battery and connect the wires from the orig-inal pump to the new one, if necessary lengthening them and fitting new connectors. Join the original pump outlet to the new pump.

*4. Remove the suction pipe from the old pump and join it to the inlet stub of the new one. If this is impracticable, fit a new suction pipe down to the bot-tom of the reservoir through a hole drilled in its cap.

3. Reconnect the battery, switch on the ignition and check the washers.

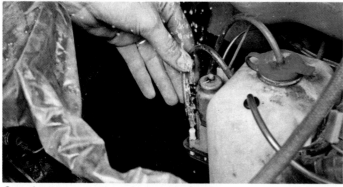
Step 1.

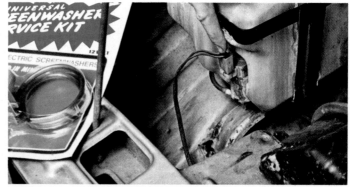
Step *1.

Step *2.

Step *3.

Wiring and electrical components

Project 51: Adding a rear window heater

Grading: ✗✗✗
Time: Approx 2hr
Tools: Drill and small bits to suit self-tapping screws in fitting kit; screwdriver; pliers; spanners and screwdriver to fit battery terminals; if necessary, hairdryer
Materials: Heated rear window kit; clean cloth; if necessary, recommended relay

A rear window heater consumes a fairly heavy current and should be wired through an ignition-controlled circuit so that it is automatically turned off when the ignition is off.

If the ignition switch already controls some electrical accessories—extra fog lamps, for instance—a relay should be used to supply the working current to the rear window heater, otherwise the ignition switch may be overloaded.

The illustrations (right) give details of alternative wiring diagrams.

Step 1. To decide the position of the heater, hold it with small pieces of tape to the outside of the rear window. Check in the interior mirror that it is in a suitable position for maximum vision, then mark its position on the outside of the glass with sticky tape.

2. Inside the car, fit the illuminated switch to the facia.

3. An ignition switch-controlled source of supply current can be found at the fusebox or at a supply wire to an ignition-controlled accessory. In each case it can be identified with a test lamp, which lights only when the ignition is on.

4. Disconnect the battery and use a splice connector to join an extra wire to the selected ignition-controlled cable, and connect the other end of the extra wire to the facia switch (see wiring diagram A).

5. Connect the switch warning-light terminal to a sound earth point on the bodywork, and connect the output terminal to a long cable. Route this behind the carpets to one end of the rear parcel shelf.

*5. On cars with other acces-

sories wired through the ignition, use a relay (wiring diagram B). Connect a wire from an ignition-controlled source (see Step 3) to the illuminated switch and connect another cable from a permanently live supply (the input terminal on the starter solenoid can be used) to the relay C2 terminal. From the switch output terminal connect a cable to the relay W1 terminal. Earth relay terminal W2 and run a cable from the fourth relay terminal (C1) to one side of the parcel shelf, passing it under the carpets to the rear window heater.

6. Clean any condensation and

dirt from the inside of the rear window with a dry cloth. If necessary, use a hairdryer to make sure that the glass is completely dry.

7. Place the heater on a flat surface, peel off the protective sheet and cut it across the centre, then refit it over the element leaving a 2in gap in the middle.

8. Align the heater with the external markings and stick the centre to the inside of the rear window.

9. Peel off the protective sheet on each side, pressing the element firmly against the glass with the palms of the hands on

the backing sheet. Remove the adhesive side strips and press down the lead-out wires. Connect one to the cable from the switch or relay, and link the other wire to earth on the body by using a short length of cable and a self-tapping screw.

10. Reconnect the battery and switch on the heater. Smooth out the element as it warms up. After about 10 minutes, peel off the backing strip and switch off the heater.

11. As it cools, press the elements against the glass with your thumb. Allow the adhesive two or three days to set before cleaning the glass.

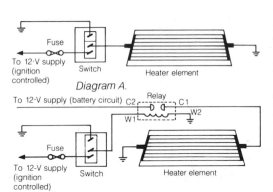

Diagram A.

Diagram B.

Step 1.

Step 6.

Step 7.

Step 8.

Step 10.

Project 52: Fitting electronic ignition

Grading: ⚒⚒
Time: Approx 2hr
Tools: Cross-head and bladed screwdrivers, drill and 9/64in (3.5mm) bit, small electrical spanner
Materials: Electronic ignition system kit to suit car; insulating tape

Electronic ignition systems can be bought to fit most makes of car. Each type of system is provided with instructions giving detailed connecting and fitting information, as well as the changes to spark-plug gaps or ignition timing that may be required. The better (and more expensive) systems are designed to be fully electronic, and replace the contact-breaker points by an electronic sensor fitted in the distributor.

The kit shown here is a typical example of a very reliable, fully electronic ignition system. A slotted disc rotated by the distributor cam chops through a tiny light beam, switching a light-sensitive transistor on and off. This produces electrical impulses that are, in effect, the same as the pulses produced by a set of contact-breaker points opening and closing. Unike the contact-breaker points, breaking the light beam does not produce any wear, so no maintenance or periodic adjustment is required.

Step 1. Disconnect the negative battery terminal. Select a position for mounting the control unit from which the cables will reach the distributor and the coil—preferably on a flat surface away from the battery and the radiator, the exhaust system and the radio aerial. Mount the unit using the self-tapping screws supplied [drill 9/64in (3.5mm) holes], securing the ring terminal of the short black wire under one of the screw heads.

2. Connect the brown wire from the control unit to the negative or 'CB' terminal of the coil in place of the distributor wire. If the car is fitted with a tachometer, connect the brown wire to the wire removed from the distributor.

3. Connect the red wire to the ignition switch, using the extra red wire supplied. This lead *must* have a 12-volt feed when the ignition is on and must be connected into the circuit before any ballast resistor.

4. Remove the distributor cap and rotor arm, following the instructions supplied for the type of car to which the unit is being fitted, remove the contact- breaker points and fit the optical switch unit and chopper disc. After fitting, make sure that there is no chance of the connecting wires being caught in the chopper disc as it turns, and that the action of the vacuum-advance mechanism is not impeded.

5. Connect the three-wire connector from the control unit to the three-wire connector from the optical unit in the distributor so that the wire colours match. Tidy up any loose wiring with insulating tape and tuck it away so that it cannot come into contact with anything hot or moving.

Reconnect the battery negative terminal.

6. Check and, if necessary, adjust the ignition timing (see Project 59), in accordance with the car's service information.

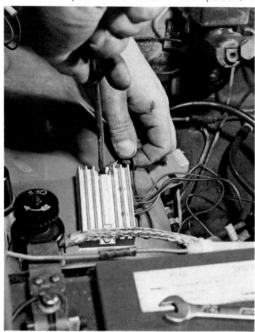

Step 1.

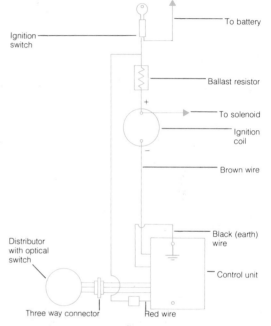

Step 2.

Step 4.

Step 5.

Ignition system

The ignition system

The ignition system is an essential part of the engine's electrical equipment. It provides the high voltage sparks which ignite the petrol and air mixture in the cylinders. The sparks are the result of passing electrical current at a high voltage across a small gap—usually between 0.025in (0.65mm) and 0.040in (1.0mm) wide—which is a resistance in its path. Each spark produces heat, and this ignites the mixture.

The spark is present for only thousandths of a second. It is this ability to provide a source of heat extremely quickly, and at exactly the right moment, that makes an electrical spark the only suitable method of igniting the fuel.

Each of the engine spark plugs is connected by a heavily insulated high-tension cable to the distributor cap. A smaller cable from the centre of the cap is connected to the ignition coil. Inside the distributor cap a rotor arm, turned by the engine, distributes the current from the ignition coil to each spark plug in the correct firing order.

To jump the gap between the spark plug electrodes at least 4,000 volts, and often as much as 10,000 volts, is required. This is produced by the ignition coil which is a pulse transformer and converts the 12 volts from the car battery or generator to the high voltage required.

The coil consists of two windings—primary and secondary—wound one over the other on a soft iron core. The primary winding consists of a few hundred turns of fairly thick wire, while the secondary winding has many thousands of turns of much finer wire. When current from the battery is passed through the primary winding, a magnetic field is produced, centred on the soft iron core. If the current passing through the primary winding is switched off, the magnetic field collapses to nothing. During the short period of time this takes, the shrinking lines of magnetic force move through both coil windings.

If a magnetic field is moved near a coil of wire, electricity is generated in the coil. The amount of electricity produced depends on how fast the field is moved, how many turns there are in the coil and the strength of the magnetic field. If 2 volts are generated in each turn of a coil of wire and there are 10,000 turns in the coil, a total of 20,000 volts will be generated. In this way, when the current passing through the primary winding is switched off, the shrinking magnetic field generates a very high voltage in the many turns of the wire which make up the secondary winding.

The coil's primary winding is switched on and off by the contact-breaker points. These are operated by cams formed on the same shaft in the distributor that is used to turn the rotor arm. The contact-breaker points appear complicated because they are designed to open and close a great number of times very quickly without failing. In a four-cylinder engine they will operate about 10 million times every 1,000 miles. They are, in fact, a simple on/off switch and every time the points open, a spark is produced by the coil. The full sequence of operation of the ignition system is as follows:

When the ignition is switched on and the contact-breaker points are closed, current from the battery passes through the primary winding in the coil, where it produces a magnetic field.

As the starter turns the engine, one of the pistons rises and compresses the fuel and air mixture in the top of its cylinder. At the same time, the shaft in the distributor is turning so that the rotor arm is pointing at the high-tension cable which is connected to the cylinder's spark plug.

At the correct moment—which is normally just before the piston reaches the top of its stroke—one of the cam lobes on the distributor shaft opens the points.

The magnetic field in the coil collapses, generating a high voltage in the secondary winding. This passes across the top of the rotor arm and along the HT cable to the spark plug.

The spark voltage continues to rise (as the magnetic field progressively collapses) until it is strong enough to 'jump' across the spark plug gap. The heat this produces ignites the fuel/air mixture in the cylinder.

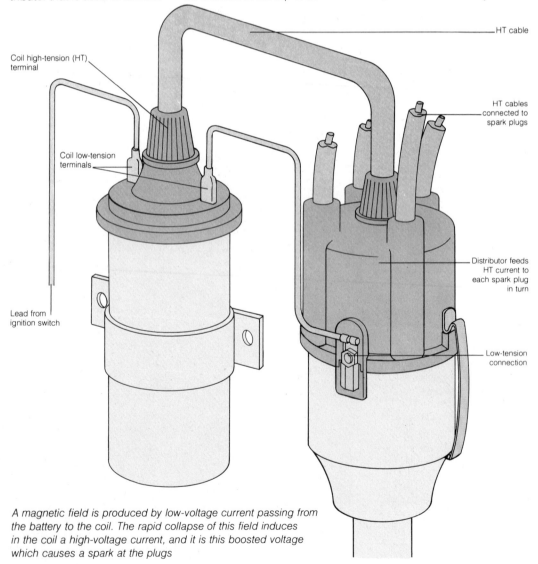

Coil high-tension (HT) terminal

Coil low-tension terminals

Lead from ignition switch

HT cable

HT cables connected to spark plugs

Distributor feeds HT current to each spark plug in turn

Low-tension connection

A magnetic field is produced by low-voltage current passing from the battery to the coil. The rapid collapse of this field induces in the coil a high-voltage current, and it is this boosted voltage which causes a spark at the plugs

Ignition system

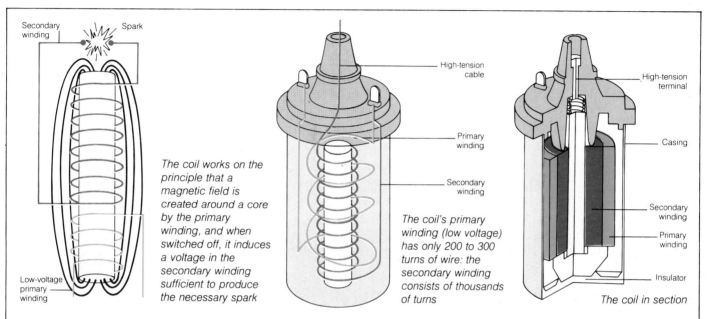

Secondary winding

Spark

High-tension cable

Primary winding

Secondary winding

High-tension terminal

Casing

Secondary winding

Primary winding

Insulator

Low-voltage primary winding

The coil works on the principle that a magnetic field is created around a core by the primary winding, and when switched off, it induces a voltage in the secondary winding sufficient to produce the necessary spark

The coil's primary winding (low voltage) has only 200 to 300 turns of wire: the secondary winding consists of thousands of turns

The coil in section

When closed, the contact-breaker allows a current to flow through the coil's primary winding. When open, and the circuit is momentarily broken, a high-voltage current is generated in the secondary winding, and this passes via the distributor to the spark plugs

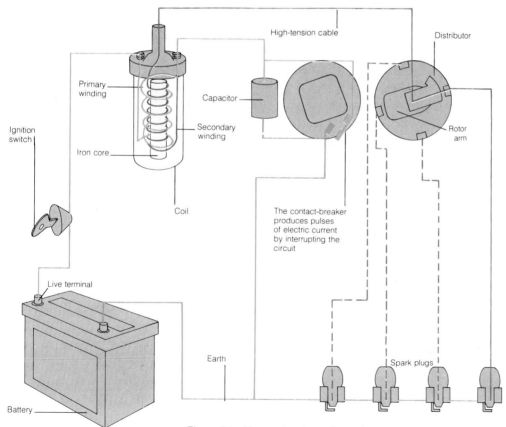

High-tension cable

Distributor

Primary winding

Capacitor

Secondary winding

Rotor arm

Ignition switch

Iron core

Coil

The contact-breaker produces pulses of electric current by interrupting the circuit

Live terminal

Earth

Spark plugs

Battery

Low-tension (12v) system
High-tension system
Earth
Plug leads not receiving current

The coil ignition system has a low-voltage current flowing from the battery, through the primary circuit, to the capacitor and contact-breaker. When the contact-breaker points are closed the current returns through the engine and car body to the battery. When the points are open, high-voltage current generated in the coil flows through the distributor to the spark plugs

Ballast resistor

When the starter motor is used it makes such a big demand on the battery that its terminal voltage drops from 12 volts to about 10 volts—sometimes as low as 7 volts if it is not fully charged. This means that the output from a 12-volt coil receiving only 7-10 volts is reduced and often, due to losses caused by dampness and dirty plugs, may not be sufficient to produce a spark at the plug electrodes. To avoid this, the ignition system fitted to most cars has a ballast resistor. The ballast resistor is fitted in the wire between the ignition switch and a coil, which is designed to operate off a supply of about 7 volts. When the engine is running, the ballast resistor reduces the 12-volt supply from the battery or generator to the 7 volts required by the coil. However, while the engine is being started, the ballast resistor is by-passed by current sent directly to the coil from the starter switch or solenoid. This provides the 7-volt coil with at least 7 volts and often more while the starter is in use, thus enabling the coil to produce sufficient high-tension current to offset losses and produce a hot spark at the plugs.

Ignition system

Contact-breaker points and capacitor

The contact-breaker is a mechanically-operated switch with a pair of contacts, or points, that are opened by small lobes on the cam which forms part of the distributor shaft. Usually there are the same number of cam lobes as cylinders in the engine, although some V8 engines have a four-lobed cam and two sets of contact-breakers.

As the shaft rotates, the cam presses against a rubbing block or shoe that forces the points apart. As the cam moves round, a spring closes the points. In this way the points continually open and close and switch on and off the circuit to the coil primary winding.

Arcing (sparking) between the points is reduced by a capacitor connected across the points between the coil's primary circuit and earth. The capacitor can be likened to a high-voltage battery that cannot hold a charge for very long.

When the points open and the magnetic field in the coil collapses, about 300 volts are generated in the primary winding.

Without a capacitor, this voltage would arc across the points, burning them. Instead it is absorbed by the capacitor which stores it until the voltage in the primary circuit drops, then discharges it back through the primary winding, helping to complete the collapse of the coil's magnetic field as quickly as possible.

Capacitors are often unfairly accused of causing poor ignition performance, but, in fact, they are rarely to blame. This is because most types have a 'self healing' action if internal short circuits occur.

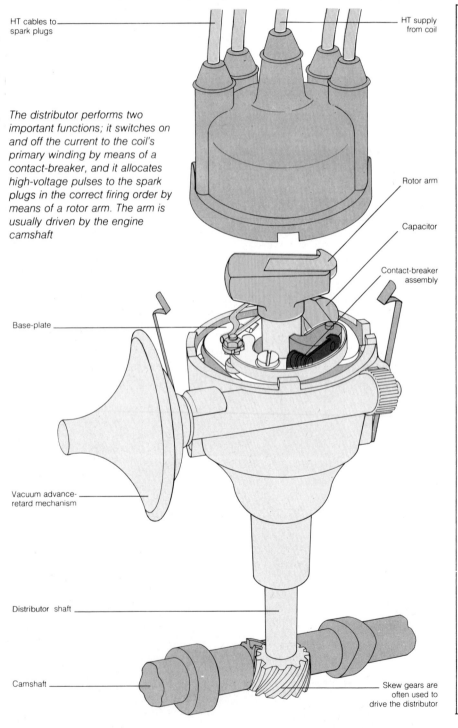

The distributor performs two important functions; it switches on and off the current to the coil's primary winding by means of a contact-breaker, and it allocates high-voltage pulses to the spark plugs in the correct firing order by means of a rotor arm. The arm is usually driven by the engine camshaft

HT cables to spark plugs

HT supply from coil

Rotor arm

Capacitor

Contact-breaker assembly

Base-plate

Vacuum advance-retard mechanism

Distributor shaft

Camshaft

Skew gears are often used to drive the distributor

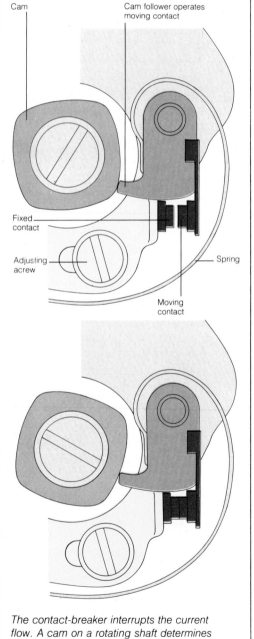

Cam

Cam follower operates moving contact

Fixed contact

Adjusting acrew

Spring

Moving contact

The contact-breaker interrupts the current flow. A cam on a rotating shaft determines whether the two points of the contact-breaker are in contact, and therefore whether current is allowed to pass through them. One point is fixed, the other is operated by the cam

Ignition system

Points gap and dwell angle

Despite the presence of a capacitor, the mating surfaces of the points erode in time because a small amount of unavoidable sparking occurs between them. Eventually they have to be replaced (see Project 55).

After fitting new points, the gap is checked by using a feeler gauge while the points are held fully open by one of the distributor cam lobes. Adjustment is carried out by loosening the fixed contact on the base plate and moving it in relation to the fully-open movable contact.

It is important to use only the points gap recommended in the car handbook.

Some car makers quote a dwell angle as well as a point gap for the contact-breaker points. The dwell angle is the number of degrees that the distributor shaft rotates while the points are in the closed position.

Although electricity moves at the speed of light, a coil of wire resists a rapid build-up of current because, as the current passes through the coil, the magnetic field it produces generates voltage in opposition. Thus when the contact-breaker points close, it takes some time for the primary winding in the ignition coil to become fully saturated and develop a strong magnetic field. The dwell angle ensures that the points are closed long enough for this to happen at the highest rpm.

The dwell angle can be measured accurately only by using special equipment; the contact-breaker points gap given in the car handbook is a compromise figure which enables the dwell angle to be reasonably accurately set without expensive tools.

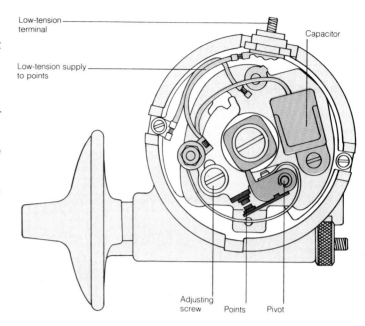

The distributor body is the low-voltage part of the distributor. Here are situated the contact-breaker points, which time the ignition; and the capacitor, which prevents excessive arcing at the points

Distributor cap and rotor arm

Both these items are made of a brittle, moulded plastic material which has very good insulation properties. The rotor arm is keyed to the top of the distributor shaft and has a metal plate moulded into its upper face. This conveys the high-tension current from the central connection in the cap to its segments which are connected to the spark plug leads. A graphite brush or a metal spring is used to make the central connection directly from the cap to the rotor arm, but no physical connection is made with the segments. High-tension current passes between them as a small spark. The distributor cap is held firmly in place sometimes by screws or, more usually, by spring clips and is keyed on its mounting face so that it can be fitted only one way round.

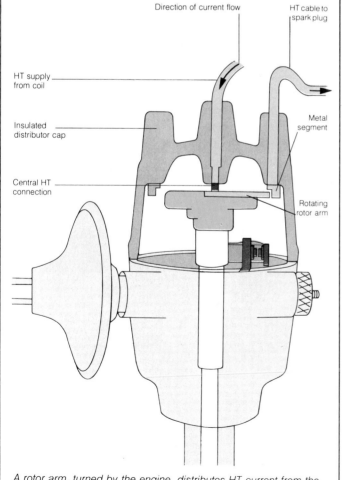

A rotor arm, turned by the engine, distributes HT current from the coil to each spark plug in turn

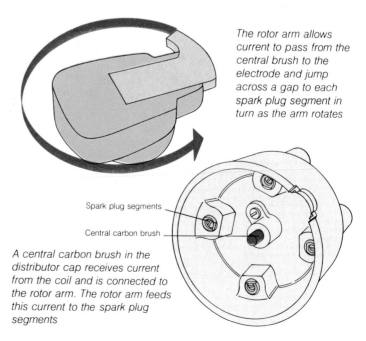

The rotor arm allows current to pass from the central brush to the electrode and jump across a gap to each spark plug segment in turn as the arm rotates

A central carbon brush in the distributor cap receives current from the coil and is connected to the rotor arm. The rotor arm feeds this current to the spark plug segments

Ignition system

Ignition high-tension cables

These have a plastic or rubber insulation about $\frac{1}{8}$in (3.2mm) thick. Instead of a copper core, modern spark plug high-tension (HT) cables have a central conductor made of graphite-coated rayon to reduce radio interference. The first types of resistive graphite-string HT cable gave a lot of trouble. Making connections was not easy, and because the insulation was of stretchable rubber, pulling the cables to remove them from the coil or the spark plugs often broke the graphite conductor.

Modern cables have plastic insulation which does not stretch easily and the end connectors are fitted by a special crimping tool. Made-up replacement sets of HT cables are sold by accessory shops.

Spark plugs

The spark plug has the job of converting the high-voltage impulses from the ignition system into sparks within the combustion chamber. It consists of a metal electrode passing down the centre of a ceramic insulator. Surrounding the lower section of the insulator is a metal casing that is screwed into the cylinder head. Fixed to the casing, and thus earthed to the engine, is a side electrode separated from the tip of the centre electrode by a small gap.

High-tension current passing down the centre electrode jumps the gap, creating a spark and igniting the mixture. Most car makers specify a gap of between 0.025in (0.65mm) and 0.040in (1.0mm) depending on the engine. The clearance should be checked and reset at service intervals because the electrodes slowly erode. Spark plugs should be renewed at recommended intervals—usually every 10,000-15,000 miles.

Each spark plug has code letters and numbers on its porcelain insulator which indicate its heat range, length and diameter, and also the shape of that part of the plug which screws into the engine.

While the length, width and shape of the plug can be matched visually, the heat range cannot be determined except by the code letters and numbers.

A spark plug is designed to operate at an engine temperature which is hot enough to burn combustion deposits off its central insulator (like a self-cleaning oven) but not so hot that the heat ignites the fuel and air mixture before the spark.

Spark plugs in some engines run hotter than those in other engines, depending on the design of the cylinder head and the efficiency of its cooling. If a spark plug is used which is physically the same as another, but is designed to be fitted in a colder-running engine, it may get red hot (incandescent) and cause pre-ignition, which can lead to the engine pistons melting. Alternatively, too cold a plug will become fouled with combustion deposits and oil, which will result in bad starting and misfiring.

The heat range is adjusted by the manufacturer by altering the length of the plug's internal insulation. The longer the insulation, the further the heat has to travel before it is absorbed by the cooling system. This means that it will become hotter than a plug with shorter insulation.

Always use the type and grade of plug recommended in the car handbook, as fitting the wrong spark plugs can cause extensive engine damage.

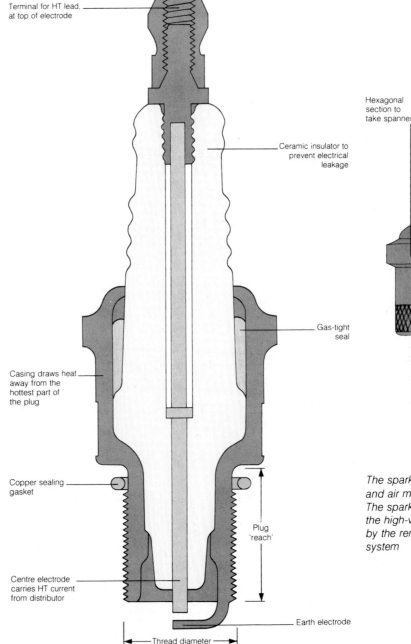

Terminal for HT lead, at top of electrode

Ceramic insulator to prevent electrical leakage

Gas-tight seal

Casing draws heat away from the hottest part of the plug

Copper sealing gasket

Centre electrode carries HT current from distributor

Plug 'reach'

Earth electrode

Thread diameter

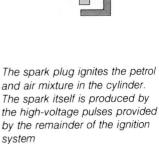

Hexagonal section to take spanner

The spark plug ignites the petrol and air mixture in the cylinder. The spark itself is produced by the high-voltage pulses provided by the remainder of the ignition system

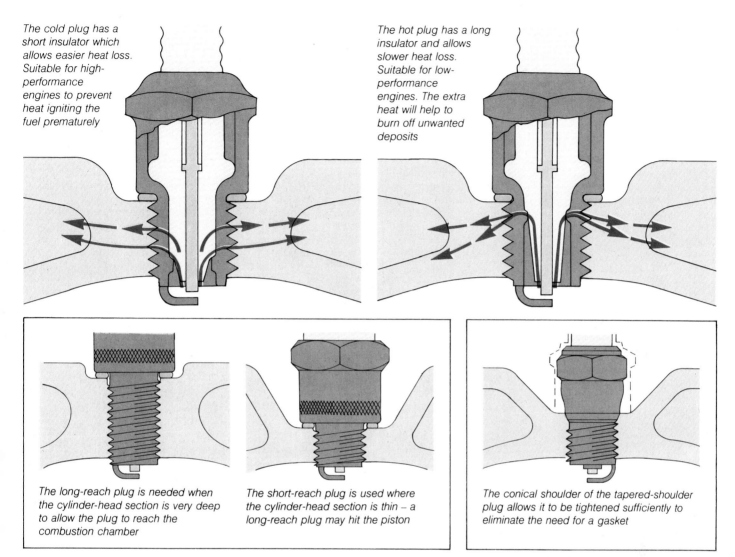

The cold plug has a short insulator which allows easier heat loss. Suitable for high-performance engines to prevent heat igniting the fuel prematurely

The hot plug has a long insulator and allows slower heat loss. Suitable for low-performance engines. The extra heat will help to burn off unwanted deposits

The long-reach plug is needed when the cylinder-head section is very deep to allow the plug to reach the combustion chamber

The short-reach plug is used where the cylinder-head section is thin – a long-reach plug may hit the piston

The conical shoulder of the tapered-shoulder plug allows it to be tightened sufficiently to eliminate the need for a gasket

Ignition timing

Because the fuel and air mixture under compression takes a short time to burn and produce full power, the spark at the plug is made to occur slightly before the piston reaches the top of its stroke (TDC—top dead centre). It is important that the timing of the spark, the ignition timing, is correct, for if the spark is too early the fuel will be burnt too soon and try to turn the crankshaft backwards, producing the characteristic pinging noises known as 'pinking', which can lead to expensive engine damage. Alternatively, if the spark is too late and the piston is already on its way down, a lot of the power of the spark will be lost. To enable the ignition timing to be checked externally, every engine has moving and fixed timing marks. The moving mark

is often a notch on the edge of the crankshaft pulley, or it may be stamped into the edge of the flywheel. The stationary mark will be a pointer or arrow on a static component next to the pulley or flywheel, see diagrams on page 108.

When these marks align, no.1 piston is in the correct position for the spark to occur. This ideal position is normally quoted in degrees of the crankshaft before top dead centre (BTDC) and is given either with the engine stationary (static timing) or with it running (dynamic). Static timing is quoted as a figure, for instance 6°BTDC, whereas dynamic timing will also include engine speed, for example 21°BTDC at 2,000rpm.

The timing marks give only half the information. It is also

essential to know exactly when the spark plug will fire. When the static timing is being checked, this is done by noting the instant that the contact-breaker points separate. Because this is difficult to see with the naked eye, a bulb is connected between the moving contacts and an earth point. With the ignition switched on, the bulb will light the instant the points separate. If ignition timing needs adjusting, the distributor body is loosened and rotated until, with the timing marks aligned, the instant that the bulb lights.

Dynamic ignition timing checks are made with two instruments—an engine revolution counter (tachometer) and a stroboscopic timing light. The stroboscope is connected into the HT cable to no.1 spark

plug. When the engine is running, it produces a bright light, like a camera flash, each time no.1 plug fires.

Aiming the flashing light at the timing marks gives the impression that the timing marks are stationary, because the eyes see them only each time the light flashes. If they do not align correctly at the appropriate speed, the distributor body is turned to make the necessary correction.

Ignition timing should be adjusted only after the contact-breaker points gap or dwell angle has been checked and, if necessary, adjusted. As all pistons are inter-connected through the crankshaft, timing is checked on only one cylinder—normally no.1. Provided this is right, the other cylinders will be correctly timed.

Ignition system

Automatic advance systems

As already stated, the fuel and air mixture takes time to burn and produce power, so if the engine speed is increased it is necessary to start burning the mixture sooner—later if the engine speed is reduced. This is accomplished by means of a mechanical, and sometimes a vacuum, automatic-advance system which is built into the distributor.

Mechanical advance

The rotor arm is moved by an engine-driven distributor shaft on which there are cams that operate the points. Below the cams there is a pair of fly-weights, held close to the shaft by springs.

As the engine speeds up, the fly-weights are progressively thrown outwards by centrifugal force against the pull exerted by their return springs. This causes the distributor camshaft to be moved in advance of its drive and the points are opened sooner, igniting the mixture earlier in proportion to the engine speed.

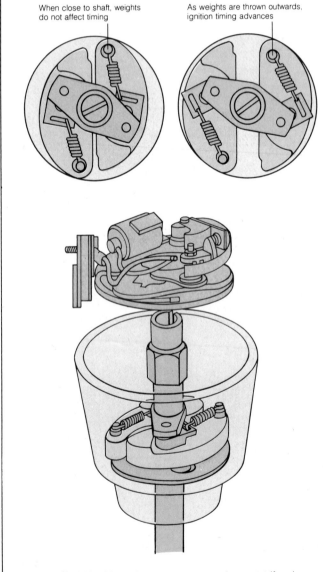

The centrifugal ignition advance system employs centrifugal force. Two pivoted weights, held close to the distributor shaft by springs, are thrown outwards as engine speed increases. As the weights move away from the shaft they turn the cam, causing the points to open earlier

Vacuum advance

Many cars have distributors also fitted with a vacuum-advance mechanism. This is used because the amount of advance required for maximum efficiency is not simply proportional to engine speed.

For instance, when the throttle is only partly open, the inlet manifold vacuum is high and less air enters the cylinders, with a resultant decrease in compression. Fuel and air mixtures burn more slowly at lower pressure, so for maximum power and efficiency, it is desirable to start the burning process sooner.

This means that the amount of advance required will be different while accelerating fast, climbing steep hills or driving along a flat road, even though the engine speed is the same.

This additional ignition advance is provided by using inlet-manifold vacuum to operate a vacuum capsule on the distributor. The vacuum capsule has a spring-loaded diaphragm which is open to atmospheric pressure on one side and subject to inlet manifold vacuum on the other.

As manifold vacuum increases, the diaphragm moves against spring pressure and a connecting link moves the contact-breaker points mechanism on its mounting plate. This moves in the opposite direction to the rotation of the distributor camshaft and causes the contact-breaker points to open earlier. In this process, vacuum-operated advance is added to any mechanical advance that occurs.

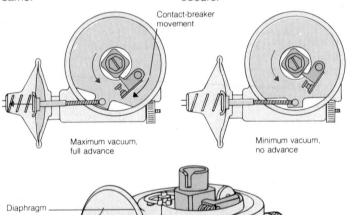

Maximum vacuum, full advance

Minimum vacuum, no advance

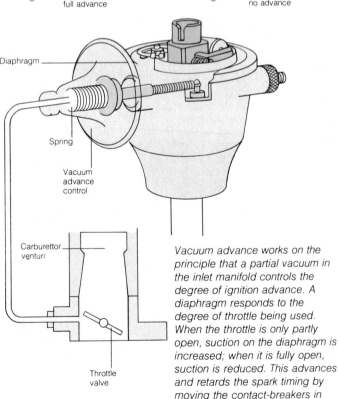

Vacuum advance works on the principle that a partial vacuum in the inlet manifold controls the degree of ignition advance. A diaphragm responds to the degree of throttle being used. When the throttle is only partly open, suction on the diaphragm is increased; when it is fully open, suction is reduced. This advances and retards the spark timing by moving the contact-breakers in relation to the cam

Electronic ignition

There are two types of electronic ignition. The most common, known as inductive storage, is the type fitted by car manufacturers. It works in exactly the same way as the ignition system described, but, instead of having contact-breaker points to switch the coil's primary winding on and off, the job is usually done by a transistor which operates as a solid-state switch. The transistor switch can be turned on and off (triggered) by a magnetic sensor or photo-electric device fitted in the distributor in place of the contact-breaker points.

The advantage of this system is that the magnetic or optical trigger device in the distributor and the transistor switch have no moving parts and so cannot lose their adjustment, become less efficient, or wear out, in the way that mechanically-operated contact-breaker points do. This means that the timing does not alter and no maintenance is required.

Another type of electronic ignition is known as capacitor discharge (CD) and, while one or two types also use the magnetic or optical trigger method, the majority use the existing contact-breaker points in the distributor. Instead of producing a spark, by switching off the primary winding and collapsing a magnetic field, the CD system switches on the primary winding and rapidly generates a magnetic field. It uses a transformer like a small ignition coil to increase the 12

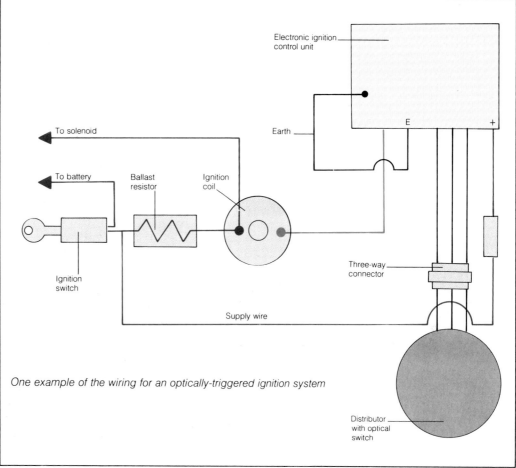

One example of the wiring for an optically-triggered ignition system

volts from the battery or generator to about 400 volts, which it stores in a capacitor.

When the contact-breaker points open, a transistor switch is operated which causes the stored electric power in the capacitor to be 'fired' very quickly through the primary winding. The rapidly produced

(expanding) magnetic field generates a high voltage in the coil's secondary winding and a spark at the plug.

The CD system produces a much shorter and a potentially more powerful spark than the inductive-storage system. However, it has more components which work harder and,

unless it is made by a competent manufacturer, it can be less reliable.

When the contact-breaker points are used, all the mechanical problems such as high speed points-bounce, wear and dirt still exist and regular maintenance is required.

Is it worth changing to electronic ignition?

The end product from an electronic ignition system is the same as that from a conventional system—a spark at each of the plugs that occurs at the right time and has enough energy to ignite the fuel and air mixture. Provided the existing

system does this, electronic ignition can do no more.

Over the years a number of claims have been made for bolt-on electronic ignition systems, including longer spark plug life, increased power and faster acceleration, but independent tests do not substantiate these.

The main benefits of a good quality electronic system that dispenses with contact-breakers (a contactless system) are reliability and the fact that, once fitted and adjusted,

it can be forgotten because it needs no maintenance.

Where contact-breaker points are used to trigger electronic ignition (transistor-assisted contacts), there are few, if any, advantages to be gained.

Fuel savings and cold starting

In the long term, a contactless electronic ignition system can give a small fuel saving compared with a conventional ignition system. This is because, towards the end of each servicing interval, a conventional system becomes less economical as the contact-breakers

wear. Under these conditions, electronic ignition can offer a fuel saving of 3-5% because it does not drift out of adjustment. When the conventional system is in good working order there is virtually no difference in fuel consumption.

So far as cold starting is

concerned, there is little to choose between a conventional ballast-resistor system and electronic ignition. Both cease to work below approximately 6.5 volts, by which time the starter has almost stopped turning.

However, when electronic

ignition is fitted, it sometimes seems to make certain engines run more smoothly and evenly at low rpm in top gear (at about 20-30mph). Also, there have been cases on some 8-cylinder engines where fitting electronic ignition has eliminated high speed misfiring.

Ignition projects

Project 53: Checking or changing spark plugs

Grading: 🔧
Time: 20min–2hr depending on spark plug location and number of plugs
Tools: Spark plug spanner or socket; old paint brush; contact file; feeler gauge; plug-gapping tool
Materials: If necessary, molybdenised grease

Spark plug electrodes are slowly eroded away and rounded off by the continual stream of sparks jumping across them. After 3,000 miles the plugs should be taken out, cleaned and the gaps reset. Most car makers recommend that plugs should be replaced every 10,000–12,000 miles.

When regapping existing plugs (the correct gap is given in the handbook) it is worth knowing that a spark jumps more easily from a sharp corner than a gently rounded surface. If, therefore, the centre electrode has become dome-shaped, the plug will work more efficiently if the end of the electrode is filed flat before the gap is set.

When fitting new plugs, it is important to use the make and grade of plug specified by the manufacturer, or a plug recommended as an alternative—incorrect spark plugs can cause engine damage. Even on new plugs, the gap should be checked, and if necessary adjusted, before fitting. Spark plugs with a centre electrode and three or four side electrodes normally need no adjustment.

Step 1. If the spark plug HT cables are not marked, tape numbers to them so that they can be refitted in the same order.

2. Grip each plug connector and pull it off the plug.

Do not remove connectors by pulling on the cable—this can break the joint at the connector.

3. Use a spark plug box spanner or socket to undo the plug. Loosen it two or three turns to begin with, and remove the spanner.

4. Using an old paintbrush, flick any dirt from around the spark plug seat—dirt can cause damage if it falls into the cylinder. This operation is not possible where the plug is deeply recessed.

5. Unscrew the plug and take it out. If it is black or coated with hard deposits, have all the plugs sandblasted at a garage, or replace them.

6. If the plug is to be refitted, check the condition of the electrodes. If the tip of the centre electrode is dome-shaped, use a small contact file to flatten it.

7. Check the gap between the electrodes with a feeler gauge.

If it is incorrect, use a spark plug gapping tool to bend the side electrode towards or away from the centre electrode until the correct gap is obtained. If you do not have a gapping tool, tap the side electrode lightly with a spanner to close the gap, or prise it away from the centre electrode with a screwdriver to widen it. Do not bear on the centre electrode when using the screwdriver—its ceramic insulation is fragile and may crack.

8. Clean the spark plug threads with a wire brush and

screw the plug hand-tight into the cylinder head. A smear of molybdenised grease on the threads helps the plug to enter easily, particularly on an engine with an aluminium head.

9. Once it is seated, tighten a plug, fitted with a separate sealing gasket, a $\frac{1}{4}$ turn with the spanner.

*9. If the plug has a taper seat and no gasket, tighten it with the spanner 1/16th of a turn from the hand-tight position.

10. Refit the spark plug HT cables.

Step 2.

Step 3.

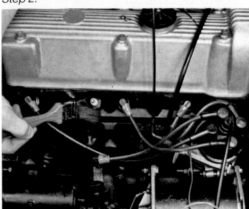

Step 4.

Step 7.

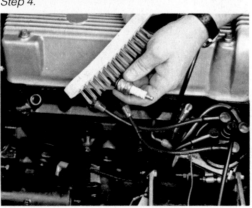

Step 8.

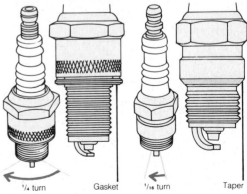

Step 9.   Gasket   Step *9.   Taper

¹/₄ turn   ¹/₁₆ turn

Looking after the contact-breaker points

Over a long period, wear and tear causes the gap between the contact-breaker points in the distributor to change. When this happens, the ignition timing alters and the engine may misfire at high speeds or become difficult to start.

If your car has contact-breaker points (some have contactless electronic ignition) the correct gap will be given in the handbook.

On most cars the points are located directly under the distributor cap. A few distributors have an upper bearing which steadies the distributor shaft immediately below the cap. On these the points must be checked and adjusted through an aperture in the bearing housing. It is important not to remove this type of bearing for adjustments, as this gives incorrect results.

The gap is measured while the moving contact is held fully open by one of the distributor cam lobes—a job which involves turning the engine crankshaft to put the cam in the right position. This can be done by using a spanner on the crankshaft pulley nut or by pressing hard on the fanbelt and turning the generator nut to rotate the crankshaft. An engine is easier to turn if you remove the spark plugs.

After long service, the faces of the contact-breaker points suffer from metal transfer and a small pile builds up on one contact, while a corresponding pit forms on the other (see diagram). The interlocking action of the faces makes it difficult to check the gap accurately with a feeler gauge. In these circumstances new points should be fitted (see Project 55).

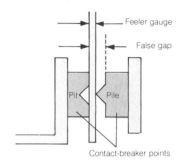

Feeler gauge
False gap
Pit — Pile
Contact-breaker points

Project 54: Checking the points gap

Grading: 🔧

Time: 15min–30min depending on position of contact-breaker points

Tools: Spanner to rotate engine; spark plug spanner if needed; feeler gauges; screwdriver; if necessary, contact file

The gap should be checked at normal service intervals (usually every 5,000-6,000 miles) and adjusted if necessary.

Step 1. Spring off the retaining clips and lift off the distributor cap. If removing the plugs, label the HT cables before detaching them.

2. Lift off the rotor arm from the top of the shaft.

*2. Some distributors have a circular rotor arm that is held by screws. Remove the screws and lift off the rotor. Underneath are the centrifugal advance weights, and beneath the weights are the contact-breaker points.

3. Turn the engine until the points are fully open, by using a spanner on a pulley nut while pressing on the fanbelt.

4. Check the gap with a feeler gauge, if necessary working through the aperture in the distributor top bearing.

5. If the contact faces are uneven, the gauge will give a false reading. Fit new points (see Project 55).

6. If the gap needs altering, loosen the screw securing the fixed contact. Do not take it out.

7. Notches are usually provided so that a screwdriver can be used to twist the fixed contact plate to alter the gap. Some distributors have an eccentric screw that is rotated for the same effect. When the feeler gauge is a light, sliding fit, retighten the fixing screw. Recheck the gap.

Step 2.

Step 3.

Step 4.

Step 6.

Ignition projects

Project 55: Changing contact-breaker points

Grading: 🔧
Time: 20min–40min depending on distributor type and position
Tools: Spanner to fit terminal-post nut; screwdriver; feeler gauges
Materials: New contact-breaker points, clean cloth or tissue

Not all contact-breaker points are the same. Most are made up as a one-piece assembly and are changed after removing one screw and disconnecting two wires. A few contact sets are in two parts, and on some cars the points come assembled in a cassette which is simply slotted into the distributor. The most common types are covered here.

Step 1. Remove the distributor cap and rotor arm.

2. On Lucas distributors, remove the terminal-post nut, lift off the insulator and the low-tension and capacitor wires.

If you are not familiar with the position of the various insulators and washers, make a drawing of their position.

*2. If the contact set is in two parts, the moving contact, complete with spring, is lifted out first, after removing the terminal-post nut.

Make a drawing of the position of the insulators and wires at the spring eye. There may be an insulating washer at the base of the terminal post and pivot pin.

3. Having removed the screw securing the contact set to the baseplate, lift out the contact-breaker assembly.

*3. On two-piece sets, remove the fixed contact.

4. Clean the faces of the new contacts with a piece of cloth or tissue to remove any preservative.

5. Fix one-piece contacts in position, using the screw to hold them, then fit the low-tension and capacitor wires so that they are insulated from the post, but make contact with the spring. Adjust the points gap (see Project 54).

*5. On Lucas two-piece contact sets, tighten down the fixed contact, and fix the moving contact on its pivot. Assemble the spring eye, insulating washer and LT and capacitor wires in their original order. Adjust the points gap (see Project 54).

**5. On some Vauxhall distributors where the points are mounted below the centrifugal weights, the low-tension and capacitor wires have push-in terminal tags that sandwich between the spring blade and a plastic insulating spacer. Press the spring away from the spacer to fit these. Adjust the points gap (see Project 54).

***5. A few distributors have a bearing housing immediately below the cap. Remove the rotor arm, undo the fixing screws and lift off the housing to change the points underneath. Adjust the contact-breaker gap (see Project 54) after the bearing has been refitted, working through the access hole.

****5. Some cars have their contacts mounted in a cassette. The old cassette is removed from the distributor after taking off the cap, rotor arm, and vacuum advance capsule. These are best fitted by a garage.

Step 2.

Step 3.

Step *2.

Step *3.

Step 4.

Step 5.

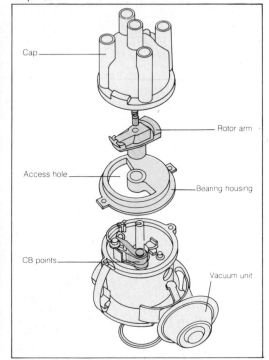

Step ***5.

Ignition projects

Project 56: Changing a capacitor

> **Grading:** 🔧
> **Time:** 10min–20min
> **Tools:** Spanner to fit terminal-post nut; screwdriver
> **Materials:** New capacitor

The capacitor is screwed to the distributor body and is connected to the contact-breaker points' spring. If it fails, the contact-breaker points burn and become covered in soot within a few hundred miles; the car then becomes difficult to start.

The illustrations show how a capacitor is changed in a Lucas distributor.

Other distributors use a similar arrangement, but because it may not be identical, it is wise to make a drawing of parts as they are dismantled to ensure correct reassembly.

Step 1. Remove the distributor cap and rotor arm. Undo the terminal-post nut, lift out the insulator and disconnect the capacitor wire from the spring.

2. Remove the capacitor screw and lift it out.

3. Refitting is a reversal of the dismantling process. When reassembling the new capacitor wire to the terminal post, make sure that the terminal (and the low-tension wire terminal) makes contact with the spring. The insulator is then fitted, and the nut is tightened on to the insulator. Finally, re-tighten the capacitor-fixing screw.

Step 1.

Step 3.

Project 57: Servicing the distributor

> **Grading:** 🔧
> **Time:** 30min–1hr
> **Tools:** Spanners to fit terminal-post nut and to turn engine; screwdriver; feeler gauges; oil can
> **Materials:** If necessary, new contact-breaker points, new rotor arm and distributor cap; engine oil; grease; dry cloth

Step 1. Remove the distributor cap and rotor arm. Examine the rotor arm for cracks—these could cause short-circuits. If any are found, fit a new rotor arm.

2. Clean inside the cap with a dry cloth. Check that the centre carbon brush is free to slide against spring pressure in its housing. If the cap has a metal terminal, make sure that it is clean and firmly fitted.

3. Check the cap for cracking and 'tracking'—this shows as a line of scorch marks between the electrodes inside the cap. If either is found, renew the cap. Do not clean the electrodes.

4. Check the contact-breaker points. If they are worn, renew them. Adjust the gap (see Project 54).

5. If the distributor cam has a small felt pad that rubs against it, put a few drops of engine oil on the pad. On distributors without a lubrication pad, put a small quantity of grease on the cam, if necessary using a screwdriver to place it. Do not let oil or grease reach the contacts.

6. On distributors with top-mounted centrifugal advance weights, twist the shaft to make sure that it moves freely, and lubricate the weights with a smear of grease.

*6. Where the weights are underneath the contact-breaker assembly, inject a few drops of engine oil through the gap in the base-plate around the edge of the cam, and temporarily refit the rotor arm. It should twist and return to its original position under light spring pressure.

7. Remove the rotor arm and lubricate the cam spindle by injecting a few drops of engine oil into the top of the shaft—there is a gap around the screw head to let it through.

8. Refit the rotor arm and cap.

Step 2.

Step 5.

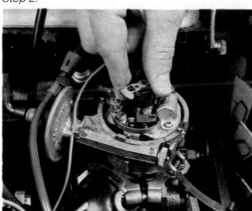

Step *6.

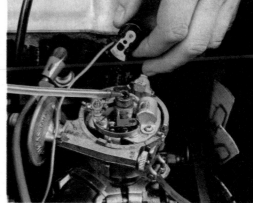

Step 7.

Ignition projects

Project 58: Renewing defective HT cables

Grading: 🔧
Time: 15min–25min
Tools: If necessary, small screwdriver
Materials: Set of HT cables

The smallest cut in the insulation of the high-voltage cables between the distributor cap, spark plugs and coil, can mean that current will escape and ignition efficiency will suffer.

Cable insulation should be checked at regular service intervals and any suspect cables renewed. Made-up cable sets, complete with the appropriate end-fittings, are available to fit most cars.
Step 1. Check the cable insulation every 5,000–6,000 miles. Even a small cut means that the cable must be renewed.

2. Most cables are a push fit into the distributor, the coil and over the spark plug insulators. On older cars the cable to the coil may be held by a screwed sleeve (which is undone by hand to release it), and distributor-cap cables (which do not have individual rubber covers), probably held by contact screws. Remove the distributor cap and undo these from the inside.
3. Because the cables are of different length, fit them one at a time to avoid confusion. Fit the spark plug cables first, detaching one at the distributor cap and plug, using it to select a replacement of the same length from the made-up set, and fitting it before moving on to the next cable. Continue until all HT cables have been renewed.

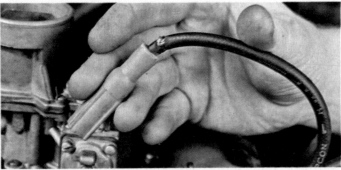
Step 1.

Step 2.

Step 3.

Project 59: Checking and adjusting ignition timing

Grading: 🔧🔧
Time: *Static timing:* 15min–20min; *Stroboscopic timing:* 5min–10min
Tools: *Static timing:* 12-v test lamp; spanner to turn engine and loosen distributor clamp; *Stroboscopic timing:* Stroboscope; tachometer; spanner to fit distributor clamp; white paint and small brush

Where the car maker quotes a static ignition setting, the ignition timing—the moment that the spark plug fires in no. 1 cylinder—can be checked with the engine stationary by using a 12-volt test lamp. If timing is quoted dynamically, the setting is made using a stroboscopic timing lamp and a tachometer, commonly called a rev-counter.

Before timing the ignition, the contact-breaker points gap must be correct (see Project 54). On cars with electronic ignition, the timing can only be checked with a stroboscope. If it needs adjustment, have this work carried out at a garage.
Step 1. First identify no. 1 cylinder. Usually it is at the generator end of the block. On less common engines, such as V4, V6 and 'flat' cylinder layouts, no. 1 cylinder is usually identified in the handbook.
2. Next identify the timing marks. It is not always obvious what they signify—some examples are shown in the drawings. If in doubt, check with a main dealer as to the car's correct ignition timing and the value of the marks.
3. To check the static timing, turn the engine crankshaft until the timing marks align at top dead centre (TDC).
4. Lift the distributor cap and check that the rotor arm is pointing to the electrode in the cap connected to the HT cable feeding no. 1 spark plug. If it is pointing in the opposite direction, rotate the crankshaft another full turn.
5. Connect one wire from a test lamp to a sound earth point (a bolt on the engine will do) and connect the other contact to the distributor contact-breaker spring.

6. Check the setting by rotating the engine crankshaft anti-clockwise about 30°, then inching it slowly clockwise with the ignition on and the test lamp connected. The lamp should light the instant that the correct timing marks align.
7. If the lamp lights before or after the marks are aligned, switch off the ignition, turn the engine anti-clockwise 30°, then turn it slowly clockwise until

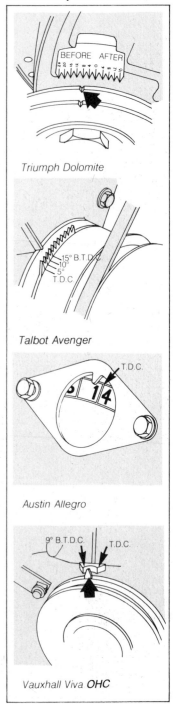
Triumph Dolomite

Talbot Avenger

Austin Allegro

Vauxhall Viva **OHC**

Step 2.

the marks are aligned once more.

8. Loosen the distributor clamp bolt.

9. With the ignition on, turn the distributor body in the same direction of rotation as the rotor arm (usually anti-clockwise) until the light goes out, then turn it in the opposite direction very slowly.

The instant that the lamp lights, stop turning. Tighten the distributor clamp.

10. Check the setting as described in Step 6.

11. Dynamic timing is checked using a stroboscope to light up the timing marks.

To help them show up, put a chalk mark or a dab of white paint (typists' correcting fluid is ideal) on the static and moving marks.

12. Connect up the stroboscope according to the maker's instructions, and connect up a tachometer if the car does not have one. Ask a helper to watch the tachometer and operate the throttle. Loosen the distributor clamp, and disconnect the vacuum advance pipe unless advised against this by the manufacturer. Refer to the manual.

13. Start the engine and aim the stroboscope at the timing marks while the helper operates the throttle to provide the correct engine speed. Take care that no loose clothing can catch in the fanbelt.

14. The timing marks should align at the recommended engine speed. If they do not, with the engine running, move the distributor body until the marks align. Stop the engine and lock the distributor body with the clamp. Recheck the setting.

Step 4.

Step 5.

Step 8.

Step 13.

Starter motor

The starter motor consists of an electric motor mounted on the side of the engine. It has a drive gear which engages with teeth formed on the edge of the engine flywheel. The motor is rated at about 5hp and when first operated—to overcome the inertia of the engine's moving components—it uses about as much electrical power as a three-bar electric fire.

Two types of starter motor are in common use: the inertia and the pre-engaged. Both use basically the same electric motor, but they each have a different method of engaging with the engine flywheel.

The electric motor consists of an armature wound with very thick, well-insulated windings, and this rotates between stationary field windings mounted inside the starter motor outer casing.

The field windings are also made of very thick wire—usually strips of copper or aluminium.

When current is passed through both the armature and the field windings, opposing and attracting magnetic fields are set up between them, which turn the armature. Each of the armature windings is connected to copper strips which form a commutator on which stationary brushes rub and provide current.

As the armature rotates, the commutator and brushes direct

current to different windings in turn so that magnetic attraction and repulsion between the armature and field windings are always present.

Armature rotation continues until the current is switched off. All DC (direct current) electric motors operate on this principle.

A car starter motor is 'series wound', which means that the

current passing through the armature also passes through the field windings.

This type of motor provides a great deal of turning force and demands more or less current from the battery as the load on it alters.

As the load decreases, the armature speeds up and current is generated in its windings (because they are moving

in a magnetic field) in opposition to the current being supplied by the brushes. This reduces the supply from the battery and is why the starter motor needs about 250amps to overcome the inertia of the moving parts of the engine. Once they are moving, however, and it speeds up, the current requirement drops to 100-150amps.

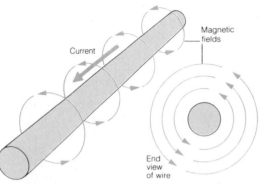

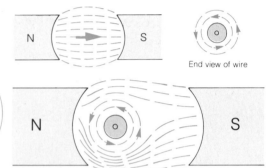

Electric current flowing through a conductor generates a circular magnetic field along its length. Depending upon the direction of current flow the lines of force of the field rotate clockwise or anti-clockwise

If a conductor with current flowing through it is put between North and South magnetic poles, the magnetic lines of force between them will be distorted

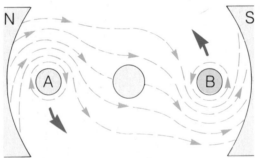

Magnetic lines of force can be likened to stretched rubber bands – when they are distorted they try to straighten themselves. Here two current-carrying conductors, A and B, seriously distort the magnetic field between two pole pieces. The lines of force attempt to straighten out, and if the conductors were in the form of a loop which could pivot, the reaction would rotate it anti-clockwise. However, as loop B neared the North pole-piece, magnetic inter-action would again distort the lines of force and it would be thrown back the way it had come. The same would apply to loop A and the South pole-piece

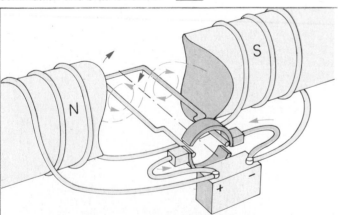

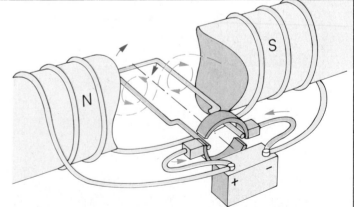

The conductor loop can be kept rotating in the same direction if the current flow through it is reversed each half-turn, reversing the rotation of its magnetic field. A commutator – separate metal segments on each end of the loop, connected to the battery through carbon brushes – does this. In the left diagram, current flowing through the loop causes it to rotate clockwise. As the loop rotates half a turn, the blue half of the conductor, originally fed by the

left-hand brush, makes contact with the right-hand brush (right diagram). Simultaneously the other half of the loop also changes brushes at the commutator. Reversing the current flow keeps the magnetic field distorted above the blue half of the loop and below the other half, continuing to drive it clockwise. In practice commercial electric motors have many separate loops on a rotating armature, each connected to a multi-segment commutator

Inertia starter motor

The inertia starter motor has its drive gear, or pinion, connected to the armature shaft by helical splines or a 'quick thread'. With the motor at rest, the pinion is held at one end of the shaft, out of engagement with the flywheel, by a weak spring. When the starter motor is operated, its armature is suddenly made to turn quite fast, and due to the inertia of the pinion, which resists such rapid movement, it moves along the 'quick thread' and into engagement with the flywheel. When the engine starts, the flywheel tries to turn the pinion faster than the starter motor armature, and this moves it back down the helical 'quick thread', out of engagement with the flywheel.

Because a starter motor draws such a heavy current from the battery, it is connected by thick, expensive copper cables. To keep these cables as short as possible, the motor is switched on and off by a

The armature shaft of the heavy-duty inertia starter is extended and carries a toothed pinion mounted on a 'quick-thread'

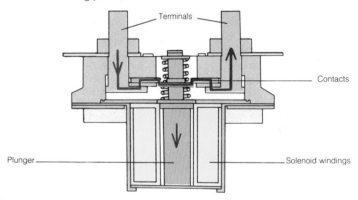

solenoid, mounted in the circuit between the battery and starter. The solenoid is a heavy-duty, magnetically-operated switch that is designed to make connections and disconnections quickly

and firmly to avoid burning and damaging its contacts.

The current to operate the solenoid is supplied by the ignition/starter-key switch. Operating the starter switch from the driving position sends

a small current to a winding inside the solenoid. The magnetic field this creates in the winding moves an iron plunger which closes heavy-duty contacts and feeds current to the starter.

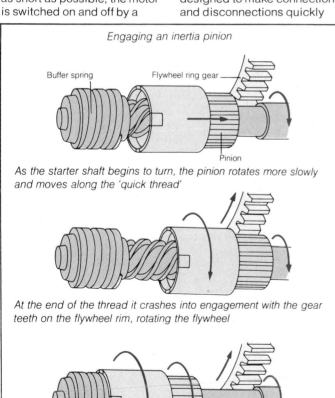

Engaging an inertia pinion

As the starter shaft begins to turn, the pinion rotates more slowly and moves along the 'quick thread'

At the end of the thread it crashes into engagement with the gear teeth on the flywheel rim, rotating the flywheel

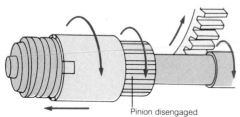

When the engine starts, the flywheel rotates the pinion faster than the shaft, screwing it back along the thread, disengaging it

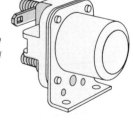

The solenoid is a magnetically-operated switch mounted in the heavy-duty cable between the battery and starter. Operating the starter key switch creates a magnetic field in the solenoid winding which moves a central plunger and closes a pair of heavy contacts that feed current to the starter motor. When the key switch is released, a spring separates the solenoid contacts

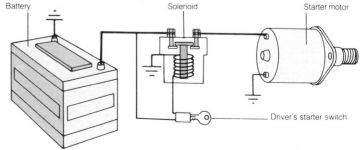

Starter motor

Pre-engaged starter motor

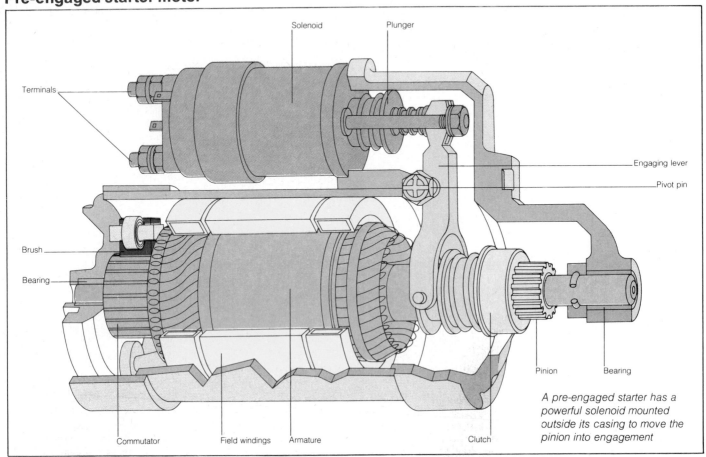

Labels: Solenoid, Plunger, Terminals, Engaging lever, Pivot pin, Brush, Bearing, Pinion, Bearing, Commutator, Field windings, Armature, Clutch

A pre-engaged starter has a powerful solenoid mounted outside its casing to move the pinion into engagement

The pre-engaged starter motor is often larger and more expensive than the inertia type. Unlike the inertia starter motor which engages with the stationary engine after its armature has started turning at high speed (which in time causes wear and damage to both pinion and flywheel gear teeth), the pre-engaged starter motor engages its pinion with the flywheel teeth *before* the armature starts to turn very fast. This is done by mounting a solenoid on top of the starter motor body—an identification feature—and using it, not only to connect the motor to the battery, but also to move the pinion into engagement with the flywheel.

When the starter switch is operated, current passes through the solenoid windings, and the resultant magnetic field moves a plunger against the pressure of a return spring. Connected to the plunger is a lever arrangement which pushes the pinion—connected by splines to the starter motor armature—into engagement with the engine flywheel. Once this has happened, the still-moving plunger closes the main contacts which supply battery current to the motor and cause it to turn.

Because the solenoid used with a pre-engaged starter has to move the pinion, it has two windings, and produces a more powerful magnetic field than the solenoid used with an inertia starter motor.

If the solenoid had only one winding, the current required to

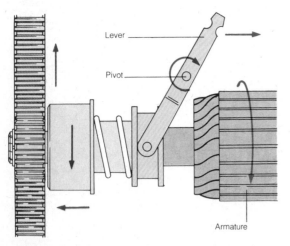

Labels: Lever, Pivot, Armature

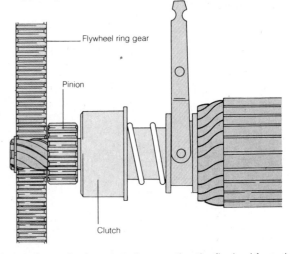

Labels: Flywheel ring gear, Pinion, Clutch

The pre-engaged starter pinion has a one-way clutch that allows it to free-wheel once the engine has started, preventing the flywheel from driving the starter shaft and damaging it. Releasing the starter key allows a spring to retract the lever which withdraws the pinion

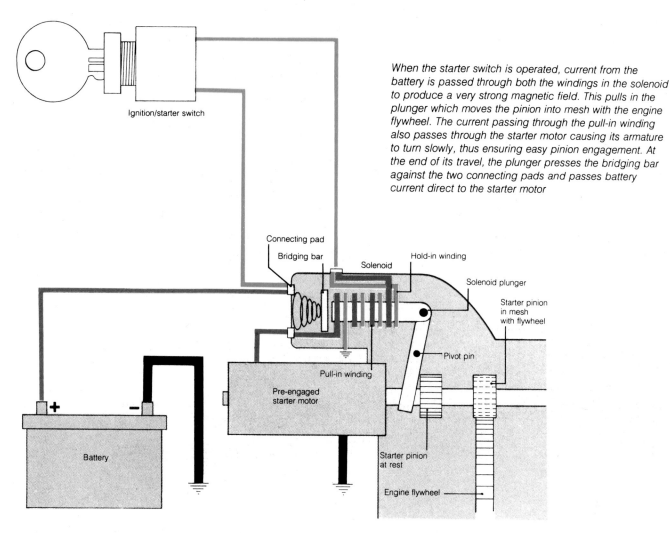

Ignition/starter switch

When the starter switch is operated, current from the battery is passed through both the windings in the solenoid to produce a very strong magnetic field. This pulls in the plunger which moves the pinion into mesh with the engine flywheel. The current passing through the pull-in winding also passes through the starter motor causing its armature to turn slowly, thus ensuring easy pinion engagement. At the end of its travel, the plunger presses the bridging bar against the two connecting pads and passes battery current direct to the starter motor

Connecting pad

Bridging bar

Solenoid

Hold-in winding

Solenoid plunger

Starter pinion in mesh with flywheel

Pivot pin

Pull-in winding

Pre-engaged starter motor

Starter pinion at rest

Battery

Engine flywheel

produce this much more powerful magnetic field would be excessive and cause the solenoid to overheat. It would also overload the starter switch and its wiring.

Both windings are energised when the starter switch is operated. One is called the pull-in winding and does most of the work. It consists of a few turns of fairly thick wire, earthed through the starter motor windings, and produces most of the magnetic field. The other, known as the hold-in winding, has many more turns of thinner wire and is earthed directly to the solenoid body.

When the starter key is turned, current passing through the pull-in winding also passes through the starter motor. This makes the armature turn slowly and ensures easy

pinion engagement. If it did not turn, the starter pinion could sometimes make tooth-to-tooth contact with the engine starter ring and prevent the teeth from meshing.

Once the main contacts in the solenoid are closed by the plunger, current from the battery is present at both ends of the pull-in winding. This prevents current from passing through it, so that the magnetic field it produced collapses. However, the solenoid plunger is still held in position by the magnetic field produced by the hold-in winding; the main contacts remain closed and pass current to the starter motor until the starter switch is released. When this happens the solenoid return spring pushes the plunger out, thus pulling the pinion out of engagement

with the flywheel.

To prevent any possibility of the starter motor being damaged if it is operated when the engine is running, there is a one-way clutch which allows the pinion to be turned faster than the starter motor armature.

As in all car electrical systems the starter motor uses the body of the car as an earth. Because the starter motor requires so much current to make it operate, its earth return system has to be in good condition. A loose earth strap can prevent the starter motor from working.

Because they are designed to operate for only a few seconds at a time, starter motors have no cooling holes or fins. If the starter motor is continually operated—when the engine refuses to start—it will soon

overheat and suffer damage. Similarly, a starter can be damaged if it is engaged when the engine is running or is used as a means of moving the vehicle when the engine will not run.

Inertia starter motors that have worked loose or have a worn pinion can occasionally jam—the pinion teeth ride up on top of the flywheel teeth, preventing either the starter motor or the engine from turning. It can be freed by using a spanner to turn the end of the armature. This draws the pinion out of engagement along the helical grooves. Sometimes a motor can be freed by selecting top gear (manual-change cars only) and, with the handbrake off, rocking the car forwards and backwards until it works free, often with a loud clonk.

Starter motor projects

If the starter does not work

There are two types of starter in use: the inertia pinion-type, which throws its pinion into engagement with the flywheel teeth as soon as the motor begins to turn, and the more sophisticated pre-engaged-type which uses a heavy-duty solenoid mounted on the casing to engage the pinion before the motor starts turning. If either type refuses to work, first check that all battery and earth connections are sound. Then connect a test lamp between the solenoid feed wire and chassis earth. Operate the starter switch. If the lamp does not light, the ignition switch is faulty; if it does light, then either the solenoid or the starter is defective.

Projects 60 and 61: Checking the solenoid

> **Grading:** 🔧
> **Time:** 5min
> **Tools:** Stout screwdriver with insulated handle

60: Inertia starter solenoid

This will be mounted in the heavy starter feed cable, not far from the starter.

When it is working, it closes with a click.

Step 1. If the solenoid has a rubber-covered push-button, press it to close the solenoid contacts. If the starter turns, the solenoid is faulty—renew it.

*1. On solenoids without a push-button, peel back the rubber caps shrouding the heavy-duty output terminals. Use a screwdriver shaft to bridge the terminals, short-circuiting the battery current directly to the starter.

2. If the solenoid is faulty there will be some sparking and the motor will turn—in which case the solenoid unit should be renewed.

*2. If the motor fails to turn, check it for jamming. If it is not jammed, remove it from the engine for checking.

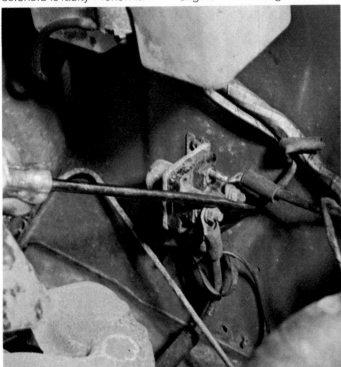

Step *1.

61: Pre-engaged starter solenoid

Step 1. This is mounted on the outside of the starter casing. If necessary remove the rubber caps from the heavy-duty solenoid terminals.

2. Use a screwdriver to join the terminals and provide current to the starter, as shown with an inertia starter solenoid in the picture above. If the motor turns, the solenoid should be replaced.

Project 62: Freeing a sticking inertia pinion

> **Grading:** 🔧
> **Time:** 30min–1hr depending on starter position
> **Tools:** Screwdriver or spanner to disconnect battery; spanners to fit starter terminal nut and mounting bolts or nuts
> **Materials:** Methylated spirit or petrol; clean cloth

The inertia starter depends upon its pinion sliding freely along a helical screw or quick-thread to make contact with the ring gear teeth on the flywheel. If the starter motor shaft is caked with dirt the pinion will not slide into engagement and the starter will rotate at high speed without turning the engine.

Step 1. To remove the starter from the engine: Disconnect the battery, remove the feed cable from the motor by undoing the terminal nut and undo two or three mounting bolts or nuts. Remove the starter to the workbench.

2. Check pinion movement. It should slide freely along the quick-thread and return to the starting point under light pressure from a restraining spring.

3. Remove dirt by brushing the pinion and shaft with methylated spirit or petrol. Do not let any fluid get into the motor. Wipe or brush off excess fluid and re-check pinion movement when it is dry. Do not oil the pinion—oil collects clutch dust which will make it stick again.

4. If cleaning the pinion does not improve its action, or some parts are obviously damaged, it must be taken off the shaft for further checking or replacement (see Project 63).

Step 2.

Step 3.

Project 63: Dismantling an inertia pinion

> **Grading:** 🔧🔧
> **Time:** 1hr–2hr
> **Tools:** Screwdriver or spanners to disconnect battery; spanners to fit starter terminal nut and mounting nuts or bolts; compressor for buffer spring; small-bladed screwdriver, pliers, carborundum stone
> **Materials:** Replacement pinion components

If the pinion refuses to slide smoothly on its thread after cleaning, or the buffer spring is broken, or the pinion teeth have been badly 'chewed' by the ring gear (some wear on the leading edges of pinion teeth is normal), the pinion must be dismantled for investigation or repair. A broken restraining spring will allow the pinion to vibrate along the shaft when the engine is running until it touches the ring-gear teeth, making a distinctive rattling sound. On most starters a spring clip or 'jump ring', held under pressure by the buffer spring, secures the pinion. To

remove it a spring compressor is needed to take the load off the clip.

Step 1. Remove the starter from the engine (see Project 62).

2. Use a compressor to squeeze the buffer spring, then prise the spring clip from its groove in the shaft using a small-bladed screwdriver.

*2 Some old starters have the pinion secured by a nut—usually with a left-hand thread. On these, extract the split pin holding the nut, with pliers, and undo the nut.

3. Remove the buffer spring (still within the compressor) then take off the quick-thread sleeve and pinion, and, where it is separate, the restraining spring.

4. Check the parts for wear. Some individual components, such as the buffer spring and retaining clip, are sold separately, but the restraining spring is incorporated in the pinion, so if it is broken a new pinion assembly must be bought.

5. Before re-fitting, use a small

carborundum stone to remove any burrs from the starter shaft.

6. Fit the pinion assembly, the compressed buffer spring and then the spring clip. Decom-

press the buffer spring to lock the spring clip in place (on old starters re-fit the nut and lock it with a new split pin). Check that the pinion slides freely.

Step 2.

Step 3.

Project 64: Freeing a jammed inertia pinion

> **Grading:** 🔧
> **Time:** 10min
> **Tools:** Bladed screwdriver to prise off cover; small open-ended spanner to fit armature shaft end

The armature shaft that protrudes through the end plate on an inertia starter has a squared end. This allows the armature

to be rotated using a small open-ended spanner to draw a jammed pinion out of engagement with the ring gear teeth.

Step 1. Prise off the cap covering the end of the armature with a bladed screwdriver.

2. Fit a spanner to the squared end. Turn it clockwise to draw the pinion out of engagement.

3. Check and if necessary tighten the motor mountings.

Step 2.

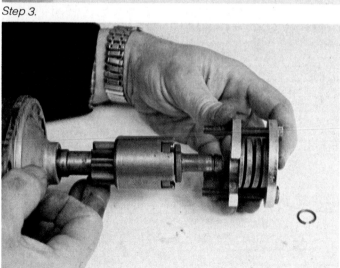

Step 6.

Starter motor projects

Project 65 and 66: Renewing starter brushes

Grading: ⌁⌁⌁
Time: 1hr–2hr
Tools: Screwdriver or spanner to disconnect battery; spanners to disconnect starter from engine; spanner to fit terminal nut; screwdriver to loosen through-bolts; vice if necessary; wire cutters or pliers; soldering iron and resin-cored solder; fine file
Materials: Starter brush set; methylated spirit; cloth; fine glasspaper

---

Because they draw such a heavy current, most starter motors have four brushes, mounted on the inside of the commutator end plate, two of them connected to terminals on the end plate and two linked to the motor field windings in the casing.

When fitting new brushes a soldering iron is required to fix the new brush wires to the terminals. Brushes need renewing when the carbon is worn down to a total length of $\frac{3}{8}$in (9.5mm).

This sequence deals with changing brushes on a motor with a drum-type commutator, similar to that used on a dynamo. Some motors have a face-type commutator, and where the procedure is different from the drum-type it is dealt with separately in the next project.

Step 1. Remove the starter from the engine (see Project 62).
2. Undo the fixing nut and washers from the terminal stud protruding through the end plate. Do not allow the stud to turn. Note the order of washers for correct reassembly. Remove the cover band from the motor casing after loosening its clamp screw.
3. Undo the two through-bolts at the end plate. If they are tight, up-end the starter, grip the side of each bolt-head in vice jaws and turn the motor to loosen it. Remove both bolts.
4. Pull the armature assembly out of the casing and remove the end plate. It will be tethered to the casing by the two field brush wires. Lift the springs and remove the brushes from their holders to release the plate.

5. Clean the commutator with a strip of fine glasspaper and wipe it clean with a cloth moistened in methylated spirit. If it is badly mis-shapen or worn, get a service exchange motor.
6. A new set of brushes will have two brushes with bare wires attached and two with

65: Motors with drum-type commutators

insulated wires. Those with insulated wires are connected to the field windings.
7. On most starters the field windings are made of aluminium and cannot be joined to the copper brush wires with ordinary solder. Therefore, to get a sound joint,

when the old brush wires are cut, leave about $\frac{1}{2}$in of the old copper wire attached to the windings, and solder the new wires to this.
8. Clean the ends of the old and new wires, and hook the cut lead through the loop at the end of the brush wire. Heat the

Step 2.

Step 3.

Step 4.

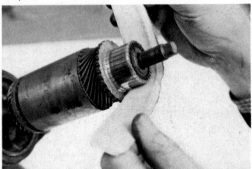
Step 5.

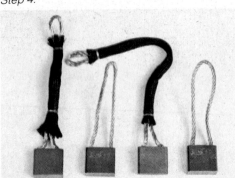
Step 6.

Step 7.

Step 8.

Step 9.

joint with a soldering iron and flow in resin-cored solder. Repeat this operation with the other brush.

9. On the end plate, remove each brush from its holder, cut through the wires of the old brush again leaving a $\frac{1}{8}$in cut end. Loop the end over the bare wire of a new brush and solder the joint.

Do the same with the other end-plate brush.

10. Move the end plate up to the casing and fit the new brushes in their holders. They should be a sliding fit. If not, remove the high-spots from the carbon with a small file. Raise each brush until its working end is flush with the bottom of the holder and prop it in place by resting the spring on the side of the brush.

11. Reassemble the armature, casing and end plate, engaging their locating notches and making sure that the terminal stud is fitted through its nylon insulating sleeve and cannot touch any metal.

Refit the terminal nut and washers and screw in the through-bolts.

12. Push a small screwdriver through the slots in the casing to lift the brush springs so that they press on the upper end of each brush. Fit the cover band so that it blocks the casing slots.

13. Refit the starter motor to the engine, making sure that its mounting bolts are fully tightened.

Because it is such a powerful motor and requires a lot of operating current, bench-testing without proper facilities is not advised.

Step 10.

Step 12.

66: Motors with face-commutators

On this type, four segment-shaped brushes in the end plate are pressed by coil springs against segments at the end of the commutator. All brush wires are insulated and the two brushes connected to the end plate are usually ready-fitted to a new terminal and do not, therefore, need soldering.

Step 1. Undo the short screws round the edge of the end plate and remove the plate from the casing.

2. Clean the commutator face with fine glasspaper, then a cloth dipped in methylated spirit.

* If the commutator segments are distorted, damaged or burned, buy a service exchange motor.

3. Remove the field brushes from the end plate, unscrew the terminal nut and pull out the terminal stud and two brushes attached to it.

4. Fit the two new end-plate brushes and new terminal stud, making sure that the stud fits into its insulating sleeve. Check that the brushes move smoothly in their holders. If they stick, file off the high-spots.

5. Cut the brush leads where they join the field winding, ensuring that the stubs are large enough to solder to the new brush leads.

6. The field brush wires are of different lengths. Check that the wires will reach from the holder to the field winding connection, then solder them in place.

7. Fit the field brushes in their holders and check that they move freely. Refit the thrust washer, then the end plate to the motor, tightening the fixing screws securely.

Step 1.

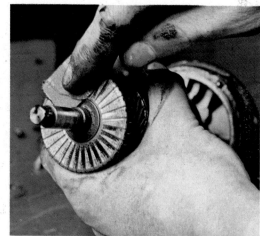

Step 2.

Step 5.

Step 7.

On the road

Wheels, tyres and suspension

The only contact a car has with the road is through its tyres. If these are defective or incorrectly inflated the car will not steer, accelerate or brake predictably. For this reason, tyres are the subject of more regulations concerning their use than most other car components.

Every tyre holds air under pressure, has a tread to grip the road, flexible sidewalls to absorb loads, and internal stiffening wires embedded in the edges—or beads—that fit on the wheel rim. Depending on its type, the tyre may or may not have a separate inner tube.

The ideal road tyre provides accurate steering but is not deflected by ridges in the road; it must be strong enough to withstand damage yet supple enough to cushion road shocks; it must provide maximum grip for acceleration, braking and cornering in the wet or dry, and it must not overheat or lose pressure during arduous driving.

It sounds a lot to ask and it is, so most road tyres are a compromise. The ultimate tyres are used on car racing circuits where 'slick' treads, which are completely smooth and slightly sticky, put the maximum amount of rubber on the track when it is dry. But when it rains, tyres with a grooved tread are used, the grooves providing drainage channels. As it is out of the question for motorists to change a set of tyres every time it rains, all road tyres have a grooved tread, and before this wears away, the tyre must, by law, be renewed.

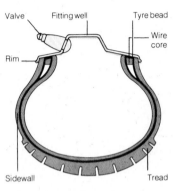

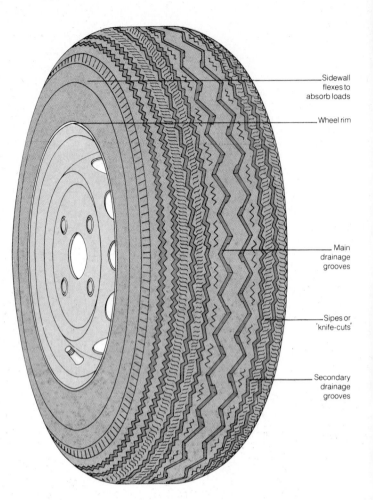

A typical tyre inside and out. Wires reinforce the beads that are held firmly against the wheel rim by pressure inside. The tread is grooved with water-displacing channels and hundreds of sipes or 'knife-cuts'

Tubed and tubeless tyres

Tubeless tyres have an inner lining of soft rubber that prevents air escaping. They are used on an air-tight wheel rim and have beads that form a seal against the rim. The valve forms an air-tight seal with a hole in the wheel.

If a tubeless tyre is punctured, the inner lining partially self-seals and the tyre usually deflates slowly. It is possible to make an on-the-spot temporary puncture repair to a tubeless tyre by inserting a plug to block the hole from the outside. Such repairs should be made permanent as soon as possible. A tyre repairer can vulcanise a patch on the inside.

Tubed tyres are fitted to wheels which cannot be made air-tight, such as wire-spoked wheels. The valve is moulded into the inner tube. Temporary external repairs cannot be made and there is no guarantee that a puncture will be a slow one. Most British cars use tubeless tyres.

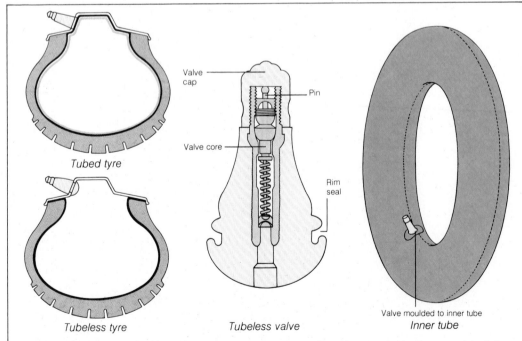

Tubeless tyres have a soft lining that partially self-seals and deflates the tyre slowly when punctured. It is used with a valve that seals in the wheel rim. The tubed tyre has a tube with a moulded-in valve and deflates quickly if punctured

Wheels, tyres and suspension

Tyre construction

There are two main types of tyre in use: cross-ply and radial-ply. Each gets its name from the method used to reinforce the tyre casing.

Cross-ply tyres are so named because the fabric bracing cords in the casing run across the tyre in overlapping layers (or plies) of cords at an angle diagonal to each other. This allows the cords to stretch in different directions, yet maintain an overall stiffness throughout the casing. In addition to cords—originally cotton but now of man-made fibres—various strips and fillers are used to stiffen the casing.

At one time, the number of cord plies in a tyre indicated its load-bearing capability. A four-ply tyre, for instance, indicated four laminations within the casing, and that the tyre could support a given load. Now, improvements in cord fibres mean that the ply-rating system is used purely to indicate the load a tyre can carry, and a four-ply rating tyre may, in fact, be made with only two plies.

Radial tyres have a more complex casing construction which reduces tread wear and gives increased tyre life. They are fitted to virtually all new cars.

The casing has two separate cord structures. A layer of cords running radially—from bead to bead across the casing—provides reinforcement for the sidewalls. On their own, these cords would provide a comfortable ride but poor steering response. However, on top of them, under the tread, there are at least two layers of breaker cords running round the tyre. The cords run at a slight angle to each other, forming a stiff reinforcing hoop.

Breaker cords—there may be two or more laminations of them—discourage the tread from squirming or shuffling when it meets the road, and thus contribute to the high mileage of which radial tyres are capable. Breaker cords are made of either fibre or steel. Steel-braced radials tend to give the greater mileage.

Safety tyres

Car manufacturers are always looking for ways of eliminating the spare wheel which takes up much-needed space and adds weight to a car, and safety organisations are conscious of the way that a car can go completely out of control if a tyre bursts and comes off the wheel.

An answer to both problems is the Dunlop Denovo, a tyre and wheel combination which ensures that the tyre cannot come off unless the wheel is deliberately dismantled. Also, when flat, it can be run for 100 miles at speeds of up to 50mph, and so does away with the need for a spare.

When an ordinary tyre deflates suddenly, the tyre beads are dislodged from their seatings on the rim, and the insides of the tread and sidewalls rub against each other, heating up the casing and eventually destroying it. In extreme conditions, the tyre beads jump over the rim, making it impossible to steer the car.

The Denovo, basically a radial with tough sidewalls, is fitted to a narrow-rimmed wheel. If it suddenly deflates, the sidewalls, which are thicker than normal, act as a cushion between the rim edge and the road.

The inside of the tyre is coated with a gel which has puncture-sealing properties. In the event of a small puncture, the gel seals the leak and the driver is unlikely to know anything about it.

Large leaks, which take longer to seal, will allow the tyre to deflate. While the sealant goes to work, the extra flexing of the sidewalls heats up the air inside the tyre. The heated air expands and partially re-inflates the tyre once the leak has been sealed. If the hole is too big to be sealed, the gel acts as a lubricant, preventing the tyre from damaging itself when run flat.

Early versions of the Denovo carried sealing fluid and a lubricant in small canisters fixed to the inside of the wheel rim. With this type, which has been superseded by the Denovo 2 with the gel coating, tyres could not jump off the rim because the two-piece wheel had no tyre-fitting well. On the Denovo 2, the one-piece wheel has a well, but the tyre beads are locked into grooves in the rim and cannot pull out.

Yet, removal of the tyre-fitting well forms the basis of a number of safety wheel designs. To allow the tyre to be fitted, a cover over the well is taken off. With the tyre on the rim, the cover is refitted and the tyre cannot then come off.

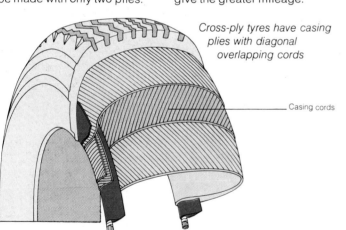

Cross-ply tyres have casing plies with diagonal overlapping cords

Casing cords

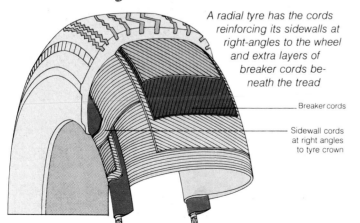

A radial tyre has the cords reinforcing its sidewalls at right-angles to the wheel and extra layers of breaker cords beneath the tread

Breaker cords

Sidewall cords at right angles to tyre crown

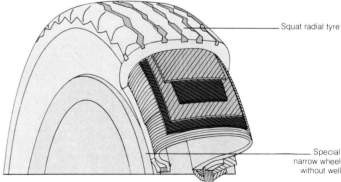

Squat radial tyre

Special narrow wheel without well

A special gel inside the Dunlop Denovo seals small punctures automatically, with very little pressure loss. If the tyre goes flat, the gel provides lubrication to prevent the tyre from overheating. The heating of the air inside partially inflates the tyre. The car can be driven at up to 50mph for 100 miles in this condition

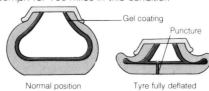

Gel coating

Puncture

Normal position   Tyre fully deflated   Partial re-inflation

Wheels, tyres and suspension

How the tread grips the road

We have seen that for maximum grip on dry surfaces the tyre must put as much rubber in contact with the road as possible. However, on a wet road, the average-size tyre must move more than a gallon of water from its path every second, in order to get a grip.

A road-going tyre therefore has a large surface area of rubber for maximum grip in the dry, but is also criss-crossed by drainage channels and small 'knife cuts', called sipes, which disperse the water when the road is wet. In effect, water is squeegeed off the road where the tyre makes contact.

Without drainage channels, even at moderate speeds, a tyre with a smooth tread will ride over surface water like a water-ski—a condition known as aquaplaning.

The way in which a tread grips in the wet depends on how much water there is on the road. It simply breaks through

a thin film of water which the sipes soak up like a sponge. With large amounts of water, the tyre pushes some of it aside and pumps a large quantity through the channels which run parallel with the wheel. These drive the water to the rear of the contact patch where it is thrown off behind the tyre. The sipes mop up residual water, providing the rubber with an almost dry area to grip.

As speed increases, the tread must disperse more water and the dry area of the contact patch gets smaller. With a half-worn tread, a tyre's grip decreases appreciably as the speed rises, and it is more likely to aquaplane.

Tyres with special tread patterns (cross-country or winter-pattern tyres, for instance) have deep grooves in the shoulder and a coarse pattern to give maximum grip on soft surfaces. These tyres wear out rapidly if used on dry roads.

Tyres with smooth or well-worn treads will skate over surface water, aquaplaning at speed and losing their grip

Tyres with deep, coarse treads are made for cross-country or winter use – sometimes with metal studs for grip on ice. They wear out quickly on normal roads

Remoulds and retreads

When a tyre tread is worn out it is often possible to re-use the casing by having a new tread vulcanised to it. Where the tread only is renewed, the tyre is called a retread; where new rubber is also put over the sidewalls, the tyre is referred to as a remould.

Retreads and remoulds use a second-hand casing, and are, therefore, less suitable than new tyres for high-speed motoring. The British Standards Institution recommends that retreads or remoulds used on private vehicles, be used only at speeds not exceeding 70mph, regardless of the size of the wheel. They are not suitable for prolonged high-speed use.

Retread or remould tyres are cheaper but have a shorter life than new tyres. When buying them, look for the British Standards mark BSI AU 144b which will be found on the better makes of tyre.

Mixing tyres

Radial and cross-ply tyres give different handling characteristics, so they should not be mixed—your car will handle and steer best with the maker's recommended tyres on all wheels.

If mixing is unavoidable, fit cross-ply tyres to the front wheels and radials to the back. It is illegal to mix the different types on the same 'axle', or to use radial tyres on the front

wheels and cross-ply tyres on the back.

Some American cars use a bias-belted tyre which has a construction midway between cross-ply and radial, with stiff sidewalls and breaker cords under the tread. When applying the above rules, regard bias-belted tyres as cross-ply. However, they must not be fitted on the front wheels with cross-plies on the back.

Tyre markings

Radial tyres are marked 'radial' or with the letter R. They also have code letters which indicate maximum recommended speeds. Radials marked SR are suitable for speeds up to 113mph, HR-marked radials

are suitable for up to 130mph, and those marked VR are good for over 130mph.

Not all cross-ply tyres are marked, and their speed rating varies depending on their size. The table gives details.

Wheel balancing

A heavy section in a tyre can set up alarming vibrations in the steering at certain road speeds. The condition can be cured by attaching small balance weights to the wheel rim to counteract the out-of-balance forces.

Do-it-yourself kits are available which allow a wheel to be balanced statically. After removal from the car the wheel is turned to a horizontal position and balanced on a needle point at its centre. Weights are added to the rim until a spirit

level indicates that the wheel is level in all directions.

Static balancing cannot cure an out-of-balance problem where the heavy section is on one side of a tyre. When this occurs, the heaviest section of the balance weight must be placed diagonally opposite the heavy section. Such calculations can be made only by using a professional dynamic wheel balancer which will indicate the position and size of weights needed to eliminate a dynamic wobble.

Rim dia	Size mark only	Speed mark		
		S	H	V
10 in	Up to 75 mph 120 km/h	Up to 95 mph 150 km/h	Up to 110 mph 175 km/h	
12 in	Up to 85 mph 135 km/h	Up to 100 mph 160 km/h	Up to 115 mph 185 km/h	
13 in and over	Up to 95 mph 150 km/h	Up to 110 mph 175 km/h	Up to 125 mph 200 km/h	Over 125 mph 200 km/h

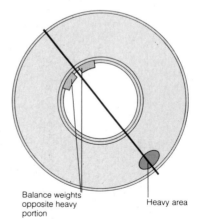

Balance weights opposite heavy portion

Heavy area

A wheel is statically balanced by placing a weight opposite the heavy portion

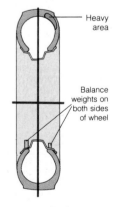

Heavy area

Balance weights on both sides of wheel

Dynamic balance involves placing the weight diagonally opposite the heavy section to iron out a wobble

Road wheels

On most cars each wheel is secured to the hub flange by four or five nuts or bolts. The wheel centre is usually shaped so that a tapered section on each of the securing nuts or bolt heads engages with a mating cone on the wheel and centres it correctly. Another method of centring the wheel is to engage a projection in the centre of the hub with a precision-machined hole in the wheel centre; sometimes the wheels will also be located by a small pin on the hub. On these, the fixings secure the wheel rather than centre it.

Some performance cars have centre-lock wheels which are held on a splined hub by a single centre nut which is tightened with a special spanner, or is shaped so that it can be knocked on and off by a copper-faced hammer. The wheel is centred by a taper on the hub and nut, and is driven by the splines. Centre-lock wheels on the offside generally have a left-hand thread.

Ideally, road wheels should be as light as possible. This reduces unsprung weight and allows them to follow the contours of the road more accurately, giving an improved ride and increased roadholding. For this reason, light-alloy wheels are used on many performance cars, usually in conjunction with wide-section tyres which give a larger contact patch and better grip on corners.

Light-alloy wheels are protected from salt spray corrosion by a coat of lacquer. If this becomes damaged, white powdery corrosion will form on the exposed metal. This can be removed with a fine grade of wet-or-dry abrasive paper. The wheel should then be re-lacquered.

The other sort of corrosion that alloy wheels suffer from is electrolytic corrosion—where the steel fixing bolts or studs are in contact with the alloy. To prevent this, the holes through which the studs or bolts pass should be greased. Self-adhesive balance weights, which do not need metal clips or screws to secure them, must be used on alloy wheels.

Wire-spoked wheels use a complex pattern of spokes to distribute the loads imposed by acceleration, braking and the weight of the vehicle. The pierced rim of a spoked wheel makes it impossible to seal, so tubeless tyres cannot be used. Because it is expensive to make, difficult to clean and heavier than a comparable alloy wheel, the spoked wheel is rarely used now.

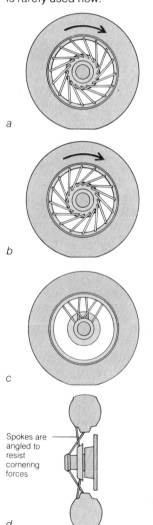

Spoked wheels use a large number of spokes, some of which are arranged to transmit acceleration (a), braking (b), the weight of the car (c), and are also triangulated to resist cornering forces (d)

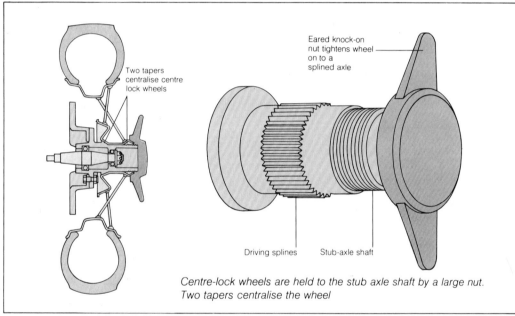

Centre-lock wheels are held to the stub axle shaft by a large nut. Two tapers centralise the wheel

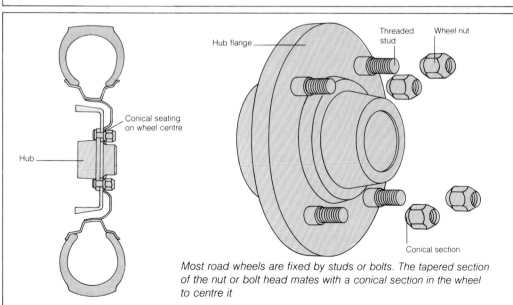

Most road wheels are fixed by studs or bolts. The tapered section of the nut or bolt head mates with a conical section in the wheel to centre it

Wheels, tyres and suspension

Suspension systems

To prevent the occupants from being jolted by every irregularity in the road, all cars have springs of one sort or another between their road wheel assemblies and the bodywork. The springs allow the wheels to move up and down over bumps and hollows while the bodywork maintains a reasonably level course.

Used on their own, springs would allow the bodywork to bounce uncontrollably over an undulating road, so all suspension systems are fitted with dampers to control spring movement.

Although suspension systems are primarily provided for the comfort of passengers, it is important that the up-and-down movement of the wheels does not adversely affect the handling of the car by allowing excessive body roll or permit-

ting wheel movement to steer the car. Therefore, in addition to springs and dampers, the suspension system has a carefully designed linkage to ensure that each wheel remains reasonably upright and points in the intended direction, regardless of road irregularities.

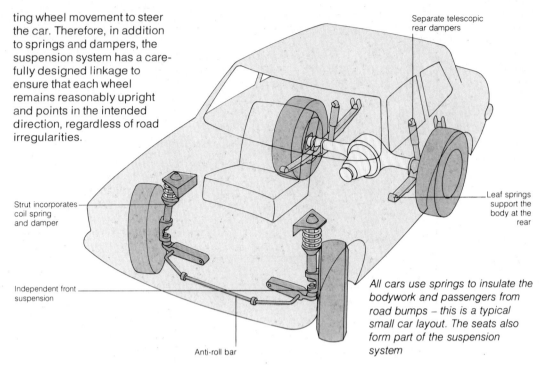

Separate telescopic rear dampers

Strut incorporates coil spring and damper

Independent front suspension

Anti-roll bar

Leaf springs support the body at the rear

All cars use springs to insulate the bodywork and passengers from road bumps – this is a typical small car layout. The seats also form part of the suspension system

Types of spring

The simplest suspension spring is the leaf spring, which was originally used on horse-drawn carts. The modern leaf spring is made from tempered steel and may be slightly curved or nearly flat. Depending on the load to be carried, it may have a number of leaves laminated together or may be in the form of a single leaf. It takes suspension loads by bending.

Because the first leaf spring resists sideways movement it is often used to locate a one-piece back axle. The leaf is bolted to the body shell at each end, and the axle is clamped near the centre.

Torsion-bar suspension, unlike the leaf spring which bends, uses the twisting loads on a steel rod to support the car. The road wheel is attached to an arm at the end of the rod, and when it hits a bump, the wheel rises. This raises the arm like a lever and the twisting of the torsion bar absorbs the load. The coil spring, used at the front on the majority of cars because of its high capacity and compact size, is, in effect, a torsion bar wrapped in a spiral, and also absorbs loads by twisting the metal.

Not all springs are made of tempered steel. Some cars

have rubber springs, others have gas springs in which an inert gas, such as nitrogen, is

trapped in the upper section of a sphere with a diaphragm below it. Suspension forces

acting on the diaphragm compress the gas, which behaves like a spring.

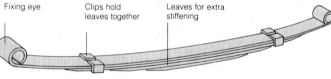

Fixing eye

Clips hold leaves together

Leaves for extra stiffening

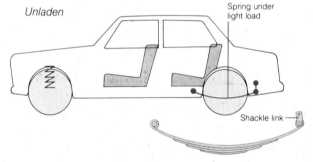

Unladen

Spring under light load

Shackle link

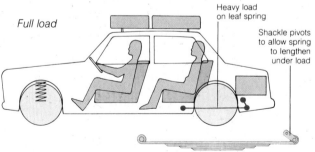

Full load

Heavy load on leaf spring

Shackle pivots to allow spring to lengthen under load

A leaf spring may have a single leaf or several laminations. To accommodate its change in length as it flexes, it is mounted at the rear on a swinging shackle

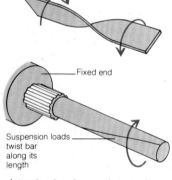

Fixed end

Suspension loads twist bar along its length

A torsion bar is a spring steel rod fixed at one end and twisted at the other by a lever attached to the suspension

The coil spring is a torsion bar wrapped in a spiral. The load is absorbed by the metal twisting

Wheels, tyres and suspension

Dampers

Early dampers relied on the resistance of a friction joint to discourage sudden movement of the suspension spring and to damp out oscillations. Now the most widely used damper is the telescopic type. It is fitted with its upper end attached to the body shell and its lower section on a major moving part of the suspension. The damper contains a piston working in an oil-filled cylinder. As the suspension moves, valves and passages in the piston control the leakage of oil past it.

In addition to controlling the flow of oil past a piston, the telescopic damper has a valve near the base to allow some oil to make a controlled escape into a reservoir or recuperating chamber surrounding the cylinder. This is used because when the damper is compressed, it cannot accept all the oil that leaks past the piston in the space above it because of the volume taken up by the piston rod. When the damper extends and the piston rises, oil from the recuperating chamber flows back into the cylinder.

Lever dampers also use pistons sliding in a cylinder to force oil through small passages. The up and down movement of the road wheel operates a lever which is engaged, through a rocker, to two opposed pistons in an oil-filled cylinder. As each piston moves towards the end of the cylinder, oil is forced through a valve in the casing, and travels to the other end of the cylinder, thereby damping the movements of the spring.

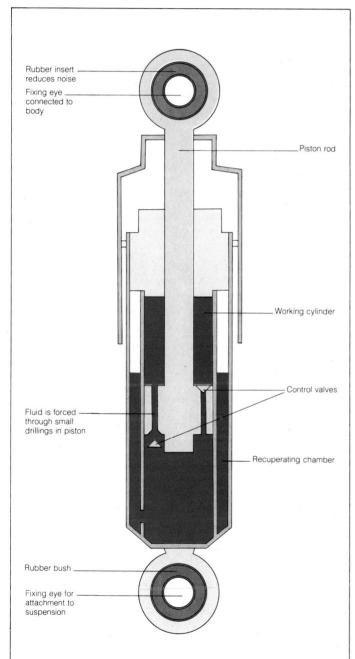

Rubber insert reduces noise

Fixing eye connected to body

Piston rod

Working cylinder

Control valves

Fluid is forced through small drillings in piston

Recuperating chamber

Rubber bush

Fixing eye for attachment to suspension

Telescopic dampers use a piston moving in oil to damp spring oscillations. Small passages and valves in the piston restrict the oil flow. A double-action damper is one that damps spring movement in both directions

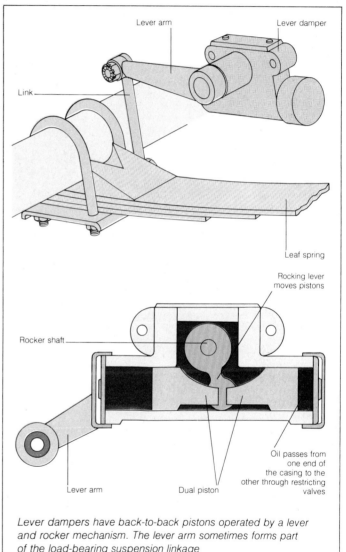

Lever arm

Lever damper

Link

Leaf spring

Rocking lever moves pistons

Rocker shaft

Lever arm

Dual piston

Oil passes from one end of the casing to the other through restricting valves

Lever dampers have back-to-back pistons operated by a lever and rocker mechanism. The lever arm sometimes forms part of the load-bearing suspension linkage

Front suspension systems

All current cars use an independent front suspension system in which each wheel has its own spring and suspension linkage and can rise and fall independently of the other. However, on many cars the suspension linkage on each side is, in fact, joined by an anti-roll bar which is added solely to discourage excessive body roll.

Because the front wheels do the steering, it is essential that the suspension linkage does not impair the steering by allowing the wheels to tilt or move backwards, forwards or sideways to any serious degree.

Wheels, tyres and suspension

Double wishbone suspension

One of the main front suspension systems is the double wishbone layout in which wishbone-shaped links are hinged at their broad ends to the car body, and at their narrow ends to the swivelling stub-axle carrying the wheel. Between the wishbone and the car body is a spring and damper. The triangular shape of the wishbones is used because it resists acceleration, braking and cornering forces.

The pivot points and the length of the wishbones control the paths of the wheels as they ride over bumps. If the upper and lower wishbones are of equal length and parallel, the wheels will not tilt (or change their camber) as they ride over bumps, but the front track of the car—the distance between the front wheels—will alter, wearing the tyres excessively and reducing cornering power because the wheels will lean with the body.

To overcome this, the upper wishbone is much shorter than the lower one, and not parallel with it. This arrangement may cause the wheel to tilt inwards at the top (called negative camber) as the spring is compressed, but the track remains the same. Negative camber during cornering compensates for body roll, keeping the wheel more or less at right angles to the road.

MacPherson strut suspension

Named after its inventor, this is a telescopic strut that incorporates a damper, carries the wheel stub-axle at the bottom and has a coil spring at the top. The strut is pivoted at its upper end on a flexible mounting on the bodywork—usually inside the front wing—and at its lower end on a swivel ball joint. It may be located at the bottom by a wishbone-like transverse link or a single track-control arm which is triangulated with an anti-roll bar to resist braking, acceleration and cornering forces.

Car manufacturers like the MacPherson strut because it is easy to fit in production, and provides suspension geometry similar to that of a double-wishbone arrangement.

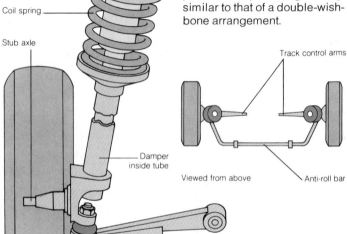

The MacPherson strut combines the stub axle, coil spring and damper in one unit. It is flexibly mounted at the top and pivots on a ball joint at its base

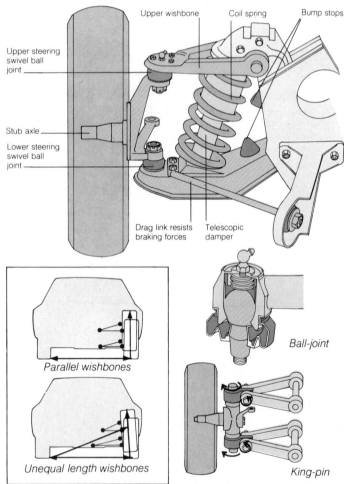

Ball-joint

King-pin

Double wishbone independent front suspension locates the wheels against the forces of acceleration, braking and cornering. The system usually includes a coil spring and damper unit mounted between the wishbones, and is usually linked to the steering swivel member by ball joints. Earlier versions sometimes use a king-pin, on which the swivel member turns in plain bearings. Parallel wishbones produce a change in track with the suspension laden, which wears out tyres and gives poor cornering. Unequal length wishbones allow the wheel to change its camber, keeping the track constant and improving the cornering power

Anti-roll bar

Centrifugal forces cause a car body to roll during cornering. This can be reduced if an anti-roll bar links the independent front suspension assemblies. As the car leans on the wheel nearest the outside of the corner, compressing the suspension, the inside wheel, in effect, drops down, 'winding up' the torsion bar. The twisting bar tries to pull the outside suspension linkage down, and in doing so, adds power to the spring, thus reducing the angle of roll.

An anti-roll bar links suspension systems on the same axle. When cornering hard, centrifugal force rolls the car body, compressing the outside suspension. Inside suspension is compressed by the action of the anti-roll bar, reducing body roll

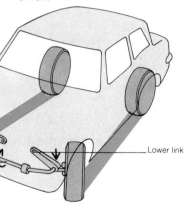

Rear suspension systems

The simplest rear suspension arrangement is the Hotchkiss drive. This uses a one-piece, live rear axle clamped to a pair of leaf springs, damped by telescopic or lever dampers. Usually, the axle is mounted slightly ahead of the centre of the springs, thus causing the axle's differential to tilt downwards as the springs deflect. This reduces upward movement of the propeller shaft and allows a shallower transmission tunnel to be used inside the car.

The snag with so simple an arrangement is that on more powerful cars, sudden acceleration causes the axle to twist and distort the springs into a shallow S-shape so that they wind-up and unwind, producing judder at the rear wheels. This is usually cured by fitting extra linkages—radius rods— which prevent axle twist.

On coil-sprung, live rear axles, additional links are needed to prevent both sideways movement and axle twisting. Most cars use a four-link system with the two centre links splayed out like the sides of a letter A, or with a one-piece A-frame to limit sideways movement. Alternatively, a Panhard rod, a long link that pivots between one side of the axle and the opposite side of the car body, may be used.

Another way of preventing rear axle wind-up on acceleration is to extend the differential housing into a long tube. Radius rods keep the axle straight and a Panhard rod prevents sideways movement.

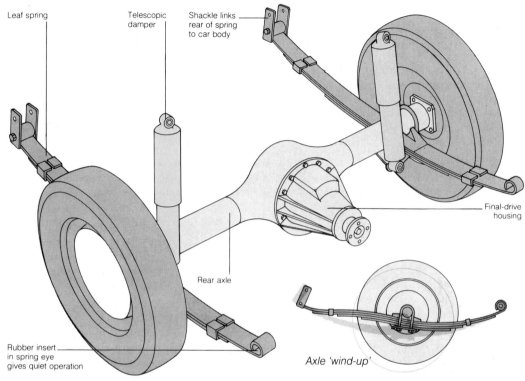

The Hotchkiss drive is the simplest rear-wheel-drive suspension system. Leaf springs locate the live rear axle and also prevent sideways movement. On powerful cars the springs can wind up, causing judder during acceleration

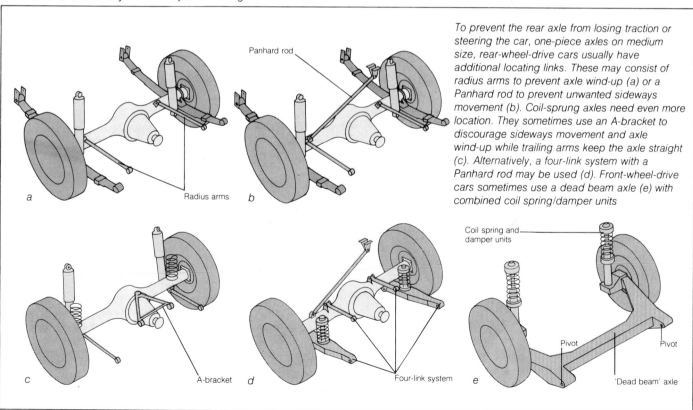

To prevent the rear axle from losing traction or steering the car, one-piece axles on medium size, rear-wheel-drive cars usually have additional locating links. These may consist of radius arms to prevent axle wind-up (a) or a Panhard rod to prevent unwanted sideways movement (b). Coil-sprung axles need even more location. They sometimes use an A-bracket to discourage sideways movement and axle wind-up while trailing arms keep the axle straight (c). Alternatively, a four-link system with a Panhard rod may be used (d). Front-wheel-drive cars sometimes use a dead beam axle (e) with combined coil spring/damper units

Wheels, tyres and suspension

Independent rear suspension systems

On rear-wheel-drive vehicles, independent rear suspension involves fixing the final drive differential to the chassis or body shell, and coupling it to the wheel with universally-jointed drive shafts. Although more complicated than a live axle, this system is used by some manufacturers because it gives improved traction.

Where the drive shafts have a single universal joint, the swinging axle effect means that the rear wheels change their camber from positive (like the sides of a W) to negative (like the sides of an A) respectively as the suspension compresses and extends. Changes in track cause accelerated tyre wear, and severe changes in camber produce unstable cornering.

The use of two universal joints in each drive shaft allows the wheels to be kept more upright. If trailing arms are used to locate the rear hubs, the wheels stay upright regardless of suspension movement.

The use of semi-trailing arms, where the arm is hinged obliquely to the car's centre line, allows the wheels to take on negative camber as the suspension compresses. This aids cornering power in the same way as an unequal-length double wishbone system.

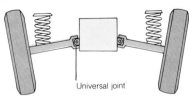

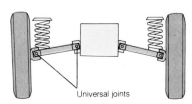

Independent rear suspension systems with a single universal joint in each drive shaft (top) cause wheel camber changes which, if excessive, wear the tyres quickly and provide uncertain cornering. Two universal joints in each drive shaft allow the wheels to be kept upright

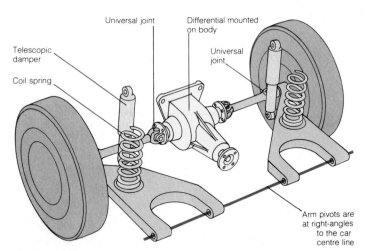

Trailing arms

Trailing arm rear suspension keeps the wheels upright and parallel. Semi-trailing arms are better because wheels adopt a slight negative camber as the suspension is loaded, increasing rear wheel grip on corners

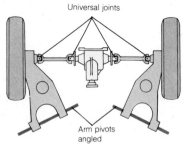

Semi-trailing arms

Linked suspension systems

If the front and rear suspension systems are linked, it is possible to arrange for upward movement of a front wheel to be matched by downward movement of the rear wheel on the same side of the car. This keeps the car level when a front or rear wheel rides over a bump. Citroen uses a mechanical linkage to do this on its small cars, while Austin-Morris uses a fluid link to provide a level ride on its Hydrolastic and Hydragas systems.

In the Hydrolastic system, each wheel transmits suspension loads to a displacer which serves as a spring and damper. The displacer is mounted on the bodywork. At one end it has a conical rubber spring, while the other end is closed by a tough, flexible diaphragm. The suspension linkage bears on the diaphragm.

Between the diaphragm and spring inside the displacer there is a two-way valve. The displacer is filled with fluid and the front and rear displacer units on each side are connected by pipes.

When a front wheel rises over a bump, the diaphragm is forced up into the displacer, pushing fluid past the damper valve. The increase in pressure inside the displacer compresses the rubber spring and forces fluid down the pipe to the rear displacer, pushing out its diaphragm and extending the rear suspension. This system ensures that any lifting of one end of the car is matched by a rise at the other end.

Current Austin-Morris cars using the fluid-link system do not have a rubber spring in the displacer. Instead, the Hydragas units employ spheres of inert gas under pressure. The gas is separated from suspension fluid by an extra diaphragm, and this provides the springing. The interconnection system works in the same way.

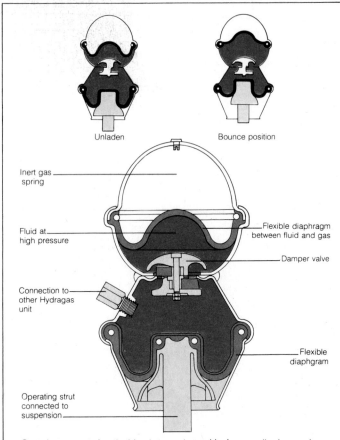

Certain current Austin-Morris cars have Hydragas displacers in which an inert gas spring, separated from the fluid by an extra diaphragm, is used. The interconnection arrangement is the same as with Hydrolastic

Wheels, tyres and suspension

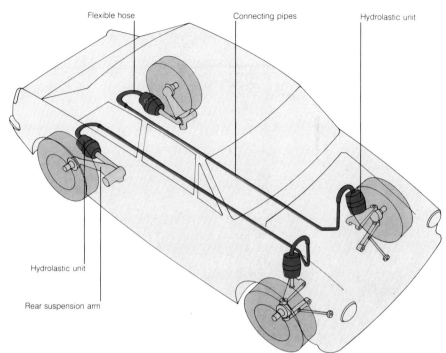

Flexible hose
Connecting pipes
Hydrolastic unit
Hydrolastic unit
Rear suspension arm

Linking front and rear suspension systems on each side makes the rear suspension drop as the front suspension rises, keeping the car body level

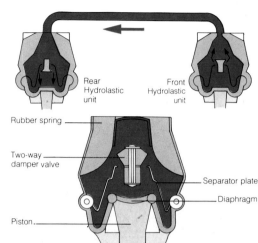

Rear Hydrolastic unit
Front Hydrolastic unit
Rubber spring
Two-way damper valve
Separator plate
Diaphragm
Piston

The Austin-Morris Hydrolastic system uses fluid to inter-connect front and rear displacers. As the suspension is compressed at the front by a bump, fluid forced down the pipe extends the rear displacer. Once the bump has passed, fluid returns from the rear displacer, restoring the normal ride height. Inside a Hydrolastic unit, fluid is forced past a damper valve by the rising diaphragm and compresses the rubber spring when the suspension is loaded

Self-levelling hydropneumatic suspension

Citroen combines a hydraulic system with gas springing in the self-levelling suspension on its medium and larger cars.

Each wheel has its own suspension unit, comprising a sphere of nitrogen gas which is separated from hydraulic fluid by a diaphragm. The lower section of the sphere houses a hydraulic cylinder containing a piston to the suspension linkage. Upward movement of a wheel raises the piston, compressing the fluid above it and pushing the diaphragm against the nitrogen, which acts as a gas spring.

In addition to the weight of the car pressurising the fluid, when the engine is running, a hydraulic pump supplies suspension fluid under pressure to a valve. When the car is heavily laden and the suspension is compressed, the hydraulic valve directs fluid under pressure to each suspension unit. This extra fluid pushes the piston down, raising the car. Once the suspension reaches its correct level, a linkage closes the hydraulic valve and the suspension height is maintained.

If the load is removed, the suspension extends and the car lowers itself. When the engine and hydraulic pump are stationary, the suspension settles to its lowest level. A valve, restricting the flow of fluid into and out of each of the suspension units, acts as a damper.

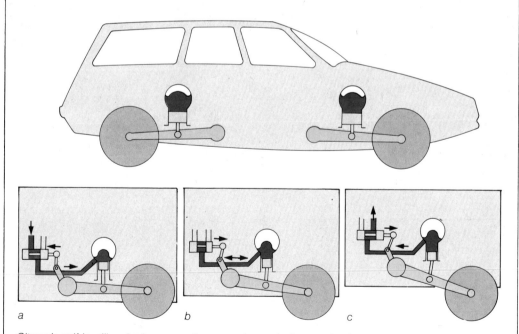

a
b
c

Citroen's self-levelling, hydropneumatic suspension works by pumping hydraulic fluid under pressure between a piston and a diaphragm below a gas spring. When the car is laden (a) a linkage opens a hydraulic valve and fluid is pumped above the piston to raise the car. As the body rises, the linkage puts the valve into a neutral position when the desired level has been reached (b). If the load decreases, and the body rises further (c) the valve is moved by the linkage and diverts suspension fluid to a reservoir, lowering the car

Wheels, tyres and suspension projects

Project 67: Checking the tyres

Grading: 🔧
Time: 10min
Tools: Tyre pump or garage airline; tyre pressure gauge; tyre tread-depth gauge

By law the tyres on your car must be in good condition, inflated to the pressure that the car maker recommends in his handbook, and the treads must not be allowed to wear beyond a minimum depth.

Check the pressure on each tyre, including the spare, once a week. If it drops more than 3-4lb sq in. in a week, the tyre or valve may be faulty. Have it checked by a tyre specialist.

Ideally the pressures should be checked and adjusted while the tyres are cold. If they are measured when the tyres are hot after a high-speed run, the air inside will have expanded, giving a false reading. If you do not have a tyre pump, keep the tyres as cool as possible by driving at no more than 30mph to the nearest garage with a tyre-inflation airline. Although all garage airlines have a pressure indicator, these are sometimes inaccurate. It is better to check the pressure with a hand-held gauge.

Step 1. Unscrew the dust cap from the tyre valve and check the pressure with a gauge. Compare it with the recommended pressure in the handbook.

2. If the pressure is low, inflate the tyre with a tyre pump or garage airline.

3. Garage airlines have a pressure gauge. Stop inflating every few seconds and check the pressure reading.

If using a foot pump, disconnect it if necessary and check the pressure with a hand-held gauge, at regular intervals.

4. If the tyre is over-inflated, use the domed end or corner of the valve dust cap to press down the valve pin and let some air out. When the pressure is correct, refit the cap.

5. When checking pressures, remember to look critically at the sidewalls on both sides of the tyres. They should be renewed if there are any cracks or bulges.

6. From time to time, use a gauge to check the depth of the tread. Measure the centre and outer grooves of the tread pattern. The legal requirement is a minimum depth of 1mm, but it is wise to renew tyres when the treads have worn to 2mm. New tyres have a tread depth of about 7mm.

Step 1.

Step 2.

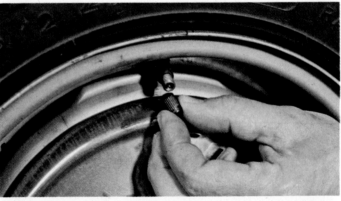
Step 4.

Step 6.

Project 68: Changing a wheel

Grading: 🔧
Time: 15min
Tools: Wheelbrace; jack; chock; lever for removing hub-cap

Every new car is provided with a simple jack and wheelbrace to enable a wheel to be changed.

The secret of successful wheel-changing is slightly to loosen the fixing nuts, bolts or centre nut while the tyre is still on the ground. The wheel should then be jacked clear of the ground, the fixings undone fully and the spare wheel fitted—the illustrations show the sequence in detail.

Sometimes cars are sent out from garages with their wheelnuts or bolts so over-tightened that the wheelbrace in the tool kit will not undo them. If this is the case, free the nuts or bolts with a long tube slipped over the handle of an L-shaped wheelbrace to increase its leverage. Loosen one nut or bolt at a time, grease the thread sparingly, and refit it, using only the wheelbrace. This will provide perfectly adequate leverage to tighten the fixings correctly, and it will make them easy to undo next time.

Some cars have centre-lock wheels fixed by a large winged nut that is 'knocked on' by means of a copper-faced hammer. The offside nuts have a left-hand thread, and most are marked with an arrow and the word 'undo', to indicate which way they should be knocked to be loosened. Always check the arrow before tackling a centre-lock wheel nut.

Changing a wheel—particularly an offside one—at the roadside can be dangerous. Before you start, park the car clear of any sharp bends and as far off the road as you can. If your vehicle has hazard-warning lights, switch them on. Listen and look out for approaching traffic when changing the wheel, and be prepared to move out of the road—a figure crouched alongside a stationary car is not easily seen, particularly at night.

Wheels, tyres and suspension projects

Step 1. Ensure that the tyre on the spare wheel is properly inflated. Take out the spare wheel and place it near the wheel to be changed. Ensure that the handbrake is applied, and chock one of the grounded wheels to prevent the car from rolling when it is jacked up.

2. Uncover the wheel nuts or bolts. Some are hidden behind plastic caps which can be pulled off by hand or prised out with a screwdriver.

3. On cars fitted with hub caps, one end of the wheelbrace may be specially shaped to remove the cap. Failing this, lever it off with a large, flat-bladed screwdriver.

4. Loosen the fixing nuts or bolts no more than a quarter-turn.

*4. If the fixings are very tight, certain types of wheelbrace can be extended to provide more leverage by sliding a long tube over the handle.

5. Fit the jack into the recommended jacking point (see the car handbook) and raise the car until the wheel is well clear of the ground. Do not get under the car.

6. Remove the wheel fixings, pull off the wheel and fit the spare.

7. Align the bolt holes with the threaded holes in the hub or brake drum. With the wheelbrace, tighten the fixings firmly, working diagonally.

8. Lower the jack until the tyre touches the ground and fully tighten the wheel fixings with the wheelbrace. Do not use an extension lever when tightening the nuts or bolts.

9. Lower the jack fully and remove it. Refit any hub caps and finishers—sprung hub caps 'snap on' with a sharp blow from the palm of the hand. Make sure that the spare wheel is made roadworthy as soon as possible.

Step 2.

Step *4.

Step 5.

Step 6.

Step 7.

Step 8.

Wheels, tyres and suspension projects

Project 69: Renewing a telescopic damper

Grading: ₤₤₤
Time: Approx 30min per damper
Tools: Wheelbrace; jack; axle stands; spanners to fit mountings and spindle end; lever or large screwdriver
Materials: Pair of new dampers; washing-up liquid

A worn telescopic damper is easy to identify because it leaks oil, which runs down the outside of its casing. If the wear is ignored, the car will bounce excessively over uneven surfaces and may become difficult to control.

Dampers should be renewed in front or rear pairs and this is done most easily if the suspension is supported on axle stands.

Telescopic dampers are stored in a horizontal position. Before fitting one to a car, the oil inside should be redistributed by holding the damper vertically and working it through its full stroke a few times.

Telescopic dampers that provide a support for a coil spring need special tools to change them. This is a job best left to a garage.

Step 1. Chock the grounded wheels, raise the appropriate end of the car and place axle stands under the suspension (see pages 14 and 15).

2. Remove the road wheel to gain access to the damper.

3. Undo the fixing nut and push out the bottom bolt from the damper mounting.

4. Disconnect any other fixing at the lower end. The damper illustrated, from a Ford Fiesta, has a bracing arm with rubber bushes that are a push fit over a pin on the suspension. The arm is levered upwards to disconnect it.

5. At the top, a nut secures the damper spindle to the body. From inside the car or in the boot, fit a spanner on the flats at the end of the spindle to stop it from turning while the fixing nut is loosened. Note the order in which the top rubber mountings and washer are fitted.

6. Remove the damper from the wheel arch.

7. Before fitting a new telescopic damper, hold it vertically and work it fully up and down three times.

8. The new damper will come with new rubber mountings assembled in their correct position. Remove the upper rubbers that fit inside the car or in the boot.

9. Enter the spindle in the upper hole, and fit the damper into its lower mounting. If the rubber bushes are a tight fit, a smear of washing-up liquid will help them to slide into place.

10. Fit the bolt and nut and tighten them fully.

11. From inside the car or boot, pull up the spindle fully and fit the rubber mountings. The rubbers are often shaped so that they hold the spindle centrally in the hole. Fit the metal washer above them.

12. Use a small spanner to prevent the spindle from turning while the fixing nut is tightened fully.

13. Repeat Steps 1-12 on the opposite damper.

14. Replace the wheels and lower the car to the ground.

Step 2.

Step 3.

Step 4.

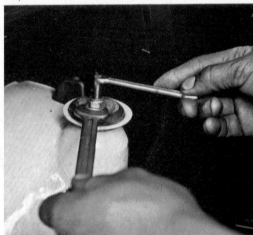
Step 5.

Step 6.

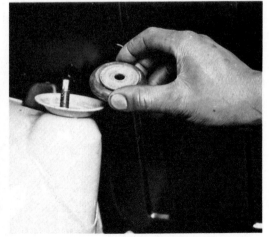
Step 11.

Wheels, tyres and suspension projects

Project 70: Replacing a lever front suspension damper

Grading: ⚡⚡⚡
Time: Approx 1hr 30min per damper
Tools: Wheelbrace; jack; axle stands; chocks; pillar jack; cold chisel; hammer; spanners to fit arm nut and damper bolts; pliers
Materials: Two new dampers; two sets of rubber bushes; new tab washers

Defective lever dampers exhibit the same symptoms as worn telescopic units: they leak fluid and the car bounces excessively on uneven roads.

Where they are used at the front, the lever-damper arms usually form part of the suspension linkage. The suspension must be supported by a jack before the damper is undone. Dampers should not be renewed individually, but as a front or rear pair.

Step 1. Chock the rear wheels, raise the front of the car and support it on axle stands (see pages 14 and 15). Remove the front wheels.
2. Place a jack under the front suspension lower link or wishbone. Jack up the suspension to compress the spring until the lower link or wishbone is approximately horizontal. Be careful not to raise the car body so high that it is lifted off the axle stands.
3. Undo the upper suspension-arm nut. If necessary, first knock down the metal tab securing it.
4. Push up the arm to disconnect it from the upper joint. There is often a taper joint, and a joint-splitter may be required.
5. Lift the arm to disengage it.
6. Remove the bolts fixing the damper to the car body. Lift out the damper.
7. Before fitting the new

damper (it comes complete with suspension arm), hold it upright and pump its arm at least ten times through its full travel in order to bleed it.
8. Fit the new damper and pull down its arm so that it sits over the upper swivel joint. Fit a new lock-washer and nut above the arm. Tighten the nut fully and bend up the tab of the lock-washer with a small hammer to secure it.
9. Remove the jack and repeat Steps 2-8 on the opposite damper.
10. Replace the wheels and lower the car to the ground.

Step 2.

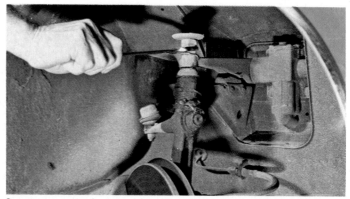
Step 3.

Step 4.

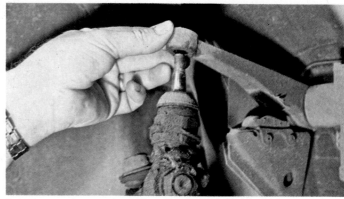
Step 5.

Step 6.

Step 7.

Steering and brakes

Steering

Because at least half the weight of a car is usually carried by the front wheels, the steering mechanism must be geared down to enable the driver to swivel the wheels. Consequently, the linkage that connects the steering wheel in the car to the road wheels incorporates a gearing mechanism that reduces the effort.

On most small cars, about $2\frac{1}{2}$ turns of the steering wheel move the road wheels a total of 60° from one lock to the other. Bigger, heavier cars may use $4\frac{1}{2}$ turns from lock-to-lock, or may use power assistance to lighten the steering.

In addition to providing a relatively light action, the steering mechanism must give precise, accurate control. It should also return automatically to the straight-ahead position after being turned, and provide enough 'feedback' to allow the driver to feel the road surface through the wheel, but without any serious 'kickback' when a road wheel hits a big bump or pot-hole.

Linkages

The road wheels are linked to the steering shaft by a system of rods, levers and joints that varies depending on the type of steering used.

The rack-and-pinion layout is popular because it is compact, gives accurate steering and uses few mechanical parts.

It consists of a small, toothed pinion on the steering shaft which is engaged with a toothed rack. When the steering wheel is turned, the rack moves sideways.

Some cars still use a steering box. This has a worm gear connected to the steering shaft. As the steering wheel is turned, the worm rotates and moves a nut or peg engaged with it, along its length.

This linkage converts the rotary motion of the steering wheel into angular movement of the front wheels by means of a shaft, attached to a drop-arm on the outside of the steering box.

To operate satisfactorily with independent front suspension, the steering linkage must be symmetrical about the centre line of the vehicle so, in layouts with a steering box, a matching slave or idler arm is fitted symmetrically opposite the drop arm.

On most cars, the swivel carrying the stub axle—the short shaft on which each front wheel rotates—is pivoted top and bottom on ball-and-socket swivel joints. A few cars still carry the stub-axle on a kingpin between upper and lower suspension wishbones, but these are becoming fewer. MacPherson strut front suspension systems have a lower ball joint and a bearing or rubber pivot at the top of the spring.

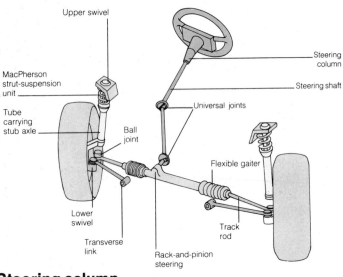

Steering column

The steering column encloses a shaft that connects the steering wheel to the linkage under the bonnet. All current cars have an energy-absorbing steering column designed to collapse or telescope in a head-on crash to prevent the driver from being injured by the wheel or column.

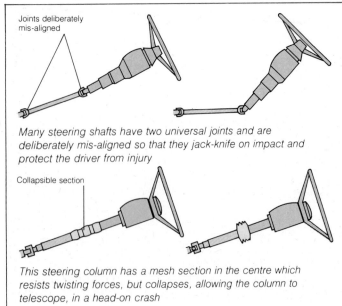

Many steering shafts have two universal joints and are deliberately mis-aligned so that they jack-knife on impact and protect the driver from injury

This steering column has a mesh section in the centre which resists twisting forces, but collapses, allowing the column to telescope, in a head-on crash

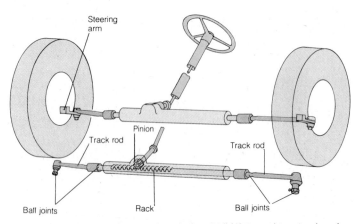

Rack and pinion steering needs only four ball joints and two track rods to connect it to the wheels

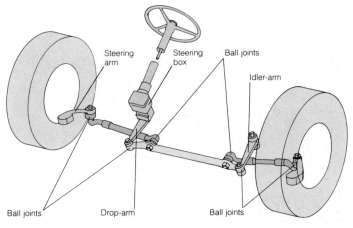

A steering box may require an idler arm and six ball joints in its linkage

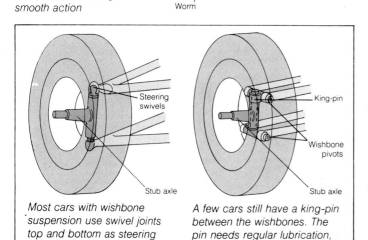

In a cam and peg steering box (above) a peg engaged with a type of worm gear on the steering shaft converts rotary movement into the back-and-forth action needed to pivot the road wheels. On a worm and nut system, recirculating ball bearings reduce friction and give a smooth action

Most cars with wishbone suspension use swivel joints top and bottom as steering and wishbone pivots

A few cars still have a king-pin between the wishbones. The pin needs regular lubrication, and extra pivots are used

Ackermann steering

When a car corners, the inside wheel makes a tighter turn than the outside one to prevent the tyres from skidding sideways.

This happens automatically on a cart with a centrally-pivoted beam axle. To obtain the same effect on a car where each stub pivots separately, the inside wheel must move through a greater angle than the outside one. By making the steering system geometrically correct (the Ackermann steering principle) the wheels describe circles all having the same centre.

The effect is achieved by carefully choosing the angle and length of the steering arms attached to the stub-axles, and by making the steering linkage shorter than the distance between the stub-axle pivots.

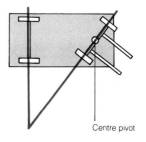
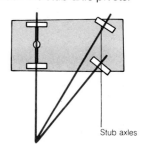

On a cart with a centre-pivoted front beam axle, all wheels automatically steer about the same centre. On a car with two stub axles, the inside wheel must swivel more than the outside one to obtain the same effect

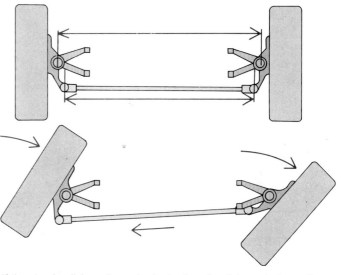

If the steering linkage is made shorter than the distance between the steering pivots, the inside wheel automatically moves through a greater angle than the outside one when steering lock is applied

Wheel alignment

It sounds obvious that when a car is travelling in a straight line the front wheels ought to point straight ahead—and they do. However, when the car is at a standstill, when viewed from above, the front wheels on most cars point in or out very slightly. This is known as toe-in or toe-out.

The small amount of deliberate mis-alignment is set to absorb the fraction of free play that inevitably exists in all suspension and steering linkages. As a rule of thumb, front-wheel-drive cars usually have their wheels set to toe-out, while on rear-wheel-drive cars the front wheels toe-in.

Wheel alignment is altered by shortening or lengthening the track rods, usually by screwing in or unscrewing the ball-joints at the ends. Because the amount of wheel toe-in or toe-out rarely exceeds $\frac{3}{16}$in (4 8mm), it must be set professionally on a special wheel alignment gauge. Even a small amount of mis-alignment can cause rapid tyre wear.

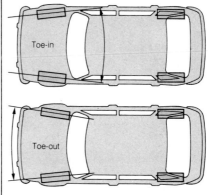

To compensate for a small amount of 'give' in all steering and suspension systems, front wheels are usually set with toe-in (top) or toe-out, when the car is stationary. On the move, the wheels point straight ahead. Toe-out is normally used on front-wheel-drive cars

Steering and brakes

Castor and camber

When a supermarket trolley is pushed, the castoring wheels automatically trail so that the trolley travels in a straight line. The same effect is desirable on a car, so that when it emerges from a corner the steering automatically centres itself.

On a trolley castor, the steering pivot is ahead of the wheel and as soon as the trolley moves, the wheel cannot help but follow. On a car, the steering pivot is near the wheel centre, but a castoring effect can be achieved if the steering pivot is tilted backwards. If an imaginary line drawn through the steering pivot to the road meets the ground ahead of the centre of the tyre contact point, the small amount of resultant castor is sufficient to provide steering that automatically self-centres.

When looked at from the front, the front wheels on most cars lean slightly inwards or outwards. This is known as wheel camber.

Most cars have a slight positive camber, where the wheels at the top are further apart than at the bottom. Wheels that are closer together at the top are said to have negative camber.

Positive camber is used to relieve the stress on the steering linkage. Unlike a bicycle, which has its steering pivot above the centre line of the tyre, a car has its steering pivot alongside the road wheel.

The heavy loading this puts on the pivot can be reduced if the wheel, or pivot axis, or both, are angled so that an imaginary line through the pivot meets the ground at the centre of the tyre contact patch. This is known as centre-point steering, and gives a light action.

Absolute centre-point steering is not used on many cars now because it has been found that a small amount of offset—in which the imaginary line through the pivot meets the ground inside the centre of the tread contact area—reduces feedback and the amount of high speed judder that the road wheels can transmit to the steering wheel, particularly if they are out of balance.

The small amount of offset, which is sometimes referred to as the scrub radius, means that each wheel would try to turn outwards, but as both wheels have the same offset, they cancel each other out under normal driving conditions. If one tyre suddenly deflates, the offset built into the opposite wheel tends to keep the car on a straight course rather than allow it to slew dangerously to one side.

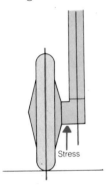
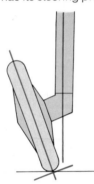

Stress

If the steering pivot is vertically alongside a wheel it is subject to considerable stress. Cambering the wheel and putting the contact area under the pivot relieves much of this

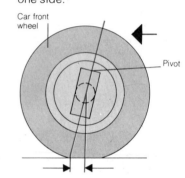

Car front wheel

Castoring trolley wheel

Pivot

Pivot

Supermarket trolley wheels automatically follow behind their pivot when the trolley is moved. A similar effect can be obtained on a car by tilting the steering pivot. Provided a line along its axis meets the ground ahead of the centre of the tyre contact patch, the wheel will castor and the steering will centre itself

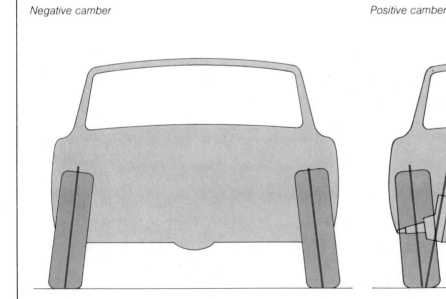

Negative camber

Positive camber

A combination of positive wheel camber and inclination of the steering pivots gives a light steering action. When the suspension is fully compressed, some front wheels adopt a negative camber attitude

Power-assisted steering

Power assistance makes low-speed manoeuvring considerably easier, particularly on large, heavy cars, and reduces the amount of kickback to the steering wheel in the event of a tyre burst.

The main components consist of a pump, which feeds hydraulic fluid to a piston in a cylinder, and a control valve.

Hydraulic fluid or light oil is supplied under pressure by the engine-driven pump to the control valve which is operated by the steering shaft. Movement of the steering column to the left causes the valve to feed high-pressure fluid to one side of the cylinder. This moves the piston, which assists the linkage to move the road wheels to the left. When the steering wheel is turned to the right, fluid pressurises the other side of the piston, moving it in the opposite direction. On some rack-and-pinion systems, the piston is incorporated in the rack unit.

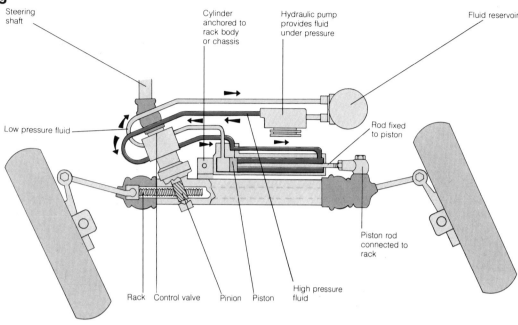

A piston in a cylinder pressurised by hydraulic fluid or light oil helps to move the steering linkage when the steering wheel is turned. Fluid is directed to the appropriate side of the piston by the control valve attached to the steering column

Cornering: oversteer and understeer

Tyres are soft and springy, and this means that the car does not necessarily follow exactly the line of the front wheels. The difference between the direction in which the front wheels point and the actual path taken by the car is called the slip angle.

At low speeds on gentle curves, the car follows almost exactly the direction of the steered wheels and slip angles are small; fast cornering results in larger slip angles, and if the cornering speed is increased sufficiently, a break-away point is reached and the tyre slides sideways.

A car understeers if the slip angles of the front tyres are greater than those of the rear tyres. The car tries to run wide on a bend, and the driver has to correct this by applying extra steering lock.

On an oversteering car, the slip angles are greater at the rear. The car responds quickly to the steering, and in some instances will respond more sharply than the driver intends, swinging the rear of the car outwards. When this happens, the steering needs to be turned in the opposite direction to correct the tail-out attitude.

Most current cars have a small amount of built-in understeer. This gives predictable cornering and better straight-line stability in crosswinds. A car that tends to oversteer usually needs constant steering corrections. This applies even when travelling in a straight line, in order to keep the car on a stable course.

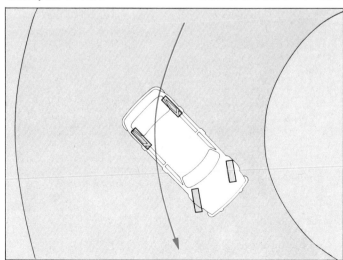

Oversteer: If the rear wheels have the greater slip angle, the car oversteers, sometimes turning into a corner more sharply than the driver anticipates. Opposite steering lock is needed to correct the oversteer

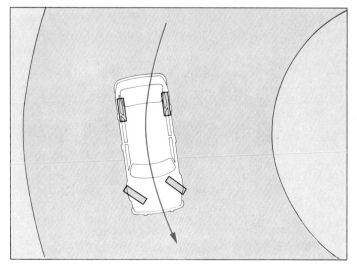

Understeer: Increased slip angles on the front tyres make a car understeer (or run wide) in a corner. The driver needs to apply extra steering lock to maintain the intended cornering line

Steering and brakes

Brakes

A car is slowed down and stopped by the friction generated when stationary lining material rubs against a metal disc or drum turning with each road wheel. Pressing the brake pedal works the brakes on all wheels. The handbrake, which stops the car moving when it is parked, operates on two wheels only.

When the pedal is pressed, it operates a hydraulic system, consisting of pipes, hoses and cylinders filled with a special fluid, which forces the friction material against the wheel discs or drums. The main advantage of hydraulics is that they apply an equal force throughout the system.

Each time the brakes are applied, the rubbing contact produces a high degree of heat, so the friction material has to be made from a temperature-stable material containing asbestos. To cool the brakes, slots in the road wheel promote a flow of air over the brakes when the car is moving.

If the brakes on an overladen car overheat, drums can distort and nearby rubber parts on the hydraulic system may be damaged. Overheating also causes a temporary reduction in brake efficiency, known as brake fade, as the drums expand and very hot friction materials lose some of their grip. Full efficiency returns after the brakes have cooled.

One of the advantages of a drum brake system is that the shoes can be arranged so that they have a self-wrapping or servo action which helps to hold them hard against the drum once they have been applied. On a disc brake, there is no self-servo effect, and a separate vacuum-operated brake servo is sometimes used to reduce the pedal effort.

Drum brakes are shielded to keep out dirt and spray, but if the car is driven through deep water the wet linings will lose their effective grip until they have dried out. Driving the car for a short distance with the pedal lightly depressed will dry them quickly. Disc brakes are not so affected by water— one or two hard applications after a soaking should restore their efficiency.

Any type of frictional contact produces wear. The linings should be examined regularly and, if necessary, renewed.

The hydraulic system

The brakes on early cars were operated by a system of cables or rods, and as the linings wore away, the linkage needed continual adjustment. Nowadays, however, only the handbrake uses a cable or rod linkage, or a combination of the two.

The basic principle of hydraulics is that fluid is virtually incompressible. This means that if a piston and cylinder arrangement, operated by a pedal, is used to generate pressure at one end of a hydraulic pipe in a car's braking system, this will move a second piston at the other end of the pipe, and apply the brake.

Increasing the cross-sectional area of the second piston increases the pressure on the brake. For instance, if the second piston is twice the area of the pedal-operated piston, it will exert twice the force, but will travel only half the distance.

When a car is being braked, about two-thirds of its weight is thrown on to the front wheels. To allow for this, the front brakes are operated by larger pistons than the rear ones.

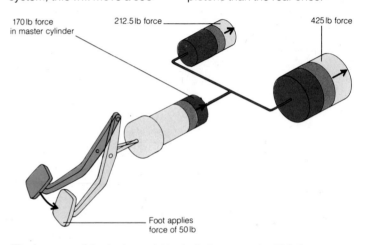

The leverage of the brake pedal typically increases the 50 lb foot pressure to 170 lb in the fluid ahead of the master cylinder piston. The wheel cylinders, here shown 1¼ and 2½ times bigger in area than the master cylinder piston, apply correspondingly more force but with less movement

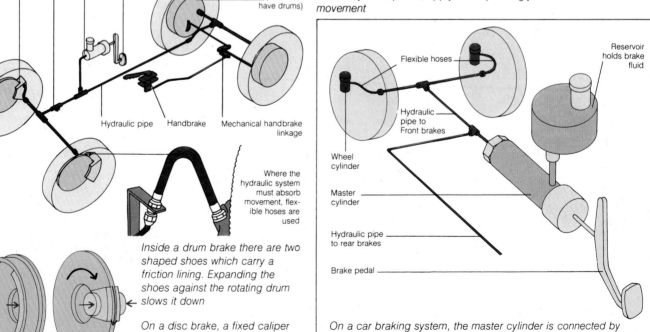

Front brakes (usually discs)
Brake lights switch
Master cylinder
Brake pedal
Rear brakes (most cars have drums)
Hydraulic pipe
Handbrake
Mechanical handbrake linkage
Where the hydraulic system must absorb movement, flexible hoses are used

Inside a drum brake there are two shaped shoes which carry a friction lining. Expanding the shoes against the rotating drum slows it down

Drum brake
Disc brake

On a disc brake, a fixed caliper squeezes two opposing pads against a disc which rotates with the wheel

Flexible hoses
Reservoir holds brake fluid
Hydraulic pipe to Front brakes
Wheel cylinder
Master cylinder
Hydraulic pipe to rear brakes
Brake pedal

On a car braking system, the master cylinder is connected by metal pipes and flexible high-pressure hoses to hydraulic wheel cylinders at each brake

Brake fluid

The hydraulic fluid used in most braking systems is a mixture of vegetable oil, alcohol and additives. It can withstand high temperatures and will not harm the natural rubber seals used in the system.

Over a period, this type of fluid absorbs moisture—mostly through the flexible hoses—which lowers its boiling point. A water content as low as 2 or 3 per cent can lower the boiling point from 428°F (220°C) to 284°F (140°C).

Continuous heavy braking heats up the brakes and causes water droplets in the fluid to vaporise and cause a vapour lock. This vapour is compressible and makes the pedal feel spongy. In some circumstances, it is possible to press the pedal to the floor without the brakes operating.

This vapour-locking can be avoided if the hydraulic fluid is changed for fresh fluid at the recommended intervals.

As a temporary measure, if the brake pedal action becomes spongy during hard use, stop the car and allow the brakes to cool for at least half an hour before continuing at a lower speed. Check that the pedal has its normal firm action before moving off.

Always use new brake fluid to top up the reservoir. Do not be tempted to use the contents of a partly used can which has stood for any length of time—it is likely to have deteriorated. For this reason it is advisable to buy only the smallest can necessary for the job.

Take great care when topping up to ensure that no fluid drops on to the car bodywork —it is a very effective paint stripper.

The master cylinder

The brake pedal is connected by a rod to the master cylinder. Operating the pedal pushes the rod against a hydraulic piston, which in turn forces hydraulic fluid along pipes to wheel cylinders that work the brakes. Hoses, which are flexible to allow for steering and suspension movements, carry the fluid from steel pipes fixed to the body, to the brake assembly at the wheel. A check valve in the end of the master cylinder ensures that there is always a positive pressure in the system when the brakes are off—this helps to prevent air from entering the lines.

When the brake pedal is released, a small passage connecting the master cylinder to a fluid reservoir is uncovered and fluid is gravity-fed from the reservoir to make good any losses. Although fluid should not leak from the system, its volume alters with temperature and some also needs to be added over a period in order to make up for disc pad wear.

It is important that the fluid level in the reservoir should be checked periodically and topped up with clean fluid when necessary.

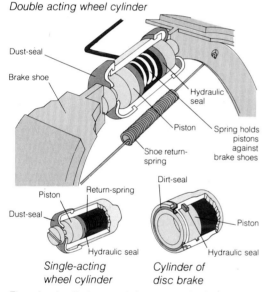

Double acting wheel cylinder

Dust-seal
Brake shoe
Hydraulic seal
Piston
Spring holds pistons against brake shoes
Shoe return-spring

Dirt-seal
Piston
Return-spring
Dust-seal
Piston
Hydraulic seal
Hydraulic seal

Single-acting wheel cylinder *Cylinder of disc brake*

The wheel cylinder expands to press the linings against the drum. Double-acting cylinders have two opposed pistons, whereas a single-acting cylinder has one piston, but the sliding body takes the place of the second piston

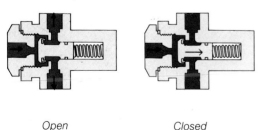

Open *Closed*

A pressure-limiting valve discourages the rear wheels from locking. When pressure in the line rises to a pre-determined level, the valve shuts off fluid to the rear brakes. Rising pressure is then fed to the front brakes which are less likely to lock

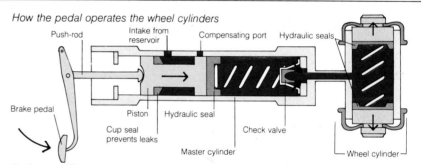

How the pedal operates the wheel cylinders

Push-rod
Intake from reservoir
Compensating port
Hydraulic seals
Brake pedal
Piston
Hydraulic seal
Check valve
Cup seal prevents leaks
Master cylinder
Wheel cylinder

Brakes on: The master cylinder piston moves forward blocking the compensating port from the reservoir and then compressing the fluid ahead of it, thereby forcing out the wheel cylinder pistons

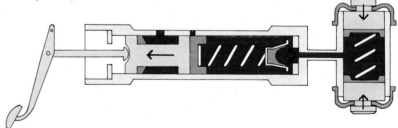

Pedal released: As the master cylinder piston retracts, fluid pushed back by the brake shoe return springs, opens the check valve and re-enters the cylinder. The spring-loaded check valve maintains a slight pressure in the fluid lines

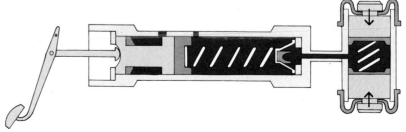

Brakes off: The return spring fully retracts the master cylinder piston, uncovering the reservoir port. The spring between the wheel cylinder pistons keeps the pistons against the brake shoe tips

Steering and brakes

Disc brakes

A disc brake consists of a cast iron disc rotating with the wheel, straddled by a U-shaped caliper which holds two friction-faced pads. When the brake is applied, one or more cylinders in the caliper clamp the pads on to the revolving disc, slowing it down and stopping the car. The principle is very similar to that of a caliper brake on a bicycle.

Because most of the disc is exposed to air flowing beneath the car, it can dissipate its heat more quickly than the more enclosed drum brake. Water spins off it, too. This is why a disc brake recovers its efficiency more quickly after a thorough wetting than a water-logged drum brake. Performance cars which may overheat conventional disc brakes, use ventilated discs with air passages between the rubbed surfaces. The flow of air through the centre keeps disc temperatures down during arduous conditions.

Most discs have a shield to protect their inner face from cross-over water splash from the opposite wheel. Without shields, the inner pads wear more quickly than the outer ones because they are constantly attacked by abrasive dirt and grit.

The friction material on the pads is bonded to a metal backing plate. Steel pins, passing through holes in the caliper and holes in the backing plate, hold the pads in place. Thin steel shims, which pack the pads against the fixing pins, are often fitted behind the backing plate, where they discourage the pads from squeaking and rattling while the brakes are off. As a rule, disc pads are easier to check and replace than brake shoes.

All current calipers have their hydraulic seal in a groove in the cylinder wall. When the brake is applied, fluid pressure moves the plated, smooth-sided piston up against the pad and the seal distorts. Releasing the brake allows the seal to straighten itself, retracting the piston a little. As the pads wear, the piston moves further out, automatically adjusting itself. When the brake is off, the pads lightly rub the disc, but not sufficiently to wear the friction material. The piston is cup-shaped and the edges bear on the backing pad. This limits the heat transferred to the fluid behind it.

Types of caliper

Originally, all calipers had two opposing pistons, each of which operated one pad. Now there are several types, including four-piston calipers used on fail-safe, dual-line braking systems, and compact inexpensive calipers that use just one piston.

Opposed-piston calipers are made in halves which are bolted together at the factory and are not intended to be separated in service. An internal drilling equalises the pressure of hydraulic fluid on the pistons.

A four-piston caliper has two pistons operating each pad. This allows a longer pad with greater frictional area to be used, and if the pairs of opposing pistons are operated by separate hydraulic circuits, a 'fail safe' hydraulic system can be fitted.

Single-cylinder calipers are popularly used on front-wheel-drive cars where there may not be room within the road wheel for an opposed-piston caliper. The single cylinder is mounted on the inner side of the disc.

This type of caliper may have two opposed pistons, one of which operates the inner pad, and the other the outer pad through a sliding-yoke. It may have only one piston, relying on the reaction of the sliding fist-shaped caliper body to apply the outer pad.

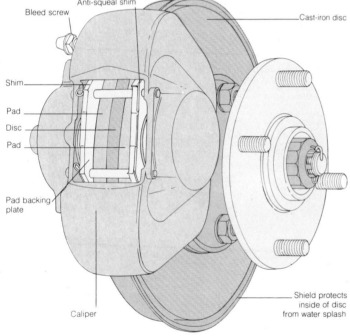

Labels: Anti-squeal shim · Bleed screw · Cast-iron disc · Shim · Pad · Disc · Pad · Pad backing plate · Caliper · Shield protects inside of disc from water splash

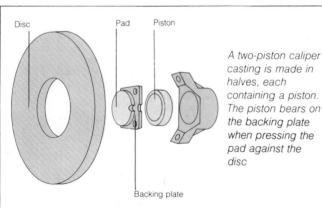

Labels: Disc · Pad · Piston · Backing plate

A two-piston caliper casting is made in halves, each containing a piston. The piston bears on the backing plate when pressing the pad against the disc

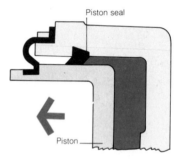

Labels: Piston seal · Piston

Brake applied

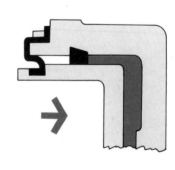

Brake released

Disc pads do not have return springs. Instead, the piston seal, which distorts when the brakes are applied, straightens and retracts the piston slightly once the pedal is released. The pads make light rubbing contact with the disc when the brakes are off

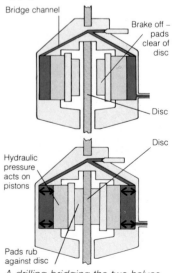

Labels: Bridge channel · Brake off – pads clear of disc · Disc · Disc · Hydraulic pressure acts on pistons · Pads rub against disc

A drilling bridging the two halves of an opposed-piston caliper ensures that each piston receives the same pressure

Drum brakes

The drum is usually made of cast iron and is carried on the revolving hub that turns the wheel. Inside the drum, but mounted on a steel backplate which is rigidly fixed to a stationary part of the axle, there are two curved shoes which have friction linings on their outer faces.

One end of each shoe bears against an anchorage point which acts as a hinge. The other end is pushed outwards by the wheel cylinder and makes contact with the inner surface of the drum when the brake pedal is pressed.

With the brakes off, return springs, stretched between the shoes, pull them away from the drum, providing a small gap between lining and drum, and allowing the wheel to spin freely.

The way in which the brake shoe is moved into contact with the drum affects the power of the brake. Where both shoes share the same hinge point and are expanded by one wheel cylinder, the system has one leading and one trailing shoe. When the linings make contact, the leading shoe is dragged by drum rotation into firmer contact with the moving surface, whereas the rotating drum tries to push away the trailing shoe.

The 'self-wrapping' or self-servo action of the leading shoe can be used to increase the power of a drum brake on the front wheels, where higher braking loads exist, by arranging for both shoes to be leading shoes.

In this case, the shoes are hinged separately at opposite points on the backplate, and two wheel cylinders are used to produce a two-leading-shoe brake system. This layout is not suitable for rear brakes, because when a car is travelling in reverse, or is parked facing up a hill, it becomes a two-trailing-shoe arrangement which needs a very high pedal pressure to apply satisfactorily. On rear wheels, therefore, a leading-and-trailing-shoe system is used.

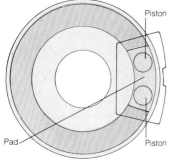

Disc — Hydraulic fluid
Pad — Pad

Piston
Pad — Piston

In four-piston calipers the upper pistons work independently of the lower ones, providing a 'fail safe' system. Longer pads can be fitted

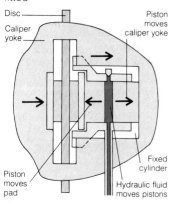

Disc — Piston moves caliper yoke
Caliper yoke
Piston moves pad — Hydraulic fluid moves pistons
Fixed cylinder

One of the pistons in this single-cylinder caliper acts on a pad. The other moves a sliding yoke, applying the other pad

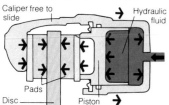

Caliper free to slide — Hydraulic fluid
Pads
Disc — Piston

The 'fist' caliper has only one piston which acts directly on one pad. Hydraulic pressure acting on the sliding caliper body applies the opposite pad

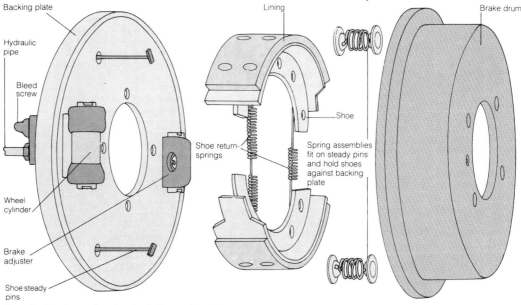

Backing plate
Hydraulic pipe
Bleed screw
Wheel cylinder
Brake adjuster
Shoe steady pins
Lining
Shoe
Shoe return-springs
Spring assemblies fit on steady pins and hold shoes against backing plate
Brake drum

Drum brake shoes, the wheel cylinder, and steady pins and springs are fitted to the stationary backing plate. The drum rotates with the wheel

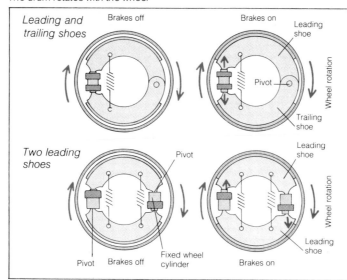

Leading and trailing shoes

Brakes off
Brakes on — Leading shoe
Pivot
Trailing shoe
Wheel rotation

Two leading shoes

Pivot
Leading shoe
Wheel rotation
Fixed wheel cylinder
Pivot — Brakes off
Leading shoe
Brakes on

On a leading and trailing shoe system, where both shoes use the same pivot, the leading shoe is drawn on to the drum by its rotation and exerts more force once it is applied, than the trailing shoe

Two-leading-shoe systems have one wheel cylinder operating each shoe and opposite pivots. The system works well in one direction, but in reverse, it has two trailing shoes and efficiency suffers

Steering and brakes

Linings

Drum brake linings, which contain asbestos, are usually of moulded construction and are riveted or bonded to the shoes. Although it is possible to buy only linings from some specialist sources, most come fitted to service-exchange brake shoes and are specially ground to conform exactly to the inner circumference of the drum.

It is important that linings are inspected by a garage at regular intervals, for if a riveted lining wears below the level of the rivet heads, the rivets will cut grooves in the drum. Once this happens, a new drum must be fitted, as well as replacement linings.

Self-adjusting drum brakes

Cars with front disc brakes, which automatically adjust themselves, often have self-adjusting drum brakes on the rear.

Early systems relied on the action of the handbrake to work an adjuster inside the drum. The problem was, however, that maladjustment or stiffness in the handbrake linkage meant that they did not work properly, and most self-adjusting systems are now triggered by the footbrake.

A popular method is to use an extendable adjuster-rod between the two shoes. A toothed nut threaded on the male section lengthens the rod when it is rotated. When the brakes operate, a small lever, connected to the trailing shoe and with its end resting on the teeth of the nut, is made to move. If brake adjustment is correct, it remains on the same tooth of the nut and adjustment remains unaltered.

As the linings wear and the shoe moves closer to the drum during each brake application, the lever eventually engages with the next tooth when the brakes are released. On the following brake application, the lever rotates the nut one tooth, extending the adjuster-rod and maintaining the correct drum-to-lining clearance.

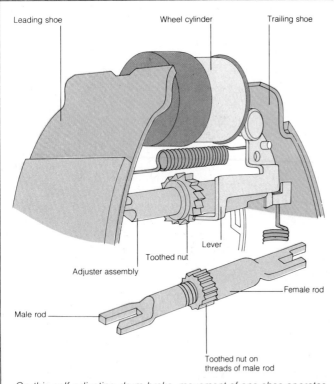

On this self-adjusting drum brake, movement of one shoe operates a lever resting on a toothed nut. As the linings wear, shoe movement increases each time the brakes are applied. Eventually, the lever moves enough to rotate the toothed nut one tooth, lengthening the adjuster assembly and re-adjusting the brakes

Fail-safe hydraulic systems

The big weakness of a hydraulic braking system is that if one pipe springs a leak, pressure is lost throughout the system and the brakes fail.

This can be minimised if the hydraulics are divided into two separate circuits. The simplest method is to fit two pistons in the master cylinder, one for the front brakes, and the other for the rear brakes. If one system fails, the other still works.

The only snag with a front/rear split is that it can leave the car with rear brakes only. This can easily cause skidding and loss of control on wet roads. A more satisfactory arrangement is the two-wheel system, where four-piston calipers are used at the front, each pair of pistons being operated by a separate circuit. If either circuit fails, the worst that can happen is loss of the rear brakes. Since the front brakes do not lock the wheels easily, the car can still be driven to a garage for repair. Some cars have a diagonally-split hydraulic layout where each front wheel shares a circuit with the diagonally opposite rear wheel.

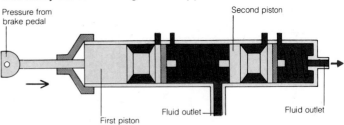

Most dual-line master cylinders have pistons in tandem, each supplying an individual hydraulic circuit

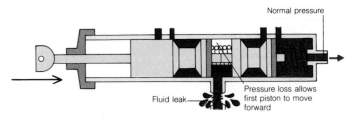

If one line fails, the first piston meets no restriction and closes up to the second, which provides pressure for the second fluid line. The driver notices an increase in pedal travel when this happens

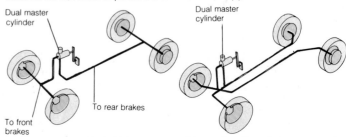

In a front/rear split, half the system remains in operation if a pipe springs a leak

Diagonal-split systems are used on cars with a negative scrub steering geometry (see page 136). Steering control is maintained if one circuit suddenly fails

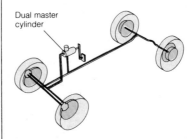

The two-wheel system has one outlet feeding all wheels and the other to half the four-piston front calipers. If one hydraulic line fails the car will have at least its front brakes intact. These provide up to two-thirds of the braking power

Handbrake systems

The handbrake, or parking brake, usually operates on the rear wheels. On most cars it is worked by pulling a lever, although some large North American cars have a foot-operated parking brake.

Where drum rear brakes are fitted, the handbrake operates the same shoes as the foot-brake, pressing them against the drums by levers or cams. The linkage consists of cables or rods, or a combination of both. A ratchet mechanism is built into the lever so that it can be locked on once it is applied.

Disc-type handbrakes are not easy to operate mechanically. One of the problems is that when it is hot, the disc expands and grows slightly thicker. If the handbrake is applied when the disc is very hot, it contracts away from the pads as it cools, easing off the brakes. A drum brake also expands when hot, but as it cools, it contracts on to the shoes, increasing the braking force.

The expansion problem has led to some cars with disc brakes all round, having small extra drum brakes operated solely by the handbrake. Other systems use two additional pads which are worked mechanically by the hand-brake, although many now use a mechanical linkage to operate the existing hydraulic pistons and press the footbrake pads on to the disc.

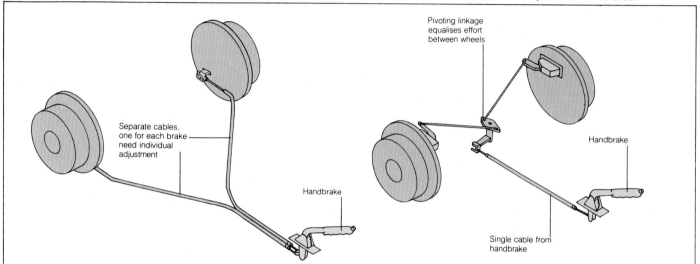

Separate cables, one for each brake need individual adjustment

Handbrake

Pivoting linkage equalises effort between wheels

Handbrake

Single cable from handbrake

Handbrake linkages with a single cable have an equalising mechanism that shares the effort between the rear wheels. Where two cables are used the load on each rear wheel must be individually adjusted. The handbrake lever is set and released with the help of a ratchet and pawl mechanism. Pressing the button at the end of the lever releases the pawl and allows the handbrake to be released. Pull-out handbrakes usually have a twist-to-release action

Power braking

A heavy car with disc brakes needs a high pedal pressure to obtain maximum braking power. Power-assisting the brakes, using a vacuum-operated servo connected into the hydraulic system, reduces the pedal effort.

The servo contains a piston or diaphragm, and is connected into the engine inlet manifold. When the footbrake is operated, manifold vacuum pulls forward the servo piston or diaphragm, moving a hydraulic piston which puts extra pressure on the brake fluid. The amount of servo assistance is proportional to the pressure the driver puts on the pedal.

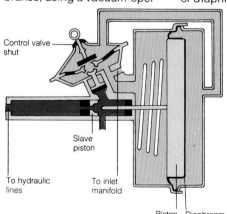

Control valve shut

Slave piston

To hydraulic lines

To inlet manifold

Piston   Diaphragm

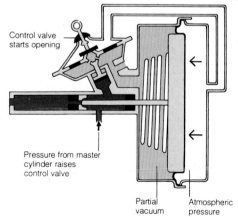

Control valve starts opening

Pressure from master cylinder raises control valve

Partial vacuum

Atmospheric pressure

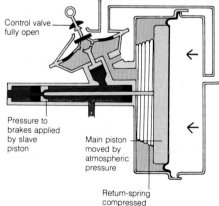

Control valve fully open

Pressure to brakes applied by slave piston

Main piston moved by atmospheric pressure

Return-spring compressed

At rest: With the brakes off, inlet manifold vacuum draws air from both sides of the main piston which is held in position by its return spring

Light braking: Hydraulic pressure from the master cylinder begins to lift the air control valve which admits air to the back of the piston. The vacuum ahead of the piston draws it forward, forcing the slave piston down its bore and adding extra pressure to the hydraulic system

Heavy braking: The air control valve has fully lifted, allowing more air behind the main piston which moves fully forward applying the maximum pressure to the brakes through the slave piston

Steering and brakes projects

Project 71: Fitting a new steering ball-joint

Grading: ⚬⚬⚬
Time: 30min–1hr
Tools: Wheelbrace; jack; axle stands; chocks; wire brush; pliers; spanners to fit ball-joint nuts; taper-breaking tool; hammer; self-grip wrench; lever
Materials: New ball-joint assembly; penetrating oil

Most steering ball and socket joints are lubricated and then sealed for life. Unfortunately the life will be a short one if the external rubber seal becomes damaged. Water will seep in and corrode and wear the joint, causing excessive slackness in the steering.

A worn joint can often be identified by its seal being damaged. It can be checked with the car stationary on level ground. Get a helper to turn the steering wheel back and forth while you reach behind the road wheel and rest a hand on the joint. Any slackness will be felt and may also be visible.

New joints usually come with a new self-locking nut on the end of the tapered pin (split-pinned nuts are no longer used on popular cars). If a joint is supplied without a self-locking nut, buy a new one.

Step 1. Chock the rear wheels, raise the front of the car and support it on axle stands (see pages 14 and 15).
2. Remove rust and dirt from the threads above the ball-pin nut with a wire brush, and apply penetrating oil.
3. Undo the nut. If it has a washer under it, keep it for reassembly.
4. Fit a taper-breaking tool between the top of the ball pin and the underside of the steering arm.
5. Tighten the bolt on the taper-breaker until it forces the pin out of the arm. If the pin is very tight, tap the head of the tightened bolt with a hammer to break the joint.
6. Remove the taper-breaking tool and separate the pin from the arm. (If a taper-breaker is not available, free the joint by impact hammering, as described in Stubborn Brutes, page 11).
7. At the track-rod, unlock the joint from its lock-nut. (Note that on cars with steering boxes, the left track-rod may have a left-hand thread.)
8. Unscrew the joint, counting the number of turns. If the track-rod starts to rotate, use a self-grip wrench to prevent it from turning.
9. Screw the new ball-joint on to the rod. Count the number of turns so that it is in the same position as the old joint. Tighten the lock-nut.
10. Insert the tapered pin into the steering arm, fit the washer, if applicable, and tighten the nut. If the pin revolves, use a lever against the joint to force the pin into the steering arm while the nut is tightened.
11. Lower the car, and have the front wheel alignment checked by a garage on specialist equipment.

Step 3.

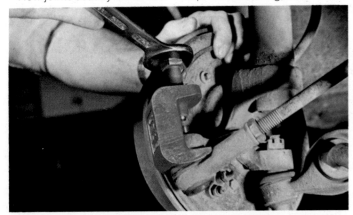
Step 5.

Step 6.

Step 8.

Step 10.

Project 72: Renewing a steering rack gaiter

Grading: ⚬⚬⚬
Time: 1hr-1½hr
Tools: Wheelbrace; jack; axle stands; chocks; pliers; wire brush; spanners to fit ball-joint nuts; taper-breaking tool; hammer; self-grip wrench; lever; wire cutters; screwdriver; oil can
Materials: New rubber gaiter; new clips; grease; paraffin; EP90 oil

A split in the concertina rubber gaiter, also called a boot, sealing each end of a rack and pinion steering unit will allow lubricating oil to leak out and dirt and grit to enter, causing premature wear.

A gaiter should be renewed at the first sign of damage. When buying a new one, remember to specify whether it fits on the left- or right-hand end of the rack housing—many housings have a different diameter at each end.

Step 1. Chock the rear wheels, jack up the car on the side where the gaiter is damaged, remove the road wheel (see Project 68) and fit an axle stand under the chassis (see page 15).
2. Place a drip tray under the gaiter and wipe oil and dirt off the surface of the rubber with a cloth moistened in paraffin.
3. Remove the steering ball-joint (see Project 71) and unscrew the lock-nut from the steering-rod, counting the number of turns.
4. Undo the clip or cut the wire holding the inner end of the gaiter to the rack housing.
5. Undo the small clip clamping the outer end of the gaiter to the steering rod.
6. Slide the gaiter off the steering rod.
7. Smear grease on the sealing surfaces of the new gaiter and slide it into position along the track-rod.
8. Engage the outer end of the

gaiter with the waisted section on the steering rod, fit and tighten the clip.
9. At the inner end, insert the spout of an oil can between the gaiter and rack housing and inject ⅓ pint (190cc) of EP90 oil.
10. Seat the gaiter correctly on the rack housing, then fit the sealing wire or clip.

11. Thread the ball-joint lock-nut on the steering rod, counting the turns to position it correctly, then refit the ball-joint to the steering rod and steering arm (see Project 71).
12. Lower the car and take it to a garage to have the front wheel alignment checked and adjusted, as necessary.

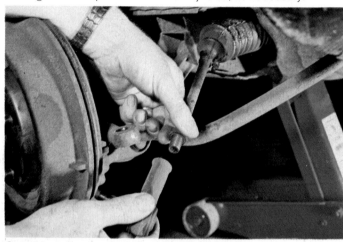

Step 3.

Step 6.

Step 7.

Step 8.

Step 9.

Steering and brakes projects

Changing front disc pads

Disc brake pads should be renewed when, on inspection, the friction material can be seen to be worn to a thickness of about ⅛in (3mm).

There are three main types of front disc brake caliper. The most common is the opposed-piston fixed caliper, in which the pads fit into a hole in the centre. It is not necessary to remove the caliper to change pads, and pad wear can usually be checked visually after removing the road wheel.

The 'fist'-type caliper has one piston and slides on a bracket fixed to the stub axle assembly. This caliper must be taken off the bracket to change pads, although pad wear can usually be checked through a small hole.

The sliding-caliper-type has a single cylinder on one side containing two pistons. It is not removed from the stub axle assembly when changing pads, but the sliding section must be repositioned to make room for a new, thicker pad. Pad wear is checked visually after removing the wheel.

Other calipers may differ in detail, but the principles of pad changing are similar. If you run into difficulties, it is worth remembering that the opposite caliper is a mirror image of the one being worked on and can be used as a reference for the position of components.

Step 5.

Project 73: Opposed-piston caliper

Grading: ♪♪♪
Time: 15min-30min per caliper
Tools: Wheelbrace; jack; pliers; old, bladed screwdriver; spanner to fit bleed screw; piston-retracting tool or approx. 1ft length of hard wood to retract piston
Materials: New disc pads and pins; methylated spirit; new brake fluid; rubber pipe to fit bleed screw; container

Step 1. Jack up the car and remove the front wheel (see Project 68).
2. Turn the steering so that the pads face towards the outside of the wheel arch.
3. If anti-rattle springs are hooked around the pad-fixing pins, make a note of their positions.
4. Remove the two spring clips from the pad-retaining pins.
5. Grip the pins with pliers and pull them out.
6. Using an old screwdriver, gently lever between the pad and the disc to loosen the pad.
7. Grip the backing plate of the loosened pad with pliers and pull it out. If it sticks, push it back into its recess and try again. Repeat Steps 6 and 7 on the opposite pad.
8. Clean dust and rust from the pad recess with an old screwdriver. Any grease can be removed with methylated spirit.
9. Remove any rust from the edge of the disc by resting an old screwdriver on the caliper and spinning the disc.
10. Put a rubber pipe on the bleed screw near the top of the caliper and lead the other end into a container—brake fluid will be expelled when the piston is retracted.
11. Loosen the bleed screw half a turn and use a piston-retracting tool to push the caliper piston fully into its bore. Close the bleed screw and remove the pipe.
12. Insert the new pad into the recess with the friction material facing the disc. If it has an anti-squeal shim behind the backing plate, fit this as well. Arrows on the shims should point in the direction of forward wheel rotation.
13. Repeat Step 11 on the opposite piston. Fit the other pad and shim (see Step 12).
14. Fit the pins through the caliper holes, and the holes in the pad backplates, and shims. Insert the spring clips to retain them. Refit the road wheel, lower the car to the ground, and tighten the wheel fixings.
15. Repeat Steps 1-14 on the opposite caliper.
16. Under the bonnet, check the level of the brake fluid. If necessary, top it up with new fluid. Never re-use the fluid taken from the caliper.
17. Before driving the car, it is essential to operate the brake pedal until normal action is restored. Recheck the brake fluid level.

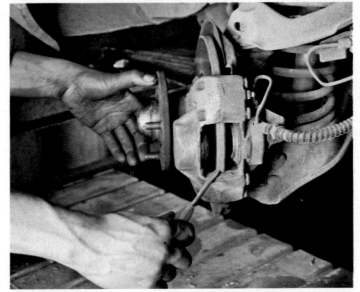
Step 9.

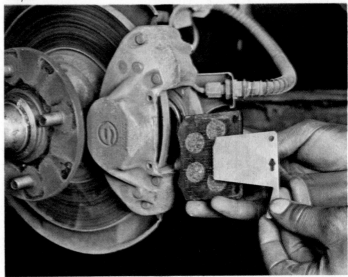
Step 12.

Step 6.

Step 7.

Step 10.

Step 11.

Step 14.

Step 16.

Steering and brakes projects

Project 73A: 'Fist' type caliper

Grading: ⚒⚒⚒
Time: 15min-30min per caliper
Tools: Wheelbrace; jack; pliers; hammer; old screwdriver; wire brush; spanner to fit bleed screw
Materials: New pads; new brake fluid; rubber pipe to fit bleed screw; container

Step 1. Jack up the car and remove the road wheel (see Project 68).
2. Use pliers to straighten the split pins, top and bottom, which locate the caliper guides, and take out the pins.
3. Use a light hammer and an old screwdriver to tap out the caliper guides, top and bottom. Take care not to spread the end of the guide.

4. Press down on the caliper and swing it forward, clear of the spring on the bracket. Lift it and remove it from the bracket.
5. It is important to support the caliper so that it does not strain the hydraulic hose—rest it on a convenient suspension link, or tie it up with string to the suspension.
6. Pull out the upper spring clip to disengage the pad from

the bracket. Remove the pad.
7. Use a wire brush to clean rust and dirt from the pad abutments and the guide seatings.
8. Rest the blade of an old screwdriver on the bracket so that it contacts the edge of the disc. Spin the disc so that the screwdriver scrapes off any flaky rust at the edge.
9 Transfer the spring clips from the old pads to the upper edge

Step 2.

Step 3.

Step 6.

Step 7.

Step 11.

Step 12.

Steering and brakes projects

of the pads to be fitted.

10. Insert the spring end of each new pad into the upper end of the recess, then swing the bottom of the pad into its correct position.

11. Connect a rubber tube to the bleed screw on the caliper and lead the other end into a container—brake fluid will be expelled when the piston is retracted.

12. Open the bleed screw half a turn, then press the caliper piston by hand fully into its bore. Close the bleed screw, remove the pipe and container.

13. Insert the caliper into the bracket. It rests against the wire springs as shown in the picture.

14. Refit the guides, pressing the caliper against the springs, and align the hole in each

guide with the split pin hole in the caliper.

15. Fit new split pins, spreading their ends wide apart and close to the caliper so that they cannot drop out or foul the road wheel. Use pliers to cut off the section overhanging the guide.

16. Refit the road wheel, lower the car and tighten the wheel fixings.

17. Repeat Steps 1-16 on the

opposite caliper.

18. Check the brake fluid level and top up if necessary.

19. Before driving the car, operate the pedal. Initially, it will probably have excessive travel as it repositions the caliper pistons. Continue pumping the pedal until normal braking action is obtained.

20. Recheck the brake fluid level and top up if required.

Step 4.

Step 5.

Step 9.

Step 10.

Step 13.

Step 15.

Steering and brakes projects

Project 74: Adjusting drum brakes

Grading: 🔧🔧
Time: 10min-20min per wheel
Tools: Jack; wheelbrace; wheel chocks; brake-adjusting spanner; if necessary, screwdriver

Some drum brakes have one or two adjusting screws or nuts. These must be turned at regular intervals to move the shoes nearer the drum to compensate for lining wear. Manufacturers usually recommend that this should be done every 5,000-6,000 miles.

Depending on the design of the brake, the adjuster may protrude through the back-plate, where it is accessible from under the car, or will be inside the drum, where it is reached through an access hole. Leading-and-trailing shoes have one adjuster, two-leading-shoe brakes have two.

Car manufacturers do not always provide information in the handbook on adjusting drum brakes. If the adjusters cannot be found, ask the local dealer where they are—the car may have self-adjusting brakes. Make sure that you do not loosen the bleed screw, which will let air into the hydraulic system, in mistake for an adjuster. The bleed screw has a hexagon head with a nipple on the end; adjusters are solid.

On two-leading-shoe brakes, used on the front wheels, the adjusters may need to be turned clockwise or anti-clockwise to move the shoe towards the drum. To avoid confusion, the steps below show how to check for correct rotation on a trial and error basis.

Always use the correct brake-adjusting spanner to rotate a screw adjuster. An open-ended spanner can slip and round off the corners of the square on the screw head, making it impossible to turn the adjuster.

Step 1. Use chocks to prevent the grounded wheel from rolling, release the handbrake and jack up the appropriate side of the car for the brake to be adjusted.
2. Rotate the wheel to make sure that it moves freely. If it does not, check that the handbrake is fully released. On driven wheels you will feel some resistance due to the transmission drag.
3. Most adjustable rear brakes have a single adjuster protruding through the backplate. Locate the adjuster and, on the screw-in type, clean the thread.
4. Rotate the wheel while at the same time turning the adjuster clockwise with a brake-adjusting spanner until the linings are felt to drag against the drum and make it difficult to rotate.

Most adjusters have a 'notch' action with four distinct tight-spots per revolution. Set the adjuster between tight spots.
5. Press the brake pedal to centralise the shoes. If the wheel spins freely, turn the adjuster again until the linings drag. From this point, turn the adjuster in the opposite direction, one notch at a time, until the wheel can be turned freely. A very light rubbing contact is permissible. Repeat Steps 1-4 on the opposite brake.
***** On a few cars the rear drum brakes are adjusted by a toothed or notched nut inside the drum. On these, follow Steps 1 and 2, then remove the plastic or rubber plug in the back-plate or drum.
***3.** Use a screwdriver blade through the access hole against the edge of the nut to rotate it, and turn the wheel. If the linings do not begin to rub the drum after several revolutions, turn the nut in the opposite direction.
***4.** When the linings drag on the drum, follow Step 4 (left).
****** Two-leading-shoe brakes have two adjusters which are set separately. First follow Steps 1 and 2.
****3.** Rotate the wheel and turn one adjuster until the lining drags against the drum.

If the lining does not make contact after half a turn, rotate the adjuster in the opposite direction until it does. Turn the adjuster in the opposite direction until the wheel rotates freely. A small amount of rubbing contact is permissible. Repeat this operation on the other adjuster.
****4.** Press the brake pedal to centralise the shoes.
6. After brake adjustment, lower the car. Check the action of both the brake pedal and the handbrake before driving the car.

Step 3.

Step 4.

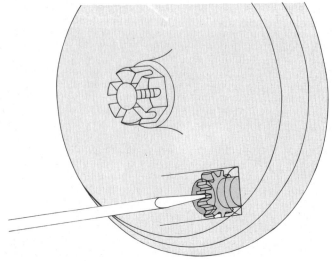

*Step *3.*

Steering and brakes projects

Project 75: Adjusting the handbrake

Grading: ✔✔
Time: 30min–1hr
Tools: Jack; wheelbrace; wheel chocks; axle stands; spanners to fit adjuster nuts
Materials: If necessary, penetrating oil

All handbrake linkages have adjusters so that they can be shortened slightly to allow for cable stretch and for slight wear in the joints.

The rule to observe when adjusting the linkage is that it must always be slightly slack when the brake is fully off. If any tension is present with the handbrake released, the brake shoes or disc pads will be prevented from returning fully to the off position. It can also cause overheating or a long pedal travel. Self-adjusting brakes triggered by the hand-brake cannot adjust themselves if an over-tight linkage prevents them from returning fully to the off position.

Most handbrakes have a single adjuster and a mechanism apportioning the braking effort equally between both wheels. A few have two separate cables—one to each wheel—and these have two adjusters. On two-cable systems the braking effort must be equal when adjustment is made.

Step 1. Adjust the brakes if they have manual adjusters (see Project 74).

2. Chock the front wheels, raise the back of the car and support it on axle stands.

3. Ensure that the handbrake is fully off, and work all the joints in the linkage to check that they move freely. Use penetrating oil to loosen any stiff joints.

4. Loosen the adjuster lock-nut and turn the adjusting nut so that it takes up some of the cable slackness.

5. Relock the adjuster and check that there is still a small amount of slackness in the linkage.

6. Test the handbrake. It should apply the brakes well before it reaches the end of its travel. If it does not, the linkage is worn and should be checked by a garage.

7. Lower the car to the ground.

* Some linkages have one cable for each wheel and two adjusters, usually at the hand-brake lever. On these, first follow Steps 1 to 3.

*4. The threaded adjuster rod will have a hexagonal section. With the handbrake fully off, hold this with a small spanner.

*5. Rotate the adjusting nut at the end of the threaded section clockwise to tighten the cable.

Count the number of turns. Check from under the car that the cable is still slightly slack.

*6. Repeat Step *5 on the other cable, rotating the adjusting nut clockwise the same number of turns.

*7. Lightly apply the hand-brake.

*8. Rotate one road wheel and note the drag on it. Rotate the opposite wheel in the same direction. The drag should be the same. If it is not, loosen the adjusting nut on the cable to the tighter wheel until the drag on both wheels is equal.

*9. Check that the handbrake applies the brakes well before the end of its travel, and that the cable is slightly slack with the handbrake off. If it is not, let a garage check the hand-brake linkage for wear.

*10. Lower the car to the ground.

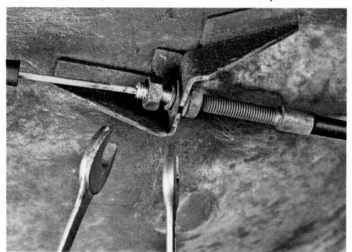

Step 4.

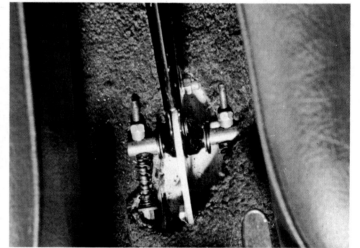

Step *4.

Step *5.

Step *8.

Transmission

The car's transmission takes power from the engine to the road wheels. On a front-engined rear-wheel-drive car it consists of a clutch or a torque converter fixed to the engine flywheel, then a gearbox, propeller shaft and final drive unit which splits the output in half, to drive each rear wheel.

Some cars dispense with the propeller shaft by combining the engine and transmission into one power-pack and mounting it between the driving wheels. This arrangement needs only two drive shafts to transmit power to the wheels.

How the clutch gets a grip

The clutch disconnects the engine from the road wheels when the driver is changing gear or bringing the car to a stop.

The clutch action can be likened to the operation of a sanding disc on a power drill. If this is rotated and brought face-to-face with a separate stationary sanding disc, as the two faces meet the initial frictional contact will make the second disc turn slowly, but as pressure is increased, both discs will turn at the same speed.

On a car engine the same effect is achieved by sandwiching a friction-lined disc (the driven plate, which is attached to the gearbox input shaft) between a pressure plate and the engine flywheel face.

The pressure plate is connected to a cover bolted to the flywheel. Operating the clutch pedal moves the pressure plate away from the flywheel, and the driven plate between them can rotate independently. When the driver lifts his foot off the clutch pedal, the pressure plate moves towards the flywheel again, clamping the driven plate and linking the gearbox shaft to the flywheel.

Although it is possible to slip the clutch by partial operation of the clutch pedal, it is essential that the clutch does not slip when the pedal is fully released. On most cars the clamping load is applied by a powerful diaphragm spring—a cone of spring steel that is fitted so that at rest its outer rim pushes the pressure plate towards the flywheel. Operating the pedal moves a thrust bearing against the centre of the diaphragm, causing it to dish away from the flywheel, thus releasing the clamping load on the pressure plate.

Before diaphragm springs became available, a circle of coil springs bearing on the rear face of the pressure plate applied the clamping load.

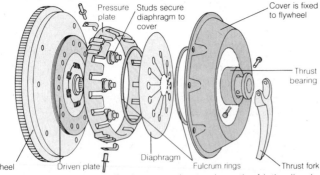

The modern clutch uses a diaphragm spring to clamp the friction-lined driven plate between the flywheel face and pressure plate

Labels: Pressure plate · Studs secure diaphragm to cover · Cover is fixed to flywheel · Thrust bearing · Flywheel · Driven plate · Diaphragm · Fulcrum rings · Thrust fork

Linking the pedal to the clutch

The clutch is operated either hydraulically or by a cable. On a cable system a heavy-duty flexible cable is routed from the pedal through the bulkhead of the engine compartment and runs down the side of the engine to a clutch-operating lever. At one end of the cable there are adjusting nuts to compensate for any cable stretching.

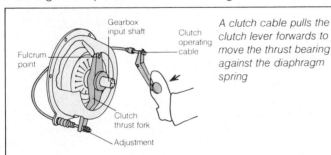

A clutch cable pulls the clutch lever forwards to move the thrust bearing against the diaphragm spring

Labels: Gearbox input shaft · Clutch operating cable · Fulcrum point · Clutch thrust fork · Adjustment

Pressure plate

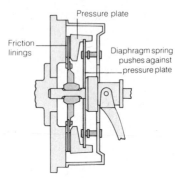

Clutch engaged

Labels: Friction linings · Diaphragm spring pushes against pressure plate

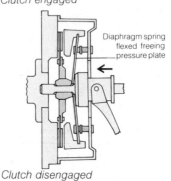

Clutch disengaged

Labels: Diaphragm spring flexed freeing pressure plate

Hydraulic clutch systems have a master cylinder connected to the pedal, attached by a hydraulic pipe to a slave cylinder which is joined to the clutch-operating lever.

In a hydraulic layout, pedal pressure on a master cylinder forces fluid into a slave cylinder which operates the thrust bearing through a linkage

Labels: Master cylinder · Directing linkage · Slave cylinder

Manual gearboxes

Because the internal combustion engine produces very little power at low speeds it cannot be directly linked to the road wheels, and must, therefore, be geared down. At 70mph, for instance, most small cars have their engines running at about 4,000 revolutions per minute while the road wheels are turning at about 1,000rpm.

The gearing-down is achieved by reduction gears in the final drive, and if the car travelled constantly at 70mph, this is all that would be needed. However, besides travelling on motorways, the car must be able to start from a standstill and tackle steep hills. In order to keep the engine working at its most efficient speed under all conditions, all cars have a gearbox. The most popular type is a manual gearbox which offers four choices of gear ratio.

Gear ratios are determined by the number of teeth on meshing gear wheels. If a gear wheel with 12 teeth is meshed with a gear wheel having 24 teeth, the smaller gear must rotate twice to turn the bigger gear once and the ratio of these two gears would be 2:1. The final drive that reduces 4,000rpm at the engine to 1,000rpm at the wheels has a ratio of 4:1.

To move it from a standstill, the average small car has a bottom gear ratio of around 3.5:1. Other typical gearbox ratios are about 2:1 in second gear, 1.4:1 in third and 1:1 in top. All these are in addition to the final-drive ratio, so with a

Pressing the pedal forces fluid into the slave cylinder which operates the clutch. The principle of hydraulic operation is explained in 'Steering and Brakes' (pages 138 and 139).

final drive of 4:1, by multiplying the ratios the *overall* gear ratios become: 1st gear 14:1 (14 revolutions of the engine to one turn of the road wheels), 2nd 8:1, 3rd 5.6:1 and top 4:1. Cars with bigger engines use slightly different ratios.

Selecting the gears

The sliding of gear wheels into and out of mesh edge-on is a difficult and potentially damaging operation needing a lot of skill. All current cars overcome this by using constant-mesh gearboxes, where the forward gears are permanently in mesh and are engaged or disengaged by locking them to the output shaft.

The freewheeling gears are engaged with the splined shaft by collars which rotate with the shaft but are free to slide along the splines. These collars have tooth-like projections on the sides known as a dog-clutch. This interlocks with mating teeth on the side of the gear wheel to lock it to the shaft. The collars are moved along

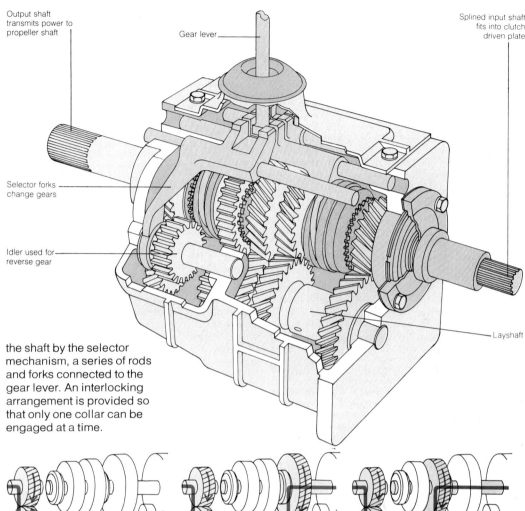

the shaft by the selector mechanism, a series of rods and forks connected to the gear lever. An interlocking arrangement is provided so that only one collar can be engaged at a time.

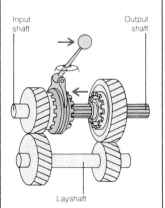

A dog clutch interlocks its teeth with mating teeth on the side of each gearwheel to lock it to the output shaft

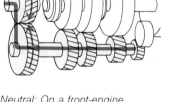

Neutral: On a front-engine rear-wheel-drive gearbox the input shaft has a single fixed gear in mesh with the layshaft where all the gears are fixed. Above it, the output shaft has gears that free-wheel. In neutral no drive is transmitted

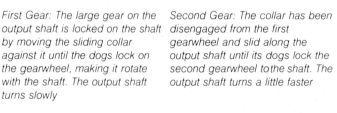

First Gear: The large gear on the output shaft is locked on the shaft by moving the sliding collar against it until the dogs lock on the gearwheel, making it rotate with the shaft. The output shaft turns slowly

Second Gear: The collar has been disengaged from the first gearwheel and slid along the output shaft until its dogs lock the second gearwheel to the shaft. The output shaft turns a little faster

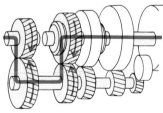

Third Gear: The second gear collar is disengaged and the dog clutch on the leading collar engages with the third gearwheel. The selector mechanism has an interlock to prevent two gears being selected at once

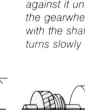
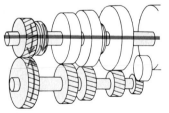

Top Gear: The input and output shafts are joined together by sliding the leading collar forward, providing a straight-through drive from the engine to the propellor shaft

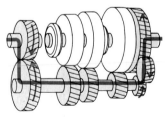

Reverse: An idler is engaged between the layshaft and the reverse gearwheel. This reverses the direction of the output shaft

Transmission

Synchromesh

One problem with a dog-clutch is that its teeth will clash if they meet at different speeds. Virtually all modern gearboxes have synchromesh—a system that gets the gearwheel turning at the same speed as the collar so that the dogs engage smoothly and quietly.

Synchromesh is commonly used on all forward gears, although a few cars have an unsynchronised first gear. It is not usual to use synchromesh on reverse. It works in the same way as a friction clutch. The collar is in two parts, and contains an outer toothed ring, spring-loaded to sit centrally on a synchromesh hub.

When the outer ring is moved by the selector mechanism towards a gear wheel, before its teeth can engage with the teeth on the gear, a conical section on the hub meets a mating cone on the gear. When the cones touch, the gear speeds up, and once it is revolving at the same speed as the collar, the dogs will engage silently.

If the gear lever is moved quickly, it is possible to 'beat' the synchromesh and grate the dog teeth. A later development is to fit a ring, called a baulking ring, between the cone on the gear wheel and the teeth of the collar. The baulking ring physically prevents gear engagement until the gear wheel is revolving at the same speed as the collar.

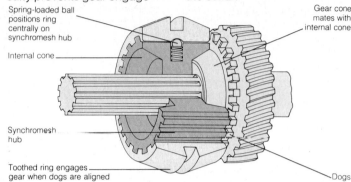

A synchromesh system uses a cone-type friction clutch to speed up the gear so the outer locking ring and dogs engage smoothly

Fluid drive systems

Instead of having a pedal-operated friction clutch between the engine and gearbox, it is possible to use an impeller and a turbine, immersed in oil, to transmit the power.

On a fluid flywheel, the engine-driven impeller faces the turbine connected to the gearbox. Each is bowl-shaped and contains a number of partitions or vanes. The impeller and turbine can be likened to two hollowed-out halves of an orange, facing each other.

When the engine is idling, oil is flung from the rotating impeller into the turbine, but because the impeller is turning slowly, the turbine does not move.

As engine speed increases, so does the centrifugal force acting on the oil. The fast-moving oil is thrown into the turbine with increasing force and the turbine begins to revolve, setting the car in motion. After giving up its energy to the turbine, the oil re-enters the impeller at the centre and is recirculated to the turbine.

As the car accelerates, the difference in rotational speeds between impeller and turbine gradually diminishes until there is only about two per cent slip between them.

One of the problems with a fluid flywheel is that it is slow to react when the car is moving off from a standstill. This can be improved if a reactor which has a number of blades just like a ship's propeller, is fitted between the impeller and turbine to redirect the oil flow at low speeds. This makes the fluid flywheel into a torque converter.

The reactor is locked to the gearbox casing by a one-way clutch. In a fluid flywheel, oil returning from the turbine tends to slow down the impeller. In a torque converter, the reactor directs the oil along a more favourable path towards the centre of the impeller, giving extra thrust to the turbine blades.

When moving off from a standstill, the torque converter can double the turning effort produced by the engine and applied to the gearbox. As engine speed increases, the torque multiplication tapers off until at cruising speed there is no increase in torque at all. The reactor then freewheels, spinning in the oil at the same speed as the turbine, and the torque converter operates like a fluid flywheel.

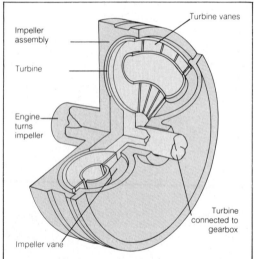

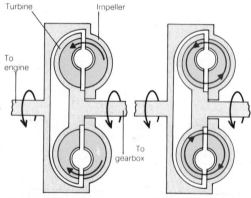

At low engine speeds, centrifugal force throws oil from the impeller to the turbine and rotates the turbine slowly

At high engine speeds, the oil moves more quickly, forming a fluid bond between the two halves with very little slip

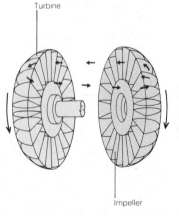

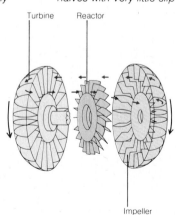

The fluid flywheel is slow to react when moving from a standstill. The torque converter has a centre reactor which re-directs oil flow at low speeds giving increased 'bite' when moving off

The automatic gearbox

The basis of the automatic gearbox is a 'gear within a gear' called a planetary or epicyclic gear train. It consists of a central sun wheel in mesh with smaller planetary gears rotating round it on a planet carrier, and an internally-toothed outer ring gear called an annulus.

Each part of the epicyclic gear—the sun wheel, planet carrier and annulus—is usually connected to a drive shaft. By holding stationary any one of these elements, the speed of the other two can be altered.

If the sun wheel is held stationary and the planet carrier rotates, the planets will roll round the sun wheel and drive the annulus in the same direction as the carrier, but at a different speed.

If the planet gears are locked, or if the sun wheel is locked to the annulus, the gear train will revolve as one unit.

If the planet carrier is held stationary, rotating the sun wheel causes the annulus to rotate in the opposite direction.

If the annulus is locked, and the planet carrier revolves, the planet gears will drive the sun wheel in the same direction as the carrier but at a different speed.

To provide the appropriate number of gears, automatic gearboxes have two sets of epicyclic gears mounted in tandem. The appropriate elements in the gear train are held stationary by a system of hydraulically-operated brake bands and clutches. They are worked by a series of hydraulically-operated valves in the bottom of the gearbox.

Oil pressure to operate the clutches and brake bands is provided by a pump in the gearbox, taking its supply from a reservoir of automatic transmission fluid in the gearbox sump.

Unless the selector valves are operated by the gear selector in the car, automatic gearchanges are made dependent upon the throttle opening (a cable relays throttle movement to the gearbox) and road speed. When the car reaches a pre-set speed, a governor allows gearbox pump pressure to take over from the throttle control and a change is made to a higher gear.

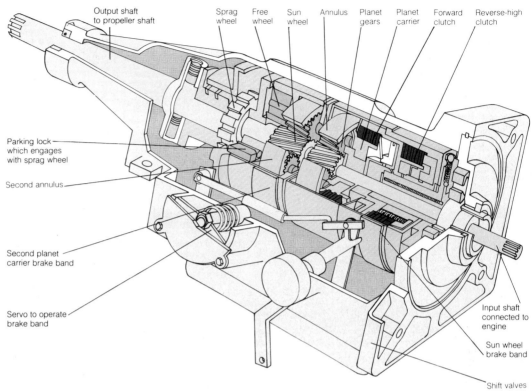

Labels: Output shaft to propeller shaft · Sprag wheel · Free wheel · Sun wheel · Annulus · Planet gears · Planet carrier · Forward clutch · Reverse-high clutch · Parking lock which engages with sprag wheel · Second annulus · Second planet carrier brake band · Servo to operate brake band · Input shaft connected to engine · Sun wheel brake band · Shift valves in base

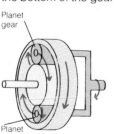

With the sun wheel locked, the planet wheels orbit around it, turning the carrier and annulus at different speeds

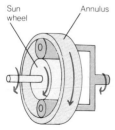

When the sun wheel is locked to the annulus, the planets cannot orbit and the complete unit turns at the same speed

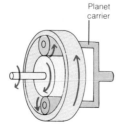

If the planet carrier is locked, the sun wheel rotates the planet wheels, turning the annulus in the opposite direction

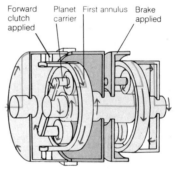

First gear: The line shows power flow through the two epicyclic gears. Driving the front annulus and braking the rear planet carrier gives two gear reductions

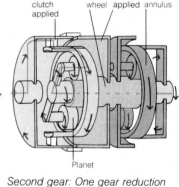

Second gear: One gear reduction is achieved by driving the first annulus and braking the common sun wheel

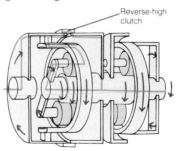

Top gear: All gears are held stationary in relation to each other, and the complete assembly rotates to provide direct drive

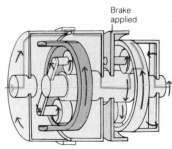

Reverse: Braking the second planet carrier causes the rear annulus and output shaft to turn in the opposite direction

Transmission

Propeller shaft

The propeller shaft that connects the gearbox of a front-mounted engine to the final drive on the rear axle not only has to transmit the full power of the engine, but must also be able to rise and fall and change its length slightly to allow for movement of the rear suspension.

The most usual way of doing this is to put a universal joint— usually of the Hooke type—at each end of the shaft, and arrange for it to slide backwards and forwards slightly where it fits on the splines of the gearbox output shaft.

On some cars the propeller shaft is in two pieces, supported near its centre by a bearing bolted to the underside of the car body. This type has three universal joints.

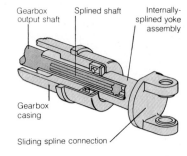

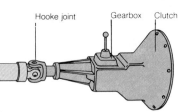

A propeller shaft has two or three universal joints and is free to slide a little along its length – usually by providing a sliding spline connection at the gearbox end

Constant-velocity joints

Front-wheel-drive cars need a joint at the outer end of each drive shaft that not only allows for suspension movement, but also permits the wheels to steer. The constant-velocity joint, which uses steel balls trapped in the internal grooves of a spherical joint, achieves this.

One of the most widely used designs is the Birfield constant-velocity joint. This has a hollow socket on one shaft, with six grooves machined inside the socket in line with the axis of the shaft.

Inside this fits a ball which is attached to the other section of shaft. There are six grooves in the sides of the ball.

Between the ball and socket

Hooke-type universal joints

The Hooke-type joint allows two shafts to be joined and rotate as one, even when they are slightly out of alignment.

The heart of the joint is a cross-shaped spider that links two yokes on each shaft at right-angles to each other.

Simple and cheap to make, the Hooke joint is widely used on articulating shafts where the angle of mis-alignment is small. At greater angles, the relative speeds of the shafts fluctuate.

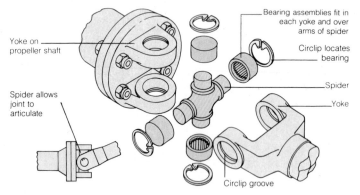

A Hooke-type universal joint uses a cross-shaped spider to link two yokes on each shaft, allowing the two shafts to rotate and articulate at the same time

Drive shafts, joints and couplings

Front-engined, front-wheel-drive cars and rear-engined cars that drive their rear wheels do not have the benefit of a long propeller shaft which twists slightly and cushions the shock of starting from rest.

Instead, the drive shafts on these cars usually have a flexible inner coupling, that allows the shaft to flex, or 'wind up' a little when the clutch is let in.

The most popular types of flexible coupling are the rubber spider joint, in which rubber sleeves surround a central cross-shaped spider to absorb transmission shock, and the hexagonal rubber 'doughnut' joint, which is bolted between two triangular flanges on the ends of the input and output shafts and allows a little end movement of the shaft, as well as cushioning sudden transmission loads.

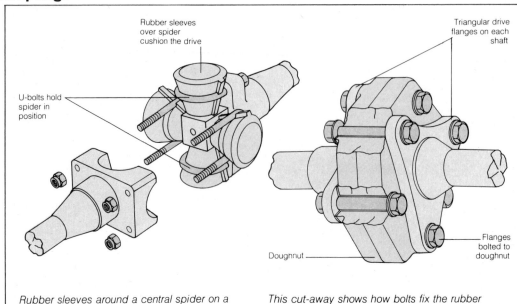

Rubber sleeves around a central spider on a universal joint absorb transmission shocks

This cut-away shows how bolts fix the rubber doughnut joint to two three-cornered flanges but do not connect the flanges directly

is a cage holding six steel balls which engage with the two sets of grooves.

One shaft drives the other through the balls, and when the shafts are out of line the balls move in the grooves. This prevents any fluctuations in speed.

The wide angles and the absence of speed variation made possible by this joint make it ideal for the roadwheel end of a front wheel drive shaft.

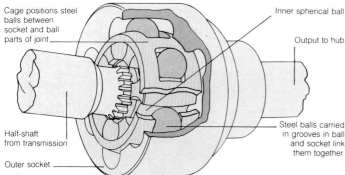

Cage positions steel balls between socket and ball parts of joint

Inner spherical ball

Output to hub

Half-shaft from transmission

Steel balls carried in grooves in ball and socket link them together

Outer socket

The Birfield constant velocity joint transmits power through steel balls linking the ball-and-socket joint

The final drive

On a front-engined rear-wheel drive car, the final drive unit does three jobs: it gears down the engine so that it can turn the road wheels at a suitable speed in top gear, it takes the drive from the propeller shaft through a right-angle and transmits it to the rear wheels, and it drives the wheels at different speeds when cornering to prevent the inside wheel from skidding.

Both the gearing down and turning of the drive at right-angles are achieved by the crownwheel and pinion.

The pinion is directly driven by the propeller shaft. On a small car it may have 10 teeth, whereas the crownwheel has perhaps 40, giving a gear ratio of 4:1. The crownwheel teeth,

on the side of the wheel, are bevelled to mesh with the pinion teeth so that the drive is transmitted through 90 degrees.

On rear axles, the pinion is below the centre-line of the crownwheel. This is known as the hypoid drive, and is designed to keep more teeth in mesh, making the final drive stronger. It also reduces noise and allows a shallower propeller tunnel to be used inside the car.

On cars with transverse engines, the drive does not have to be turned through 90 degrees and the crownwheel and pinion are replaced by two spur gears which mesh in the same way as the constant-mesh gears in the gearbox.

How the differential provides traction

When a car travels round a corner, the outside wheel travels further than the inside one. If both wheels were driven at the same speed, the inside wheel would skid as it attempted to make the same number of revolutions as the outer one.

To prevent this, each driving wheel is rotated by its own half-shaft and the two shafts are driven by a differential connected to the crownwheel. The differential consists of two pinions mounted on a spindle fixed to the crownwheel and in mesh with a bevel gear on the inner end of each half-shaft.

On a straight road, the diff-erential pinions remain stationary and the half-shafts are driven at the same speed. On a corner, however, when the inside wheel has less distance to travel, its reluctance to turn at the same speed as the outside wheel is transmitted along the shaft to the differential and the pinions rotate, allowing the inside wheel to slow down and the outside wheel at the same time to speed up.

On corners, the crownwheel turns at the average speed of the two road wheels. If the inner wheel turns at 70rpm and the outer one at 80rpm, the crownwheel will turn at 75rpm.

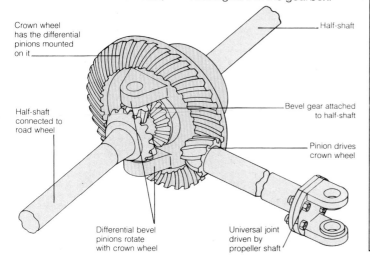

Crown wheel has the differential pinions mounted on it

Half-shaft

Half-shaft connected to road wheel

Bevel gear attached to half-shaft

Pinion drives crown wheel

Differential bevel pinions rotate with crown wheel

Universal joint driven by propeller shaft

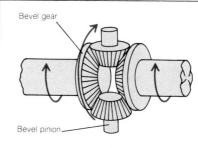

Bevel gear

Bevel pinion

When both drive shafts are travelling at the same speed, the bevel pinions orbit with the bevel gears, but do not rotate on their axes

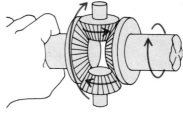

If one shaft is stopped, the bevel gears turn on their axes, orbiting round the stationary gear and driving the other half-shaft

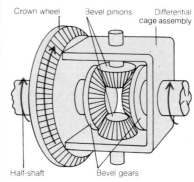

Crown wheel

Bevel pinions

Differential cage assembly

Half-shaft

Bevel gears

In the final drive the differential is in a cage driven by the crown wheel. When the car is travelling in a straight line the bevel pinions orbit, but do not spin on their axes, and the unit drives both half-shafts equally

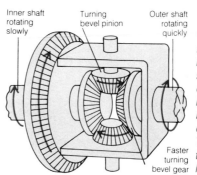

Inner shaft rotating slowly

Turning bevel pinion

Outer shaft rotating quickly

Faster turning bevel gear

When taking a bend, the bevel gear on the inner half-shaft turns more slowly than the crownwheel, and the outer half shaft, driven by the bevel pinions turns correspondingly faster. The crownwheel turns at the average of the half-shaft speeds

Transmission projects

Project 76: Adjusting a clutch cable

Grading: ∽∽
Time: 10min-20min
Tools: Axle stands or drive-up ramps; chocks; feeler gauges; steel rule; spanners to fit clutch-adjusting nut and lock-nut; pliers; screwdriver
Materials: If required, timber to wedge up pedal

Many popular cars have cable-operated clutches, where the cable is provided with a screwed adjustment at one end to allow for clutch lining wear and a small amount of cable stretch.

Although there are many different methods of adjustment, almost all aim for the same result. There must be a small amount of slackness in the cable when the pedal is released. The actual amount of slackness varies from car to car (it will be given in the handbook) and is measured either from under the car, where the cable meets the bell-housing, from under the bonnet, where it abuts with the bulkhead, or from inside the passenger compartment, at the clutch pedal. Some typical examples are illustrated.

Step 1. Raise the front of the car on drive-up ramps or on axle stands, apply the handbrake and chock the rear wheels (see pages 14 and 15).
2. On smaller Ford cars, use a block of timber to wedge the clutch pedal fully upwards.
3. From under the car, pull the outer cable away from its seating on the bell-housing and measure the gap between the adjusting nut and the bell-housing. It should agree with the measurement given in the handbook.
4. If adjustment is needed, unlock the nuts by undoing them in opposite directions, rotate the nut nearest the bell-housing to obtain the correct clearance, then lock it in position with the other nut. Recheck the gap.
*2. On some cars the adjustment is checked at the clutch-operating arm. On the Talbot Avenger, for example, raise the front of the car (see Step 1) and remove the external coil spring

hooked on to the operating lever.
*3. With pliers, pull the inner cable towards the rear of the car—this fully raises the pedal—and check the gap between the ball-ended adjustment nut and the arm. If it needs adjusting, loosen the lock-nut and turn the adjuster, locking it when the correct clearance is obtained. Recheck the clearance before refitting the coil spring.
**2. If the car has an adjuster at the bell-housing, the free play is measured at the pedal. On

the Fiat 128, for example, the adjuster is unlocked and turned until there is 1in (2.5cm) of free play between the pedal pad in the fully released position and the moment when the clutch cable begins to tighten.
***2. The Vauxhall Cavalier is one of the few cars with no free play in the clutch-operating linkage—its clutch-release bearing is of the constant-contact type. With the car on ramps or stands (see Step 1), a squared adjuster in the bell-housing is turned to give a specific measurement between

the operating arm and the cable abutment.
***3. There is a second adjustment at the bulkhead where the cable has a circlip and groove adjuster. Prise out the circlip with a screwdriver. Ask a helper to switch on the ignition and watch the clutch-wear indicator light in the facia, while from under the bonnet the clutch cable is pulled away from the bulkhead, exposing more grooves. When the light goes on, fit the circlip in the third groove away from the bulkhead mounting.

Step 2.

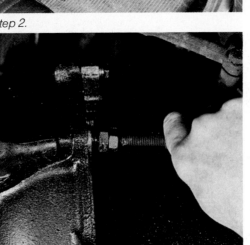
Step 3.

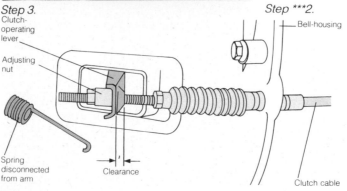
Step *3.

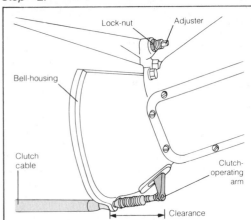
Step **2.

Step ***2.

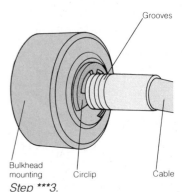
Step ***3.

Project 77: Renewing a clutch cable

Grading: ✧✧✧
Time: 30min-1hr
Tools: Axle stands or drive-up ramps; chocks; pliers; screwdriver; spanners to fit cable-adjusting nut and lock-nut
Materials: New clutch cable

If a clutch cable is seen to have a broken strand, the complete cable should be renewed

before the inner cable snaps.
Step 1. Before attempting to renew a frayed cable, lift the bonnet and make a sketch of the route that the cable takes between various components. If the new cable is mis-routed, either it will not fit, or it will break quite soon.
2. Raise the front of the car, supporting it on axle stands or drive-up ramps. Apply the handbrake and chock the rear wheels (see pages 14 and 15).

3. Slide the driver's seat right back, wriggle under the facia and disconnect the cable from the top of the pedal. It may be held by a clevis pin or a clip, or it may simply be hooked on. Keep any pins and clips in a safe place for reassembly.
4. Underneath, uncouple any external springs tensioning the clutch-operating arm, and remove the cable from the operating arm. If there is a rubber cover, peel it back. The cable may be attached to the arm by two nuts, or might have a soldered nipple on the end which is slid along a slot and through a hole to release it.
5. Pull the outer cable from its mounting point on the bell-housing, saving any spacers and insulators. From under the

bonnet, pull it forwards away from its mounting at the bulkhead.
6. Thread the new inner cable through the hole in the bulkhead mounting.
7. Inside the car, connect the inner cable to the top of the clutch pedal, refitting the pins and clips as appropriate.
8. Route the cable through the engine compartment to the bell-housing. Fit it on its abutment at the bell-housing, fitting any spacers or insulators, and connect it to the clutch-operating arm. If necessary, wind back any adjusting nuts on the cable to allow it to reach. Refit any tensioning springs to the arm.
9. Adjust the cable (see Project 76) and refit any rubber covers.

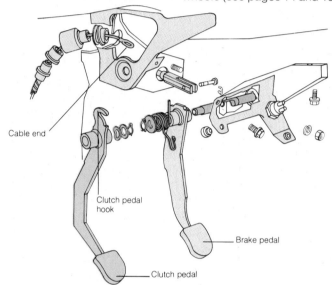

Step 3.

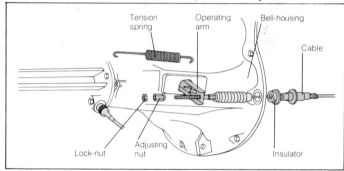

Step 4.

Project 78: Renewing a 'doughnut' joint

Grading: ✧✧✧
Time: 1hr-2hr, depending on the amount of dismantling needed
Tools: Jack; axle stands; chocks; spanners to fit nuts and bolts on joint; large screwdriver; snips; wire brush
Materials: New rubber doughnut joint; new fixing bolts, nuts and washers

Some cars use a Rotoflex rubber coupling, commonly called a 'doughnut' joint, instead of a Hardy-Spicer universal joint in the propeller shaft or drive-shaft.

A worn 'doughnut' coupling distorts under acceleration and braking, and at times the yokes hit the fixing nuts in front of and behind them, causing a knocking or clicking sound.

If you can see the doughnut joint with the car on the ground,

it can be checked for distortion by engaging bottom gear and rolling the car back and forth, preferably with the aid of a helper. A small amount of movement is permissible, but if the shaft yokes move more than a fraction of an inch in relation to each other, the coupling should be renewed.

If the coupling cannot be checked in this way, it can be checked statically. Levering it sideways with a large screw-

driver will indicate if it has softened (it will probably be covered in oil if this is the case) and will show up any cuts in the rubber.

New couplings are supplied encased in a metal band, and they must be fitted with this in position. The band is removed only after all the bolts have been tightened.
Step 1. Chock the front wheels, jack up the rear of the car and fit axle stands.

2. Wire-brush any dirt from around the fixing nuts and bolts and undo them. Remove the doughnut joint from between the two yokes.
3. Clean the faces of the yokes with a wire brush, then slide the new joint between them. Align the bolt holes and fit the new bolts and nuts. Tighten the nuts alternately on each side.
4. Use snips to cut through the outer metal band and remove it from the joint.

Step 2.

Step 4.

Transmission projects

Project 79: Overhauling a Hardy-Spicer universal joint

Grading: ᘓᘓᘓ
Time: 1½hr-2hr
Tools: Jack; axle stands; chocks; large screwdriver; spanner to fit flange nuts and bolts, and centre bearing fixings, where applicable; soft-faced mallet or copper hammer; circlip pliers; large vice; two small sockets; old paint-brush; small screwdriver; rat-tail file; draining tray for gearbox oil
Materials: Universal joint overhaul kit; paraffin; high-melting-point grease; gearbox oil

A faulty universal joint in the transmission makes a clonking noise when the drive is taken up, or when the accelerator is released.

From under the car, check to see if the four bearing cups on a Hardy-Spicer joint are secured by circlips. If they are, the joint can be overhauled by fitting a DIY bearing kit. Do not attempt to overhaul a Hardy-Spicer joint unless you have a large engineers' vice.

Some propeller shaft joints have just two circlips, or none at all. These use staked-type joints, and if a joint fails, the complete propeller shaft must be renewed. The illustrations show how to overhaul a universal joint retained by circlips.

Step 1. Chock the front wheels, jack up the car at the rear and fit axle stands (see pages 14 and 15).

2. To check for wear, use a large screwdriver to try to lever the centre spider away from each yoke in turn. If the spider and yoke move, the joint should be overhauled.

3. Mark the flanges of the propeller shaft and the final drive so that they can be refitted in the same position. If there is a centre bearing, scribe a line round the bearing housing.

4. Place a tray under the gearbox to catch any oil. Remove the nuts and bolts holding the propshaft and final drive flanges together. If the shaft has a centre bearing, remove any bolts holding it to the underside of the body. Pull the flanges apart, lower the prop-shaft, and then pull it from its

attachment splines at the gearbox end.

5. Clean the joints with a brush dipped in paraffin. Use circlip pliers to squeeze together the ends of the circlips and lift them out of their grooves in the yokes. Broken or rusty circlips can be chipped out with an old screwdriver.

6. Rest the journals of the horizontal yoke on blocks or on an open vice and tap the vertical yoke with a soft-faced hammer. This will drive the upper bearing cup from the yoke.

7. Turn the shaft through 180° and repeat the operation to drive out the other bearing cup. If there is insufficient spider

travel to drive the cups right out of the yoke, use a pipe wrench or the vice jaws to complete their removal. With both cups out, the spider can be disengaged from the yokes on the shaft.

8. Clamp the two free ends of the spider in the vice and hammer the remaining yoke down-

Step 3.

Step 4.

Step 5.

Step 6.

Step 8.

Step 12.

Step 13.

Step 14.

wards to drift out the top cup. Turn the spider through 180° and repeat the process to remove the last cup.

9. Clean out the circlip grooves in the yokes with a small screwdriver blade, and file away any burrs.

10. The new spider assembly will have its bearing cups fitted with pre-greased needle rollers. Take off two opposite bearing cups and thread the bared journals of the spider through the holes in one yoke.

11. Make sure that the needle rollers are kept clean—dirt will considerably shorten their life—and that they are positioned evenly around the inner surface of each bearing cup.

12. Place the yoke in a vice with one bearing cup entered into its housing. Squeeze the cup into position by closing the vice jaws. Remove the yoke from the vice, insert one spider journal into the open end of this bearing, then position the opposite bearing cup. Again use the vice to press in the new cup, entering the spider journal into it as it is squeezed into place. Repeat the process with the other yoke.

13. The vice will press in the bearing cups only flush with the yoke. To press them in sufficiently to fit new circlips, use two sockets between the cups and vice jaws to tighten the cups further. Check frequently that they are not squeezed too far—they must only just uncover the circlip grooves.

14. Fit new circlips, making sure that they are fully seated in their grooves. Rest each yoke on the bench and tap the web of the opposite yoke to drive each bearing cup up against its circlip—this ensures correct free movement.

15. Oil the leading end of the shaft before sliding it into the gearbox—this will avoid damaging the oil seal—and refit the flanged ends so that the scribed marks align. If there is a centre bearing, align this with the scribed mark when refitting it.

16. If oil has been lost, top up the gearbox to the correct level (see next project).

Project 80: Checking the transmission oil level

Grading: 🏊🏊
Time: Approx 30min
Tools: Jack; axle stands; chocks; wrench to fit filler/ level and drain plugs
Materials: Transmission oil; cloth; container

The level of oil in the transmission should be checked when the engine oil is changed. On front-engined, rear-wheel-drive cars, this involves getting underneath and removing two filler/level plugs, one at the gearbox and one at the back axle.

Some front-wheel-drive cars have a separate oil supply for the gearbox and final drive, but most use a common filler/level plug. On British Leyland front-wheel-drive cars, the transmission is lubricated by engine oil and does not need to be checked separately.

Before changing the gearbox oil, the car should be driven a few miles to warm the oil so that it drains quickly and easily. It is not usual to drain the back axle—most axles do not have a drain plug.

Hypoid-type EP (extreme pressure) oil is usually used in the highly-stressed back axle, and a special oil may be recommended for the gearbox. Oil of the correct grade and type must be used and will be specified in the handbook. If the transmission needs regular topping-up, a garage should check the car.

Step 1. Look under the car and check the type of filler/level and drain plugs used on the transmission—you may have to buy a special combination wrench to undo them. If there is more than one plug on the gearbox, identify the filler/level plug from the handbook or workshop manual; undoing the wrong plug may cause parts to drop into the gearbox, making complete dismantling necessary.

2. Raise the car on axle stands so that it is level (see pages 14 and 15).

3. Remove the filler/level plugs. The oil inside should be level with the bottom of the hole

4. If the manufacturer recommends draining the gearbox, remove the drain plug and catch the oil in the container. Wipe the plug with a cloth before refitting it.

5. Use a flexible plastic bottle filled with the recommended oil for topping-up or refilling. Place a container under the gearbox or axle and squeeze the bottle to force lubricant through the filler hole.

6. Keep filling until the oil level reaches the bottom of the filler hole. If it is over-filled, allow the surplus to run out before wiping the plug with a cloth and refitting it.

Note that some older cars have a dipstick attached to the filler plug. In this case fill only to the FULL mark.

7. Lower the car to the ground.

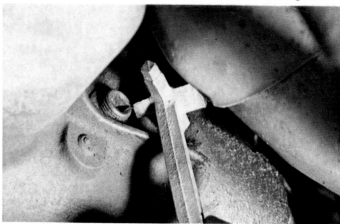
Step 3.

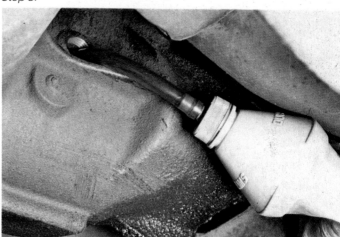
Step 5.

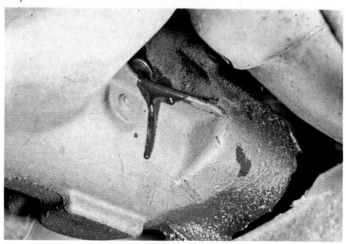
Step 6.

Outside and in

OUTSIDE AND IN

Panelwork

When the passenger car was first conceived, its body construction was little more advanced in design than the horsedrawn carriages it superseded. A strong chassis of iron or steel formed the platform on which the engine and the remainder of the running gear were mounted. On top was a minimal body, wood-framed and with wooden panelwork offering little shelter to the occupants. The use of wooden panelwork quickly gave way to lightweight materials like doped and varnished canvas stretched over seasoned, and very shapely, wooden frame members. It was not until after World War 2 that all-metal bodies became the predominant form of car construction.

The major breakthrough in car assembly came with the introduction of the unitary, or monocoque, bodyshell. Instead of mounting a separate body on a steel chassis, the bodyshell was assembled as one unit by welding together built-up metal panel sections. Now most cars are built this way.

Load-bearing components are still required to support, for example, suspension units, the engine and the steering gear, which cannot be mounted direct to thin steel panels. Thicker gauges of steel are used in areas where added strength is needed, and the metal is formed into box sections or shaped channels to make it even stronger.

The main shell is put together like a large box, in which the floor section and roof are welded to two main side sections. The side units generally form the inner surface of the wings, and the welded joint along the roof above the windows is usually concealed by making it the drip channel or rain gutter. The scuttle section or bulkhead, between the engine and front compartment, is then welded into place. There may be another bulkhead between the back seat and the boot.

As the components come together—still with no doors fitted—the structure gains in strength. Sturdy cross-members, welded and bolted in place at the front, provide heavy-duty anchorages for the front suspension and the engine bearers. Reinforcement around the sills and other box sections under the floorpan gives the body the necessary strength to prevent it from twisting when a wheel hits a severe bump.

Another technique is the use of a sub-frame to carry mechanical components—almost a return to the days of the separate chassis. Nowadays, however, the sub-frame is in separate front and rear parts, and the car designer still depends on the main body structure to provide the overall torsional strength (resistance to twisting) and beam strength (resistance to bending). A car with separate sub-frames is usually easier to repair after an accident, as the sub-frame can be removed, realigned and refitted. If necessary, it can be replaced. Because the sub-frame can be insulated from the body by rubber mounts, it is easier to suppress the noise and vibration created by the road wheels. Construction is also simpler and potentially cheaper. The disadvantages are that there is a greater risk of corrosion, and extra weight and material cost.

Some manufacturers use a sub-frame at the front only to carry the engine and front suspension components.

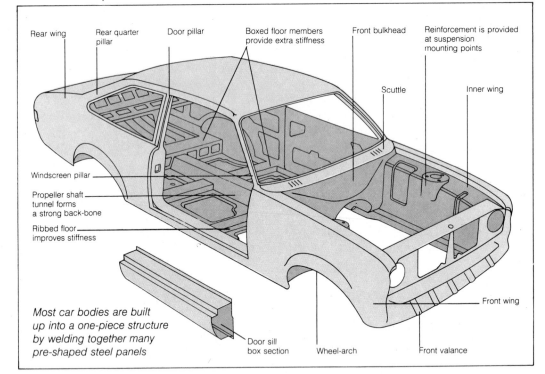

Most car bodies are built up into a one-piece structure by welding together many pre-shaped steel panels

Rear wing

Rear quarter pillar

Door pillar

Boxed floor members provide extra stiffness

Front bulkhead

Reinforcement is provided at suspension mounting points

Scuttle

Inner wing

Windscreen pillar

Propeller shaft tunnel forms a strong back-bone

Ribbed floor improves stiffness

Front wing

Door sill box section

Wheel-arch

Front valance

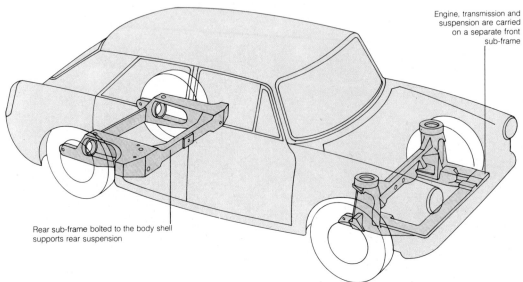

Engine, transmission and suspension are carried on a separate front sub-frame

Rear sub-frame bolted to the body shell supports rear suspension

Sub-frames, which carry the major mechanical components, simplify construction and make it easier to suppress road noise

Instead of steel

At one time it was widely thought that resin-bonded glass-fibre (glass-reinforced plastic) and other plastics had great potential in car construction and would perhaps displace steel as the major bodywork material. The difficulties of mass production and rising costs of the oil-derived raw materials put a different complexion on the future of grp and other plastics. Even so, they are still used for specialist cars such as Lotus and Reliant, made in smaller production runs. Glass-fibre-bodied cars usually have a separate steel chassis.

The special appeal of a grp bodyshell is that it is comparatively light and easy to repair. As the same glass-fibre and resin materials will bond directly to clean steel, grp also has special attractions as a means of repair for minor damage to steel bodies. While grp cannot be used to replace metal in areas where structural strength is needed, non-load-bearing sections of a steel body, such as wings and boot-lids, can be made from it. Fibre and resin materials are most useful when there is a cavity or tear in metal to be bridged. This sort of repair is within the scope of the amateur and needs no special equipment.

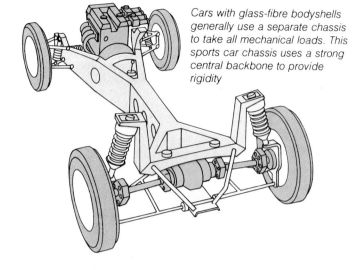

Cars with glass-fibre bodyshells generally use a separate chassis to take all mechanical loads. This sports car chassis uses a strong central backbone to provide rigidity

Structural repairs

Car makers build their vehicles as light as possible because excess weight means greater material cost and needs a bigger engine and more fuel to move it. Current cars are therefore built using the latest computer techniques to avoid unnecessary weight. The result is that they are no stronger than they need to be. They will bear the normal loads, deal with bad roads and cope with reasonable extra loadings.

Nevertheless, in some conditions they can be very fragile indeed. It is not only bumps and knocks on the bodywork that can damage the modern car. Some body designs are very intolerant of the use of jacks or suspended tow equipment at any points other than those designed by the manufacturer.

Despite its light construction, the modern car bodyshell must maintain the alignment and precise positioning of suspension mountings and

wheels. It is therefore most important that after any suspected accident damage a professional check is made to ensure that the structure has not been either weakened or distorted, and that the alignment of all the suspension and steering parts is correct. Even the most competent do-it-yourself repairer should not be tempted to bolt on a new wing without having these checks made.

Tests for correct alignment

are made by a bodywork specialist or a garage equipped with a special jig.

This is an accurately constructed framework provided by the manufacturer, with datum points which must coincide with precise suspension and body points.

If any misalignment is revealed, powerful hydraulic rams may be used to force everything back in place. In bad cases, major new sections can be welded in.

The hinged components

All cars have a hinged bonnet or engine cover, hinged doors, and a hinged boot lid or tailgate at the rear. When damage has been caused, these non-load-bearing parts can be renewed by a competent amateur. It is worth remembering, however, that structural damage might have occurred if a door is driven forward by impact, distorting the post to which it is attached.

In mass production, there can be small variations in the size of a major component like a door, and there is also need to allow for wear of hinges and door latches. All cars, therefore, have some sort of provision for adjusting door hinges.

Adjustment of the bonnet and boot lid is also important to ensure that latches fasten securely, and that the panel sits evenly against its rubber seal. When bonnet or boot

panels are replaced, it is normal to transfer the existing locks or catches, unless they have been damaged.

In all but the simplest cars, doors are complex structures, carrying locks, interior release handles, windows and a window-winding mechanism. When a new door is ordered for

an accident repair, it is supplied as a steel panel and window surround, in primer. All sound mechanical components and window glass have to be transferred to it at the repair stage. This involves heavy labour costs, and where the damage is restricted to the door panelwork, a cheaper

repair system has been developed, in which only the outer skin of the door is replaced. A grinding wheel is used to separate the outer skin of the door from the main structure, along the seam. A new panel can then be spot-welded in place and primed and painted to match the rest of the car.

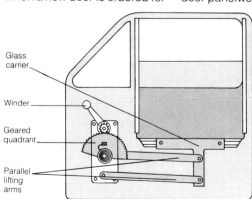

Glass carrier
Winder
Geared quadrant
Parallel lifting arms

A quadrant-and-parallelogram linkage converts rotary movement of the window winder handle into up-and-down movement of the glass

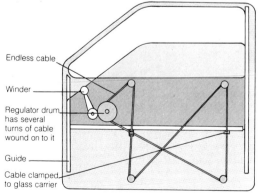

Endless cable
Winder
Regulator drum has several turns of cable wound on to it
Guide
Cable clamped to glass carrier

Some cars have a system of pulleys and a cable that raises and lowers the glass when the winder handle is turned

Panelwork

Windscreens and windows

Most British cars have their windscreen and windows made from toughened glass. This is pre-stressed by heat treatment during manufacture so that if it is broken, the whole windscreen or window breaks into tiny pieces, designed to be too small to cause serious cuts.

The size of the broken fragments makes it difficult to see through a damaged toughened windscreen—particularly for the first few seconds after it breaks. To overcome this, most current cars are fitted with a zone-toughened windscreen which, when it breaks, has a patterned area of larger fragments in front of the driver to provide improved vision.

Laminated windscreens consist of two sheets of glass bonded together with a plastic interlayer. A stone hitting a laminated windscreen will crack it or cause a star-shaped blemish at the point of impact, but will not usually affect the remainder of the glass. Although the interlayer is designed to retain the glass during a breakage, it was possible on early types of laminate for sharp fragments to break off and injure the occupants in the event of a serious impact.

The latest laminated screens have ordinary glass on the outside which prevents a 'white-out' when hit by a sharp object, while the inside lamination is of toughened glass, which cannot break into sharp pieces.

If a windscreen breaks, it should be replaced by a windscreen specialist. Do not be tempted to do it yourself.

Accident safety

A car's bodywork is the final protection for its passengers if all other safety systems fail and the car is involved in a crash. Safety legislation and the use of advanced methods of research have forced the pace of car body development forward in many ways.

As more has been discovered about what happens to cars and their occupants in accidents, it has been learned that it is the severity of the deceleration throwing people forward as the car comes to a sudden impact-stop that causes death and injury. The rate of deceleration can be reduced by deliberately introducing weakness into the front and rear sections of the body, so that they crumple progressively, absorbing the energy of the collision.

Cut-out sections of the body metal are designed so that, under impact, the car's front and rear zones will not offer so much resistance to crumpling. Preliminary creases are formed in the stronger parts of the body structure to encourage boxes and panels to collapse more readily on impact. On the other hand, the passenger compartment is designed to be as strong as possible to prevent penetration by anything the car hits, or by major rigid units of the car like the engine. Doors are provided with latches that will not fly open in a crash, yet can be opened after the impact. Screen and roof pillars are strengthened to reduce the risk of the roof collapsing if the car rolls over. Another safety measure is additional side reinforcement for doors and door sills, to protect the occupants from the effects of a side impact.

Whenever possible, interior projections are made of pliable material, or are deliberately arranged to snap off when struck. Padding on top of and beneath the facia panel prevents many of the injuries to knees and faces that used to occur in accidents. Seat belts have to be fixed to strong areas of the structure, so that their mountings will not tear out in an accident. To avoid danger to pedestrians, car frontal areas are increasingly being designed to reduce injury and prevent anybody hit by the car from falling underneath.

Another safety factor that is taken into consideration by manufacturers is the design of exterior door handles. On most modern cars these are recessed in the door panel to prevent further injury to anybody struck by the side of the vehicle.

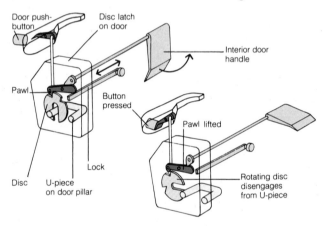

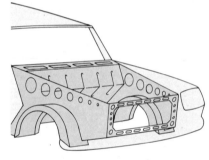

Most doors now have a disc latch which shuts the door against a U-fitting or a pin in the door frame, and has good anti-burst characteristics. The U-fitting engages with a slot cut in the disc which turns through 90 degrees to shut the door. A mechanical linkage of levers and rods locks and unlocks the disc

One method of constructing the front of a bodyshell to ensure progressive collapse on impact. To protect the strong passenger compartment from side damage, many doors have box sections of steel tubes beneath the outer panel

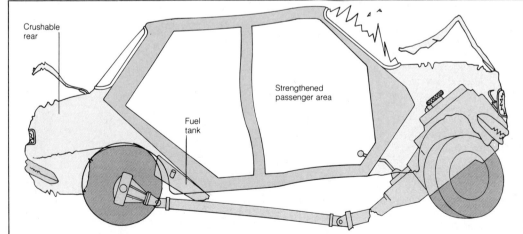

Front and rear sections of one-piece bodyshells are built to crumple progressively and absorb some of the energy of an impact. The engine and transmission are mounted so that they will not break into the strong passenger compartment. The fuel tank is positioned in a protected area

Decorative trim

For styling to meet market demands, to distinguish models apart (when they may actually have the same body shape), and to cover vents in the body, cars are embellished with a variety of decorative trims. A car will normally have at least one plastic or metal badge or motif bearing the maker's name and the model, plastic grilles over ventilation holes, the main front grille itself to allow air into the engine compartment, and headlamp surrounds to disguise the gap between the glass lens and the surrounding panelwork.

Decorative paintwork is another feature of many modern cars. Only in the case of a luxury car like a Rolls-Royce are the handsome coachlines along the side hand-painted. On more mundane cars they are sprayed on over special masking tapes, which are increasingly available to the enthusiastic amateur. Even easier to apply, however, are coachlines which are ready printed on a self-adhesive backing. These are a cheap-to-apply cosmetic addition, also used by many car manufacturers.

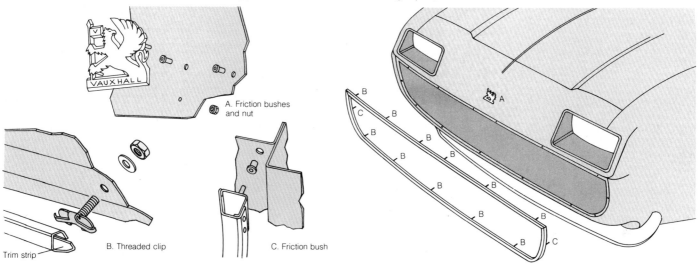

A. Friction bushes and nut

B. Threaded clip

C. Friction bush

Trim strip

Before trying to remove any brightwork, check behind the panel to see the type of fixings that hold it. Most small badges are held by plastic friction bushes and can simply be prised out. but a few also have a self-threading nut to make them vandal-proof. If this is not undone, the badge will be damaged. Trim strips are usually fitted to clips

Making good

One of the most important products used by the do-it-yourself enthusiast faced with panelwork repairs is the rubbing-down agent. While rubbing down itself is a process that sounds easy, like smoothing a piece of wood, it is, in fact, where the main skill of the repairer and the ultimate success or failure of the job begins to emerge. The material used is wet-or-dry abrasive paper. Never use sandpaper as it sheds particles of abrasive. The degree of coarseness of the wet-or-dry paper is shown by the numbered density of the grit, printed on the back of the paper. The higher the number, the more the number of particles and the finer the abrasive. The grit on the paper is normally silicon-carbide, and the job of flatting the filled work usually begins with a fairly coarse grade of abrasive, such as 80 or 120-grit. As the treated surface comes closer to a fine finish (and nearer to a level with the surrounding paintwork) you can graduate to smoother 300 or 400 papers. Final finishing should be made with 600-grit paper.

Abrasive paper of this kind is best used wet—hence the name wet-or-dry. The water acts as a lubricant, and prevents the paper from clogging with paint or filler. Rubbing down is done with the paper wrapped round a sanding block in order to keep the surface flat, and there should be a container of water handy into which the paper can be dipped from time to time.

Wipers and washers

By law all cars must be fitted with windscreen wipers and washers. The rubber strip that squeegees water off the glass is held against the windscreen by a spring-loaded arm and a flexible metal or plastic carrier which is designed to make the rubber follow the curve of the windscreen.

Most modern cars use electrically-operated windscreen washers in which a small motor-driven pump draws water through a one-way valve from a reservoir, and sprays it on to the windscreen through two jets.

Hatchback cars, which tend to drag road spray on to their rear end in the wet, are frequently fitted with a rear window wash and wipe system.

All wiper rubbers depend on a thin straight edge of rubber to wipe the glass clean. If this edge is damaged, it cannot remove water effectively and the rubber must be renewed. Wax polish or oil-based materials must be kept off the windscreen, otherwise they will cause smearing and loss of vision. The addition of a proprietary additive to the washer fluid will help to keep the glass smear-free and prevent the system from freezing in winter.

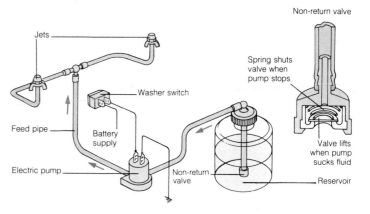

Jets

Feed pipe

Washer switch

Battery supply

Electric pump

Non-return valve

Non-return valve

Spring shuts valve when pump stops

Valve lifts when pump sucks fluid

Reservoir

Small-bore plastic pipes link the key components in a windscreen washer system. A few washer layouts use a plunger-type hand pump

Panelwork projects

Windscreen wipers and washers

As a general rule, wiper blades should be changed every 12-18 months if they are to clear water from the windscreen efficiently.

Wiper arms last longer. The sign that they are due for renewal is when they allow the blades to lift off the screen at high speeds.

Legally, windscreen washer systems, like wipers, must be in efficient working order, and the water in the reservoir must be prevented from freezing in winter.

Project 81: Renewing wiper blades.

Grading: 🔧
Time: 5min for two arms
Materials: New wiper blades

Step 1. To disconnect a push-on blade, angle the spring-loaded connector to disengage it from the protrusion on the arm and pull it off.
* Some push-on blades have a clip at the connector. Depress this to release the blade from the arm.

** With hook-type arms, hinge the arm away from the screen, turn the blade through a right-angle and uncouple the hook.
*** Some blades have a pin fitting. On these, a two-piece plastic insert fits inside the hook enclosing the pin. To remove the blade, hinge the arm away from the screen and slide the plastic insert and blade out of the hook.

Spread apart the two parts of the plastic to remove the wiper blade.

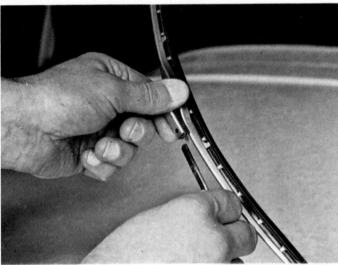

Step 1.

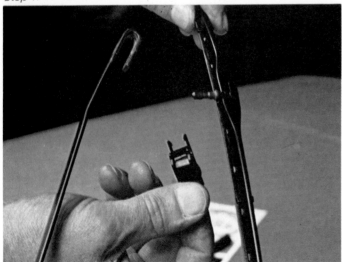

Step ***

Project 82: Caring for windscreen washers

Grading: 🔧
Time: 10min
Tools: Screwdriver or pin to aim jets
Material: Windscreen washer anti-freeze

Windscreen washers should be aimed so that they squirt a jet of water in the centre of the wiped area, approximately five inches down from the top of the screen.
Step 1. Jets fitted in plastic holders are aimed on a trial-and-error basis by using a pin pushed into the jet and levered in the appropriate direction.
*1. Some jets can be adjusted while the washer is in action. Ask a helper to operate the washer while you alter the aim with a screwdriver.
2. In winter, add a windscreen washer anti-freeze to the reservoir. Do not use engine anti-freeze as it can damage paintwork. In an emergency, add two tablespoonfuls of methylated spirit to one pint of wash water.

Step 1.

Step *1.

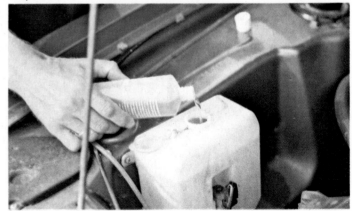

Step 2.

Panelwork projects

Project 83: Changing a wiper arm

Grading: 🔧
Time: Approx 10min for two arms
Tools: Screwdriver; spanner; small adjustable spanner; coin to release arm
Materials: New wiper arms

Step 1. To change an arm with a central screw at the base, take out the screw.
2. Lift the arm off the drive spindle. The spindle is splined to engage with splines in the arm-fixing socket. Fit the blade, line it up in the parked position, engage the arm on the spindle and refit the centre screw.

*1. If there is no centre screw and the arm does not have a lift-up cover over the spindle, it will be held on the splines by a spring clip. Use a coin to prise the arm forward.
*2. Fit the blade and make sure that the clip sits on the side of the spindle when the blade is in the parked position. Push it firmly on to the spindle so that the spring clip engages under the bottom edge of the spindle.

**1. Some wiper arms are secured by a nut beneath a hinged cover. Lift the cover, undo the nut and remove the spring washer underneath. The arm can then be lifted clear.
***1. On arms secured by a nut fitted on a tapered and splined spindle, the socket of the new arm may not have any splines at all. Attach the blade, slip the arm on the spindle and loosely fit the nut and spring washer. Align the arm and blade in the parked position.

**2. Tighten the nut fully. It will cut matching serrations in the arm.
3. If the arms are not parallel with the screen, the blades may judder noisily across the glass. To cure this, start the wipers and stop them when the arms are vertical by switching off the ignition.
4. Remove the wiper blade.
5. Using a small adjustable spanner, twist the arm so that, when viewed end-on, it is parallel with the surface of the glass.

Step 2.

Step* 1.

Step* 2.

Step** 1.

Step** 2.

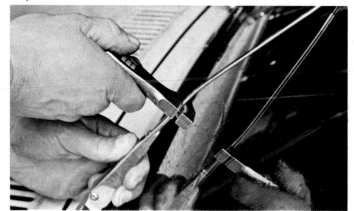

Step 5.

Panelwork projects

Project 84: Smoothing out a small dent

Grading: 🔧🔧
Time: 1hr-2hr
Tools: Hammer or mallet; power drill; small bit; rotary wire brush or sanding disc; screwdriver; perforated file
Materials: Body-filler kit; mixing board; self-tapping screw; wet-or-dry paper (grades 120, 240, 320 and 400-grit)

Small dents in the bodywork are best smoothed out by filling them with a two-part plastic filler. With proper surface finishing and painting, this type of repair is virtually undetectable.

There are a few golden rules: to adhere properly, filler must be applied to bare metal, the surface must be dry, and the air temperature should be at least 59°F (15°C) for the filler to cure quickly. In winter it helps to warm the damaged area with an electric fire.

The most time-consuming part of the project is shaping the hardened filler to blend with the bodywork. The job can be speeded up if rough shaping is done with a perforated file, and subsequent finishing is done with progressively finer grades of wet-or-dry paper, used wet. The abrasive paper grades quoted are only approximate—a grade of paper near the numbers quoted will do just as well.

Sometimes rubbing down the filler uncovers pin-holes in the surface—the result of air bubbles in the mix. These can be filled with a thin coating of filler once the correct shape has been obtained; make sure that the original filler is cured before filling the pin holes.

A dent that has stretched the metal cannot be successfully hammered out. It is better to level if off using plastic body filler.

Step 1. To save filler, make a deep dent as shallow as possible. If you cannot tap the dent from behind with a mallet, drill a hole in the deepest part, insert a self-tapping screw, then use a claw hammer on the screw head to draw the dent outwards. Use a piece of wood for the hammer to bear on.

2. Remove all paint down to bare metal with a rotary wire brush or sanding disc, treating an area extending at least 2in beyond the edge of the dent.
3. Feather the edges of the old paint so that it blends smoothly with the exposed metal, using wet-or-dry abrasive paper. Begin with 240-grit paper, then use a finer grade—around 320-grit—to obtain a smooth finish. Wet the paper frequently.
4. Score the dented metal with the tang of a file to provide a

key for the filler.
5. Squeeze out the correct quantities of filler and hardener (check the maker's instructions) on to a small piece of smooth hardboard or stiff card. Mix them thoroughly.
6. Working quickly, spread filler into the dent so that it stands proud of the surrounding bodywork.
7. Once it has hardened (it should take about 30 minutes, depending on air temperature), use a coarse file or sandpaper to rough-shape it. Do not try to

level it with the bodywork at this stage—leave it about $\frac{1}{16}$in proud.
8. Blend the filler into the surrounding metal, using progressively finer grades of wet-or-dry paper, used wet. Start with coarse grade (about 120-grit) then change to a finer grade as the final shape is reached. The progression to aim for is 120 followed by 240, 320 and lastly 400-grit paper. This will avoid scratches on the finished surface. Paint the repair (see Project 87).

Step 1.

Step 2.

Step 3.

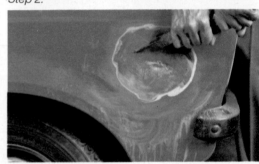

Step 4.

Step 5.

Step 6.

Step 7.

Step 8.

Panelwork projects

Project 85: Sealing leaking window rubbers

Grading: 🔧
Time: Approx 30min for one leak-point. Allow extra time to trace leaks
Materials: Sealing compound; methylated spirit; wooden wedge; soft cloth

Leaking rubber seals can be cured fairly easily by using a sealant, but finding the leak is more difficult than curing it. Car manufacturers use ultrasonic detection equipment to pin-point tiny gaps in rubber seals. Without this, one must rely on keen eyesight.

Examine the outside of the seals around the area of the leak, looking for damage, cracks, perishing or lifting of the edges. A patch of dampness that lingers after the rest of the seal has dried out indicates a water-entry point.

Check a good length of the seal on each side of the leak-point, as water often travels along a seal before dribbling through. On windscreens, in particular, examine the seal at its upper corners, even though the leak may appear at a bottom inside corner.

Step 1. Prepare a seal for treatment by making sure that it is completely dry, then cleaning it with a cloth dipped in methylated spirit. If necessary, force a cloth between seal and glass with a wooden wedge.

2. Windscreen seals are always a tight fit. Lift the edge with a wooden wedge (metal may cut the rubber) and then inject silicone-based sealant.

3. Side window seals are usually more flexible. After cleaning, insert the nozzle of the tube between seal and glass and apply a line of sealant to fill the gap. Use a dry cloth to clean off the surplus sealant before it hardens.

Step 2.

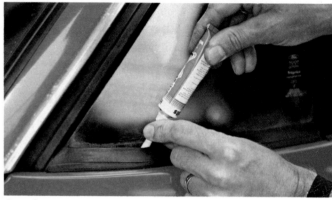

Step 3.

Project 86: Fitting mudflaps

Grading: 🔧
Time: Approx 1hr for two mudflaps
Tools: Stiff brush; handyman's knife; chalk; spanner or screwdriver to fit clamp screws; drill and bit for self-tapping screws
Materials: Mudflap kit; if necessary, self-tapping screws

Most car manufacturers offer mudflaps as an accessory. On cars where the body shape curves under at the sides, flaps behind the front and rear wheels protect the paintwork from stone chipping.

Accessory shops sell universal mudflaps which usually need trimming exactly to shape to fit the wheel arch. This project covers the fitting of these flaps because they are more awkward and take longer to fit than the custom-made type.

Step 1. Mudflaps are clamped or screwed to the wheel arch flanges, which on most cars are turned inwards. First remove accumulated dirt with a stiff brush.

2. Ask a helper to check the alignment of the mudflap from behind the car. When the base of the flap is parallel with the ground, mark the outline of the edge of the wheel arch flange on to the rubber.

3. Cut off surplus rubber with a sharp knife. Use the cut flap as a template to cut the same amount from the opposite flap.

4. Use the clamps supplied to hold the mudflap securely against the wheel arch flange.
*On cars where the clamps will not fit, drill through the mudflap and the flange, and secure the flap with two or three self-tapping screws. Make sure that the flap is properly aligned when drilling the holes.
**On certain cars the wheel arch shape skews the mudflap. Some flaps are, therefore, supplied with small wedges which are packed between the wheel arch and the flap to straighten it. If no wedges are supplied with the fitting kit, use some of the rubber offcuts as packing pieces.

Step 3.

Step 4.

Paint repairs

Never did the old adage about a stitch in time hold so true as in the need to apply rapid repairs to the most minor body damage, or even a paint scratch. Paintwork certainly enhances the appearance of a car, but its primary function is to protect the bodywork metal. Once the protective paint finish has been pierced through to the metal by minor damage, corrosion begins at once if the damaged area is neglected. There will be visible rust within days, sometimes even hours. The earlier the work is started, before rust action spreads out from the scratch and under surrounding paintwork, the easier it is to carry out repairs.

It helps, in repairing paintwork, to understand how the car's outer skin is built up because it is, in fact, not so much a simple lick of colour as a sophisticated system. In a typical paint process, bodies coming off the production lines are first washed in a de-greasing solvent to remove any grease, metal dust particles and grit left on the bare metal after assembly. Inside the bare shell are hung any other metal parts that will later be bolted to the finished body so that they too receive the same level of corrosion protection.

Slung on a hooked conveyor, the bodywork is then pulled, totally immersed, through a tank of etching fluid (zinc phosphate is a major chemical used) which deposits an anti-corrosive layer on the metal surface and provides a good key for subsequent paint layers. The chemicals are then washed off in a chamber with high-powered sprays of pure (de-ionised) water, and the body is conveyed through a blast of drying air.

The first actual paint coat is a primer layer about one thousandth of an inch thick. It is applied by attaching high-power electric cables to the car body and immersing it once more in a bath of paint particles suspended in a solvent. Because the body is highly charged, the paint particles are attracted to the metal surface, even into those nooks and crannies that could not possibly be reached by a brush or a spray. This stage is called the electrophoretic process and is followed by further washing and drying.

After priming, many manufacturers have a robot spray to apply the underbody protection, a thick bituminous or PVC paint, although this may be done after the paint process has been completed.

Final colour painting is also carried out by robot sprays, making two passes over the entire body. This is not quite the same as giving it two coats —some parts of the car will get two layers, but the rather irregular shape of the bodywork means that some areas may receive only a partial coat on each pass. Any areas missed by the automatic process are rectified by hand-sprays operated at the exit of the paint booth. This final colour coat, two thousandths of an inch thick, is baked on to the car in a 30 minute oven treatment which thoroughly dries and hardens the finished gloss surface.

An XJS receives one of the eight-stage pre-treatment processes

250ml box-section wax
400ml plastisol sealer
400ml weld cream sealer
500ml metal adhesive
1 litre rubber resin cement
2.4 litres dip primer
3 litres underbody wax
3.6 litres primer surfacer
10.7 litres acrylic colour
11.5 litres underbody sealer/deadener
16 litres thinners

One of today's popular cars is given about 50 litres of protective coating, in the quantities shown here

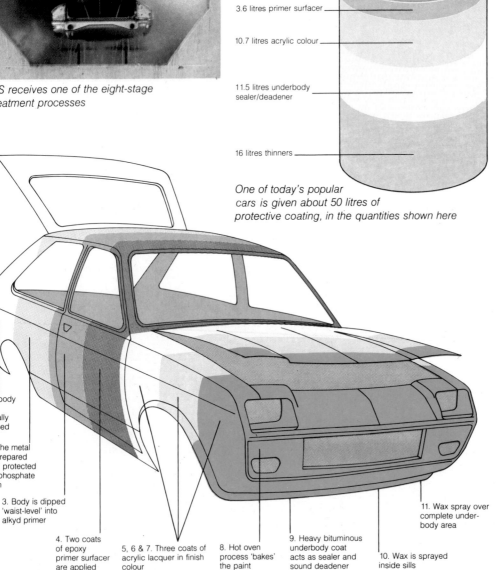

1. Raw body shell is chemically degreased

2. The metal is prepared and protected by phosphate etch

3. Body is dipped 'waist-level' into alkyd primer

4. Two coats of epoxy primer surfacer are applied

5, 6 & 7. Three coats of acrylic lacquer in finish colour

8. Hot oven process 'bakes' the paint

9. Heavy bituminous underbody coat acts as sealer and sound deadener

10. Wax is sprayed inside sills

11. Wax spray over complete underbody area

The illustration shows the protective process, stage by stage, which one leading manufacturer uses to achieve a lasting paint finish and to combat bodywork corrosion

Paint repairs

Before painting

There are some basic rules to be borne in mind in order to make a good repair to a car finish. The first is that paint alone is not enough to keep out the weather. A paint surface is naturally porous and allows some water through. This would create rusting below the surface if no other protective coat was applied. Once rust has formed to any appreciable depth it must be neutralised, otherwise further rusting will take place, the paint applied on top of it will bubble up, and the blemish will reappear in a very short time.

Remember that paint is simply a convenient method of applying colour: it is *not* a filler. If paint is applied to a damaged or irregular surface, all it does is to change the colour of the damage—the blemish remains. Paint should be applied only to a smooth and filled surface.

The first step in any paint repair is to cut down to the bare metal. It will make more work if you enlarge the area to be painted, so take care when tackling any areas of rust that you do not slip and damage surrounding paintwork. Stick masking tape around the area to be worked on, and use a sharp implement to scratch away at the rust until you get down to shiny steel. Larger areas can be tackled more confidently with a flap wheel used in a power drill, a rotating wire brush or using just sandpaper.

The repair can then be built up from the bare metal, reproducing as exactly as possible the process that the manufacturer uses. If there is no rust at all on the area to be treated, a good foundation coat with excellent anti-corrosion properties is a zinc-based primer obtainable in aerosol or brush-on form. Where extensive rusting has taken place

—and there may be a few minute pores of corrosion remaining after the best of metal treatments—a brush-on rust-removing and inhibiting primer should be applied. This type of treatment should be allowed to dry thoroughly for a day or two before carrying out the finishing work.

Blemishes remaining after this anti-corrosion treatment then have to be dealt with. Large dents or holes have to be levelled off with a filler paste – many brands are available in tubes and cans. Some brands come as a two-component mixture, consisting of a tin of resin/filler putty and a small tube of chemical hardener. These materials should be used in exactly the same way as the glass fibre materials explained in Project 91.

Scratches and small areas of paint damage are best made good with cellulose putty or filler. This is a quick-drying

paste, supplied in a tube or tin, which contains identical solvents to those in the primer and paint that will be used to make the final surface finish. It can be smoothed into the blemish with the flat edge of a pallet knife or other blade—sometimes a small plastic spatula is supplied. When the filler has been built up to stand very slightly higher than the surrounding paintwork and it has hardened (4 to 5 hours for cellulose putty—at least a day for resin-based fillers) it is time for the most painstaking job of all—rubbing down.

Wet rubbing down becomes a messy job, with water running everywhere and scoured-off material congealing on the paper and the paint.

This must be thoroughly washed off the surface to be painted with clean water, and the area must be completely dry before primer and paint are applied.

The 'no-go' areas

Perhaps the most tedious part of the preparatory work for vehicle painting is the masking of parts that are not to be painted, but this is essential when using both aerosol paint cans or spray guns. Large items like wheels are easily covered with newspaper securely stuck down with masking tape so that it cannot blow up and contact the new paint. Wherever possible, trim should be removed rather than masked. This ensures that stray paint does not get on it, and that paint is applied to the area beneath. Painting against masked-off rubbing strips, for example, causes an ugly build-up of paint along their edges. A much neater effect is achieved by spraying the whole area and refitting the strips when the paint is dry.

When spraying around doors and windows it is a good idea to cover seats, carpets, facia and so on inside the car, because a fog of paint may form in the interior which will be sufficient to mark them. Windows themselves are best covered with newspaper cut to size and stuck on with masking tape so that all the rubber

surrounds are covered. Small items that are very fiddly to mask, such as protruding door locks, can be protected with a carefully applied smear of grease or petroleum jelly. This

is wiped off when the surrounding paint has completely dried.

Overspray of paint on to areas not sufficiently well masked can be removed by light application of a cutting

compound, as explained later. Paint oversprayed on glass or chrome trim, can be cleaned off by light rubbing with a little cellulose thinner on a cloth (never use this on window surrounds or vinyl upholstery).

Masking off adjacent paint areas that are not to be treated is best done at a prominent 'break line' such as a seam in a door, or the junction of a wing with the rest of the body. If just a small area has to be painted, the overspray can be feathered into the original area on completion of the job, using a cutting compound.

Before beginning any painting make sure that the whole of the area on which paint is likely to settle is scrupulously clean. It is impossible to do a neat job if dead insects and road dirt still adhere to the surface. Painting calls for calm, clean air, free from dust and insects. It is not a job to be done on a breezy, hot summer day when insects will land on the new work before it is dry, or when a neighbour is having a bonfire. Really professional-looking results can be achieved only with care and patience, especially in the preparatory work.

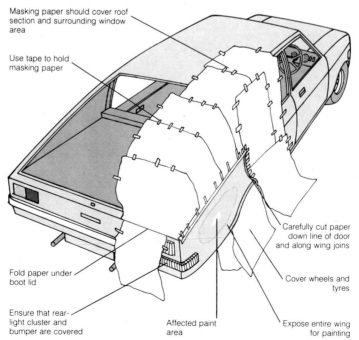

Masking paper should cover roof section and surrounding window area

Use tape to hold masking paper

Fold paper under boot lid

Ensure that rear-light cluster and bumper are covered

Affected paint area

Expose entire wing for painting

Carefully cut paper down line of door and along wing joins

Cover wheels and tyres

Protect the sound paintwork with masking paper before spraying the affected area

Paint repairs

Aerosol paint sprays

Aerosol paints can match almost every standard colour offered by most of the world's motor manufacturers. If the required paint colour is not available from a DIY car repair or accessory shop, a main agent or dealer should be able to supply it from a particular manufacturer's range.

This popular form of paint application needs a little inside knowledge for the best results to be obtained. Inside every aerosol paint can there is a mixture of paint pigment, solvent and propellant. The pigment tends to settle out of the solvent/propellant mixture even in a very short time, so inside the can there is also an agitator—usually a small, steel ball-bearing. When you shake the can to mix the paint, you may not at first hear the rattle of the agitator, as it will be stuck to the can in a goo of thick pigment. When it finally shakes free, continue rattling it about inside for a further two or three minutes to ensure even mixing.

The propellant in the can is a fast-evaporating liquid which boils at ordinary room temperature. The resultant vapour forces the paint/solvent mixture out of the specially designed delivery nozzle when the valve is opened. Within limits, the warmer the can is, the better the propellant evaporates and the better the dispersal of the paint within the vapour stream. Do not use a can straight from a cold garage—warm it first by the radiator at home (never *on* the radiator) or in an overall inside pocket.

After the can has been used, turn it upside down and give the delivery button a quick press. Only propellant vapour should emerge, cleaning any remaining minute drops of paint that could dry and block the tiny nozzle. If the nozzle is blocked, pull it off the can and soak it in cellulose thinner solvent. You may be able to poke a fine wire or a nylon brush bristle down the nozzle to clear any obstinate debris.

While the manufacturers of aerosol paints have done their best to ensure that their paints and solvents are compatible with the standard finishes applied to cars, it is still possible that the application of new paint and solvent could pucker the existing paint surface surrounding the repair area. This often happens when, unbeknown to the DIY repairer, the panel he is spraying has previously been resprayed using inferior, non-standard paints.

To avoid this problem it is best to make a small test before starting the main work. Spray a little of the paint on a hidden area of paintwork as close as possible to the area to be repainted—inside the boot lid, behind removed trim or under a door are useful spots. If there is a marked puckering of the test area when the paint is dry, the best solution is to take the car to a paint specialist for advice.

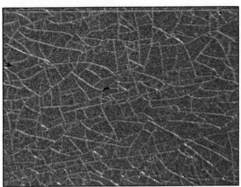

LEATHERY SURFACE
Cause: Surface cracks in very old paint
Remedy: Remove the paint using 400-grit wet-and-dry paper, respray

CRACKED SURFACE
Cause: Over-heavy application of top-coat
Remedy: Strip colour coat, re-prime if necessary, clean area and repaint

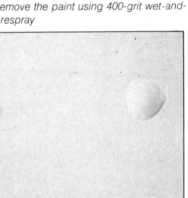

BLISTERED SURFACE
Cause: Poor adhesion between top-coat and primer – probably because of water between them
Remedy: Remove top-coat using 400-grit wet-and-dry paper, respray

'PICKLED' SURFACE
Cause: Cellulose top coat applied over oil-based primer
Remedy: Remove all paint to bare metal and respray with compatible primer and top-coat

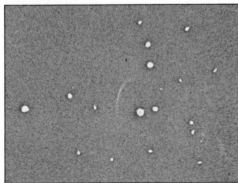

WHITE SPOTTED SURFACE
Cause: Tiny projections caused by dirt trapped between the primer and top-coat are knocked off, revealing white or grey primer during car cleaning
Remedy: Remove top-coat, respray

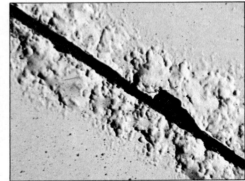

RUST EROSION
Cause: Rusting of bare metal has crept under the paint on each side of a scratch.
Remedy: Scrape away rust, treat with rust preventive, prime and paint small areas with a touch-up brush. Spray larger areas

The first coat

Following the same steps as the manufacturer's original paint protection system, the next stage after cleaning up and masking is the application of primer. This is a special type of paint, designed to have excellent adhesion properties on a treated metal surface as well as providing a smooth yet bonding or keying surface for the top coat of colour. It is widely available in brush-on or aerosol-spray forms. While it is considerably cheaper to buy, the brush-on primer is much more difficult to apply in an even coat. Much harder rubbing down is required to eradicate brush marks and variations in paint thickness which could show through the top coat.

It is during the application of the primer that you can practise the very difficult job of laying down an even paint coat. With an aerosol it is usual to hold the can about 12in from the area to be treated and move it parallel to the body surface, starting this scanning movement a moment before you press the delivery button. Aerosols, like all paint sprays, cover a fairly well defined area—a circle about 2in-3in across, fading out towards the edges. The trick is to use your hand movement to spread this circle into an even band of painted surface. Make only light applications at a time, allowing a few minutes for the paint to dry between each burst. Do not aim to cover the treated area completely in one burst of spray. The paint is quite likely to run and quickly dry into unsightly ripples or tear-drops which will have to be flatted down.

The final coat

The primed surface is now ready to receive the final coat.

By now your spraying technique should be good enough to apply a smooth and consistent layer of colour. It will usually be necessary to give at least three coats of the final colour for it to match the surrounding paintwork and so totally obscure the patch of primer underneath.

Final surface treatment

Once the top coat is dry, in about 15 minutes, the masking tape and interior covers can be removed. The finished work should have a high gloss, and in running a finger over it no surface imperfection should be noticeable. You may find, however, that the sheen of the new paint picks it out from the surrounding paintwork and that a slight overspray, fine mist particles of paint, lies in a noticeably matt layer around the repair. The visible difference in the nature of the paint surfaces, old and new, can be removed quite easily by the use of rubbing-down compound.

This is a very mildly abrasive cream which, when mixed with water and applied with a damp cloth, restores the surface of the old paint affected by overspray. An even shine to the surface can then be restored by treating the whole area to a good coat of wax polish. It is wise to leave the final polishing for at least a week after repainting to allow the new surface to harden.

Finally, give the surface an even shine by treating the whole area to a coat of wax polish.

Alternatives to aerosols

When dealing with minute scratches in the paint layer that do not go as deep as the body metal, all the lengthy preparation work will not be necessary. Most car manufacturers supply small cans of touch-in paint to deal with these blemishes. Liquid paint is flowed on to the scratch with a fine-bristled brush, usually provided as part of the touch-up kit.

Much larger repairs will need the use of professional or semi-professional equipment. If you have to repaint an area, say, the size of a door, a small aerosol paint spray will not provide very much more than a single coat. Three or four small cans, or two of the larger size, will be required to do the job properly, which makes it a fairly expensive job. Professional repairers use compressed-air spray guns and are able to make tremendous economies by buying paint in bulk. With skill the DIY paint restorer can come close to professional standards of finish at realistic prices by using one of the many airless types of spray gun available to amateurs.

Airless spray guns

An airless gun has a paint container and a mains or battery-operated high-pressure pump that delivers a cone-shaped spray of paint from a specially designed nozzle. The weight of the electro-magnetic pump behind the nozzle makes the gun heavier than the average all-aluminium compressed-air spray gun—particularly when the reservoir is full of paint—so that it can be hard to keep the gun steady when tackling a big job.

The heart of an airless gun is a close-fitting piston that slides back and forth in a cylinder and pushes the paint towards the nozzle. The close fit of the parts makes it absolutely essential to clean the gun after use, otherwise paint will dry inside the pump and jam it.

During spraying, the gun should be cleaned by passing neat thinners through it each time there is a pause in the work. Before the gun is put away, the dip tube should be removed, two drops of thin oil applied to the exposed side of the piston and the gun operated briefly to distribute the oil. This prevents the gun from seizing during storage.

Airless guns come in many sizes and prices. Cheap ones often have a feeble output and will spray only very thin paint. Excessively thin paint tends to run easily, and as it will require more coats to obtain the depth of colour needed than thicker paint, the chance of failure is increased.

Air-driven guns

Spray guns used by professionals operate at about 60 lb/sq in (4.20kg sq cm) air pressure and can deliver paint fast enough to enable the whole side of a car to be coated in less than half a minute.

Air-driven guns sold for do-it-yourself use are usually powered by a small mains-operated compressor and have a more modest output. The compressed air is pumped into the paint container on the gun and a mixture of paint and air comes out of the nozzle when a trigger is operated. Most guns produce a cone- or fan-shaped spray about 5 or 6 inches wide. The spray shape is altered by changing the nozzle. Like airless guns, they must be cleaned after each use by spraying thinners through them.

Thinning paint

No spray gun can cope with vehicle paint straight from the tin—the paint is too thick and must be diluted by adding the correct type of paint thinners.

Most small do-it-yourself spray guns operate satisfactorily on a 50-50 mixture of paint and thinners. You can test the mixture by aiming the spray on to an old piece of board, but a more scientific method is to check the paint viscosity. There are two devices in popular use for doing this. One is a viscosity cup, a small funnel with an accurately-sized lower orifice, which gauges the viscosity of the paint by allowing you to time (with a stopwatch) how long it takes a full measure of thinned spray to empty out through this hole. The other device is a ball in a glass tube filled with a sample of the paint. With this device, viscosity is determined by the time it takes the ball to fall through the fluid between two marks on the tube.

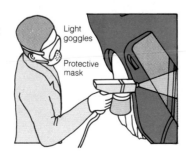

When spray-painting, mouth and eye protection is essential

Paint repairs projects

Project 87: Dealing with minor paint blemishes

Grading: ℒℒ
Time: 15min-1hr
Tools: Knife; old hacksaw blade
Materials: Tar solvent; cutting compound; rust preventive; cellulose stopper; wet-or-dry paper (400-grit); cloth; tissue; touch-up paint

A car naturally gathers small paintwork blemishes—spots of tar from the road, the occasional light scratch and chips of paint removed by a flying stone. These can be repaired quickly and easily.

Step 1. Tar spots should not be left on for too long, or the paint underneath becomes discoloured. Once a fortnight, check the car for tar and remove it with a proprietary solvent, available at accessory shops. A neat alternative is to use a dab of butter. It softens the tar and after ten minutes the spot can be wiped away with a dry cloth.

2. Polish out any surface scratches with a mild cutting compound. The compound contains a fine abrasive which removes a thin film of paint. It will remove light scratches entirely, and it will feather the edges of deeper scratches, making them less conspicuous.

3. Touch up chips and deep scratches in the paintwork as soon as possible as rust quickly attacks bare metal.

4. Use a knife blade to remove any flaky paint, then, using wet-or-dry paper, clean the damaged area down to shiny metal.

5. If rust has developed, clean off as much as possible with the knife and thoroughly clean the area with 400-grit wet-or-dry paper, used wet.

6. Clean and dry the area with a tissue and apply a proprietary anti-rust treatment, following the manufacturer's instructions.

7. After the treatment has had time to work, apply a smear of cellulose filler to bring the bare metal area up to the level of the surrounding paint. An old hacksaw blade makes a useful spatula for applying filler.

8. When it is dry (in about 20 minutes) smooth off any imperfections by rubbing them very lightly with 400-grit paper, used wet. Wipe dry with a tissue.

9. Brush the correct shade of touch-up paint over the blemish.

Project 88: Painting with an aerosol

Grading: ℒℒ
Time: 1hr-2hr
Materials: Wet-or-dry paper (400-grit); masking tape; soft cloth; wax remover or methylated spirit; newspaper; aerosol primer; aerosol top coat; mild rubbing (cutting) compound

Damaged paintwork areas up to about 12in across can be resprayed with a small aerosol can of matching paint.

To ensure that you get the correct colour, always quote the year, make and model of your car if you have to order paint and, if the car has one, quote the paint code number from the under-bonnet identification plate. As well as top coat, buy a suitable primer—most paint makers recommend a grey primer under light colours, and red primer under dark tones.

Paint should be sprayed on to a clean dry surface in a well ventilated, dust-free area. If painting in a garage, sprinkle water on a concrete floor to lay the dust, and leave the doors open to provide ventilation. In winter, the work area can be warmed with an electric fire to speed up the paint drying time—the quicker it dries the less chance there is of it picking up dust. For safety, switch off the fire when using inflammable materials and during the actual painting.

Step 1. Isolate the area to be painted by sticking masking tape to the bodywork. Once this border is established, use tape to stick newspaper up to the tape boundary to cover the surrounding paintwork.

2. Shake the aerosol canister thoroughly before use—see the instructions on the can.

3. Before painting the car, test the spray on a vertical piece of card. A faint covering, with paint forming separate droplets, means that the spray is too far from the surface.

*3. If the paint builds up too quickly and runs down the surface, the spray head is too close. The ideal distance is when the paint is fluid enough for the droplets to merge on the

Step 4.

Step 6.

Step 7.

Step 9.

surface without excess paint running off the panel—this can be achieved with a little practice.

4. The first coat is primer. It must overlap the edge of the old paint. When it is dry, lightly rub down the surface with dry 400-grit paper, then put on a second primer coat, again removing any blemishes when it is dry.

5. The first coat of gloss paint should be a light one—do not attempt to obtain a brilliant gloss at this stage. Follow it with subsequent coats, letting each coat dry before adding another, until the required depth of colour and shine is obtained.

6. If the shine of the new paint does not match the rest of the finish, leave it a week to harden, then rub it with a soft cloth and mild rubbing (cutting) compound. This will remove small surface irregularities and give a good gloss finish, making it difficult to distinguish a repaired area from the original paintwork.

Step 1.

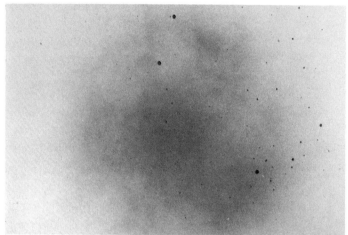

Step 3.

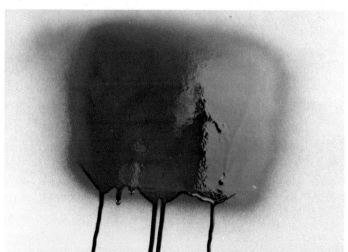

*Step *3.*

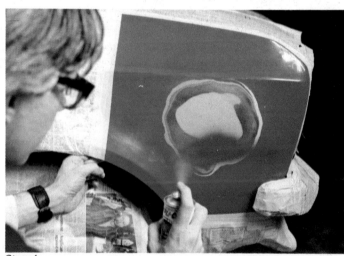

Step 4.

Step 5.

Step 6.

Paint repairs projects

Project 89: Painting with a spray gun

Grading: ✎✎✎
Time: Approx 1½hr for a front wing
Tools: Spray gun; viscosity cup
Materials: Primer, top-coat and suitable thinners; 400-grit wet-or-dry paper; lint-free cloth; 'tacky rag'.

When painting a large area, such as a complete wing, it is more economical to buy paint in bulk and apply it with a spray gun, than to tackle the job with a number of aerosol cans.

Metallic paints, which are difficult to match, are best left to professionals.

The paint used must be suitable for spraying and air-drying (some vehicle paints dry satisfactorily only in a low-bake oven). Because the paint will be too thick to spray directly from the tin, buy an equal quantity of suitable thinners. If you are spraying inside a garage, buy a small mask to cover your nose and mouth to prevent spray from being inhaled.

There are two types of spray gun which can be bought or hired: airless or air-driven (see page 175). Both operate at their full output the instant that the trigger is squeezed. Because of this, it is important to know how the gun is going to spray when the trigger is operated.

At first, some guns spatter blobs of paint on the work; the gun should be aimed away from the work when starting the spray, and moved to the area to be painted only when the spray is consistent.

If you are not familiar with the art of spraying, it is better to avoid the professionals' 'wet on wet' application. Without experience it is all too easy to apply too much paint which will sag and cause tear-drops as it runs down the panel. Instead, each coat should be allowed to dry until it is slightly tacky (check by touching the overspray on the masking paper) before applying the next coat.

When painting a door, for example, it is easiest to spray the edges first, then fill in the centre with horizontal strokes of the gun, overlapping all the edges by about 2 inches. Stop and restart the gun each time you change its direction, to avoid a build-up of paint.

When painting horizontal surfaces, hold the gun at an angle of about 45°. Keep the paint reservoir well filled—if the level drops too low, the pick-up pipe will draw in air, and blobs of paint will come out of the nozzle.

For best results, painting should be carried out in a warm, dry atmosphere. If working inside, make sure that the area is well ventilated, and sprinkle water on the floor to lay the dust before spraying. If working outside, pick a still day.

When painting big areas, it is important to eliminate dust. Wiping it off with a dry cloth actually attracts *more* dust because static electricity builds up on the surface. A special 'tacky rag', sold by paint suppliers, prevents this problem. It has a slightly sticky surface that picks up the finest dust film, and should be used immediately before paint is applied.

Step 1. Prepare the panel to be sprayed (see Project 88) and mask off the surrounding bodywork. It is best if the new paint ends at a body join, as this will disguise any slight mis-match.
2. Stir the paint thoroughly—in storage, darker pigments settle, and if they are not mixed in, the paint will be the wrong colour.
3. Some spray-gun instructions recommend a specific viscosity for the paint, and quote a time—for instance, 22-28 seconds. This is the time taken for a mixture of paint and thinners

Step 1.

Step 2.

Step 3.

Step 6.

Step 7.

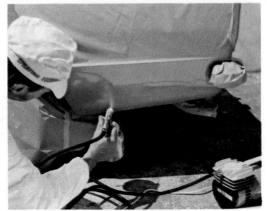
Step 8.

Paint repairs projects

Project 90: Brightening up shabby road wheels

to pass through a viscosity cup (see page 175). Adjust the consistency of paint with thinners until the correct viscosity is obtained.

4. If no viscosity is recommended, begin with a 50-50 mixture of paint and thinners, and test the gun by spraying a piece of vertical board. If the coating is semi-transparent and runs off the surface, the paint is too thin. Paint is too thick if it is reluctant to atomise and causes blobs to build up in the centre of a narrow spray.

5. Once the correct viscosity has been achieved, practise on a piece of board to assess the correct distance to hold the nozzle from the work (see Project 88).

6. Spray two coats of primer over the damaged area. Once it has dried, remove any imperfections from the surface by lightly rubbing with 400-grit wet-or-dry paper, used wet. Dry the area with a clean cloth.

7. Immediately primer painting is finished, empty the reservoir, pour in a small quantity of thinners and clean the nozzle by operating the gun. Remove the reservoir and clean the inside with fresh thinners. Fill the reservoir with the correct mixture of top-coat and thinners.

8. Start the spray away from the work until it is consistent, then move it on to the panel, keeping the nozzle parallel with it. Move the gun so that the spray gives an even coating without excessive paint build-up, which will cause a 'run'. Try to make the first coat even, and do not try to obtain a gloss finish at this stage.

9. If a run develops on a small area, it is best to wipe off the wet paint with a cloth dipped in thinners, and start again. On a bigger area, allow the run to dry, and smooth it out with 400-grit wet-or-dry paper, used wet. Make sure that the panel is thoroughly dry before applying the next coat.

10. Apply subsequent coats until the colour has the same depth as the original paint.

11. Remove the masking tape and paper. If the new paint lacks gloss, leave it for a week to harden, then polish it with rubbing compound.

Grading: 🔧
Time: Approx 30min per wheel
Tools: Wheelbrace; jack; power drill and rotary wire brush
Materials: Aerosol paint; masking tape; newspaper

Painted road wheels inevitably collect surface chips and rust spots. A once-a-year clean-up and repainting session makes a surprising difference to the car's appearance.

As the paintwork is so vulnerable, it is hardly worth spending a lot of time preparing the surface. Most wheels look almost new after the dirt, loose paint and rust have been removed and they have been given a coat of aerosol wheel paint. Allow one small can of paint for each wheel (or use the very large cans sold specially for treating five wheels).

Step 1. Inspect the wheels. Any that show cracks are dangerous and must be replaced.

2. Take off each wheel in turn (see Project 68) and lie it on the ground. Use a rotary wire brush to remove loose paint and rust.

3. Cover the tyre with newspaper and tape it into place, leaving the rim exposed.

4. Give about three generous coats of aerosol wheel paint.

5. Allow the paint to dry, then remove the masking tape. Refit the wheel to the car.

Step 1.

Step 2.

Step 3.

Step 4.

Step 5.

OUTSIDE AND IN

Corrosion

It has been called 'the red menace', 'the rust-bug', 'the tin-worm' and a score of other disparaging names, all describing the creeping rot of corrosion which can, eventually, totally destroy a car's bodywork. Costing motorists millions of pounds a year, rusting, the result of a simple chemical reaction between the car's steel panelwork, water and air, is aggravated by some of the very conditions that are designed to prevent it.

Poor application of under-body sealants and the overnight garaging of damp cars are examples. Corrosion is made worse by the application of salt to winter roads, it will bite at any unprotected chip or scratch in the car's paintwork,

and its occurrence has even been linked to the use, in certain areas, of high levels of agricultural fertiliser.

So great is the threat of rusting to the value of a car that a whole industry devoted to protecting car bodywork against corrosion attack has grown up in the last ten years. Initially, one or two entrepreneurs made fortunes by selling anti-rust treatments of dubious efficacy, and car manufacturers have had hard-won reputations destroyed almost overnight by public reaction to the poor corrosion resistance of their cars. There is even a motoring mythology attached to the curing of this modern-day plague: 'spray on old sump oil', 'never garage your car', 'always use a

cold-water wash', are the sort of tips passed around the public bar as panaceas for the common enemy.

It is a fact that cars built prior to 1950 suffered less from the debilitating effects of corrosion. Steel panelwork on these cars was much thicker than on those of today, salt had made only a limited appearance on winter roads, and cars were built on very strong chassis, so that it did not affect the strength of the car very much if a small section of the body corroded through.

Rust became a serious problem to car manufacturers and owners only when the advance of body design into the age of unitary (or monocoque) construction was complete. Bodies

built to this design have a fully integrated structure in which the strength and rigidity of the metal shell relies upon the complex relationships between the shaping and jointing of up to 200 individual body panel and reinforcing components.

As a result, there are very few sections of the body which play no part at all in the distribution of the forces acting on the shell. A weakness in a single panel, due to corrosion, has far-reaching effects on the car's ability to withstand accident damage or to cope with the everyday pounding. Panelwork has also become thinner, to reduce manufacturing costs and weight, so it is all the more susceptible to corrosion damage.

Anxiety about rust

Corrosion is unwelcome in any form because it looks so ugly, and because, once it has started, it is not easy to halt its progress. But it is important to distinguish between corrosion which is just unsightly, and that which may lead to structural weakness.

Owners who do not worry too much about their cars' appearance learn the penalty for neglect when it is found that water has made its way into the vehicle. Only later will the structural weakening due to corrosion show in a more dramatic form, with the collapse of a suspension mounting or the failure of a jacking point the next time an attempt is made to change a wheel.

Rusting that may affect a vehicle's safety is one of the more important examinations made in the annual MoT vehicle test for cars more than

three years old. While this test does at least ensure that those cars most at risk from corrosion damage are checked, the first test may be the first time an owner is made aware of the fact that his car is rusting away. Damage which can eventually result in failure of a major system of the car can start early in the car's life, and the sooner an owner spots it, the more there is the possibility to apply a cure. Unfortunately, MoT testers have no brief to tell owners of potential rust damage. All too often it is revealed only when a car is failed at a later stage in its life, requiring very costly repairs. On an older car this may be completely uneconomical and the next trip the car makes is to a scrapyard.

Corrosion attack can make its first appearance to the rear of the car, where the suspen-

sion is bolted on. Here the panelwork and suspension mountings are vulnerable to the corrosive effects of water and the abrasion of grit thrown up by the front wheels. This part of the car does not have the advantage of protection by the oil film leaked or vented from the engine which can give the front body parts a vital edge in the fight against rust.

On any part of the car which does not get a regular oil bath or that lacks good underbody protection, rusting is made much worse by the accumulation of mud and dirt. These deposits of grime, which build up in any open cavity of the underbody, lie in traps created by turned-up body flanges. They silt up the crevices behind parts fitted close to the body metal, retain moisture and may never properly dry out at any stage in the car's life.

The moisture, in contact with the body steel, has ideal conditions in which to accelerate rust attack. Mud poultices will also retain concentrations of road salt and other corrosive chemicals to add to the potential damage.

There is an obvious solution, and one that every motorist can carry out for himself with real benefits. Clean the underbody of the car in the early spring after the worst of the winter's corrosive onslaught, and thereafter, every few weeks. A high-pressure water-hose jet is needed, played inside the wings, including the inside of the flanges and in any traps at the front and rear. Ensure that the water jet penetrates and flushes away the mud. Obstinate patches of mud can be shifted with a piece of wood or plastic, as neither of these will damage the underbody.

Protecting the underbody

In the days when few cars arrived at the dealers with a factory-applied layer of underbody sealant, motorists paid extra to have cars treated with a heavy bituminous sealant. It was with dismay that some owners found that this treatment had not succeeded in keeping rust at bay. In many cases it even appeared to have hastened the rot. The sealant that remained on the car after a

few years was often shown to be concealing rust damage between the protective layer and the metal.

There are several reasons for this. Firstly, the paint-on sealants used then did not have the long-term elasticity necessary to maintain an unbroken protective layer for year after year in the face of bombardment by stones and grit. The material slowly dried out and cracked.

Inevitably, water and salt gained access to the underlying metal. Once rust had got a slight hold, its attack on the metal caused the surface around the crack to bubble, forcing the sealant away from the metal and allowing the corrosive solution to spread in contact with the metal surface, which may have been coated only with primer. As the car had already travelled from the fac-

tory to the dealer, some road dirt, and even salt, may have been present on the underbody, and been inadequately cleaned off before the sealant was applied. It is almost impossible to ensure complete cleanliness when cavities are inaccessible to steam and water-spray lances, and an already-assembled car is laced with cables, brake pipes and other underfloor fittings.

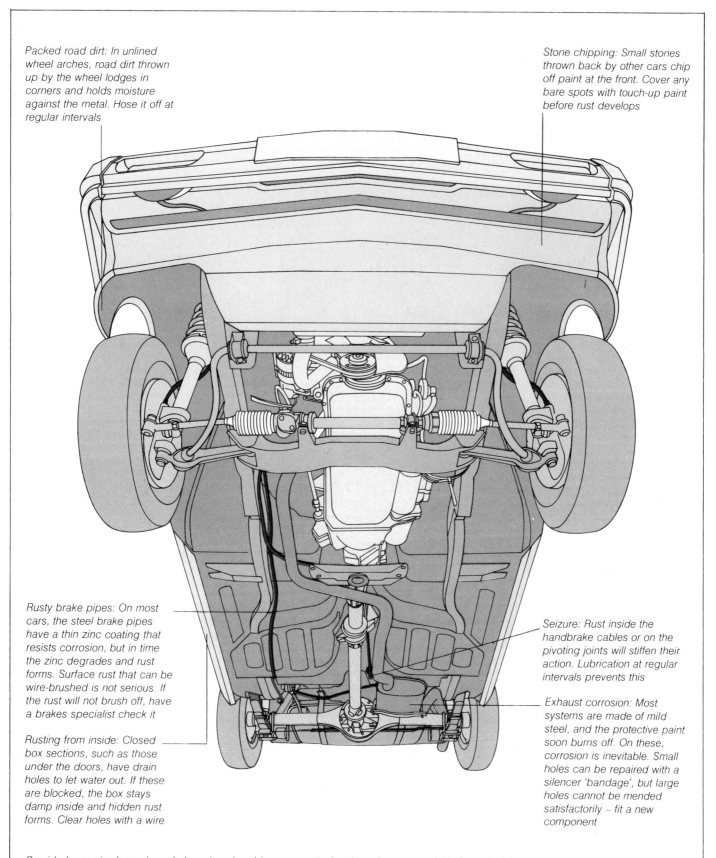

Packed road dirt: In unlined wheel arches, road dirt thrown up by the wheel lodges in corners and holds moisture against the metal. Hose it off at regular intervals

Stone chipping: Small stones thrown back by other cars chip off paint at the front. Cover any bare spots with touch-up paint before rust develops

Rusty brake pipes: On most cars, the steel brake pipes have a thin zinc coating that resists corrosion, but in time the zinc degrades and rust forms. Surface rust that can be wire-brushed is not serious. If the rust will not brush off, have a brakes specialist check it

Rusting from inside: Closed box sections, such as those under the doors, have drain holes to let water out. If these are blocked, the box stays damp inside and hidden rust forms. Clear holes with a wire

Seizure: Rust inside the handbrake cables or on the pivoting joints will stiffen their action. Lubrication at regular intervals prevents this

Exhaust corrosion: Most systems are made of mild steel, and the protective paint soon burns off. On these, corrosion is inevitable. Small holes can be repaired with a silencer 'bandage', but large holes cannot be mended satisfactorily – fit a new component

Provided a car is cleaned regularly, external rust is soon spotted and can be corrected. Underneath, it is not so obvious. The drawing shows where to look for corrosion – even on cars treated with underbody sealant

Corrosion

The anti-corrosion treatment on your car

Nowadays, the majority of cars are supplied with some factory-applied anti-rust treatments. Many are given a spray with a clear waxy film, supplemented by a tougher coat of a bituminous sealant in areas vulnerable to stone and grit damage—under the wheel arches for example. Some cars are sprayed all over the underbody with a bitumen-derived substance. Other manufacturers have developed even more specialised coatings which are baked on to the primed and painted surface for lasting protection.

Unfortunately, the speed of mass-production, and the methods used, result in cars leaving the production line with patchily applied sealants. The waxy-oil type of preparation that is used on many cars does not stand up to much physical attack either, so there is still a great need for caring motorists to check the protection applied and to deal with any early signs of rust.

It is not beyond the scope of the do-it-yourself enthusiast to protect the car's underbody, but it can be an unpleasant job, and it is difficult to do without equipment such as steam guns, ramps or a hoist. For those unwilling to tackle the task there are many professional treatment companies who are skilled in this type of work (see later).

If you do tackle the work, the key to success is to ensure that the surface is properly prepared, and that it is completely dry. Rust-proofing cannot be carried out on a damp or dirty surface.

All dirt must be removed, ideally with a rotary wire brush in an electric drill. Use a large cup-brush, and a small pointed one for scouring into the corners of seams. Flaking rust must also be removed, and the cleaned metal treated with a de-rusting agent to inhibit further corrosion. Any remaining areas of loose sealant from an earlier application should be cleaned away. Without these preparations, even the best bituminous coating will soon begin to flake off and corrosion will resume, with the new coating retaining the damp and aiding the process it is supposed to be preventing.

Once the surface has been adequately prepared, a protective mastic can be painted on liberally with an old paint brush. Thorough coverage is important, and it may be found helpful to use two coats, allowing sufficient drying time between applications. Care should be taken to avoid splashes on flexible brake hoses, the propeller shaft or front-wheel-drive shafts. On brake hoses, the splash could conceal warning signs of cracking; on a propshaft it can upset the balance of this fast-rotating part.

Inaccessible areas

Moisture penetrates and rust occurs in areas which are not visible when inspecting the underneath of the car. Examples are the box-section reinforcement areas of the chassis and the sills, and the interior of doors. Applying effective anti-rust protection to these cavities is impossible for the amateur.

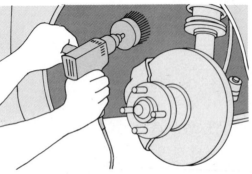

Before applying undersealant, have the car professionally steam-cleaned. Then raise it on axle stands, remove the wheels, and brush any dirt from the wheel arches

To keep undersealant off the paintwork, stick masking tape to the edges of the body at the wheel arches, under the doors and under the front and rear bumpers

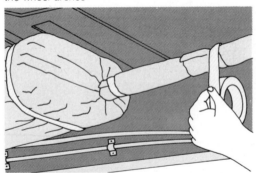

Underneath, use masking tape and newspaper to shield the exhaust system, the transmission moving parts, suspension dampers and brake components

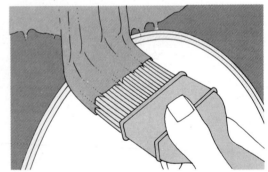

Brush on undersealant, taking care to stipple plenty into the crevices that trap dirt, such as the wheel arch inside edges and around headlamp shells

Professional rust protection

Professional rust-proofing specialists are geared up to flow-line principles of car treatment, and are able to achieve a more effective result than any DIY enthusiast can hope to accomplish.

The treatment starts by steam cleaning the underbody to remove all accumulations of dirt and oil. The car is then dried by forced air, and the sealant or rust-proofing is sprayed on by high-pressure gun. Various types of sealant material are used in each operator's process. A very heavy viscous material is put on the floorpan, but cavities and less exposed panels are usually treated with a thinner coating material.

Some anti-rust layers have 'self-healing' properties. This means that if part of the treated underbody is hit by a stone and the protection is penetrated, the layer creeps over the damaged spot and reforms the protective skin.

To treat blind sections, such as sills and the inside of doors, the specialist will drill small holes, spray in the appropriate rust protective under pressure, and then cover up the hole with a small bung. (These, incidentally, will tell the used-car buyer that the car has been rust-protected.) A long lance is used to ensure that the spray is applied to the whole of the internal area.

A specialist's work on a new car is usually guaranteed for several years, subject to periodic re-inspection which gives the company a chance to make good any defective work. Few specialists, however, will give a guarantee for the protection of a used car over three months old, as they cannot then tell how advanced the corrosion may be in blind areas.

The rust-proofing business is highly competitive, and the larger firms generally value their reputations too highly to do other than a first-class job.

When rust has taken hold

By the time rusting has shown through exterior paintwork, the panel may be seriously weakened. Rust may be well advanced on the unseen side of the metal, so a much larger area than is first suspected could be damaged.

Severely rusted metal loses its strength until eventually any pointed implement, such as a screwdriver, will pass right through it. It will have little structural strength for some time before this stage is reached. If there is evidence of extensive rusting in the region of any parts of the underbody to which major suspension components are attached, professional advice should be sought.

If the damage has been caught in time, repairing it need not be so devastatingly expensive as might be feared. New parts (whole panels or small sections) can be welded in, provided that there is sound metal to which the welder can cut back for a strong seam. Some dismantling of suspension parts may be necessary, and there are special problems if any welding needs to be done in the region of the fuel tank or pipe.

Provided your examination, or that of a garage, shows that the damage does not affect the structural strength of the car, certain DIY methods can make a sound repair. Areas like the body wings, the lower parts of doors and the junction between the lower trim and the floorpan at front or rear can safely be regarded as non-structural.

Here, kits of glass-fibre materials can be used (see Projects 91 and 91A).

When working with glass-fibre and resin bonders, the area to be treated must be thoroughly prepared first. DIY glass-reinforced plastics (grp) will cling to anything, and even bond firmly on to rusty metal, but such a repair will be short-lived, because rust will soon begin to spread to the surrounding area, and in only a very short time the panel will be as weak as ever.

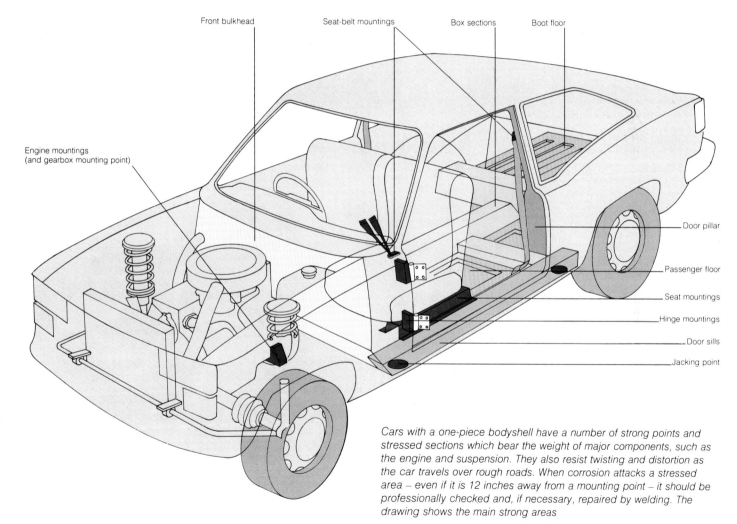

Front bulkhead · Seat-belt mountings · Box sections · Boot floor · Engine mountings (and gearbox mounting point) · Door pillar · Passenger floor · Seat mountings · Hinge mountings · Door sills · Jacking point

Cars with a one-piece bodyshell have a number of strong points and stressed sections which bear the weight of major components, such as the engine and suspension. They also resist twisting and distortion as the car travels over rough roads. When corrosion attacks a stressed area – even if it is 12 inches away from a mounting point – it should be professionally checked and, if necessary, repaired by welding. The drawing shows the main strong areas

Corrosion problems—on the way out?

Volkswagen set a new trend in 1979 with the introduction of a six-year warranty against body corrosion. Most other manufacturers are more generous and confident in the offer of anti-rust warranties than they have ever been in the past. Treatments made to new cars, and the materials used, are becoming more effective at preventing corrosion. An example is the application of a baked-on PVC coating to all exposed areas of the underbody as an integral part of a car's construction. More makers are sealing body cavity surfaces with wax coats, and at the vital design stage more is now understood about the avoidance of the dirt traps which used to exacerbate the problem of rusting.

Even with long-life warranties, however, manufacturers rightly insist that early signs of rusting are treated before structural damage has been allowed to occur. An annual inspection is likely to be one of the conditions of maintaining the warranty in force. While tomorrow's cars are unlikely to rust away to the scrapheap in quite the same way as today's, care and rapid action to retard the rusting process will remain the best way actively to prolong a car's life.

Corrosion projects

Project 91: Patching a hole with glass-fibre

Grading: 🦶🦶
Time: Approx 1½hr
Tools: Power drill; rotary wire brush or sanding disc; ball-pein hammer; pliers; tin-snips; old paint brush; file
Materials: Glass-fibre body-repair pack, body filler kit; for larger holes, expanded or perforated metal; wet-or-dry paper (120, 240, 320 and 400-grit); methylated spirit

On older cars, what seems to be minor surface rust sometimes turns out to be serious corrosion that has eaten right through the metal. Provided the weakened area is not load-bearing, the hole can be invisibly mended by using resin-bonded glass-fibre and plastic body filler.

Where the hole is a large one, the glass-fibre needs some support while the resin cures. A piece of expanded aluminium mesh or perforated zinc (sold by most iron-mongers) fitted into the hole, is the best means of support.

The glass-fibre patch provides strength and a base for a top-coating of plastic body filler. To make an even coating of filler, it is very important that the top surface of the glass-fibre is about ⅛ in below the level of the surrounding body-work.

Glass-fibre resin, like body filler, cures more quickly in a warm atmosphere. If necessary, use an electric fire to warm the working area to around 60°F (15°C).

Step 1. First masking the unaffected part of the damaged area, grind away surface paint using a rotary brush or power sanding disc, then cut out the weakened metal with tin-snips.
2. Hammer the edges of the hole down until they are about ¼in below the level of the surrounding bodywork.
3. Large gaps must be bridged to support the glass mat. Make up a fast-setting mix of body filler with double the quantity of hardener, and use this to secure a piece of expanded or perforated metal to the underside of the hole.

4. Cut two pieces of glass mat of a size and shape to fill the hole and make contact with the turned-down metal edges.
5. Mix the appropriate quantity of resin and hardener according to the maker's instructions. Because it cures quickly, mix only the quantity you need.
6. Put the first layer of glass mat into the hole and stipple on plenty of resin. When it is saturated, apply the second layer, adding more resin until the glass mat has a translucent appearance. If any resin drips on to the surrounding body-work, wipe it off immediately with a rag soaked in methylated spirit.

7. Once the resin has cured, use a file to trim off any surplus. Mix a suitable quantity of body filler and spread this over the glass-fibre patch so that it is slightly proud of the bodywork. Once it is hard, smooth it to the body shape (see Project 84) and paint the repair (see Projects 87 and 88).

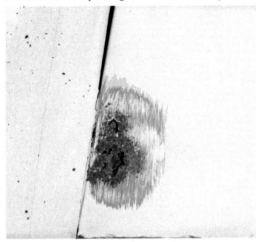

Step 1.

Step 2.

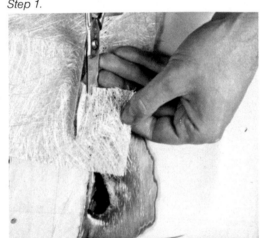

Step 4.

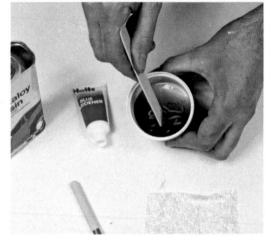

Step 5.

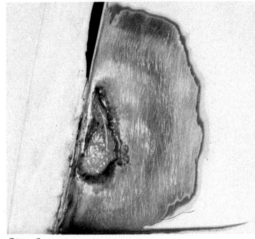

Step 6.

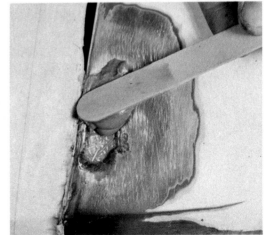

Step 7.

Project 91A: Repairing corroded metal with a fibre filler

Grading: 🖋🖋
Time: Approx 2hr
Tools: Power drill and rotary wire brush; hammer; tin-snips
Materials: Fibre-filler body-repair kit; masking tape; abrasive paper; rust preventive; wet-or-dry paper (400-grit); materials for painting (see Project 87)

To speed up and simplify the repair of rust holes, certain plastic body fillers have glass fibres mixed with them. The fibres increase the strength of the filler, so that the repair of a large hole can be tackled in one operation without the need to bond in a glass-fibre support, as explained in the previous project.

Adding fibres to the filler means that it cannot be rubbed down without the risk of uncovering 'hairs' of glass, so fibre-filler kits contain a flexible plastic sheet that is used as a mould to ensure that the filler surface conforms exactly to the shape of the bodywork.

The mould is taped into position to hold the filler over the hole until it hardens. Peeling off the plastic then leaves a repair with a smooth surface that blends with the surrounding area.

Steps 1 and 2. Refer to the previous project.

3. Treat the area with a rust-preventive fluid, following the instructions on the container.

4. Fix the flexible plastic sheet over the hole with masking tape, and use a felt-tipped pen to mark the edge of the hole on the plastic.

5. Using the recommended quantity of hardener, mix the appropriate amount of fibre filler. Do not mix more than is needed to fill the hole.

6. Unstick one end of the plastic sheet and peel it back. Spread fibre filler within the area previously marked on the plastic.

7. Replace the plastic sheet over the hole and tape it down so that it sits smoothly on the bodywork. The filler will block the hole in the panel. If necessary, gently smooth the plastic sheet so that it conforms

exactly to the contour of the panel. Allow time for the filler to harden.

8. Once the filler has hardened, peel off the plastic.

9. Mask the surrounding area and spray-paint with primer. Small blemishes can be removed with 400-grit wet-or-dry paper, used wet. Do not

shape the filler by rubbing down—this should not be necessary.

10. Paint the area as detailed in Projects 87 and 88.

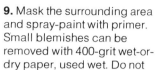

Step 3.

Step 4.

Step 5.

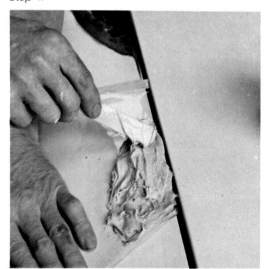

Step 6.

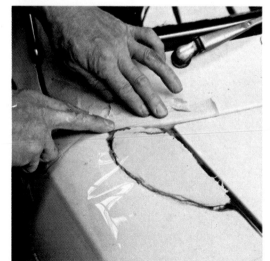

Step 7.

Step 9.

Corrosion projects

Project 92: Renewing a bolt-on front wing

Grading: ∫∫∫
Time: 1½hr-3hr
Tools: Spanners and screwdrivers to fit bumper, wing and lamp fixings; blunt knife; wire brush; rat-tail file; if necessary, nut splitter
Materials: New wing and set of fixing bolts, nuts and screws; rust preventive; mastic sealant; paint; cloth

About half the cars in current production have bolt-on front wings. This means that if a wing becomes corroded, or is badly damaged, it can be taken off and a new one bolted on in its place. Welded-on wings should be professionally replaced.

A bolt-on wing can usually be identified by a line of bolt heads visible in the bonnet drain gulley. Further bolts or screws hold the wing to the door pillar and to the body below the headlamp. On a few cars the upper bolts are mounted horizontally and can be seen only from inside the wheel arch.

A front wing that has rusted is usually held on by rusty bolts, so where a corroded wing is being replaced, the job is made easier if the bolt threads in the underwing area are wire-brushed clean and dosed with penetrating oil every 24 hours for at least three days before the wing is removed. Give the bumper fixings the same treatment.

A new wing will come finished in a thin coat of primer and will need repriming and painting immediately after it has been fitted.

Step 1. Disconnect the battery and the wiring to the sidelamps, direction indicators and headlamps—wiring connectors are usually under the wing or inside the engine bay.

2. If necessary, undo the bumper-fixing bolts and take off the front bumper. Remove any trim strips.

3. Undo the screws holding the side and headlamps and any repeater flashers to the wing, and remove the units.

4. Slacken the screws and bolts holding the wing. If necessary, ask a helper to hold any nuts that turn. Seized nuts are best broken off with a nut-splitter (see page 10).

5. Check that the wing is free to move, then take out all the fixings and separate it from the body.

6. Scrape any remains of sealant and dirt from the flanges to which the wing is bolted, with a blunt knife. Use a wire brush to clean off any flaky rust, then treat the area with a rust preventive prior to painting (see Projects 87 and 88).

Step 2.

Step 4.

Step 5.

Step 7.

Step 8.

7. Allow the paint to dry, then offer up the new wing, temporarily holding it with three or four bolts. Check that all its mounting holes align with the holes in the flanges. If necessary, loosen the wing and use a rat-tail file to elongate the holes.

8. With the wing removed, apply an even coat of mastic sealant to the body flanges.

9. Refit the wing using new nuts and bolts, if necessary, and tighten them evenly. Wipe off any surplus sealant.

10. Prime and paint the new wing (see Projects 88 and 89).

11. Refit the bumper and any trim; fit and connect the lights.

12. Check headlamp alignment (see Project 42).

Project 93: Patching the underbody sealant

Grading: 🔧🔧
Time: Varies, depending on the area covered
Tools: Drive-up ramps or jack and axle stands; chocks; wheel-brace; old paint brush; wire brush
Materials: Underbody sealing compound

In time, some sealing compounds become brittle and crack. The cracks trap water which can eventually seep between the layer of sealant and the body metal, setting up hidden corrosion.

To prevent this causing serious damage, a yearly inspection of the underbody sealant should be made. Probe any cracks with an old screwdriver and peel away any sealant that has lost its hold.

First check the wheel arches one at a time. Jack up the car, remove the wheel and use a powerful torch to check in the arch (do not get under the car at this stage). Wire-brush away caked-on dirt (use a hose if necessary) to expose the sealant underneath.

The underside of the car is best checked by driving the front and rear wheels in turn on to ramps or by supporting the car on axle stands (see pages 14 and 15).

This is a very messy job. Wear old clothes, an old hat and eye protection.

Step 1. Once loose underbody sealant has been located, peel it off, then remove any rust with a wire brush.

2. Coat the damaged area with fresh sealant, using an old paint brush to apply it with a stippling action. Sealant is available in aerosol cans—convenient to apply, but much more expensive. Try to use a sealant that contains rust inhibitors and remains tacky. This type is self-healing and will not crack.

Step 3.

Step 6.

Step 9.

Step 1.

Step 2.

Interior furnishings

It is not just in the mechanical and electrical areas that the car has progressed in recent years. Interior furnishings have undergone changes that result from the same major influences on modern car design. Most significant has been the emergence of cheap modern materials and processes to replace costly wood, leather and natural-fibre fabrics for upholstery. Science has also advanced knowledge about the role furnishing plays in important areas such as occupant safety, seating comfort, ergonomics, noise reduction and market appeal.

As recently as the late fifties, even a modestly priced car would have been fitted with seats upholstered in leather; and one did not have to move very far up the price ladder to enjoy the luxury of polished walnut-veneered facia panels and window sills.

However, as labour and material costs have increased, manufacturers have had to find other ways of fitting out the interior. Imitations of real wood in plastic rapidly became so good that it was very difficult to tell whether one was looking at a synthetic material or not.

A major consideration has been that of occupant safety. The highly impressive wood cappings along the top of facia panels on older cars could cause horrific injuries in an accident. In a modern car interior all protruding fittings have to be padded, and even small projections such as electric switches have to be shrouded or designed to have no sharp edges.

At the lower end of the price scale, the quality of interior furnishing has improved even more markedly. There are few cars still in production with painted metal window sills and facia panels. Safety considerations alone outlaw this simple finish, even if buyers were still prepared to accept it. Covering up metal panelwork also helps to suppress noise.

Moulded facias

The development of techniques to make intricate plastic mouldings and the superb results achieved have meant that cars soon passed through the era of plastic trim bonded to metal. Almost all cars today have one-piece facia mouldings in plastic, with excellent safety characteristics and a high quality surface finish.

These full-width panels often have an instrument binnacle as part of the moulding. In early designs it was soon found that the disadvantage of having to remove the complete panel to gain access to wiring or a faulty instrument was unacceptable. More modern facia mouldings overcome this by having instruments on a separate panel inset into the binnacle, or by having a separate instrument binnacle, removable to make access to the wiring much easier.

However, this is about the only concession to the needs of service and accessibility found in the facia area. The simplicity of working on cars like the old Jaguar Mk II, on which only two nuts had to be unscrewed to hinge forward the centre part of the facia panel, is just a fond memory. Nowadays, wiring, connections, fixing screws and clips tend to be buried away, with no means of gaining access to them being immediately apparent.

Matters are made worse by the manufacturers' attempts to give the facia a neater appearance. Where previously designers were content to fix the instrument panel or its surround with visible screws, every available technique is now used to avoid having any screw-heads on show.

For the DIY repairer who needs to gain access to the rear of the facia, the only reassurance is the certain knowledge that there *must* be a way. But in facia removal, take great care. It is all too easy to spoil the appearance of the trim by forcing components apart with improvised tools.

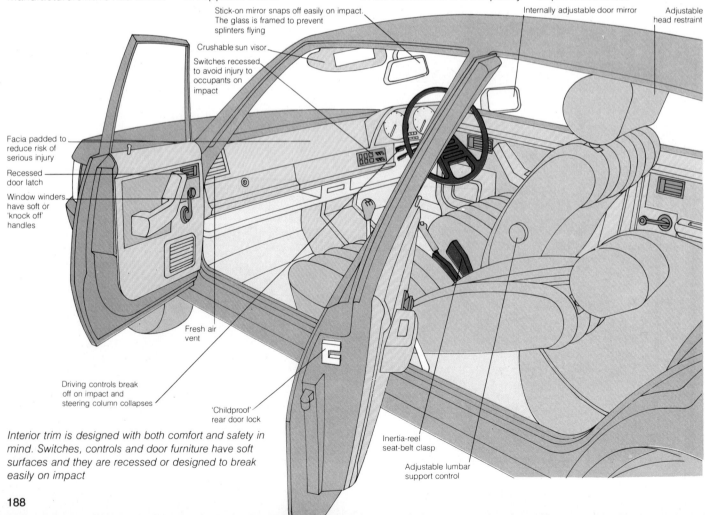

Stick-on mirror snaps off easily on impact. The glass is framed to prevent splinters flying

Crushable sun visor

Switches recessed to avoid injury to occupants on impact

Internally adjustable door mirror

Adjustable head restraint

Facia padded to reduce risk of serious injury

Recessed door latch

Window winders have soft or 'knock off' handles

Fresh air vent

Driving controls break off on impact and steering column collapses

'Childproof' rear door lock

Inertia-reel seat-belt clasp

Adjustable lumbar support control

Interior trim is designed with both comfort and safety in mind. Switches, controls and door furniture have soft surfaces and they are recessed or designed to break easily on impact

Getting behind the facia

As a first approach, a very careful check should be made for concealed screws. Sometimes the manufacturer buries screws in the underside of facia lips, behind the locking lid of a glove box or under tiny plugs of plastic, matching the facia material. The positions of any screws revealed by a close inspection may enable you to guess at a procedure for dismantling.

The next stage is to examine the projecting controls and other fittings to assess how many need to be undone. Heater controls may protrude through slots formed in the facia panel itself, or they may be mounted on a separate removable panel which simplifies the task. Control knobs are often fixed to the spindle by a buried grub screw; this can be removed only by using a small screwdriver.

If there is no concealed screw on the fitting there may be a spring catch reached through a small hole in the base of the knob or lever. A small pointed instrument pressed into the hole will release the catch, allowing the fitting to be pulled off. If there appears to be no visible means of positive attachment, try gently pulling off the unit. A surprisingly large number of fittings are designed to be removed in this way.

Next, remove the part of the facia to which access is required. Carefully examine the shape of the moulding for the join in individual pressings. It may well be that access to an instrument, for example, is obtained simply by lifting off the surround without removing the complete panel.

If a careful check has revealed no screws, there are two other possible methods of fixing. One is for the manufacturer to have used spring clips, into which a panel or facia section is firmly pressed home. The other method is the use of bolts or screws fixed to the underside of the facia. In either case it will be necessary to reach the underside of the facia by removing whatever trim is fitted.

A technique favoured by some foreign manufacturers for under-facia trim fixing is the use of plastic rivets. These take the form of a plastic surround like a button, into the centre of which a plastic pin is pressed. The presence of the pin forces outwards the inner flanges beneath the button, and locates the trim. The best way to remove this type of fastening is to take hold of the centre pin with a pair of long-nose pliers. If this is not possible, a pointed narrow instrument must be used to push the pin right through the fixing. It can then be recovered after the trim has been removed. With a torch or inspection light, it should now be possible to track down the main facia-fixing points.

If it is necessary to remove a steering column surround, you will find that the commonest method of fastening is to bury screws in deep sockets, accessible from under the wheel. There may also be clips to hold the upper and lower halves of a column surround together.

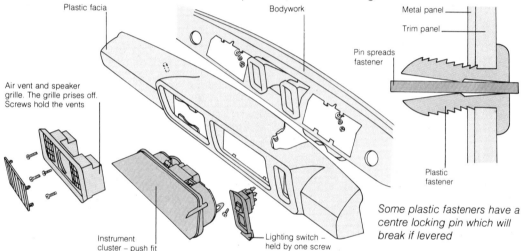

Plastic facia

Air vent and speaker grille. The grille prises off. Screws hold the vents

Instrument cluster – push fit

Bodywork

Lighting switch – held by one screw

Metal panel

Trim panel

Pin spreads fastener

Plastic fastener

Some plastic fasteners have a centre locking pin which will break if levered

On most cars the facia is a large plastic moulding. The instrument cluster is usually fitted separately so that it can be removed easily to change instrument lighting bulbs. This one is a press fit and is pushed out from below the facia

Windows, handles and trim

Behind door trim panels there are some very complex mechanisms. The window-winding system alone, designed to move a heavy piece of glass up and down by the light rotary action of a winder handle, is a fairly sophisticated mechanism. The door release and lock controls have to be operated by an interior handle as well, sited in a position which does not correspond with the outside handle.

It is rarely necessary to remove the trim and gain access to the mysteries that it conceals. Nevertheless, if something goes wrong with the window-winding mechanism, or if a door lock jams, it is an all-important first step in the repair. You may also wish to fit stereo speakers in the door. At first glance this seems a daunting task, as door trims usually give no clue to the repairer as to how they can be removed.

Begin with the armrests if any are fitted. Usually a careful check reveals at least two deeply recessed screws. In some cases it may be necessary to remove a snap-fastening section of trim in the armrest to gain access to the securing screws. Next, examine the window-winding handle. There are two popular methods of fastening: there may be a concealed pin through the shank of the winding handle, or a countersunk screw, often covered by a detachable section of cosmetic trim on the shoulder of the handle.

Door trim is generally held in place all the way round by spring clips which plug into holes in the door. They are fairly firm, and gentle levering away with a wide-bladed screwdriver or pallet knife is called for. Sometimes the door trim can be removed without disturbing a recessed internal door handle.

Window-winding mechanisms are usually of the rack-and-pinion type, in which the handle is geared to a large, quadrant cog-wheel. A lever attached to this provides the vertical movement while a parallel arm steadies the mechanism so that the window rises smoothly. Another type consists of centre-pivoted scissor levers—the angular movement of the scissor arms gives vertical travel of the window pane. In both these types there are a number of sliding surfaces and fulcrum points which benefit from lubrication—a smear of grease—when access to the door interior makes it possible.

In another type of window-lifting gear, an endless wire cable is used, wrapped round a drum and travelling round a lower fulcrum. Rotating the handle winds the cable, which is linked or geared to the window carrier to provide vertical lift.

Interior furnishings

Draughts and seals

Car doors and windows require effective sealing to keep out draughts, prevent the entry of rain water and to reduce wind noise at speed. Quite a small imperfection in the door seal, perhaps because the seal is not fitted correctly or the door catch is not adjusted sufficiently tightly to maintain the seal, can result in irritating wind hiss.

Adjustments to the fit of the door are fairly easy to make, provided you have a screwdriver to fit the very large crosshead screws used to fix the lock striker plate—the part fitted to the door frame. Adjustment is always made by experiment, first by moving the striker plate inwards until the fit

becomes too tight and the door will not close properly, and then by easing it back a little to achieve a snug fit.

The system used to seal the doors on most cars consists of two different types of material. On the door itself, often located in a retaining channel, there is a thick band of specially shaped spongy rubber material. It may be stuck in place with impact adhesive as well as being crimped into the holding channel. The door seal is supplemented by a second type of trim, clipped and/or glued over the flange of the door frame. The two are clamped together when the door is closed.

The most common fault of

this sealing system is that the seal comes away from its location and becomes distorted when it is pinched between the door and the frame. The soft

Sticking metal to glass

To save time and money during production, some car manufacturers fix the interior mirror and window catches and hinges directly to the glass with an adhesive specially made for the purpose.

If one of these components comes off, a suitable adhesive for refixing it can be bought from accessory shops. The most popular type sets hard within seconds of being exposed to the ultra-violet rays in sunlight, and when applying

foam rubber (or it may be a rubber tube) on the door may also harden with age, so that it no longer makes a good contact with the frame.

it, the area being worked on should be shaded by sticking brown paper over the glass with masking tape. Remove the paper when the component has been coated with a thin film of adhesive and you are confident that it is correctly positioned.

This type of adhesive is not satisfactory on tinted glass, which filters out ultra-violet light. In this case, it will be necessary to have the job done professionally.

Interior soundproofing

One has only to rev an engine hard with the bonnet open, or to stand on a bridge over a motorway, to appreciate how much noise has to be suppressed in a fast-moving car if the interior is to be acceptably quiet. The most important contribution to this is the fitting of thick felt and other damping materials beneath the carpets and against the engine compartment bulkhead.

Some manufacturers even fit a double bulkhead between the engine bay and the passenger compartment, but this takes precious space and can be accepted only in a large car. Other soundproofing measures include the filling of all holes in the passenger compartment with rubber plugs and mastic putty, the use of anti-drumming pads of heavy, adhesive mastic on door panels, and the isolation of major mechanisms, like the gearbox, from the body by rubber bushes.

Accessory kits of sound-damping material are available for most popular cars, to supplement the minimal insulation installed by the makers of less expensive models. The kits consist of ready-cut and shaped pieces of fibre mat, reconstituted foam rubber sheet and anti-drumming pads. Sections are provided to cover all the metal panelwork of the car that may resonate or

transmit engine noise, transmission whine or road and tyre rumble. This may include the panel beneath the rear seat, the boot floor and the rear bulkhead, all of which may be

transmitting resonance from the suspension. When a noise-reduction kit is fitted, a check should be made on the fit of door seals, as already mentioned, and on tightness

of the window glass against its surrounding seals when the windows are closed. Opening quarter-lights are particularly prone to noisy air leakage.

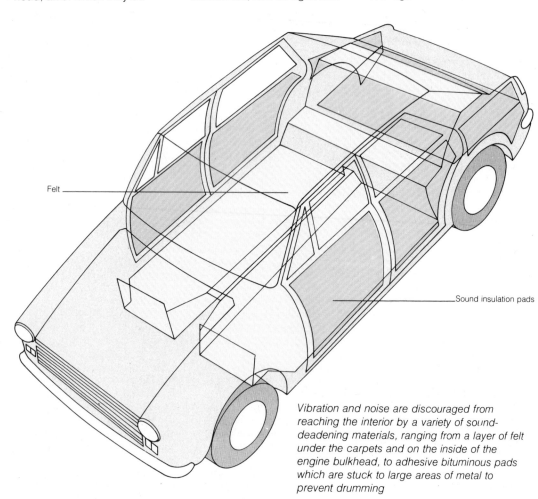

Felt

Sound insulation pads

Vibration and noise are discouraged from reaching the interior by a variety of sound-deadening materials, ranging from a layer of felt under the carpets and on the inside of the engine bulkhead, to adhesive bituminous pads which are stuck to large areas of metal to prevent drumming

Removal of seats and head-restraints

Seats are built up on a sturdy frame, usually of tubular steel. A sophisticated combination of various densities of foam rubber, fibre pads and webbing is used for the cushioning and springing. Metal springing mats are also used. The front seats have fore-and-aft adjustment for driver and passenger comfort, and often there is also provision for the backrest to recline. Sometimes this is in the form of a cogged wheel into which a locking peg engages, in whatever position is chosen. A more satisfactory, infinitely adjustable system is operated by gears linked to a handwheel.

Firm seat mountings are a vital part of car safety design. The mounting runners are usually secured to the floor by bolts at each end of the runner. Generally the nuts into which these bolts fasten are of the captive type—they are located by a welded-on trap underneath so that they cannot turn. If they do not undo easily, beware of over-exertion with the spanner (see Stubborn Brutes, pages 10 and 11). In a few cars, the locating nuts are welded to the floor inside the car and corrosion is less likely. It helps, when undoing these nuts and bolts, to slide the seat fully forward first, and undo the rear ones from the back; then slide it back for access to the front ones. While the seats are out, take the opportunity to clean the newly revealed carpet thoroughly, and to clean and lightly grease the runners.

A growing number of cars are fitted with headrests—more correctly called head restraints, since their main function is to prevent whiplash injury to the neck if the car is run into from behind. A head restraint may form an integral part of the backrest, but by far the most common type consists of a pad of upholstered plastic, supported above the seat back on a metal pillar (or pillars) which slides into a socket so that the height can be adjusted. For maximum safety the head restraint should be adjusted so that its centre point is in line with the centre of the back of the head—about eye level.

Some drivers find that the presence of head restraints is an obstruction to vital all-round vision, particularly in city traffic, and may wish to remove them. On many cars they simply pull straight out of their sockets, although the seat backrest may first have to be reclined to give sufficient clearance.

Inside a seat: As well as supporting the springs and upholstery, the steel frame of the driver's seat will carry the latching mechanism for fore-and-aft adjustment. It may also include a mechanism for adjusting the backrest rake and sometimes, as on this one, have an adjustable lumbar-support pad, which slightly alters the shape of the backrest

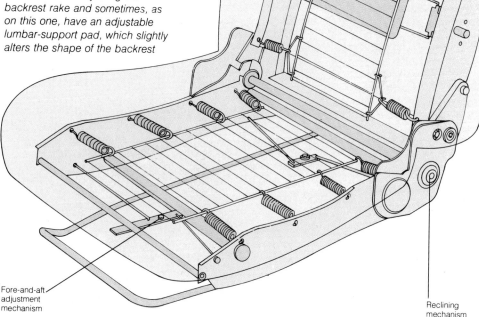

Head restraint frame

Lumbar support adjustment

Fore-and-aft adjustment mechanism

Reclining mechanism

Keeping it clean

Cars can be repainted, engines and mechanical components can be rebuilt, but once the interior of a car has been allowed to fall into a state of prolonged neglect it may be impossible to restore it even with the most vigorous cleaning. Regular valeting of the interior will help to maintain the value of the car.

Not to be forgotten when carrying out regular cleaning tasks are the top edges of the windows, the instrument glasses, the inside surface of the windscreen and back window (take care not to damage heated rear window elements), and the top of the facia. Smokers in particular need to clean the headlining and the tops of sun visors with a spray-on foam or emulsifying type of upholstery cleaner, to prevent the heavy yellow discolouring which can form there.

A small tear in a vinyl seat or headlining can be almost invisibly mended by using a vinyl repair kit, available from most accessory shops.

The kit includes special adhesive and colouring, and a compound for making a mould. This is used to match the surface of the repair to the texture of the surrounding vinyl.

Interior furnishings projects

Project 94: Renewing old carpets

Grading: ⟋⟋
Time: 3hr-5hr
Tools: Spanners and screw-drivers to remove interior fittings; pencil; scissors; chalk; sharp knife
Materials: New carpet; carpet adhesive; impact adhesive; press-studs

Where the car manufacturer uses an intricately moulded, one-piece floor covering, it will not be possible to duplicate it from a flat piece of carpet. In this case, all you can do is to use the old carpet as a rough guide to cutting the replacement at awkward curves. Then machine-sew the cut edges together.

On cars with a shallow transmission tunnel and not too many awkward contours, new car carpeting can be cut to shape fairly easily, using the old carpet as a pattern.

Step 1. Remove as many floor fittings as possible. Unbolt and remove the front seats and take out the seat-belt anchorages.

2. Unscrew the gear-lever knob and remove the gaiter. If the transmission tunnel has an oddments tray or console, undo the fixing screws or bolts and remove it.

3. Take out the screws holding the door-sill trims and remove them.

4. Take out all the carpet, lay the pieces on the ground and mark out the shape(s) on to pieces of paper.

5. Trim the paper slightly over-size and fit it into position in the car. Trim it exactly to shape with scissors. Mark each pattern with any shaping cuts or holes needed for floor fittings.

6. Lay each pattern the right way up on the new carpet and mark the edges with chalk.

7. Cut along the chalk lines with a sharp knife. If the carpet begins to fray, coat the backing edges with carpet adhesive.

8. Stick the carpet on the transmission tunnel and side sills, using impact adhesive.

9. Carpet in the footwells can be laid in position or secured with special press-studs, available from upholsterers.

10. Refit the seats, seat belts and interior furniture.

Step 1.

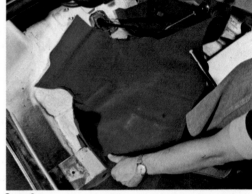
Step 3.

Step 4.

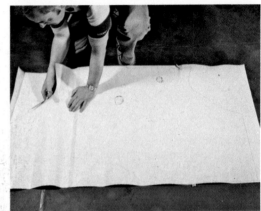
Step 5.

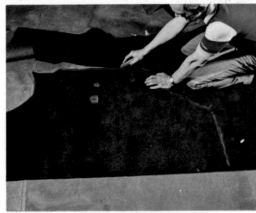
Step 7.

Step 8.

Step 9.

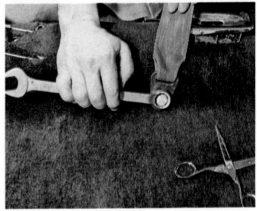
Step 10.

Interior furnishings projects

Project 95: Tracing and curing water leaks

(For leaking window rubber seals, see Project 85)

Grading: 🔧
Time: Up to a day
Tools: Watering can
Materials: Impact adhesive; mastic sealer; stiff wire; talcum powder

Cars are designed so that water, which inevitably leaks into some of the body cavities, is channelled away without reaching the passenger compartment, and without collecting in places where it might cause corrosion. Rain can seep into a door interior through the window seal, so the door is fitted with drain tubes and/or holes to let it out. Similarly the heater intakes, and perhaps the wiper spindle recesses immediately in front of the windscreen, have channels to drain water harmlessly into the engine compartment or out under the front wings.

There are, however, a number of faults which can allow water into the passenger compartment where it soaks the carpet or underlay, causing mould and rot, and creates ideal conditions for corrosion of the metal floor.

It can be very difficult to find where water gets in. Start by ensuring that all the door and heater-intake area drain holes are not blocked. Next examine the door seals for obvious signs of displacement or damage.

If there are no obvious signs of entry, choose a dry day and remove all the damp interior trim, carpeting and underlay. This may involve removing and refitting the front seats and seat belts. Most have straightforward bolt or screw fixings.

Once the carpet is out, put it somewhere to dry, then clean and dry the wet floor.

You now need a helper and a lot of rain. The nearest rainstorm is at the local car-wash. With your helper in the back seat, ask him to watch the rear door and window seals while the car-wash is in operation. Check the front doors and watch under the facia for water seeping down from the wiper spindles and heater intake.

Step 1. It is a good idea to check the car for interior leaks every time it is cleaned. If you can, peel back the floor covering and look for moisture underneath. If the car has a fixed floor covering, and the windows persistently mist up when the vehicle is parked, suspect water ingress.
2. The efficiency of the door drain holes can be checked by playing water from a watering can or a hose on the outside of the closed window. Water should drain through the holes immediately.
3. Behind the door trim (see Project 98) there is a layer of plastic that acts like a shower curtain to keep water off the trim. If water seeps from the bottom of the door trim into the car, the plastic layer is broken.
4. Cut a small piece from a polythene bag and stick it in place with mastic sealer or adhesive to provide a waterproof patch.
5. Fibreboard trim panels distort if they get wet. To straighten one, thoroughly dampen the back of the panel by wiping it with a wet cloth, then lay the panel on a dry, flat surface, using weights to press it flat. Allow about 48 hours for it to dry.
6. Displaced door and window seals will let in water and must be refitted. Carefully clean out the seating slot and dry it thoroughly, if necessary, using a hair dryer.

7. Coat the body flange with impact adhesive or mastic sealant and push the seal firmly into position with the palm of the hand.
8. If the seals appear to be sound but still leak, try the car-wash test. To highlight water leaks, dust talcum powder on the door seals.
9. After the car-wash, open each door carefully and note any water entry points. The leak may be cured only by renewing the complete seal.
10. A car-wash will not help in detecting leaks in the floor. A helper inside the car may spot the leak if you spray a strong water jet from a garden hose into each wheel arch and under the car.

Step 2.

Step 3.

Step 4.

Step 6.

Step 7.

Step 9.

Interior furnishings projects

Project 96: Taking a seat apart

Grading: ✿✿✿
Time: 2hr-3hr, depending on seat construction
Tools: Large-bladed screwdriver; pliers
Materials: Hooked wire

If the metal frame inside one of the seats breaks, it can be difficult to get it repaired. Few professional garages want to involve themselves in the time-consuming business of stripping off the upholstery and refitting it afterwards; most will try to sell you a new seat.

With patience and common sense, however, it is possible to remove the upholstery yourself—and put it back. Once the frame is uncovered, it can be taken to a garage, engineering workshop or blacksmith for repair. Usually only a small, inexpensive welding job is involved.

Here we show how a typical front seat comes apart:

Step 1. If the seat has a reclining backrest, separate it from the cushion. This one has small clips at the end of each pivot—they are prised out with a screwdriver.

2. Once the clips are out, disengage the backrest, if necessary, levering the hinge plates off the pivot pins with a large screwdriver.

3. On this seat, four spikes fix the backrest cover at the base. They can be levered straight with a screwdriver.

4. The cover can then be disengaged from the spikes and taken off the backrest. This seat has a sliding control on the outer edge to unlatch the seat-locking mechanism—the covering is simply tucked under this, and is pulled out by hand as the cover is removed.

5. Underneath, the padding consists of a layer of felt on a firm fibre base. The semi-rigid fibre is bent over the frame and is easily removed.

6. This frame is broken at the top. It is a simple welding job to repair it.

7. If the seat cushion is damaged, the upholstery is more complicated to remove. In this case, the bottom edge of the upholstery is stiffened by a wire with its ends wrapped round the frame. This should

be carefully unhooked.

8. Usually, spikes or spring clips hold down the rest of the fabric edge. Straighten any spikes (see Steps 3 and 4) and carefully prise out any clips with a screwdriver. Do not force plastic clips; if they break, replacements have to be ordered and they can often

Step 1.

Step 4.

Step 5.

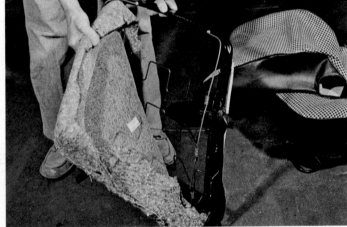
Step 9.

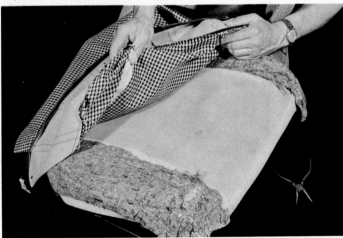
Step 10.

take a long time to arrive.

9. If the cushion is shaped, the cover may have trim rods—wire inserts that are pulled down on to the spring base by split-rings. Before prising the split-rings apart, make a note of their position on a sketch pad.

10. Once the split-rings are removed, the cover can be taken off.

If necessary, cloth covers can be cleaned by soaking them in a biological detergent—this will remove most of the stains.

11. The felt, foam and fibre padding will usually be fixed to the spring base by bending over the edges of the fibre. If any of the foam is stuck to the base, peel it off carefully with an old knife, taking care not to damage the foam. It can be restuck with double-sided adhesive tape.

12. Reassembly is a reversal of the dismantling process.

The most difficult part will probably be refitting the split-rings. It will help if you make up a small hooked tool from an old wire coathanger to pull the trim rods towards the spring base of the seat when fixing each split-ring.

13. Once it is in the correct position, close the ring with pliers.

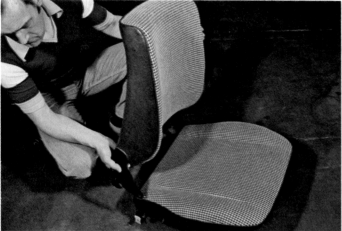
Step 2.

Step 3.

Step 7.

Step 8.

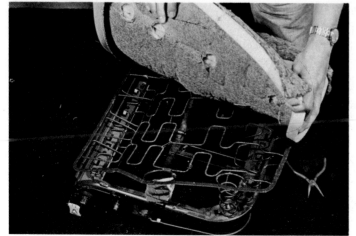
Step 11.

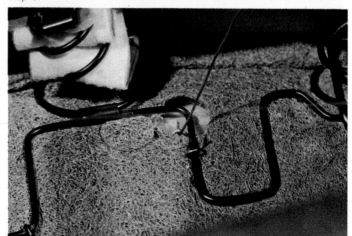
Step 12.

Interior furnishings projects

Fitting a child safety seat

A safety seat to carry a small child must be mounted on fixings attached to a suitably strong section of the car bodywork, or the steel frame of a glass-fibre-bodied car. The two front mountings are fitted under the rear seat, and on cars with a fixed back seat the rear fixings for the child seat are bolted to the metal rear parcel shelf.

On cars with an opening tailgate, where the rear shelf is removable and made of plastic or board, the rear mountings for the child seat must be fitted to metal bodywork in the luggage compartment.

Project 97: Fixed back seat (illustrated)

> **Grading:** 🔧🔧
> **Time:** Approx 2hr
> **Tools:** Screwdriver to undo rear seat-mounting screws; drill; suitable bits; centre punch; spanners to fit mounting nuts and bolts
> **Materials:** Safety seat and mounting kit

Step 1. Undo the screws securing the seat cushion and lift it out. If the car is a hatchback, see under Fold-down seat.
2. Undo the screws holding the bottom of the seat backrest, unhook the upper edge from the parcel shelf and take it out.
3. Most new cars have rear seat-belt mounting points under the seat cushion. Where these are provided, remove the blanking plugs.
4. Bolt the two lower fixing straps to the seat-belt mounting holes.

If there are no holes, see Fold-down seat, Steps 2-4.
5. The slope of the rear window may make it difficult to drill down into the parcel shelf. If so, drill from the underside, inside the boot. Mark the two holes, drill a $\frac{1}{8}$in (3mm) pilot hole, then use a large bit to enlarge each hole to the recommended size.
6. From inside the car, fit the seat-mounting bolts with the recommended spacers and washers.
7. Underneath the shelf, thread a large washer and nut on to the bolt. You will now need a helper to hold a spanner on the bolt inside the car while the nut is fully tightened.
8. Refit the seat backrest, pull the lower mounting straps upwards and refit the cushion. Connect the four mounting straps to the seat and adjust them as tightly as possible.

Project 97A: Fold-down seat (not illustrated)

Step 1. If there is a rear parcel shelf, remove it, and take out the floor covering in the luggage area.
2. Refer to the manufacturer's fitting instructions, and mark the mounting holes. Look behind the panel to make sure that the drill will miss the fuel tank, fuel and brake pipes and electrical wiring. If necessary, reposition the holes slightly.
3. Drill a $\frac{1}{8}$in (3mm) pilot hole. Enlarge it to the recommended size with a larger bit.
4. Bolt on the anchorages, using the recommended spacers and washers. Ask a helper to stop the bolt head from turning while the nut is fitted.

Step 1.

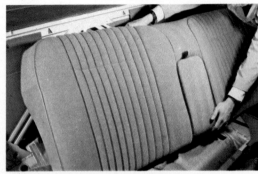

Step 2.

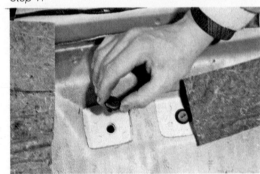

Step 3.

Step 4.

Step 5.

Step 6.

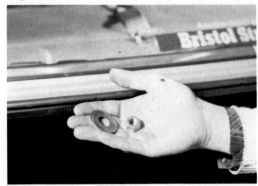

Step 7.

Step 8.

Interior furnishings projects

Project 98: Getting behind the trim

Grading: ♫♫
Time: Approx 30min-1hr
Tools: Screwdriver; skewer; hooked wire or shaped metal to remove door handle; screwdriver to fit armrest screws; large and small flat-bladed screwdrivers

To fit a radio speaker or cure water leaks it is sometimes necessary to remove an interior side-trim panel, either in the door or the body.

To remove a door trim, some surface 'furniture', such as the window-winder and perhaps an armrest and door handle, must be taken off before the panel will come away.

The picture sequence shows how the door furniture and panel are removed from the majority of cars, but if the panel does not readily respond to the treatment illustrated, seek expert help. The backing is usually only fibreboard, and excessive force can distort or tear it.

Step 1. Window-winder handles are held by a screw, pin or clip to the winder shaft. Fixing screws are usually concealed by a plastic finisher —prising this up will uncover the screw head.

2. Where door handles are retained by a spring clip or a cross-pin, press the trim panel towards the door to uncover it. A cross-pin can be pushed out with a long skewer or a very small screwdriver. Depending on its shape, the clip can either be hooked out with a piece of stiff wire, or may need to be pushed out with a piece of shaped metal. Once the fixing is removed, pull the handle off the shaft.

3. Armrests are less complicated and are normally held by long screws. Look for screw-holes under the armrest if they are not immediately apparent.

4. On some cars the edging round the interior door handle must come off. Plastic surrounds may be held in place by clips that are disengaged by slightly distorting the moulding. Others are retained by pegs and can be prised off.

5. On cars where the trim hooks over the top of the door, it may be necessary to unscrew the interior button lock—this can be done by hand.

6. Most trim panels are secured by hidden retaining clips. Use a large screwdriver blade to prise the panel gently from the door. If the trim is a tight fit, first ease the edge up with a small screwdriver to make it easier to insert the big one.

7. Slide the screwdriver alongside each retaining clip in turn, and lever carefully to prise the trim away from the door. On some cars, one edge of the trim will be slotted into a metal channel. Undo the clips on the other three sides before sliding the trim clear of this channel.

8. Remove the trim.

Step 1.

Step 2.

Step 3.

Step 4.

Step 7.

Step 8.

Diagnosis

DIAGNOSIS

Sensing trouble

Breakdowns on the road rarely happen without some form of warning. Usually it is a light glowing on the instrument panel, an unusual noise or an unexpected vibration that will tell even the most non-mechanically-minded driver that something is wrong with the car. When the cause is not obvious at first sight, however, diagnosing the warning signs usually needs a little detective work.

All cars have instrument-panel warning lights that will give an instant indication of a slipping or broken generator belt or lack of engine oil pressure. Some cars with more comprehensive instrumentation will have an oil-pressure gauge, an ammeter or a battery-condition indicator that will give advance warning of trouble.

However, because the parts of a car wear and deteriorate gradually, the onset of any serious faults may be difficult to detect. The steering and braking systems are good examples of areas in which gradual wear can lead to sudden failure if the warning signs are not heeded in time. If the steering feels slack and imprecise, or the brake pedal feels spongy, or the car pulls to one side when braking, it is a sure sign of impending failure; but these may be symptoms a driver ignores in daily use.

A knocking noise, on the other hand, is a much more obvious sign, and although it can prove elusive to find, methodical elimination of possible causes will eventually track down the fault.

Warning signs should never be ignored. By making use of them in good time you will be able to avoid the inconvenience of a breakdown and much more expensive repairs later. Some of the most common warning signs and their possible causes are given below.

Unusual engine noises

Problem:
Rattling noise from the engine which occurs only when the car is cornering

Likely causes:
Low engine oil level, sometimes the noise may be accompanied by a flashing oil-pressure warning light, or fluctuating oil-pressure gauge. Air cleaner assembly loose or touching the underside of the bonnet. Exhaust pipe loose. Engine mountings worn, loose or broken.

Problem:
Heavy knocking noise as the engine is revved

Likely cause:
Big-end bearings worn. The symptoms are sometimes accompanied by a flickering oil-pressure warning light or fluctuating oil-pressure gauge.

Problem:
Rumbling noise under load

Likely causes:
Worn crankshaft main bearings. Flywheel bolts loose—in severe cases, the noise may also be accompanied by engine vibration at high revs.

Problem:
Light tapping noise when the engine is idling

Likely causes:
Valve clearances need adjustment. Worn camshaft or tappets. Crankshaft pulley loose, or pulley-locating keyway worn.

Problem:
Pronounced tapping noise when the engine is hot

Likely causes:
Worn connecting rod or piston small-end bearings. Excessive tappet clearances.

Problem:
Rattling noise from the front of the engine

Likely causes:
Worn timing chain or chain-tensioner assembly. Broken tensioner, or tensioner in need of adjustment. Worn water-pump bearings. Loose fan assembly. Loose generator mountings. Loose crankshaft pulley.

Problem:
Rattling or slapping sound when starting the engine from cold

Likely causes:
Slow oil-pressure build-up due to low oil level, worn crankshaft bearings or incorrect type of oil filter. Sticking or broken oil-pressure relief-valve spring inside oil pump or cylinder block. Piston slap, caused by excessive piston-to-cylinder-bore clearance (not necessarily serious).

Problem:
Rattling noise at slow speeds

Likely causes:
Distributor components worn, or centrifugal advance-weight springs detached or broken. Crankcase emission-valve spring weak or broken.

Problem:
Screeching noise from the front of the engine

Likely causes:
Generator drive belt slack and/or slipping. Seized or frozen water pump. Seized or dry generator bearings. On power-steering systems: slack or worn drive belt.

Problem:
Bumping or bubbling noise when the engine is switched off

Likely causes:
Engine coolant boiling. Air locks in the cooling system or heater system.

Problem:
Hissing noise coming from near the carburettor

Likely causes:
Inlet manifold gasket leaking. Carburettor-to-inlet-manifold gasket leaking. Crankcase emission-valve hose leaking. Brake vacuum-servo hose leaking. Vacuum advance pipe detached from carburettor. Air cleaner assembly loose or badly fitted.

Problem:
Chuffing sound from the engine under acceleration

Likely causes:
Leaking exhaust pipe or silencer. Blown exhaust manifold gasket. Loose or broken exhaust manifold-to-pipe-clamp joint. Engine oil filler cap missing.

Clutch

Problem:
Grinding noise when the clutch pedal is depressed

Likely causes:
Clutch release bearing worn (or, on carbon thrust-types, broken). Misaligned thrust pad on pressure-plate release fingers.

Problem:
Rattling noise during clutch engagement

Likely causes:
Engine mountings or steady-bar mountings loose or broken. Exhaust pipe mounting

slack or broken. Detached or broken clutch-operating arm. Loose or broken clutch springs.

Problem:
Screeching noise when the clutch pedal is fully depressed

Likely causes:
Worn, seized or broken clutch spigot bearing in flywheel. Worn clutch release bearing.

Problem:
Clanking or knocking noise when the clutch is engaged

Likely causes:
Propshaft or drive-shaft universal joints badly worn. Worn drive-shaft coupling splines. Loose propshaft coupling bolts. Worn or loose propshaft centre-bearing mountings. Loose or worn rear axle mountings.

Problem:
Whirring sound that stops when the clutch pedal is depressed

Likely causes:
Gearbox constant-mesh gear or bearing noise, possibly caused by low gearbox oil level.

Problem:
Clutch judder during engagement

Likely causes:
Worn clutch plate. Worn or broken clutch pressure-plate fingers or diaphragm. Oil on clutch plate. Worn or broken engine or steady-bar mountings.

Problem:
Engine speed increases on hills but the car does not accelerate

Likely causes:
Clutch slip due to worn clutch plate or insufficient clutch-operating clearance. Oil on clutch plate.

Brakes

Problem:
Brakes judder when applied

Likely causes:
Worn brake linings. Warped brake discs or brake drums. Accumulation of lining dust inside brake drums. Brake pads sticking in caliper on disc brakes. Broken shoe-return springs inside brake drums. Loose or worn suspension.

Problem:
Brakes pull on one side

Likely causes:
Incorrect front drum brake adjustment. Unequal front tyre pressures. Contaminated brake shoe linings due to leaking hydraulic wheel cylinder. Brake pad seized in caliper on disc brakes. Caliper piston or wheel cylinder seized. Air in system.

Problem:
Brakes squeal when applied

Likely causes:
Accumulation of brake lining dust. Excessive rust build-up on brake disc. Worn brake pads or linings. Glazed pads or linings. Anti-squeal shims missing or incorrectly fitted on disc pads.

Problem:
Loss of efficiency during heavy braking or on a long descent

Likely causes:
Brake fade due to worn or incorrect pad or lining material. Hydraulic fluid boiling, producing vapour lock in hydraulic system (caused by old or contaminated fluid). Handbrake accidentally left on. Air in hydraulic system.

Problem:
Grinding noise when the brakes are applied

Likely causes:
Brake pads worn down to the backing plates. Brake linings worn down to the shoes. Stone lodged between caliper and disc. Rust on discs or drums.

Problem:
Grinding noise when the brakes are off

Likely causes:
Stone lodged between caliper or splash shield and disc. Excessively slack or worn front wheel bearing.

Wheels

Problem:
Rubbing or grinding noise at low speeds

Likely causes:
Brakes binding, due to seized disc caliper or wheel-cylinder pistons. Brakes binding due to over-adjustment. Damaged, worn or dry wheel bearings. Tyres touching wheel arch or bodywork due to damage, overloading or faulty tyre sidewall. Mud flaps scraping the road, due to overloading.

Steering

Problem:
Vibration through steering wheel or body at moderate and high speeds

Likely causes:
Wheels out of balance. Tyres damaged or out of round. Buckled wheels. Wheel nuts loose. Propshaft or drive-shaft out of balance.

Problem:
Knocking noise on full steering lock (front-wheel-drive cars only)

Likely causes:
Drive-shaft constant-velocity joints worn. Front wheel bearings worn.

Problem:
Steering wander

Likely causes:
Steering linkage joints or couplings loose or worn. Steering box or rack mountings slack or worn. Steering wheel loose on splines. Loose wheel bearings. Unequal tyre pressures. Worn suspension or steering dampers.

Problem:
Steering column rattles or feels slack on rough roads

Likely causes:
Steering column universal joints worn or loose. Steering column inner bushes worn. Steering wheel loose on column splines. Adjustable steering column mechanism worn.

Problem:
Steering unusually heavy

Likely causes:
Front tyre pressures too low. Incorrect wheel alignment. Castor or camber angle wrong (after a collision). Where applicable, lack of lubrication. On power-assisted steering systems: broken drive belt to hydraulic pump.

Problem:
Excessive free play apparent at the steering wheel

Likely causes:
Steering wheel loose on splines. Steering column joints worn. Wear in steering linkage. Steering box or rack and pinion assembly worn or loose. Wear in road wheel stub-axle swivel joints. Slack wheel bearings. Loose wheel fixings.

Sensing trouble

Noise is not the only valuable warning sign which it pays the motorist to heed. He can also sense trouble ahead by following his nose. Smells are a very important aid to diagnosing impending problems—some of the most common causes are listed below. The wise motorist will also not ignore what he can learn from instruments. In a modern car, some of the tell-tale meters and gauges are standard equipment, others can be bought from accessory shops. They are simple to use, providing an accurate means of double-checking the condition of the car, and are detailed on the next page.

Unusual smells

Problem:
Acrid burning smell

Likely cause:
Electrical wiring short-circuit. Switch off the ignition—look for smoke.

Problem:
General burning smell

Likely causes:
Paint or cloth smouldering on exhaust manifold or pipe. Handbrake accidentally left on. Brakes binding. Clutch slipping. Cigarette or paper smouldering in ashtray. Dropped cigarette burning the upholstery or floor covering.

Problem:
Petrol smell

Likely causes:
Carburettor flooding due to sticking needle valve. Leaking fuel pipe connections. Fuel tank clumsily filled or over-filled. Leaking fuel tank. Fuel tank vent pipe detached inside the boot.

Problem:
Oily smell

Likely causes:
Engine oil filler cap missing. Blocked or disconnected crankcase vent, emission valve or connecting pipe. Excessive engine fumes due to worn pistons or rings.

Is it the weather?
Although the engine is housed under a virtually weatherproof cover, it is still vulnerable to extremes of heat, cold and damp. In heavy rain, for example, the front wheels can splash water over the engine from underneath, and the spray from passing cars can be drawn in through the radiator grille.

Moisture droplets settling on the spark plug leads, the coil and distributor cap in these conditions can cause the engine to misfire or cut out completely. The moisture

Problem:
Sluggish starter motor action

Likely causes:
Battery in a low state of charge, unable to cope with cold, stiff engine.

Problem:
Steam coming from under the bonnet

Likely causes:
Burst or leaking radiator or hoses. Leaking water pump. Faulty by-pass pipe between cylinder head and block.

Instrument warnings

Problem:
Ignition warning light stays on above idling speed

Likely causes:
Generator brushes worn or sticking—sometimes during or after a high-speed run. Fanbelt broken or slipping. No generator output, due to disconnected wires or an internal fault. Short-circuit in wires from the generator to the battery. Voltage regulator contacts burnt or faulty. On alternators, regulator pack faulty.

Problem:
Both fuel and temperature gauges show higher than normal readings

Likely causes:
Faulty instrument voltage-stabiliser unit.

Problem:
Excessive speedometer needle waver

Likely causes:
Worn, damaged or sparsely lubricated cable. Outer cable run disturbed.

allows the HT current to leak away steadily. Thoroughly drying the ignition components and then spraying them with a proprietary ignition sealer will usually cure the trouble. Dense fog and condensation can cause the same problem.

At the other extreme, hot weather takes its toll of the cooling system. A slack fanbelt reduces cooling fan and water pump efficiency, so the radiator water is not cooled sufficiently and the engine overheats. Check the belt tension periodically and especially before a long, high-speed

Problem:
Loud screech when the engine is started from cold

Likely cause:
Fanbelt slipping due to frozen water pump.

Problem:
Oil light stays on above idling speed

Likely causes:
Lack of engine oil. Low oil pressure due to worn crankshaft bearings, worn oil pump. Faulty oil-pressure warning light switch on engine. (On certain cars such as early Minis, the oil filter may be blocked.)

Problem:
Oil-pressure light flickers when cornering

Likely causes:
Low engine oil level. Short in switch wiring.

Problem:
Water temperature gauge reading higher than normal, then drops

Likely causes:
Engine overheating followed by complete loss of coolant.

Problem:
Fuel gauge does not work

Likely causes:
Wire disconnected at tank sender unit. Fuel gauge or sender unit faulty—test by disconnecting wire from sender unit and touching it to an earth point with the ignition on. If the gauge then reads 'full', the sender unit is faulty. If the gauge reads 'empty' it is faulty.

journey. The radiator should be checked for blockage by lime deposits which build up in older cars. A car with a furred-up radiator can work perfectly well on short runs, but on a long motorway journey or at high altitude its cooling efficiency will be greatly reduced.

Winter brings its own problems. Without anti-freeze in the coolant severe frosts will completely ice-up the radiator and block it, causing overheating. At its worst, a frozen engine means a cracked cylinder block, and an expensive repair bill.

Problem:
Brakes drag or will not free completely when released

Likely cause:
Handbrake cables frozen. Seized clevises.

Double checking

Diagnosing faults is made all the easier, and more precise, if you have access to the kind of equipment professional mechanics use. With today's boom in the market for cheaper DIY diagnostic aids, the instruments detailed below need not cost the enthusiastic car tuner much more than £30 for the set. Combined tachometer, dwell meter, voltmeter and ammeter instruments are widely available. In one small hand-held unit you have the means to check faults on the engine and in the car's vital electrical circuitry, as well as to give the car a regular ignition tune-up.

Tachometer/dwell meter

Tachometers, or rev counters, are fitted as a standard instrument and driving aid on many high-performance or higher-priced cars, but for many drivers a tachometer is useful only as a tuning aid. It makes it possible to set the engine idle speed accurately after adjustments to the ignition and the carburettor. As an accessory it is best bought as a combined instrument which doubles as a dwell meter.

A dwell meter is designed to make the accurate setting of contact-breaker points in the distributor much easier. If you use the normal method of gap setting with feeler gauges, you are, in effect, measuring only the length of time for which the ignition coil is switched off. Far more important to the efficient operation of the coil is the time it is switched on. This is directly related to the number of degrees turned by the distributor cam while the points are closed—the dwell angle. With a dwell meter, which gives a reading of the degrees of dwell angle, it is possible to set the contact-breaker points at the most effective gap, with the added advantage that any slight wear or eccentricity, which affects distributor rotation, is taken into account. You can also adjust more successfully slightly worn points which defy accurate feeler gauge setting.

At the roadside, a dwell meter will greatly simplify the detection of distributor faults. For instance, damaged points or a loose base plate, contributing to misfire, will show as a widely varying dwell reading.

Voltmeter

A voltmeter can be bought as a facia-fitting accessory or as a separate tuning instrument. The facia-fitting type is sometimes called a battery-condition indicator. This gives a rough-and-ready picture of the battery voltage when the ignition is switched on. When the engine is started,

however, the voltage that it shows is that of the generator. This type of voltmeter will give some indication that the battery is retaining a reasonable charge (the reading will be about 12-13 volts) and that the generator is giving sufficient output (13-14.5 volts). It will also spot gross overloads of the electrical system (eg short-circuits) or overloading by the use of too many electrical accessories. In both cases the voltage will fall below the satisfactory 12-volt level. It is, however, a rather inaccurate and sluggishly-moving instrument, and it cannot be used for other diagnoses.

A separate tuning voltmeter will be of the moving-coil type and can be used to check the voltage at points throughout the car. Like the circuit-testing lamp described on page 9, it will determine whether power is reaching a particular part of the electrical circuit, and tell what voltage that power is. Generally the voltage available throughout a car's system, when the engine is switched off, should be that of the battery (12-13 volts). If the power supply to a component is lower than that, it suggests a poor connection, either to earth (the car body) or in the supply lead from the switch. No voltage at all indicates a break in the supply. A tiny voltage (just a flicker of the needle in many cases) when the voltmeter leads are connected on either side of a lead connection shows that this point is lowering the voltage in the supply wire.

Ammeter

Like the voltmeter, an ammeter, which measures current, can be bought quite cheaply as a facia instrument or as a tuning instrument which is sometimes combined with a voltmeter. While the facia instrument has a small scale and is not generally as accurate as a hand-held unit, for anybody but the keenest car electrician the permanently installed instrument is the best buy. Correctly fitted it shows the rate of charge applied to the battery by the generator, and makes it possible to spot overloads caused by short-circuits (even temporary ones will cause the dial to flick) and by too many electrical accessories being used at once.

Ammeters show charge and discharge readings on a scale of about −30amps (discharge) through the zero resting point of the needle to +40amps (charge). It is normal for a slight discharge to show when the ignition is switched on, rising to a charge of about 8-10amps when the engine is first revved up, and then falling after a few minutes to a charge of about 1-2amps. As more electrical accessories are

switched on (particularly the heated rear window and the headlights) the generator may not be able to cope and the reading may fall to show a slight discharge. Any deviation denotes a possible fault.

Vacuum gauge

A vacuum gauge, which measures the vacuum created in the inlet manifold when the engine is running, is often marketed as an aid to economical driving. A driver attempting to maintain the needle of the instrument as near to the 18-21in Hg (inches of mercury, which is a unit of pressure) reading—sometimes shown as a green band on the instrument face—by light-footed driving, will be achieving the best economy from his car.

The gauge will also reveal engine wear problems and many different signs of impending trouble. For example, a fluctuating needle will indicate valve problems, and a low reading may indicate a leak in one of the inlet manifold gaskets.

Compression gauge or tester

Many types of compression tester are available to the DIY tuner. Some resemble large tyre-pressure gauges, and others are instruments with a dial readout. In either case they are fitted with a tapered rubber seal which is forced into the spark plug hole of a cylinder while the engine is cranked through a few revolutions on the starter. The recorded reading is the maximum pressure in the cylinder at the point when the petrol and air mixture would normally be fired by the spark. Readings from all the cylinders, measured one at a time, should all be within about 10psi. A lower reading on one or more of the cylinders will indicate damage to, or wear in, the pistons, piston rings or cylinders, worn or poorly seated valves or worn valve guides. Tests should be carried out with the engine warm and all the spark plugs removed to lessen strain on the starter motor and battery. The accelerator pedal should be pressed to the floor by the helper who operates the starter.

Further deductions can be made about apparently faulty cylinders by feeding a tablespoonful of oil into the cylinders and repeating the test. A much higher reading on the second test will indicate that the fault lies with the piston rings or cylinder bore area, rather than with the valves. If two adjacent cylinders give near identical low readings, and the second test shows no change, the most likely cause is a failed cylinder head gasket.

DIAGNOSIS: Your at-a-glance fault-finding chart

Chart 1

When the engine will not fire

▼ Start here

If your car breaks down or develops a fault, and the cause is not immediately obvious, the two quick-reference fault-finding charts will help you to reach a quick diagnosis of the trouble and how to rectify it. Chart 1 tells you what to look for and check when the engine fails to start, and Chart 2 is for when the engine starts but does not run properly. For example, if the engine has a fault when idling but not on acceleration, then the fault should be found by following the diagnosis procedure in Chart 2.

Both charts are laid out in the same way and consist of a series of boxed questions, requiring either a simple YES or NO answer. Follow the green channel for a YES answer, and the red channel for a NO. Each box has a number relating to a numbered section in the following text where the possible causes are detailed.

The charts are designed to be followed *from the beginning* and logically lead to the point where your car's fault will show up. For example:

If your engine does not fire go to the starting point (on the extreme left) in Chart 1. Does the starter turn the engine?, asks Box 43. First read the note in section 43. Then, if you answer YES, follow the green line to Box 44. Does the starter turn the engine briskly? Turn to section 44 for further symptoms.

With this additional information you should be able to give a second YES or NO answer and follow a line on to the next question. This procedure is continued until you reach a diagnosis of the trouble given by the chart or the text, or a deduction made from both these pieces of information.

If, however, you cannot locate the trouble, call in professional help.

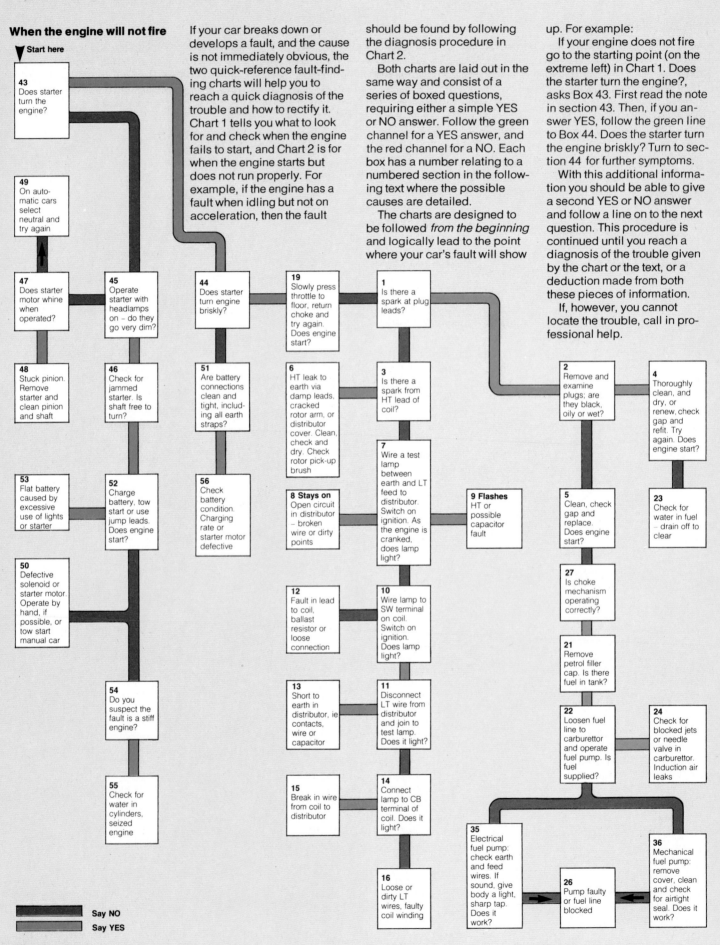

43 Does starter turn the engine?

49 On automatic cars select neutral and try again

47 Does starter motor whine when operated?

45 Operate starter with headlamps on – do they go very dim?

44 Does starter turn engine briskly?

19 Slowly press throttle to floor, return choke and try again. Does engine start?

1 Is there a spark at plug leads?

2 Remove and examine plugs; are they black, oily or wet?

4 Thoroughly clean, and dry, or renew, check gap and refit. Try again. Does engine start?

48 Stuck pinion. Remove starter and clean pinion and shaft

46 Check for jammed starter. Is shaft free to turn?

51 Are battery connections clean and tight, including all earth straps?

6 HT leak to earth via damp leads, cracked rotor arm, or distributor cover. Clean, check and dry. Check rotor pick-up brush

3 Is there a spark from HT lead of coil?

5 Clean, check gap and replace. Does engine start?

23 Check for water in fuel – drain off to clear

53 Flat battery caused by excessive use of lights or starter

52 Charge battery, tow start or use jump leads. Does engine start?

56 Check battery condition. Charging rate or starter motor defective

7 Wire a test lamp between earth and LT feed to distributor. Switch on ignition. As the engine is cranked, does lamp light?

8 Stays on Open circuit in distributor – broken wire or dirty points

9 Flashes HT or possible capacitor fault

50 Defective solenoid or starter motor. Operate by hand, if possible, or tow start manual car

27 Is choke mechanism operating correctly?

12 Fault in lead to coil, ballast resistor or loose connection

10 Wire lamp to SW terminal on coil. Switch on ignition. Does lamp light?

21 Remove petrol filler cap. Is there fuel in tank?

54 Do you suspect the fault is a stiff engine?

13 Short to earth in distributor, ie contacts, wire or capacitor

11 Disconnect LT wire from distributor and join to test lamp. Does it light?

22 Loosen fuel line to carburettor and operate fuel pump. Is fuel supplied?

24 Check for blocked jets or needle valve in carburettor. Induction air leaks

55 Check for water in cylinders, seized engine

15 Break in wire from coil to distributor

14 Connect lamp to CB terminal of coil. Does it light?

35 Electrical fuel pump: check earth and feed wires. If sound, give body a light, sharp tap. Does it work?

26 Pump faulty or fuel line blocked

36 Mechanical fuel pump: remove cover, clean and check for airtight seal. Does it work?

16 Loose or dirty LT wires, faulty coil winding

■ Say NO
■ Say YES

Ignition

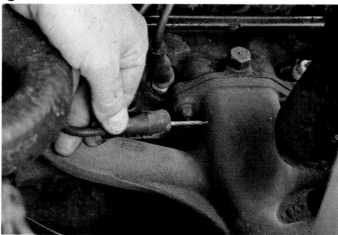

Checking for spark with the help of a nail

BOX 1 To test for a spark, two people are needed; one to operate the ignition switch, and the other to check the plug leads. Remove the plug lead from one spark plug and hold it about ⅛in away from a good earth. A bare patch of metal on the engine block is a good place, but do not hold it close to the carburettor or rocker cover.

With the gear lever in neutral, operate the starter for a few turns of the engine and look and listen for a spark jumping between the lead and earth. If a plug lead has a deeply shrouded cap push a piece of wire or a nail into the connector and let the spark jump from the end of the improvised conductor to a good earth.

2 Label the order and note the position of the plug leads before detaching them. Unscrew and remove the spark plugs from the cylinder head, keeping them in order too.

Examine the plug electrodes and the gap, to see if they are heavily carboned (sooty) or black and oily. A plug in good condition will be light brown or grey in colour, possibly with light flaky deposits. A sooty or oily electrode may not allow a spark to pass. Sooty electrodes indicate that the carburettor mixture is too rich. Wet plugs are usually a sign of excessive choke use, which causes petrol flooding. Wet and oily plugs indicate worn piston rings or valve guides in that cylinder.

3 Disconnect the HT lead from the distributor centre terminal, then pull back the lead-end insulating sleeve to expose the metal end of the lead. Switch on the ignition and carry out the spark test as detailed in section 1.

Look for a spark jumping between the lead and a good earth point on the engine block. If you can see and hear a spark, then the coil is operating correctly.

4 If the spark plugs are sooty or blocked with carbon deposits, a special plug sand-blasting machine, used by garages, will clean them thoroughly.

Check the condition of the plug outer electrodes. If the inside edges show signs of erosion with similar wear on the centre points the plugs should be replaced with a new set—always replace plugs in sets if possible.

Wet plugs and a smell of petrol indicate that fuel is reaching the cylinders. A wet plug without a petrol smell may indicate a water leak in the cylinder head gasket, or water in the fuel system.

Before fitting used or new plugs, check and adjust the electrode gap by bending the side electrode to the figure specified in your car's handbook—usually about 0.025in (0.6mm).

Check that the plug sealing washers are in good condition, then refit and tighten the plugs.

Plugs with tapered, cone-shaped seats do not have sealing washers and should be tightened just enough to form a good seal. Do not over-tighten this type of plug. Reconnect the plug leads in the correct order.

5 Check the electrode condition. If the plugs are light brown or grey, or there are heavy carbon deposits, clean them. It is best to have them sandblasted by a garage but make sure they are washed clean with petrol afterwards. Reset the gap if necessary. Refit as in section 4.

6 If a check reveals that the coil is operating correctly (section 3), but there is no spark from the plug leads (section 1), the HT current is leaking to earth somewhere between the coil and plugs.

Operate the starter and listen for a clicking sound along the leads, especially near points where they may be secured by a clip. At night, a spark or blue-coloured flash may indicate the position of the fault. If not, remove the distributor cap and thoroughly dry it inside and out. Also dry the plug leads and insulator shrouds, and the coil top.

While the cap is removed, check the rotor arm and the inside of the cap, looking for fine random lines or cracks which indicate that the HT current is 'tracking' to earth. If there are cracks, a new cap or rotor arm should be fitted.

Examine the plug leads, looking for cracked insulation and for broken or detached terminal ends. Carbon-string type plug leads become disconnected from the terminal ends if you pull on the lead instead of the terminal sleeve when taking them out.

Check the condition of the centre contact inside the distributor cap to the rotor arm. The rotor can be tested by removing the distributor cap and seeing if a spark can be made to jump from the coil lead to the centre of the rotor—see section 3. If it does, the rotor arm is faulty.

7 Connect a test lamp (see page 9) between a good earth and the LT (low tension) wire from the coil to the distributor (at the coil terminal). Operate the ignition/starter and observe the test light. It will do one of three things—light and stay on, flash on and off, or not light at all.

8 If the test lamp stays on, it indicates that the distributor contact-breaker points are dirty, not closing, or that there is a break in the LT circuit in the distributor. Check that the gap between the contact points is not excessive when the heel of the moving contact is on the peak of one cam lobe. The contact gap size is given in the car handbook—it is usually about 0.018in (0.45mm).

Check that the spring strip bearing on the contact is not broken, or that the moving contact has not seized on its pivot post. Make sure that all LT wire connections are secure and that no wires are broken.

9 If the test light flickers as the engine turns, it indicates that the ignition LT circuit is in good order. The lack of any HT spark from the coil lead could be due to a distributor capacitor or internal coil fault.

10 If the test light fails to light, check that the bulb and the wiring are in order by connecting it between the battery and earth. If the light works, connect it between the coil LT terminal marked SW or +ve and earth. Switch on the ignition and leave it on.

11 If the test light comes on when test 10 is conducted, disconnect the LT wire from the distributor and connect the light between the wire and earth.

12 If the test light does not come on when test 10 is conducted, it indicates that there is no LT current reaching the coil from the ignition switch even though the ignition is switched on. This may be caused by failure of the ignition switch, a loose connection, or failure of a ballast resistor. Do

DIAGNOSIS: Your at-a-glance fault-finding chart

Chart 2

When the engine fires

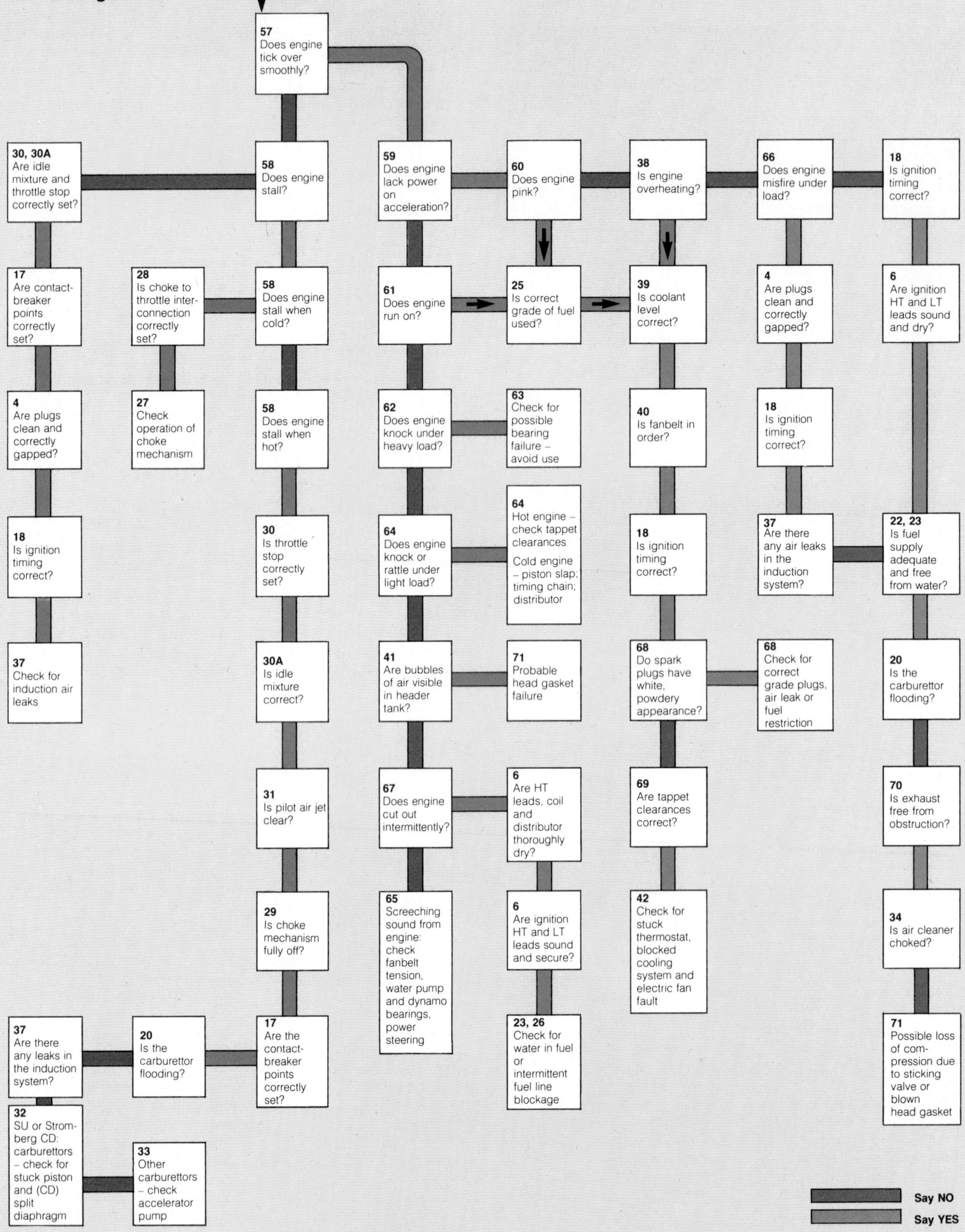

▼ Start here

57 Does engine tick over smoothly?

30, 30A Are idle mixture and throttle stop correctly set?

58 Does engine stall?

59 Does engine lack power on acceleration?

60 Does engine pink?

38 Is engine overheating?

66 Does engine misfire under load?

18 Is ignition timing correct?

17 Are contact-breaker points correctly set?

28 Is choke to throttle inter-connection correctly set?

58 Does engine stall when cold?

61 Does engine run on?

25 Is correct grade of fuel used?

39 Is coolant level correct?

4 Are plugs clean and correctly gapped?

6 Are ignition HT and LT leads sound and dry?

4 Are plugs clean and correctly gapped?

27 Check operation of choke mechanism

58 Does engine stall when hot?

62 Does engine knock under heavy load?

63 Check for possible bearing failure – avoid use

40 Is fanbelt in order?

18 Is ignition timing correct?

18 Is ignition timing correct?

30 Is throttle stop correctly set?

64 Does engine knock or rattle under light load?

64 Hot engine – check tappet clearances Cold engine – piston slap; timing chain; distributor

18 Is ignition timing correct?

37 Are there any air leaks in the induction system?

22, 23 Is fuel supply adequate and free from water?

37 Check for induction air leaks

30A Is idle mixture correct?

41 Are bubbles of air visible in header tank?

71 Probable head gasket failure

68 Do spark plugs have white, powdery appearance?

68 Check for correct grade plugs, air leak or fuel restriction

20 Is the carburettor flooding?

31 Is pilot air jet clear?

67 Does engine cut out intermittently?

6 Are HT leads, coil and distributor thoroughly dry?

69 Are tappet clearances correct?

70 Is exhaust free from obstruction?

37 Are there any leaks in the induction system?

20 Is the carburettor flooding?

17 Are the contact-breaker points correctly set?

29 Is choke mechanism fully off?

65 Screeching sound from engine: check fanbelt tension, water pump and dynamo bearings, power steering

6 Are ignition HT and LT leads sound and secure?

42 Check for stuck thermostat, blocked cooling system and electric fan fault

34 Is air cleaner choked?

32 SU or Strom-berg CD: carburettors – check for stuck piston and (CD) split diaphragm

33 Other carburettors – check accelerator pump

23, 26 Check for water in fuel or intermittent fuel line blockage

71 Possible loss of com-pression due to sticking valve or blown head gasket

■■■ Say NO
■■■ Say YES

206

not attempt to make a connection between the battery and ignition coil. Have an auto-electrician make any necessary repairs.

13 If the lamp lights up in test 11, there is a short-circuit to earth in the distributor. Remove the cap and check that the LT wire connections are sound and that the insulating washers under the contact assembly are in position.

14 If the test light does not come on in test 11, connect it directly between the distributor contact terminal on the ignition coil and an earth connection.

15 If the test light now comes on, it indicates a break in the LT wire between the distributor and the coil. As an emergency repair, a length of insulated wire can be connected between the two terminals to replace the original wire.

16 If the test light does not light in test 14, and the LT terminals on the coil are clean, then the coil is faulty and should be replaced.

17 With the ignition switched off, remove the distributor cap, then turn the engine until the heel of the distributor moving contact is on top of one of the cam lobes. This can be done either with a spanner on the crankshaft pulley bolt or by pushing the car to and fro in top gear.

The contact points should now be open, allowing the gap to be checked with a feeler gauge placed between the contacts. The gap on most cars is about 0.018in (0.45mm)—check with the car handbook for the correct gap figure.

Examine the condition of the contact-breaker points. They should be free from any pitting or pipping on the surfaces. In an emergency, badly pitted or pipped points can be dressed flat with a file, but as a general rule a new set should be used. Before removing the points, note the assembly order to ensure that the parts are

replaced in the order that they were removed.

An occasional check of the contact-breaker points in between normal servicing intervals will reveal any undue wear and enable them to be renewed before they fail.

18 The static ignition timing setting can be checked quite easily with the aid of the test lamp. Connect one lead of the test lamp to the distributor LT lead connection at the coil. Connect the other lead to a good earth point on the car body or battery.

Remove the distributor cap, noting the position of no.1 plug lead on the cap in relation to the distributor body, and marking it if necessary.

Switch on the ignition and turn the engine in its direction of rotation with a spanner on the crankshaft bolt, or by moving the car in top gear, until the timing marks on the crankshaft pulley flywheel are aligned —the exact location of them should be given in the car handbook. The test lamp should now light. Turn the engine in the opposite direction until the test lamp goes out—indicating that the contacts have closed. Turn the engine back again until the test lamp just comes on, stopping the engine the moment it does.

The position of the timing marks relative to each other will indicate whether the setting is correct or not. Check in the car handbook for the correct setting, eg 5° BTDC. This means that the contacts should just be opening and lighting the test lamp when the crankshaft has 5° to rotate before reaching the Top Dead Centre position (TDC).

If the timing marks are correctly aligned with the setting given in the handbook, then all is well. If the test lamp came on before the correct timing marks, then the ignition is too far advanced and should be retarded. To do this depends on the type of distributor fitted. On some distributors there is a vernier-adjuster screw on the side of the distributor which, when turned, will advance or retard the ignition by small

amounts. If there is no adjusting screw, the distributor clamp bolt should be slackened a little so that the distributor body can be turned a little, until a check with the test lamp shows that the timing marks are correctly aligned. To retard the ignition by this

method, turn the distributor body in the direction of rotation of the rotor arm; to advance the ignition, turn it in the opposite direction.

When you have adjusted the timing, check it again with the lamp, re-adjusting it if necessary.

Fuel

Tuning the carburettor for performance and economy

The carburettor mixes fuel with air, and the resulting mixture is then drawn into the engine, compressed by the pistons and ignited by the spark plugs.

The engine will stop if the fuel mixture does not reach the cylinder combustion chamber and it will misfire if the mixture is not delivered in the correct quantity or the right mixture ratio.

Lack of fuel mixture can be caused by a faulty petrol pump, blocked jets in the carburettor or an air leak between the carburettor and the cylinder head. The only air to enter the combustion chamber should come through the air cleaner and, on some cars, the crankcase emission valve.

It is very important to guard against the risk of fire when working on any part of the fuel system. Naked lights and sparks are dangerous, so do not smoke. It is best to disconnect the battery if possible. Take extra care to avoid sparks when disconnecting wires. If you are working on an electric fuel pump, make sure that the ignition is switched off.

If the carburettor has to be dismantled, ensure that parts do not drop into the inlet manifold. Some carburettors have a small steel ball which is released when the float chamber is removed. This can jump out and fall into the combustion chamber if the throttle butterfly is open when the float chamber is removed. Before removing any jets, note their location and the assembly order of any other carburettor parts. Always blow through the jets to clear them or poke out any obstruction with a bristle —never use wire to clean a jet.

BOX 19 The engine can become flooded with excess petrol from the carburettor (particularly fixed-jet types) if the accelerator pedal has been depressed a few times during starting with the choke out. The fuel excess can usually be cleared—if the battery is well charged—by slowly depressing the accelerator to the floor and holding it there while operating the starter with the choke in. After a few revolutions, the engine should start. On automatic-choke carburettors, remove the air cleaner and get a helper to hold the choke flap in the fully open position until the engine fires, then release it, after which the engine should idle normally. Persistent flooding is usually caused by a jammed open float needle valve or a punctured float.

20 Petrol flooding can also occur while the engine is running. The symptoms of this will be a rhythmical misfire and blackish exhaust fumes. Sometimes, the engine will turn slower and slower until it finally stops. Another clue will be found on the carburettor—flooding will be visible or telltale stains of fuel leaking from the float chamber will be seen.

Inside the float chamber a needle valve, operated by the float, controls the fuel flow into the carburettor. If the valve is worn or sticking, or if the float is punctured, the needle will be prevented from shutting off the feed from the fuel pump and flooding will occur.

Check the float and needle valve assembly by removing the float chamber or the cover from the carburettor. Remove the float pivot pin and detach the float—shake it to see if there is any fuel inside. If there is, it is leaking and should be renewed. Unscrew the needle valve, and holding it in the closed position with one finger, try to blow through the valve. A leak will be detectable by a hiss of air past the valve. A worn valve needle usually has a distinct wear ridge near the point.

21 Always check that there is petrol in the fuel tank before starting to dismantle the carburettor or fuel pump, as the fuel gauge may be faulty. Check for fuel in the tank by removing the filler cap and rocking the car from side to side. If there is fuel there, you will hear it sloshing around the inside of the tank. **Never use a naked light to look into the fuel tank.**

22 To test that fuel is reaching the carburet-

tor from the fuel pump, detach the fuel feed pipe or hose at the carburettor. Place the pipe end into a container to prevent petrol being sprayed over the engine. If the car has an electric fuel pump, this should operate immediately the ignition is switched on. With a mechanical fuel pump a helper is needed, who should use the starter to turn the engine. In either case, fuel should spurt out of the feed pipe if the pump works.

23 If water has been found on the spark plugs (section 4), the most likely causes are water in the petrol tank or a blown cylinder-head gasket. Check for water in the petrol by removing the float chamber on the carburettor. As it is heavier than petrol, water collects at the bottom of the float chamber. If water is found, empty out the contents of the float chamber by removing it, or by soaking up the contents with a piece of fluffless rag. Blow through the jets to clean them. Take care not to lose any parts of the carburettor when dismantling it.

If there is no sign of water in the float chamber, check the water level in the radiator. If it is low, top it up, then run the engine. If it misfires and overheats, and there are bubbles near the filler cap hole, the head gasket has probably blown.

24 If fuel reaches the carburettor but does not appear to reach the engine, remove the float chamber or cover from the carburettor and check the operation of the float needle valve (section 20).

In the case of SU or Stromberg/Zenith carburettors, make sure that the suction piston inside is not stuck in the open position. These carburettors often have a lifting pin which, when lifted, raises the piston slightly. When released it allows the piston to fall with a distinctive 'clunk'. If there is no pin, remove the air cleaner and lift the piston with a screwdriver. If no noise is heard, remove the piston suction chamber from the top of the

carburettor and free the piston by sliding it up and down. Remove and clean it if necessary, taking great care not to bend the jet needle.

25 If the octane rating of the fuel is lower than recommended the engine may make a 'pinking' noise under hard acceleration. 'Pinking' is best described as a tinkling noise coming from the engine. Occasional light pinking will not damage the engine, but continual pinking produces excessive combustion chamber temperatures which may burn the pistons or valves. This may also cause the engine to run on after the ignition has been switched off. The correct octane fuel should always be used, but where this is not possible the ignition timing should be retarded by 4-5° (section 18) and speed reduced.

26 Check that there are no fuel taps in the system that may have been accidentally shut off, especially on cars with a reserve petrol tank. See that the fuel tank vent is clear and if a new petrol filler cap has been fitted, ensure that it is of the correct type.

Examine any fuel-line filters for blockage or leaks and watch out for dents or squashing of the pipes.

If there are no obvious faults, disconnect the inlet pipe from the fuel pump and blow down it —a length of rubber hose, such as a radiator overflow pipe, is ideal for this. Listen for air bubbling into the petrol tank. No bubbling noise means that there is a blockage in the pipe, which can often be cleared by blowing extra hard down the pipe. If the fuel pump works, but petrol does not reach the carburettor, the cause will be a blockage in the fuel pipe between the pump and the carburettor. Check the pump-to-carburettor feed pipe by disconnecting it at both ends and blowing through it. Blow through the fuel pump (from the tank side). If the car has previously run out of petrol, it is possible that grit is jammed under one of the fuel pump

valves. After reassembly, blowing into the fuel tank will help to prime the system.

27 If, after checking the ignition and finding nothing wrong, the engine still will not start and all the spark plugs are dry, it is possible that insufficient mixture is being drawn into the cylinders. Make sure that the choke is operating correctly at the carburettor. On automatic-choke carburettors, remove the air-cleaner cover and see that the choke plate is closing properly. If the plate is in the vertical (hot) position you may be able to close it by lightly touching it—never force the plate. Have the choke mechanism checked by a dealer as soon as possible.

28 Trouble in starting a car when the engine is cold is quite a common occurrence. Check that the choke mechanism works (see section 27) and that the linkage opens the throttle slightly to a fast-idle position. There is normally a cam mechanism on the side of the carburettor that turns the throttle slightly as the choke control is pulled out. The fast-idle position can usually be adjusted in an emergency, either by bending the choke interconnecting rod or turning the small screw which bears on the cam. The clearance between the end of the screw and the cam is normally about 0.015in (0.4mm) with the choke control fully in.

29 If the engine stalls when hot, check that the choke plate is vertical with the control knob fully in. On automatic-choke carburettors, remove the air-cleaner cover and see that the choke plate is in the vertical position. If it is not, touch it lightly. If it is stuck it may open; if not, the mechanism is faulty and should be repaired by a garage. Resist any temptation to tie the choke plate into the vertical position.

30 Both the throttle stop and the idling volume-control screws should be adjusted with the engine at normal operating temperature—and other adjustments, like the valve clearances and the ignition, set correctly. Set the idling speed by screwing the throttle stop screw in or out until you get a reasonable idling speed of around 800rpm.

On fixed-jet carburettors where there is an adjustable volume screw, which sets the idling mixture, the amount of fuel and air is metered at idling speed. The volume control is a small sprung screw on the side of the carburettor body. Set the idling mixture by turning the screw in until the engine speed drops and then turning it out until the engine runs smoothly at the highest engine speed. If necessary, readjust the throttle-stop screw to give the correct idle speed.

30A Some variable-jet carburettors have a jet-adjusting nut under the carburettor. Screwing the nut upwards weakens the idling mixture, and screwing it downwards richens it.

To set the idling mixture, screw the adjusting nut upwards by small amounts at a time until the engine slows; then screw it downwards until the engine idles smoothly at the highest speed. Check the mixture strength by raising the piston lifting pin about 1/16in. The engine should speed up slightly, then idle normally. If the engine speed rises and continues to do so, the mixture is too rich. If the engine speed drops, the mixture is too weak.

The condition of the crankcase ventilation valve on most cars can affect the idling. Pinching the tube should slow the engine noticeably. Releasing it and removing the oil filler cap should cause the engine to run faster.

31 On some Solex by-pass carburettors there is an additional screw, which allows air to mix with the fuel and makes it easier to control the idling mixture. The screw is normally situated about halfway down the side of the carburettor body and it is screwed in or out by a small amount to give the correct idling speed and mixture. On these car-

burettors, the normal volume-control screw is factory-set and should not be touched.

32 The piston inside the upper part of the carburettor body on SU and Stromberg/Zenith types controls the air/fuel mixture. Make sure that the piston is free to slide up and down, falling with a metallic 'clunk'. Remove the air cleaner and ensure that the piston is free by inserting a finger into the air intake or removing the top of the carburettor. Sometimes the piston will stick because the jet assembly is off-centre. If this is the case, the complete jet assembly should be unscrewed and recentralised by a mechanic.

On Stromberg/Zenith carburettors, check that the diaphragm attached to the air valve body is not perforated or damaged.

33 Fixed-jet carburettors have a small piston or diaphragm accelerator pump in the side of the carburettor body. This injects extra fuel into the airstream when the throttle is depressed quickly. A 'flat spot' can develop if the piston or diaphragm is worn or if the linkage is disconnected.

34 Remove the air cleaner top cover and examine the condition of the air filter. If the filter is choked with dirt it will restrict the air supply and make the mixture richer, thus upsetting the carburation. As an emergency measure only, the engine can be run with the filter removed. Put in a new filter, however, as soon as possible.

35 If an electric fuel pump is not working, it can sometimes be started by giving the pump body a light tap with a spanner. If it is 'clicking' fast, it may mean that there is an air leak in the supply pipe, or that there is no fuel in the tank. If the pump is dead, test the supply and the earth connections, using a test lamp across the connections (with the ignition switched on).

36 If a mechanical fuel pump does not deliver fuel to the carburettor when the engine is turned, first check that the pump filter-cover sealing ring is fitted properly. Test for correct pump operation by removing the pipe from the tank on the inlet side and blocking it to prevent loss of fuel. Place a finger over the pump inlet pipe and have a helper turn the engine again. You should be able to feel moderate suction with your finger. If you cannot, the pump is probably faulty and should be replaced (see Project 29).

37 Any air leaks into the inlet manifold between the carburettor and the cylinder head will upset the carburation by weakening it. This may damage the engine by increasing the combustion chamber temperatures. Make a thorough check for leaks around the inlet manifold and carburettor flange gaskets, vacuum pipe connections, brake servo pipe or connections, or the crankcase emission valve connection. Use oil or washing-up liquid rubbed over a pipe or joint to pin-point the leakage. Renew the relevant faulty parts.

Cooling System and Starter Motor

Topping up the radiator

Two types of starter

BOX 38 Overheating is one of the main causes of breakdown and engine damage. To guard against it, any fault that develops in the engine or cooling system must be corrected immediately. A water temperature gauge is a most useful guide. However, if you fail to notice a rise in temperature and coolant leaks away, there may be insufficient liquid in the system to surround the gauge sender unit in the cylinder head. The engine may then continue to overheat without the correct temperature showing on the gauge. Loss of coolant can be detectable by the heater inside the car running cold when switched to the hot position.

A burning oil or paint smell, steam or a bubbling sound heard when the engine is idling are signs that the engine is overheated. Switch off the engine immediately, but do not remove the radiator pressure cap until the engine has cooled down.

39 If you suspect engine overheating, check the water level in the radiator, after allowing the engine to cool for about 10-15 minutes. Release the pressure cap slowly to allow pressure remaining in the system to escape, then check the water level. If it is low or non-existent, do not fill up with cold water immediately as this may damage the radiator or engine block. Wait another 10 minutes then pour the water in.

Check for leakage from the radiator water pump or hoses as the water is poured in. If a leak cannot be repaired temporarily, and you have plenty of water on board, the car can be run a short distance to the nearest garage. Leave the radiator pressure cap loose to avoid excessive coolant loss.

40 The water pump is driven by the fanbelt. If the belt is broken, the ignition warning light will come on to warn of trouble. It will only be a short time before the engine overheats.

If a spare belt is not available, a temporary one can sometimes be made from thick string or nylon doubled-up. Run the temporary belt only between the crankshaft pulley and the water pump pulley. If you drive slowly, watching your temperature gauge, this might get you to a garage for a new belt.

41 If, when the radiator pressure cap is off, you find many small bubbles floating to the top of the coolant, but the coolant is not boiling, there is probably a leakage in the cylinder-head gasket. A blown gasket allows combustion gases to enter the engine water jacket, and hence to the radiator. It may also allow water to run into the sump.

42 Although the generator belt, the hoses and the coolant level in the radiator have been checked, there are other faults which can affect the efficiency of the cooling system.

Many modern cars have electric cooling fans. These are operated via a relay, controlled by a temperature-sensitive switch on the radiator. With insulated wire, connect the switch terminal to earth (or connect between the switch terminals if there are two). The fan should operate. If the radiator is still very hot and the fan is not working, suspect the switch. If the fan does not work in the test, suspect the fan-operating relay or a break in the fan supply circuit. In each case, check the connections.

See that the radiator core is clean and free from leaves, dirt or other obstructions, to allow a proper air-flow. The thermostat may stick in the closed position, so remove it and check its operation. A build-up of sediment inside the radiator core over a number of years can block or slow down the circulation of the coolant inside the radiator. This should be flushed out of the system at regular intervals, preferably with the radiator removed.

43 Check that the gear lever is in neutral, then switch on the ignition and try to turn the engine with the starter motor.

44 If the starter turns fairly fast, it indicates that there is nothing wrong with the starter or battery. Do not operate the starter too much if the engine refuses to start. You will only add to the trouble by flattening the battery.

45 Switch on the headlamps and operate the starter motor. If the lights go dim, current is being passed to the starter motor.

46 If the lights go very dim and the starter does not operate, or if the solenoid makes a rapid clicking sound, the battery is flat and needs charging or replacing.

If the starter solenoid makes a single loud click but the motor does not turn, this means that the starter motor is jammed or is faulty.

A jammed starter can be freed by rocking the car backwards and forwards in top gear, or by turning the squared end of the armature shaft with a spanner.

47 A droning noise when the starter is operated means that the starter motor is working but the pinion gear is not engaging with the flywheel ring gear.

48 A starter motor pinion that will not engage can sometimes be freed by tapping the motor body with a heavy object, while a helper operates the starter. If this fails, the starter must be removed from the engine.

Clean the Bendix pinion gear on the end of the shaft with paraffin to remove any oil or metal particles, and dry thoroughly. Check that the Bendix assembly is free to rotate on the shaft and returns to its stop position under the return-spring pressure. Do not lubricate the pinion threads as this is quite likely to lead to recurrence of the sticking trouble.

49 On automatic cars there is a gear-selector inhibitor switch to prevent the engine from being started other than in the Neutral or Park positions. If this switch is faulty or out of adjustment, moving the gear selector lever through all gear positions may free it.

50 If the starter motor does not operate, test the starter solenoid. Older cars may have a button on the solenoid to operate the starter manually. With the gear lever in neutral, switch on the ignition and press this solenoid button.

Battery and Electrics

Removing battery post corrosion with a wire brush

If the starter now operates, there may be a fault in the wiring to the solenoid from the ignition switch, or the ignition switch or solenoid may be faulty.

Modern cars do not have a solenoid button, and in this case it will be necessary to bridge the two large terminals on the solenoid with heavy gauge wire. With the ignition on (gear lever in neutral) just touch the wire between the two terminals (it may get very hot). If the starter still does not turn, the fault is in the starter motor itself.

BOX 51 If a battery connection is loose or badly corroded, it can sometimes fail to pass the large current needed for the starter motor. Normally a terminal in this condition will feel hot to the touch after trying to operate the starter. Check all battery leads, clean off any corrosion of connections down to bare metal and remake connections firmly. The engine and battery earth connections to the car body should also be examined for tightness and cleaned, as these also affect starting.

52 If necessary, a garage can give a flat battery a boost charge. About 30 minutes of charge will be enough to start the engine. If you have a small home battery charger, an overnight charge of 3-4amps should give enough power in the battery to start the engine. Failing this, the car can be started by pushing or towing it (not automatic models). Battery jump leads can be used to start an automatic car with a flat battery.

53 The battery is one of the few components that actually benefits from use and the occasional complete discharge will not damage it so long as the discharge, or charge, is not too rapid, and provided that the unit is never left in a discharged condition.

54 Trying to start a very stiff engine imposes an excessive load on the starter motor. If the cause of the stiffness is not discovered and the fault not remedied, no further attempt should be made to start the engine—damage to the starter motor may result.

Your motoring organisation should be called for roadside help, or contact a garage.

55 If you suspect that the engine is unusually stiff, switch off the ignition immediately. Place a spanner on the crankshaft drive-belt pulley bolt and try to turn the engine. If it needs considerable leverage on the spanner to turn, the engine is partially seizing. Remove the spark plugs and check for water in the combustion chambers. If it spurts out as the engine is turned, the head gasket is leaking.

56 When a battery goes flat after a recent full charge, it could be that it is old and unable to hold its charge. Alternatively the generator may not be charging at the correct rate. Worn brushes, a faulty voltage regulator, a slipping fanbelt or a fault within the generator are common causes. Where both battery and generator are in good working order, check the starter motor brushes and engine earthing connections.

General Checks

Adjusting fanbelt tension

BOX 57 Ensure that the engine idles smoothly at the correct speed; make allowance for the weather if it is very cold. If there is a fault when idling that cannot be detected when the engine is under load, see Boxes 30 and 30A and follow the checking procedures.

58 If the engine stalls when the clutch is let in, or on initial acceleration, refer to the next box.

59 If the fault persists above idling speed, or becomes apparent only on acceleration, rev up the engine when stationary (but do not race it) and note the result. Defects such as misfiring and rattling will often show up at higher engine speeds.

A carburettor flat spot (hesitation) when the throttle is opened quickly can be due to a weak mixture, blocked jets or venturi progression holes, or a worn accelerator-pump piston, jet or diaphragm. On variable-jet SU and Stromberg/Zenith carburettors the trouble may be a sticking piston. Retarded ignition, or an air leak in the carburettor or inlet manifold are the other possibilities.

60 'Pinking' is a term used to describe a metallic tinkling noise heard from the engine during hard acceleration or when climbing a steep hill. This fault, if it continues for a long period, can damage the pistons and valves. Causes of pinking are over-advanced ignition timing, and using lower octane fuel than that specified for the car. Some cars are prone to pinking. An overheated engine may also show this symptom.

61 'Running-on' is a term used when the engine continues to run (irregularly or lumpily) after the ignition has been switched off. Common causes of this fault are excessively high combustion chamber temperatures due to incorrect ignition timing, incorrect fuel grade, weak carburettor mixture, and too high an idle speed.

A cause of running-on that is not so common, now that fuels and oils contain special additives, is the build-up of carbon deposits inside the combustion chamber. These can glow incandescently and continue to ignite the fuel until the deposits cool down. The old term 'decoke' refers to the removal of these deposits.

62 Knocking noises from the engine can be worrying, but before looking any further, check the engine oil level. A diagnosis of noises and their possible causes and sources is given in Sensing Trouble (pages 200-203).

63 Damage to the engine may not be too bad at first, but it can get rapidly worse and may result in a broken connecting rod and further harm to the block. Do not use the car until the noise has been thoroughly investigated.

64 Light tapping or rattling noises from the engine are usually less serious, but the cause should be checked before the car is used on the road.

65 A high-pitched screaming noise coming from the front of the engine usually comes from a worn or slipping fanbelt. Slipping overheats the belt, which rapidly disintegrates.

If you hear this noise, check the tension of the belt and replace it if it is worn. If the belt tension is correct, the noise may arise from a squeaking or frozen water pump. A squeaking pump can usually be cured by pouring a water-soluble lubricant into the coolant. Power-steering drive belts or pumps sometimes squeak and, if the belt tension and reservoir oil level are correct, the pump fault should be investigated by a garage.

66 Engine misfiring on hard acceleration can be caused by a breakdown of the spark plugs or coil. This can be due to the higher combustion pressures exerting a greater strain on the ignition system. Spark plugs should be changed after 10,000-12,000 miles.

67 If an engine cuts out intermittently without warning, checks are difficult because the engine may work satisfactorily when you come to check it. An examination of the ignition or fuel systems might reveal clues. Possible causes are a blockage in the fuel tank venting system or a vapour lock in the fuel line (on a very hot day).

68 If the spark plug tips are white and powdery (section 2) they have been subjected to extreme operating temperatures. Check with the handbook that they are of the correct grade for the engine. A very weak carburettor mixture or an air leak at the inlet manifold will also cause the plugs to overheat. An overheated, incandescent plug can damage both the piston and the valves, so make sure that the fault is rectified before driving at speed.

69 A valve with too little rocker or camshaft clearance will overheat. Make sure that the valve clearance settings are correctly adjusted, as specified in the car handbook. If the valve clearance should be set cold, the engine must not be noticeably warm when the settings are adjusted. If a hot setting is specified the engine should be at normal operating temperature.

70 An exhaust can become partially blocked if you reverse the end of the tailpipe into a roadside verge, so affecting engine efficiency. Check that it is clear of grass and soil.

71 A blown or defective cylinder-head gasket will usually display the following symptoms: chuffing or similar noises when idling, rough running and loss of power. A sticking valve will also make the engine misfire and, unless found in time, will burn, with subsequent loss of power.

Check the compression of each cylinder by placing a spanner on the crankshaft pulley bolt and turning the engine. With a four-cylinder engine you should feel the compression on all four cylinders. On six-cylinder units, the same principle applies.

For a more accurate check a compression tester should be used (see page 203).

Be prepared

Emergencies on the move: Burst or flat tyre

If you have a blow-out at high speed, the primary consideration is to steer the car to a convenient point off the road, or at least out of the main traffic flow, as quickly as possible, but do not make sharp changes in direction.

Do not worry about damaging the tyre further in the process as it will probably be ruined anyway in the first few seconds after deflation.

Before starting to change the wheel, it is important to switch on the hazard-warning lights (if fitted), and to give approaching traffic some indication of your car's position, either by leaving the boot lid open or by placing a warning triangle at least 50 yards away from the vehicle, where drivers of oncoming cars can see it.

For instructions on changing a wheel, see Project 68.

Brake failure

If the brake pedal sinks to the floor without stopping the car, it can be an unnerving experience. Nevertheless, keep a cool head, because there are a number of things you can do which may stop the car or reduce its speed.

First, try pumping the brake pedal repeatedly—this may restore at least some braking effect. The handbrake should be applied in a series of short, firm applications. Do not apply the handbrake fully all the time, especially when descending a hill, as this may lead to failure caused by the rear drums expanding with the heat generated.

Change down through the gears to slow the car as well, and engage first gear as soon as possible. If you use a combination of the handbrake and gears, and the road conditions are suitable, in most cases you will be able to steer yourself out of trouble and stop the car

Clutch failure

If the clutch fails, as a result of either faulty hydraulics or a broken cable, there is very little you can do. As there is usually no way of repairing a faulty hydraulic system or a broken inner clutch cable at the roadside, you must call for garage help. Push the car off the road as soon as possible.

In the rare case of an outer cable coming adrift from its abutment at the bulkhead or gearbox, a self-grip wrench can be used to hold the outer cable in position.

Broken windscreen

Toughened glass windscreens fracture into small rectangular nuggets, with larger fractures giving a wide, clearer zone across the centre of the screen. If the screen breaks on the move, the clear zone can be used to see through until it is safe to stop. Do not attempt to punch a hole in the glass to see through, as the flying glass in the airstream may cut your face, as well as scattering glass all over the inside of the car. When the car is stationary, place a cloth over the whole upper surface of the facia to stop pieces of glass from falling into the demister and radio speaker slots. Using a covered or gloved hand, gently break

off and remove the glass from the remains of the screen. To prevent loose fragments from falling out as you drive, clear as much glass as possible from the rubber surround, then remove the cloth with the debris.

If you carry an emergency plastic windscreen, fit it according to the manufacturer's instructions.

It will allow you to continue your journey at a reasonable speed.

Before driving off, put a coat on to protect yourself from the draught, close all the car windows and drive slowly to the nearest garage.

A laminated screen does not shatter, so if your car is fitted with one and it breaks, you should be able to drive on without vision being impaired.

An emergency repair kit to carry in the boot of the car
In addition to the car's basic tool kit, there are several tools and replacement parts that every driver should carry for emergencies.

Although you can, of course, carry a large stock of tools, equipment and spares in your boot, the items listed below will form a reasonable kit which will be sufficient to tackle the majority of normal roadside

repairs. The cost will be only a few pounds, but as the parts will be needed sooner or later anyway, it is a wise investment to buy them all at one time in case they are required unexpectedly.

Parts
Fanbelt
Contact-breaker points
Spark plugs
Radiator hoses
Length of heater hose
Bulbs—spares for front and rear lights, indicators, and headlamps, if replaceable bulb-type
Fuses and fuse wire
Emergency windscreen

Tools
Screwdrivers—1 large, 1 small, and 1 small cross-head

Spanners—set of A/F, or metric open-ended and ring type—depending on the make of car

Spark plug spanner
Pliers
Feeler gauges
Tow-rope
Torch
Self-grip wrench
Tyre pressure gauge
Jump leads
Roll of insulating tape
Approx 3ft of coiled mild steel wire

Approx 3ft of insulated wire
A ball of thick string
Assorted nuts, bolts and washers
Wide wood block—for wheel chock and jack support

In addition, it is always advisable to carry a first-aid kit and a fire extinguisher inside the car to help others, if not yourself.

For Continental trips, special spares kits are available from the motoring organisations or franchised dealers, on a use or return basis.

Be prepared

Leaking or burst coolant hose

The first thing to do with cooling system leaks is to switch off the engine and, with a folded cloth to prevent scalding, slowly remove the radiator or expansion bottle pressure cap as soon as is safely possible. This will reduce the pressure in the cooling system which will be forcing coolant out of the leak.

Having located the leak, proceed as follows:

Leaking hose joint

Tighten the hose clip until the leak stops, or is reduced to an occasional drip. Do not overtighten a hose clip as this will distort the rubber and make the leak worse. In stubborn cases, where tightening the clip has no effect, disconnect the hose, trying to save as much coolant as possible, clean the inside of the hose-end and wrap a small amount of insulating tape around the joint stub. Reconnect the hose and tighten the clip. Refill the cooling system.

Burst or split hose

If you do not carry a hose repair kit (see Project below), a faulty hose can sometimes be repaired, at least as a get-you-home measure, by binding the affected area with insulating tape. Make sure that the tape overlaps an area well beyond the damaged part.

If only a small amount of coolant has been lost, the cooling system can be topped up with water from the screen-washer bottle. Do not use all the water, but leave just enough for the washers to work—it is a legal requirement.

Remember to refit the pressure cap loosely—tightening it fully will pressurise the system and could force water past the temporary repair.

Jammed thermostat

Overheating and a boiling radiator without any obvious cause could be due to a faulty engine thermostat jamming in the closed or partially-closed position. In an emergency, the car can be driven with the thermostat removed.

To dismantle it, first switch off the engine and allow it to cool for 15 minutes before removing the radiator or expansion bottle pressure cap with a covered or gloved hand.

The thermostat is normally located under a domed cover at one end of the cylinder head, attached by two or three bolts.

Unscrew the bolts evenly and remove them. Carefully lift off the cover, taking great care to avoid damaging the sealing gasket in the process. Remember that coolant will start to leak out as soon as the gasket seal is broken.

Lift out the thermostat and discard it. Check the condition of the flange gasket to see whether it is fit for re-use. If it is, then refit the cover and refill the cooling system. If the gasket is too badly damaged to be used again, and a new one is not available, another can be made up from thin cardboard or several layers of writing paper. Use the cover flange as a template and cut the gasket to shape. Make the holes for the bolts or studs with a pencil or any other sharp tool.

Fit the gasket and cover, then refill the cooling system as detailed earlier.

Note The 'E'-series OHC engine on the latest BL Marina and Princess models should never be run with the thermostat removed, as this will cause the engine to overheat. In this case you must call a garage for help.

Broken fanbelt

If you carry a replacement belt, there is no problem here; fit it as described in Project 3.

A length of thick string can be used in an emergency. Tie as many windings of it as practicable tightly around the crankshaft and the water pump pulleys only, not the generator pulley as this will increase the risk of the string slipping. The engine will still run without the generator if the battery is in good condition, but it will overheat if the water pump is not turning.

Missing wiper blade

If a windscreen wiper blade or arm flies off when you are on the move, the chances of finding it again are pretty slim. If it is the important one on the driver's side, the best thing to do on a wet day is to swop the passenger's wiper over. The blade is usually secured to the arm either by a clip or by a locating dimple. The arm is attached to the spindle by splines—simply pull off the arm, or undo the pinch-bolt at the base of the arm. Make sure that the wiper motor is in the parked position before fitting the arm to the spindle (see Project 83).

Flat battery

If the starter motor does not turn the engine or the headlamps are very dim on main beam, a flat battery is the likely cause. It could also be due to battery terminals being corroded or loose. Sometimes overnight condensation on the terminals—especially if they are dirty—can cause a bad connection and give the impression of a flat battery.

Once the battery is too exhausted to turn the starter, the easiest way to start the engine is with jump leads. You will need to connect them to a helper's car battery which is in

Project 99: Repairing a burst hose

> **Grading:** 🔧
> **Time:** Approx 20min
> **Materials:** Hose-repair kit

A burst hose will allow scalding water to escape into the engine compartment. It is often the top radiator hose, which runs hottest and usually suffers most vibration, that bursts.

As a temporary measure, small splits can be repaired with the self-adhesive rubber bandage in a hose-repair kit sold for the purpose. This kit also contains emery cloth and plastic clips.

Step 1. Wait until water and steam have stopped escaping, then locate the fault in the hose.
2. Dry the outside of the hose, then roughen the surface around the damaged area with emery cloth.
3. Peel the backing off the tape. Wind the tape tightly round the hose, allowing a generous overlap at the split.
4. Tighten the clips to prevent the ends unwinding.
5. Top up the cooling system and replace the filler cap before driving on. Renew the hose at the earliest opportunity (see Project 7).

Step 1.

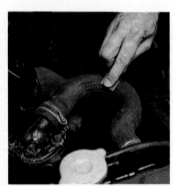

Step 2

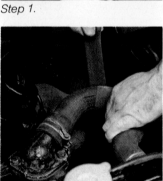

Step 3.

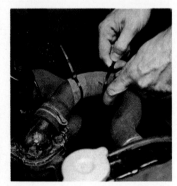

Step 4.

a good state of charge, but be careful how you do this. Make sure that the jump leads are connected Positive (+) to Positive and Negative (−) to Negative. You will find the + and − marks on the battery near the terminals. Never connect them the wrong way round. If you do, there will be a bright flash as the second terminal is connected, and serious damage may be done to an alternator or other polarity-sensitive components. Make sure, also, that your car and your helper's do not touch.

Once the two batteries have been wired together properly, operate the starter on your car until the engine turns. You should advise your 'good Samaritan' to keep his engine running to ensure that his battery stays charged.

Another way to start the engine is to push-start or tow-start the car. This can be done only on cars with manual gearboxes, not automatics.

The procedure for starting a car this way is as follows:

With the driver seated at the wheel, pull out the choke control (if the engine is cold), switch on the ignition, select second gear and hold the clutch pedal down. Push or tow the car to a fast-walking speed and then release the clutch pedal. If the first attempt does not succeed, the second or third should be enough to start the car, which will probably jerk forward as the engine fires. Keep the engine running at a fast-idle speed, or drive the car for some distance to recharge the battery.

Towing a car and being towed

There comes a time when a driver will need either to be towed or to tow another car, and it is as well to be aware of a few legal points and some sensible techniques before the event.

Whenever possible, tow ropes should be attached to the towing eyes provided by the manufacturer. If the car has not got proper welded-on towing points, tie the rope round a bumper mounting point (but not the middle of a bumper), an

anti-roll bar mounting or on another firm point under the front or rear of the car. Do not put ropes on moving suspension members and never attach them to points where they will foul the steering mechanism, the exhaust pipe or the number plate. If the rope runs over a sharp body edge, pad this point with a piece of cloth. Tie a coloured rag in the middle of the tow rope to ensure that pedestrians and other road users can see it.

By law, the maximum length of tow rope between two vehicles is 14ft 7in (4.5m) and it will help if your rope is as near to this maximum as possible. There is no legal requirement to put an ON TOW sign in the rear of the towed vehicle, but it does help other road users. You should cover the towed vehicle's number plate with a piece of card showing the towing vehicle's number.

If you are towing

Arrange a code of signals with the other driver for events like stopping, pulling off the road, and any other things that the towed driver would like to tell you. If possible, both vehicles should have their headlights on to warn other road users that you are a slow combination and that your vehicles might behave in a slightly abnormal manner. To help other people, and the towed driver, reinforce your normal electrical direction signals by using hand signals, which should be repeated by the towed driver.

Although the law allows towing up to 40mph, it is wise to stay below 25mph to lessen the strain on the tow rope if the vehicles jerk apart. Drive smoothly, accelerating with a very light foot, and stop as gently as possible.

When you are being towed

If your car has a steering lock, you must use the ignition key to disengage the lock. If possible turn the key only to an accessory position so as to be able to use most of the car systems without the ignition coil staying on and possibly overheating.

Where there is no accessory

position on the switch, turn the ignition on and, if the tow is to be a long one, disconnect one of the two ignition coil leads.

Remember that if your car is fitted with power steering and/or power-assisted brakes, considerable effort will be required to steer and brake when the engine is not running.

Arrange a code of signals with the tow car driver, particularly one that enables the towed car to do most of the

braking. This keeps the rope taut, and so avoids snatch.

Towing automatics

Considerable damage can be done to an automatic car if it is towed. In a real emergency some automatics can be towed up to 10mph for a maximum of 5 miles with the selector in the Neutral position.

For towing over longer distances, the rear end of the propshaft must be disconnected and securely tied up under the car.

Project 100: Plugging a leaking exhaust

Grading: 🔧🔧
Time: Approx 1hr
Tools: Drive-up ramps or axle stands and jack; chocks; wire brush; pliers
Materials: Exhaust repair kit

As well as being anti-social and illegal, a leaking exhaust can be lethal. The carbon monoxide in exhaust gas is toxic even in moderate amounts, and in small quantities it can cause drowsiness and dizziness which slow down a driver's reactions.

Small holes or splits in the exhaust system can often be

Step 2.

Step 3.

patched by using a proprietary repair kit. Usually the kit consists of metal foil to cover the hole, and a heat-resistant bandage to wind over the foil. The bandage is impregnated with a compound which hardens as the exhaust heats up.

Intended as a temporary measure, a repair of this type is acceptable so far as the MoT test is concerned, provided the exhaust is not weakened. However, this type of repair cannot be considered permanent.

Some silencers have small water-drain holes of about $\frac{1}{16}$in (1.6mm) diameter at their lowest point. These should not be covered.

Step 1. Raise the car on axle stands (see pages 14 and 15).
2. With a wire brush, remove any loose rust from around the hole to be plugged.
3. Wrap metal foil over the hole, then tape it into position with the heat-resistant bandage.
4. Secure the bandage with twisted wire. Lower the car to the ground, and run the engine at tick-over speed for several minutes to harden the repair.

Step 4.

ECONOMY MOTORING
Buying hints

Since the motor car was conceived, engineers and designers have placed their faith in the widespread availability of one particular type of hydrocarbon fuel—petrol. For the engine designer it is a fuel with many advantages. Petrol vaporises at relatively low temperatures, it is easy to ignite and therefore the release of its stored energy, compared with many other fuels, is easily attained.

There *are* other fuels. Diesel is cheaper to refine from crude oil, it produces fewer harmful exhaust emissions and it is capable of releasing its energy more efficiently than petrol. The result is up to 30% better mpg from diesel cars than their petrol equivalents. It has drawbacks, however. The performance many motorists have come to expect from their cars is not easily attainable using diesel engines, people object to the clatter of the engine (a curable factor), and the fuel can be smelly and messy to handle. Frequent oil changes are not needed on modern small diesels, however. On the design front, diesel engines have to be a little stronger than today's petrol engines, and the fuel-injection system used is complex and expensive to manufacture. Hence diesel cars cost an extra £400-£600 more than their petrol counterparts. It is money that few of today's motorists are prepared to pay.

Now, the supply of the base material for both these fuels—crude oil—is in question. World reserves of this valuable commodity are shrinking, and even the most confident experts can predict only a further 100 years in which man can enjoy the many benefits derived from oil. It is sensible to consider many kinds of measures to economise on the rate at which we are draining the remaining reserves. Of all end-uses of oil, the combustion of petrol and diesel by cars is considered to be one of the most wasteful processes. It is one of the first areas in which cutbacks appear whenever suppliers run short of crude oil, and it is the first area to be hit by rationing of petrol supplies.

Already at advanced stages of research are many different types of engine that minimise the squandering of petrol and diesel, and some that use completely different forms of propulsion or alternative fuels.

Developed from military engines are those power units which will use anything combustible as a fuel—vegetable oil, Scotch whisky and peanut butter have been tried with success. Electric cars are a serious proposition provided that the electrical energy can be supplied economically without using oil as the generating fuel. Diluting petrol with alcohol, cheaply distilled from replenishable crops like trees or sugar beet, is another solution, while at least two inventors have had some success in running cars with mixtures of petrol (or alcohol) and up to 80% water. The world's enormous coal reserves can also be converted, albeit expensively, into car fuels.

Developments like these will almost certainly mean that private cars, and the tremendous advantages of personal mobility that they bestow, will be with us for a long time to come. In the meantime there is a great contribution to be made to the world's energy problems by the motorist himself. Economies of up to 20% in fuel usage, easily within the grasp of any caring motorist, will not only stave off the day when the pumps run entirely dry, but also give a tremendous fillip to the household motoring budget. A modest 10% saving over a year's motoring means an extra £30 or so in the pocket of the average motorist—more if fuel prices continue to rise at present rates.

The suggestions and hints given below, and the techniques used to save fuel, do not involve drastic changes in your style of driving and need not mean travelling any slower or reaching your destination later. But they are designed to add interest in your car and motoring that will certainly increase as the considerable benefits mount up. There are other spin-offs, too. The greater care with which you treat the car should be reflected in a higher resale value, wear on expensive components like the tyres, brake linings and clutch will be reduced, and your passengers should almost certainly enjoy a smoother ride.

Buying an economical car
Of the many factors affecting a buyer's choice of a particular model of car, fuel consumption figures have probably been, until recently, the most confusing. Understandably so, because the only available figures shown to the potential customer were those produced by the manufacturers themselves. What was badly needed was a reliable, independent source of information to make the figures not only intelligible, but also to make comparisons more meaningful.

Now, however, the buyer can make direct mpg comparisons between cars by referring to the Department of Energy's list of approved petrol consumption test results, which give a kind of respectability to consumption figures.

The tests, conducted on practically every model of car under strictly standardised conditions must, by law, be available for inspection at all new car salerooms. This list gives for each car at least two results of tests which simulate a short ride in town traffic conditions (the 'urban cycle') and at a constant cruising speed of 56mph (the 'constant-speed test'). Any fuel figures quoted in advertising must also, by law, come from this list.

While the Government figures are a useful guide and an important first reference check when buying a new car, the tests do not take into account several other potential sources of fuel economy. A quick engine warm-up on cold mornings is the most important of these. Keen buyers can check this kind of detail by reading magazine road test reports, or those produced by consumer and motoring organisations, to see the effect this has on fuel economy under true driving conditions.

It may seem obvious, but it should be stated, that the smaller and lighter a car is, the more economical it will be to run. Every 100lb of car weight takes about 15 gallons of petrol a year to propel it. You may find that some makers are more adept than others at providing adequate family space within a small frame. Shape can also play an important part. Lower, leaner and more streamlined cars with low frontal areas save fuel, especially at higher speeds.

Worthwhile fuel-saving equipment, such as an overdrive or a five-speed gearbox, may look uneconomic because of their relatively high extra cost, but it should be possible to recover some of the money on resale. Avoid automatic gearboxes if you possibly can, as they use up to 10% more fuel than manual gearboxes.

Do not necessarily go for a car with a smaller engine, as fewer ccs may mean a lower ratio between power and weight. In a choice between two models offered in almost identical specification but with an 1,100cc engine or a 1,300cc engine, it is often the larger-engined car that has the greater potential for fuel economy. However, that is only if you drive economically enough to restrain the extra power available so that the engine works under less stress than the smaller engine would do.

False economies
A poorly maintained car is a fuel waster. Few aspects of car maintenance and tuning have *no* effect at all on fuel economy. While it is tempting to prop up your motoring finances by neglecting servicing or extending the intervals between vital jobs, it really is false economy to do so.

All the key jobs which save fuel are detailed in projects in this book. These are: replacing and adjusting contact-breaker points (Project 55); carburettor servicing (Project 26); air filter servicing (Project 25); ignition timing (Project 59); spark plug cleaning, gapping and replacement (Project 53); battery care (Project 31); brake adjustment (Projects 74 and

75); tyre inspection and inflation checks (Project 67).

Get these jobs right—they are the bare minimum for successful economy—and the saving can amount to as much as 10% in a year's motoring.

There is also one more 'saving' that cannot be recommended. Almost since cars began, both genuine engineers and garden-shed tinkerers have developed an amazing variety of so-called economy devices. Despite the fact that hardly any two devices look

Extra work on the car

As mentioned earlier, a lighter car saves fuel—and most motorists will admit that the boot is often piled high with the aftermath of a family holiday or a fishing or golfing weekend. Clear out all the non-essential items from the car in order

alike, or act in the same way, they have one thing in common—none of them works well enough for the motorist to recover the cost of the device (and its fitting) within a reasonable time. Thorough investigations by the Automobile Association have proved that many of the devices have no effect whatsoever on fuel consumption and some even increase fuel usage.

Excluded from this comment is the vacuum gauge, which is an accessory more correctly

to reduce the weight carried.

Under the car there is excess baggage, too. The road dirt that accumulates and dries on, not only hastens corrosion, but is costing fuel as well. Hose out the mudtraps as often as you can and the car will stay pounds lighter and will be in

described as an economy aid, and it is equally useful for engine tuning and diagnosis. It records, in mercury inches, the difference in pressure between the outside atmosphere and the inlet manifold. At cruising speed, it should read 10-18in Hg—the higher the better. It may be worth buying if you feel unable to cope with the advice given later on simple ways to drive economically.

Electronic ignition system kits are also claimed to give fuel economy. Fully electronic

better condition when the time comes to sell it.

Roof-racks wreck a car's aerodynamic performance and even driving with an empty one burns up to 4% of the petrol you are using. Take off the rack whenever it is not in use, and consider very carefully whether

ignition, completely replacing the contact-breakers, certainly saves money by avoiding the need to service the ignition system for long periods (plus the straight saving in replacement contact-breakers). Also, because the ignition stays in tune, it is possible to save up to 5% of the fuel bill. These savings will not be anything like as big if the system does not replace the contact-breakers. Fitting a fully electronic ignition set is described in Project 52.

or not you really need to use it at all. Load a roof rack with smaller packages or cases to the front and larger ones at the rear to give the load a stepped wedge shape. Smooth the profile by tying a heavy plastic sheet or special luggage cover firmly down over the cases.

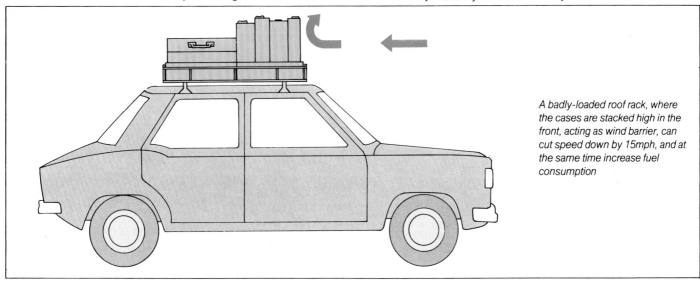

A badly-loaded roof rack, where the cases are stacked high in the front, acting as wind barrier, can cut speed down by 15mph, and at the same time increase fuel consumption

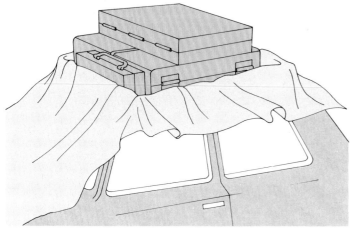

To hold the cover firmly in position on the roof rack, lay the cases on top and 'parcel' them up

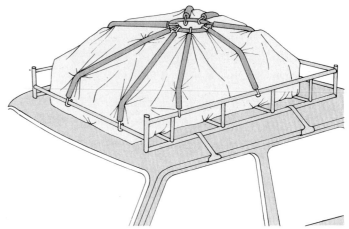

A strong eight-stranded elastic spider will keep the cases secure and reduce wind resistance

Driving hints

During the important weekly maintenance checks, pay particular attention to the smooth action of the choke control. Ensure that when the knob is pressed fully home the linkage on the carburettor, to which it is connected, fully opens the choke butterfly in the throat of the carburettor. This will prevent excessive choke use. Owners of automatic choke cars can sense the mechanism's malfunction only by experience during morning starts. If it appears to be on choke for too long, refer to Project 27 for checks to be made, or seek expert advice.

A warm car is an economical car and there are steps you can take on most cars to ensure that the engine gets hotter faster and stays at the most efficient temperature. On many older cars it may be possible to fit a 'winter' thermostat which opens at a slightly higher temperature than the original one (see Project 6). This can speed winter warm-ups. Cars with engine fans (rather than the electric type) can be overcooled in winter, and blanking off part of the radiator grille with firmly secured board or metal sheet

keeps up engine temperatures. Up to 90% can be covered —but do not cover air intakes for electric fans or the car's ventilation system.

Keep the carburettor air intake at the summer position for as long as possible, provided your car starts and initially runs smoothly. Colder, denser air gives more efficient combustion than when it is slightly warmed by the exhaust manifold.

When you have to buy a new set of tyres, buy radials instead of cross-plies—radials wear up to 10% less and offer less rolling resistance to the car's progress. This can contribute up to 4% on fuel savings. In addition to regular tyre inspections, you might consider raising the inflation pressure to that recommended for high-speed and high-load conditions. This measure will also lower rolling resistance and save fuel without significantly affecting tyre life. Never exceed the tyre or car manufacturer's maximum recommended pressure, however. If you do, the car's handling could be seriously affected and tyre life will be reduced.

Getting on the road

Never start the engine without being thoroughly prepared to set out on your journey. If it is to be an unfamiliar trip, write out a memory-jogging route card and equip yourself with a good road map—every mile (or minute) spent getting lost or trying to work out directions is

fuel down the drain. A good map will help you navigate around unexpected traffic delays, but the real economiser will have planned a route to avoid likely jam spots and listened to the local radio station for news of any accidents or road-works that could impede progress.

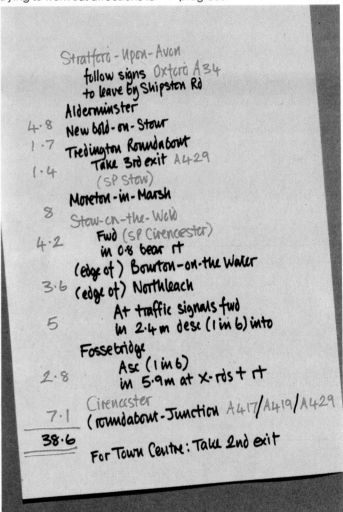

When setting out on a long journey it is a good idea to plan the route beforehand and to write out a 'route card'. This should help to avoid taking wrong turns and wasting precious petrol on the extra miles

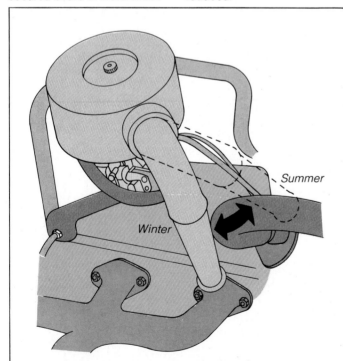

Many carburettor air-cleaners have an adjustable air-intake nozzle so that it can be turned away from the hot exhaust manifold in summer when the carburettor needs cold air

Try to park the car so that a straight drive-off is possible —time spent manoeuvring a cold, choked car is fuel thrown away. Do all the manoeuvring while the car is warm at the end of the previous journey. Provided you have a well-ventilated garage, reverse the car into it. And when you move off the next morning get someone else to close the doors so that you don't leave the engine literally idling. A

properly-tuned car should be simplicity itself to start—but pay close attention to your technique. Avoid blipping the throttle pedal (before or after starting, it will pump fuel into the cylinders), crank the engine in only 2-3 second bursts, allowing a few seconds for the battery to recover between each attempt, and feed the choke in as quickly as you can. Try pushing it fully home a lamp standard or gate-post earlier each day until you find the earliest point at which the engine still functions smoothly on your morning run.

Always start off from rest in first gear—second-gear starts will entail higher engine revs

On the road

Greatest fuel savings of all come from sensitive use of the throttle. It is, in effect, a fuel tap so that the more it is opened, the more fuel flows. Any fuel in excess of the exact amount that the engine needs goes to waste. Therefore, never accelerate simply by ramming down the right foot and waiting for the engine to sort itself out. Feed the pedal in a minute amount at a time until you reach the speed you require and then back off a fraction—you will be surprised how far you can lift off the pedal and still maintain the required speed.

Remember, although you can save fuel by going slower (a considerable amount, in fact —see later) many drivers will not wish to do so. The savings are almost as big by reaching your required speed gently. Look out for any developing traffic or road situation that will allow you to take your foot off the throttle completely and coast in top gear—it is pointless to continue pedal pressure if, eventually, you will have to apply the brake to slow down. Timely slowing down in this way also gives you more time to appreciate the next move. When approaching congested traffic, a roundabout or traffic lights, it may enable you to select the correct gear to keep moving and take advantage of any gaps that occur.

For corners and bends, judge your speed carefully to avoid the need to brake. Select a turning radius that will carry the car smoothly round the bend without violent mid-course corrections that scrub off speed and make it necessary to abuse the accelerator.

Take hills with the minimum of extra accelerator pressure, if possible, holding your foot steady on the pedal. Change down only if absolutely necessary, and then keep the foot at a fixed throttle position. Coast

and costly clutch wear. Accelerate smoothly, using the throttle gently, changing up to a higher gear as soon as possible. Generally, first gear need be used only to get the car rolling, and second can be

down the other side without accelerating, but always stay in gear for control.

Spend as much time in top gear as you can—if your car has overdrive or a fifth gear, all the better. Savings of up to 10% can be made by wise use of an overdrive gear.

As mentioned above, an overall reduction in your driving speed will make a tremendous saving. Engines are most economical when running at speeds close to the point at which maximum torque is developed (see your handbook). This usually falls in the 2,000-3,200rpm rev range, equivalent to top gear road speeds of 30-50mph, depending on the car's overall drive ratio (sometimes usefully expressed in road test reports as mph per 1,000rpm). If it is at all possible, keep your driving down to these speeds.

You can switch off petrol, too, but only when you have stopped the car. If traffic jams look like lasting, turn off the ignition to make a straight fuel saving, but under no circumstances take the ignition key out of the lock, as on most cars it will lock the steering.

Do not turn off the ignition too often, either—frequent restarts might flatten the battery.

While on the road, turn off every non-essential electrical accessory. No energy comes for nothing, and the electrical power used in the car is generated at the expense of fuel. So do not use headlights, heated rear windows or heater fans a second longer than the law or safety make necessary.

Sooner or later even the best economy driver will have to visit the pumps. It will not save any fuel—but it will save a lot of money—if you always ensure that you buy the correct grade of fuel for your car. It simply should not be necessary, if the car is properly maintained, to

engaged almost immediately. Gear change points through the rest of the range vary widely from car to car, with many modern cars being quite happy in top gear at speeds as low as 20mph. Experiment to

give the engine a higher octane petrol than that recommended, to keep it running smoothly. It is even possible to run some cars on a lower star-rating, using petrol from blender pumps which offer extra

find the lowest speed in each gear from which the car will continue to accelerate smoothly. A good starting point for your tests is to halve the manufacturer's recommended maximum speed in each gear.

grades in the 3- and 4-star category. If you detect any pinking (see page 101) when using a lower octane fuel, go back up one star grade as soon as possible to eliminate it.

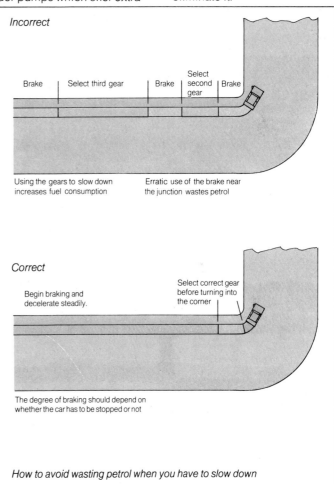

Incorrect

Brake | Select third gear | Brake | Select second gear | Brake

Using the gears to slow down increases fuel consumption

Erratic use of the brake near the junction wastes petrol

Correct

Begin braking and decelerate steadily.

Select correct gear before turning into the corner

The degree of braking should depend on whether the car has to be stopped or not

How to avoid wasting petrol when you have to slow down

The vacuum gauge is an instrument which indicates how economically a car is being driven. It does this by measuring the pressure in the inlet manifold. If the vacuum gauge shows a high reading (low manifold pressure) the amount of petrol entering the combustion chamber is being restricted, reducing acceleration and fuel wastage. This is the ideal reading for economical motoring. The instrument usually has to be fitted as an accessory

INDEX AND GLOSSARY

Wheel alignment *135*
See toe-in and toe-out

Wheelbase –
Distance between the centres of the
front and rear wheels

Z

Zone-toughened windscreen *166*
Toughened glass with a specially
treated area in front of the driver
which, if broken, fractures into larger
fragments than the rest of the glass,
ensuring reasonable forward vision

Most of the glossary boxes refer to a
specific mention in the text of the
book. Where no page numbers are
given, the terms have been included
for information only.